Diversity and Contact
among Singer-Poet Traditions
in Eastern Anatolia

ISTANBULER TEXTE UND STUDIEN

HERAUSGEGEBEN VOM
ORIENT-INSTITUT ISTANBUL

BAND 40

Diversity and Contact
among Singer-Poet Traditions
in Eastern Anatolia

Edited by
Ulaş Özdemir
Wendelmoet Hamelink
Martin Greve

BADEN-BADEN 2018

ERGON VERLAG
IN KOMMISSION

Umschlaggestaltung: Taline Yozgatian

Cover photo:
Musicians during the "Festival of Folk Poets in Sivas", 1931.
Tecer, A. K. (1932). Sıvas Halk Şairleri Bayramı. Sivas: Kamil Matbaası.

Bibliografische Information der Deutschen Nationalbibliothek
Die Deutsche Nationalbibliothek verzeichnet diese Publikation in der Deutschen
Nationalbibliografie; detaillierte bibliografische Daten sind im Internet über http://dnb.d-nb.de
abrufbar.

Bibliographic information published by the Deutsche Nationalbibliothek
The Deutsche Nationalbibliothek lists this publication in the Deutsche Nationalbibliografie;
detailed bibliographic data are available in the Internet at http://dnb.d-nb.de.

ISBN 978-3-95650-286-6 (Print)
ISBN 978-3-95650-481-5 (ePDF)
ISSN 1863-9461

Ergon – ein Verlag in der Nomos Verlagsgesellschaft, Baden-Baden

Gedruckt auf alterungsbeständigem Papier

Contents

Introduction

Ulaş Özdemir, Wendelmoet Hamelink, Martin Greve

The photo on the cover of this book was probably made on 7 November, 1931 during the first "Festival of Folk Poets in Sivas" (*Sivas Halk Şairleri Bayramı*) (Tecer, 1932). It depicts a number of participating folk singers, including (upright from left) Âşık Ali, San'ati, Yusuf, Talibi (Hacı Bektaş Coşkun), Yarım Ali, Âşık Müştak, (sitting from left) Hikayeci Ağa Dayı, Karslı Mehmet, Âşık Süleyman (Süleyman Fırtına), the two famous brothers Suzani (Vahap Bozkurt) and Revani (Kurtveli Bozkurt), and finally, (on the right outside) the at that time still completely unknown Âşık Veysel (Veysel Şatıroğlu). This festival marked a turning point for the singer-poet tradition in the young Republic of Turkey. Here, Ahmet Kutsi Tecer discovered folk poets who from then on would become the most important symbols for national Turkish literature and music.

The Diversity of Singer-Poets in Anatolia

The tradition of singing shorter or longer poems or even epics, accompanied (or not) by the singer himself/herself on instruments such as a long-necked lute or a bowed fiddle is widespread in a large area reaching from the Balkans over Anatolia, through the Caucasus, Iran until Central Asia. Within this larger context, a great number of languages are used, including Turkic, Persian, Kurdish, Armenian, Arabic, Slavic or Caucasian languages, further complicated by bilingualism or multilingualism, an important issue that still needs to be studied more in-depth. However, even within Anatolia, the diversity, communication and interaction of singer-poets of different ethnic groups have not been explored enough to date. Only exceptionally did researchers pay attention to diversity leaving nationalistic debates on the side. The following are the most important examples: Greek folk poets writing and singing in Turkish (Salcı, 2004); Turkish folk poets writing and singing in Greek (İslamoğlu, 1994; Öztürk, 2006); Armenian *aşug*s writing and singing in Turkish (Pamukciyan, 2002; Bayrak, 2005; Koz, 2014); Kurdish tales in Armenian folk literature (Seropyan, 2017); Turkish folk songs from Karaman Greeks (Stravridis, 2017); *âşık* poets with Turkish, Kurdish, Armenian verses (Hakobyan, 2016); comparable characteristics of Armenian and Kurdish lullabies (Bilal & Estelle, 2013); *âşık*s influenced by *dengbêj*s and vice verse (Hamelink, 2016). With these examples showing what a large variety of forms existed, we most probably only know a small part of them.

Furthermore, the content of the songs might be influenced by different religions and denominations including Sunni and Shia Islam (Fa in this volume),

Alevism, Yezidism (Amy de le Bretéque, 2012; Allison, 2001), and Armenian (Xi in this volume) or Syriac Christianity. Some performers "sing" (in the narrow sense) while other rather recite or tell stories, possibly with inserted sung passages or songs. Moreover, similarities, transitions and exchange between singer-poets and traditions such as *hikaye* (story-telling; Boratav, 2002; Başgöz, 2008), *ağıt* (laments; Esen, 1982; Gökçen, 2015), *destan* (epic; Esen, 1991) or religious poetry of different denominations have rarely been discussed.

We might conclude that the relationship and interaction of the singer-poets belonging to different ethnicities or religions and speaking different mother tongues are important topics affecting the poetry and musical performance. As a contemporary example of interaction between different regions and languages, two female singer-poets, Dengbêj Gazîn from Van and Âşık Leyli from Armenia, performed together at concerts, and released an album together.[1]

Nationalistic Discourses of Singer-Poets

Despite this obvious diversity, during the twentieth century, several (newly founded) nation-states tried to turn singer-poet traditions into political symbols of their respective national culture with the rather absurd consequence that the so-called *âşık* tradition was accepted three different times by the UNESCO as Intangible Cultural Heritage, that is for Turkey (2009), Azerbaijan (2009) and Armenia (2014)–not to mention the UNESCO recognition of other epic traditions in the region, such as the *Akyn* Epic tellers in Kyrgyzstan (2008), the Meddah theatrical storytellers in Turkey (2008), or epic singing to the accompaniment of the fiddle *gusle* in Serbia (2018). In Turkey, in particular Turkish literature studies have described the tradition of *âşık* or *ozan* (also refered to by some other names) as a homogeneous national Turkish tradition (Balkılıç, 2015; Öztürkmen, 1998), widely ignoring non-Turkish influences and related traditions. Turkish folk literature and music scholars used terms such as *halk şairi* (folk poets), *saz şairi* (poets with the *saz/bağlama* instrument) or *âşık* within a general nationalistic discourse, claiming them to be the most important carriers of a Turkic cultural memory supposedly originating in Central Asia (Köprülü, 2004). This later notion deeply changed both the tradition and its perception.

While the cover photo of 1931 shows some poor rural singers of the region of Sivas, without any indication of the high prestige and honours which they would receive in the following decades, Âşık Veysel later became the most prominent representative of the Turkish *âşık* tradition. Interestingly, even though his life and

---

[1]   For more information about this project and the album see: http://www.anadolukultur. org/tr/calisma-alanlari/ermenistanla-kultur-sanat-diyalogu/kadin-asik-ve-dengbejler/152 (accessed: 24 February 2018); https://kalan.com/audio/vandan-yerevana-dengbej-gazin-ve-asik-leyli (accessed: 24 February 2018).

work was studied in-depth, his possible Armenian roots have never been mentioned in studies on Turkish folk literature (Bayrak, 2017), and even his Aleviness was only mentioned many years after his death. Since the *âşık* tradition was part of the ideological mission of the Turkish nation-state to nationalize, Turkify, and unify its citizens, affiliation with different ethnicities or faiths of *âşık*s were mostly ignored in official Turkish discourse. As one of the few exceptions to this subject, studies on Turkish folk literature and music did mention that the Armenian *aşug*s were often influenced by Turkish *âşık*s (Köprülü, 1999; Gazimihal, 1962). However, the opposite possibility has never been suggested (Kerovpyan & Yılmaz, 2010).

Meanwhile a number of encompassing studies have been published on the *âşık* tradition and its poems (e.g. Artun, 2014; Kaya, 1994; Reinhard & de Oliveira Pinto, 1989). However, its exact regional and historical scope is still unclear, for example western periphery (Şenel, 2007), possible transitions to traditions on the Balkan (Bohlman & Petković, 2012), its connection with related traditions at the Black Sea coast and those in Iran (Allison & Kreyenbroek, 2013) and further east (Küchümkulova, 2016). In some few studies, the multilingual character of different traditions has been examined (Pamukciyan, 2002; Salcı, 2004; Bayrak, 2005; Öztürk, 2006). These latter studies form an interesting example of how some local researchers moved into the opposite direction of the Turkish state, not conforming to the "nationalization" process of the Turkish state. Generally, however, non-Turkish traditions were (and still are) ignored by most Turkish scholars, of which the Kurdish *dengbêj* is the most notable example because of its recent revival. During the early 2000s a process of Kurdish nationalization of the *dengbêj*s took place in the Kurdish political movement, this time excluding non-Kurdish traditions and actors in the region, and disregarding the vast variety of Kurdish singer-poet traditions (Turgut and Schäfers in this volume).

Main Contribution of this Book

The present volume, focusing on the widely neglected but extremely rich cultural area of eastern Anatolia, suggests that six major steps are needed to enrich and strengthen the research on singer-poets:

1) Almost all articles in this volume question the nationalist narratives of homogeneous traditions connected with one (and only one) nation or ethnic group. Even if languages create serious borders for both the performance and perception of songs and epics, similarities and exchange regularly crossed (and still cross) these borders. Singer-poet traditions rather have to be investigated as local, regional, sometimes super-regional phenomena that developed their individual styles in interaction with different traditions in their local environments. Under the influence of media and politics, however, some recent actors have become effective over a much larger area. Such internationalization was accelerated

by the many migrants settling outside of Anatolia, building new communities in which there continued to be a demand for singer-poets from the region of origin. This mediazation was often influenced and reinforced through the construction of social and political identities of the different ethnic groups, both in the "homeland" and abroad. And even though social and political homogenizing currents strongly influenced the way in which Anatolian traditions exist today, the artistic power of individual creativity should never be neglected.

2) In order to understand the place and role of traditions or individuals, a comparative approach, which bridges the traditions from different ethnic and linguistic groups, is essential. Because of the politicization of this topic, not only the traditions itself, also the works written about them often do not relate to each other, thereby missing the chance to understand mutual influences and exchange. In addition to the "major" traditions of *âşık*, *ozan* or *dengbêj*, also smaller, today lesser known traditions should be taken into account, including *destan*, *hikaye*, the *sa* from Dersim, *finnans* in Antakya, and religious singers of Sunni, Shia, Alevi, and Christian traditions. Since the short but pioneering article of Ursula Reinhard (1997), hardly any serious comparison has been published. Obviously, before an encompassing overview and comparison can be achieved, numerous small-scale case-studies need to be conducted. Future field research would need to be sensitive to the necessity of a comparative approach both regional and historical, to which the chapters in this volume give a first incentive.

3) Gender is a topic that needs much more attention in research on singer-poets, as this has been lacking in much of the writing up to this date (Köksel, 2012; Birkalan, 2013; Çınar, 2008; Erdener, 1995; Hamelink, 2016). Important themes that need investigation are the participation (historical and contemporary) of women in singer-poet traditions, their specific contribution to the repertoire and genres, and their acceptance as professional singers by the public as well as by the music market (see Marlene Schäfers in this volume).

4) Instead of the wide-spread assumption of timeless "traditions" which are assumed to have remained basically unchanged over centuries, this volume takes on a historical, source-based approach, encompassing methods of oral history as well as the analysis of historical music recordings. Furthermore, the study of oral tradition needs to include the study of political choices and developments regarding its "heritage-making". Recent works, such as that of Christine Allison (2001), Metin Yüksel (2011), Clémence Scalbert-Yücel (2009), Marlene Schäfers (2015), and Wendelmoet Hamelink (2016), have paid attention to these aspects.

5) This volume demonstrates the rich results of interdisciplinary research and exchange, including disciplines such as cultural anthropology, which might focus on issues such as cultural meaning of traditions and identity (Schäfers), (socio-)linguistics (Ağbaht), (ethno-) musicology (Sağlam, Özdemir, Greve), organography (Shidfar), and literature studies. It also brings together the works of local and foreign researchers, who have a different history of collecting.

6) Finally, an important subject discussed throughout the book is the role that singer-poets play in popular music, especially since the 20th century. Singer-poets came to the fore when cultural identities were expressed through music in different communities. Recent works related to the subject are increasingly showing the role of radio, television, music industry and social media (Fidan, 2017; Özdemir, 2017).

Almost naturally these six aspects are mutually interlinked. For example, a focus on the regional cultural history of present-day eastern Anatolian singer-poets, combined with a historical approach, will necessarily force the researcher to investigate contacts and exchange with Armenian singer-poet traditions that were influential in the region previously, in particular during the nineteenth century.

The concept of this volume was initially developed for a panel held at the *Turkologentag* in Hamburg in 2016. The editors, struck by the unexpected large field and approaches, decided to contact further scholars working in the field. During this process the field more and more enlarged, and today we even consider a second volume on the issue.

The editors would like to thank the Orient-Institut Istanbul for its support.

References

Allison, Ch. (2001). *The Yezidi Oral Tradition in Iraqi Kurdistan*. Richmond, Surrey: Curzon Press.

Allison, Ch. & Kreyenbroek, Ph. (Ed.). (2013). *Remembering the Past in Iranian Societies*. Wiesbaden: Harrassowitz Verlag.

Amy de le Bretéque, E. (2012). Voices of Sorrow: Melodized Speech, Laments, and Heroic Narratives among the Yezidis of Armenia. *Yearbook for Traditional Music*, 44, 129–148.

Artun, E. (2001/ 2014). *Âşıklık Geleneği ve Âşık Edebiyatı*. Ankara: Akçağ Yayınları.

Balkılıç, Ö. (2015). *Temiz ve Soylu Türküler Söyleyelim: Türkiye'de Milli Kimlik İnşasında Halk Müziği*. Istanbul: Tarih Vakfı Yurt Yayınları.

Başgöz, İ. (2008). *Hikâye. Turkish Folk Romance as Performance Art*. Bloomington: Indiana University.

Bayrak, M. (2005). *Alevi- Bektaşi Edebiyatında Ermeni Âşıkları (Aşuğlar)*. Ankara: Özge Yayınları.

— (2017). Kadim Ermeni Yerleşkelerinde Hüzünlü Bir Gezinti. *Kürt Tarihi Dergisi*, 29.

Bilal, M. & Amy de le Bretéque, E. (2013). The Oror and the Lorî: Armenian and Kurdish Lullabies in Present-day Istanbul. In Kreyenbroek, Ph. & Allison, Ch. (Eds.). *Remembering the Past in Iranian Societies*, 125–140. Wiesbaden: Harrassowitz Verlag.

Birkalan, H. (2013). Reconsidering Gender and Genre: Female Aşıks, Tradition and Tactics. In Shankland, D. (Ed.). *Archeology, Anthropology and Heritage in the Balkans and Anatolia*, 123–153. Istanbul: Isis Press.

Bohlman, Ph. V. & Petkovi'c, N. (Eds.) (2012). *Balkan Epic. Song, History, Modernity*. Lanham (etc.): The Scarecrow Press.

Boratav, P. N. (1996). Giriş. In Esen, A. S. *Anadolu Ağıtları*. Istanbul: İletişim Yayınları.

– (2002). *Halk Hikayeleri ve Halk Hikayeciliği*. Istanbul: Tarih Vakfı Yurt Yayınları.

Coşkun, Zeki (1995). *Aleviler, Sünnüler ve ... Öteki Sivas*. Istanbul: İletişim.

Çınar, S. (2008). *Yirminci Yüzyılın ikinci Yarısında Türkiye'de Kadın Âşıklar*. (Unpublished doctoral dissertation). Istanbul Technical University. Istanbul.

Erdener, Y. (1995). *The Song Contests of Turkish Ministrels. Improvised Poetry Sung To Traditional Music*. New York: Garland Publishing.

Esen, A. Ş. (1982). *Anadolu Ağıtları*. Istanbul: Türkiye Kültür Bakanlığı Yayınları.

– (1991). *Anadolu Destanları*. Istanbul: Türkiye Kültür Bakanlığı Yayınları.

Fidan, S. (2017). *Âşıklık Geleneği ve Medya Endüstrisi: Geleneksel Müziğin Medyadaki Serüveni*. Ankara: Grafiker Yayınları.

Gazimihal, M. R. (1962). Ermenicede Turani Ses Unsurları. In *Türk Folklor Araştırmaları*, 7 (150), 2604–2605.

Gökçen, A. (2015). *Kadim bir ses: Ezidi Ağıtları*. Istanbul: İstanbul Bilgi Üniversitesi Yayınları.

Hakobyan, A. (2016). *Arapgir: Songs*. Retrieved from http://www.houshamadyan. org/mapottomanempire/vilayetofmamuratulazizhrput/kaza-of-arapgir/lochal-characteristics/songs.html (last accessed 24 February 2018).

Hamelink, W. (2016). *The Sung Home: Narrative, Morality, and the Kurdish Nation*. Leiden: Brill..

İslamoğlu, M. (1994). Kıbrıslı Türk Âşıklar ve Rum Halk Edebiyatına Katkıları. *Kıbrıs Türk Kültur ve Sanatı*, 105–124.

Kaya, D. (1994). *Sivas'ta Âşıklık Geleneği ve Âşık Ruhsatî*. Sivas: Cumhurriyet Üniversitesi Yayınları 55.

Koz, S. (2014). *Gül Ağacı Boy Vermez: Ermeni Harfli Türkçe ve Ermenice Maniler*. Istanbul: Turkuaz Yayınları.

Köksel, B. (2012). *20. Yüzyıl Âşık Şiiri Geleneğinde Kadın Âşıklar*. Ankara: Akçağ.

Köprülü, M. F. (1999). Türk Edebiyatı'nın Ermeni Edebiyatı Üzerindeki Te'sirleri. In Köprülü, M. F. *Edebiyat Araştırmaları*, (239–269) Ankara: Türk Tarih Kurumu Yayınları.

– (2004). *Saz Şairleri*. Ankara: Akçağ Yayınları.

Küchümkulova, E. (2016). Introduction to Central Asian Epic Traditions. In Levin, Th.; Daukeyeva, S.' & Küchümkulova, E. (Eds.). *The Music of Central Asia*. Bloomington: Indian University Press.

Özdemir, U. (2017). *Senden Gayrı Âşık mı Yoktur: 20. Yüzyıl Âşık Portreleri*. Istanbul: Kolektif Kitap.

Öztürk, R. (2006). Sözlü Anlatımların Bir Başka Dil İle Anlatılması: Rumca Anlatılarda Türk Halk Verimleri. *İlmî Araştırmalar: Dil, Edebiyat, Tarih İncelemeleri*, 26, 187–203.

Öztürkmen, A. (1998). *Türkiye'de Folklor ve Milliyetçilik*. Istanbul: İletişim Yayınları.

Pamukciyan, K. (2002). *Ermeni Harfli Türkçe Metinler*. Istanbul: Aras Yayıncılık.

Reigle, R. (2013). A Brief History of Kurdish Music Recordings in Turkey. *Hellenic Journal of Music, Education and Culture*, 4. www.hejmec.eu (last accessed 4 May 2018).

Reinhard, U. (1997). Dichtersänger im Nordosten der Türkei, in Armenien und Aserbaidschan. Ein Vergleich. *Jahrbuch für musikalische Volks-und Völkerkunde*, 16, 71–92.

Reinhard, U. & de Oliveira Pinto, T. (1989). *Sänger und Poeten mit der Laute. Türkische Aşık und Ozan*. Berlin: Museum für Völkerkunde, Veröffentlichungen des Museums für Völkerkunde Berlin. Neue Folge 47, Abteilung Musikethnologie VI.

Salcı, V. L. (2004). Türkleşmiş Hristiyan Bektaşî Şairler I-II. *Türk Kültürü ve Hacı Bektaş Velî Araştırma Dergisi*, 31–32.

Scalbert Yücel, C. (2009). The Invention of a Tradition: Diyarbakırs's Dengbêj Project, *European Journal of Turkish Studies*, 10. http://ejts//revues.org/index 4055.html (last accessed 4 May 2018).

Schäfers, M. (2015). Being Sick of Politics: The Production of dengbêjî as Kurdish Cultural Heritage in Contemporary Turkey. *European Journal of Turkish Studies*, 20, 2–16.

Seropyan, S. (2017). *Aşiq û Maşûq: Ermenice Kaynaklardan Kürt-Ermeni Aşk Masalları*. Istanbul: Aras Yayıncılık.

Stravridis, St. (2017). *Anatol Türküleri. 1896 Osmanlı İmparatorluğu'nda İlk Türkü Mecmuası*. Istanbul: Literatür Yayıncılık.

Şenel, S. (2007). *Kastamonu'da Âşık Fasılları*. Kastamonu: Kastamonu Valiliği.

Tecer, A. K. (1932). *Sivas Halk Şairleri Bayramı*. Sivas: Kamil Matbaası.

Kerovpyan, A. & Yılmaz, A. (2010). *Klasik Osmanlı Müziği ve Ermeniler*. İstanbul: Surp Pırgiç Ermeni Hastanesi Vakfı Kültür Yayınları.

Yüksel, M. (2011). *Dengbêj, Mullah, Intelligentsia: the survival and revival of the KurdishKurmanji language in the Middle East, 1925–1960*. Unpublished PhD dissertation. Chicago: University of Chicago.

History and Organization of the Anatolian
Ašuł/ Âşık/ Aşıq Bardic Traditions

Xi Yang

Introduction

Sources about the *ašuł/âşık/aşıq* bardic tradition, especially before the seventeenth century, are deplorably poor and the situation does not significantly improve until the nineteenth century, when modern scholarly practices were introduced into the area. Therefore, much information concerning the bardic tradition during the sixteenth to eighteenth centuries has to be pieced together or even conjectured from later sources, which inevitably raises certain questions about the reliability of the resulting construction.

For the sake of brevity, whenever the context is clear, I will refer to "*ašuł, âşık, and aşıq*" as "bardic tradition" and the exponent as "bard". In many cases the term *ašuł/âşık/aşıq* will be individualized to refer purely to ethnic Armenian, Turkish or Azarbaijani bards respectively. The terms Azerbaijan/Azerbaijani/ Azeri are used without any political implications. "Azerbaijan" refers to both the territory of the current Republic of Azerbaijan (called "Tartary" in Russian in the nineteenth century) as well as the region in the Northwest of Iran, which bears this name from ancient times. "Azerbaijani" as a noun refers to the Turkic inhabitants of both territories mentioned above in addition to those Turkic inhabitants who used to live, or still live in the Republic of Armenia and the mostly eastern and southern parts of the Republic of Georgia, which belonged to the Persian Empire in the early modern period, since from Russian Imperial times onward these people are identified as "Azerbaijanis". As an adjective, "Azerbaijani" pertains to the Azerbaijanis. "Azeri" refers to the Turkic language spoken by the "Azerbaijanis" as defined above. For Armenian, Georgian and Russian, the Library of Congress system of transliteration is followed; while transliterations of Arabic, Persian, and Ottoman follow the system of the *International Journal of Middle East Studies* (IJMES).

The *ašuł/âşık/aşıq* type of bard is associated with a composite performing art, a unity of narration and song to instrumental accompaniment with the appropriate use of gesture. On the whole the requirements for becoming a bard resemble those in other bardic traditions, i.e. that the candidate should possess a good memory and be able to master the art of singing and playing musical instruments (primarily strings; especially the *saz*) (Başgöz, 2008: 98). There seems to have been no prescription regarding their family background, and only a few hailed from a well-off family[1] while even rarer individuals could lay claim to high rank.[2] Blind bards are found from time to time, e.g. the famous early nineteenth-century Armenian *ašuł* Širin[3] or the twentieth-century Turkish Âşık Veysel,[4] but the claim by some scholars that bards were frequently blind is unsupported,[5] as established by Garegin Levonyan's list of Armenian *ašuł*s up to the late nineteenth century (Levonyan, 1892: 16–132) and Erman Artun's list of famous sixteenth-to-twentieth-centuries Turkish *âşık*s (Artun, 2011: 273–488), most of whom do not belong to that category.[6] On the contrary, a number of bards were orphaned at a very early age, losing at least one parent, e.g. Ašuł Širin and Jīvani, but here, too, it is hardly possible to draw any significant correlations between their family situation and their becoming a bard (Başgöz, 2008: 104–109). There are reports that Armenian Christian *ašuł*s learned the art from Turkic masters, such as the example of the nineteenth-century Armenian *ašuł* Zahri who studied with the Turkish *âşık* master Necmi (Levonyan, 1944: 39),[7] though I have not encountered any example in the opposite direction.

Judging from extant written sources, there were hardly any women bards before the nineteenth century,[8] when Armenian and Azerbaijani female *ašuł/aşıq*s first appeared in what are now the republics of Armenian and Azerbaijan. From

---

[1]   For example, the late nineteenth-century Armenian *ašuł* Šahir-Xačʻatur, on whom see Grigoryan's chapter in: *Hay nor grakanutʻyan patmutʻyun*, vol. 4, 1972, p. 704, or the Turkish *âşık* İsa Kemali, on whom see: Başgöz, 2008: pp.72–73.

[2]   For example, Kul Mehmed, a sixteenth-century Turkish *âşık*, was born into the family of a pasha (Köprülü, 1962–1965: 59–60).

[3]   (1827–1854) Born as Yovhannēs Karapetean in Kołb, lived and performed in Alekʻsandrapol and Vałaršapat. See Š. Grigoryan's chapter on him in: *Hay nor grakanutʻyan patmutʻyun*, vol. 1, 1962, pp. 273–289.

[4]   (1894–1973) Born in the village of Sivrialan in the Sivas province, he first attracted the attention of the local teacher Ahmet Kutsi Tecer (1901–1967, a Turkish scholar and politician) by a song composed for the tenth anniversary of the Turkish Republic, and later won nation-wide fame. See Artun, 2011: 389–391.

[5]   Abovean's description in *Verkʻ Hayastani* (Abovyan, 1948: 4). See also Von Haxthausen, 1982: 11, as excerpted from Taylor 1854. See also Levonyan, 1892: 32.

[6]   However, among the four Armenian *ašuł*s known for their storytelling to Levonyan, three of them were blind: Tʻujjar, Bangi, Feyradi (Fahrad). In the case of Abovean and von Haxthausen, the blind *ašuł*s are reported more for their story-telling as well. Therefore, it might be possible that among the Armenian *ašuł*s who lived more on storytelling in the nineteenth century, a significant percentage of them were blind. See Levonyan, 1963: 109–110.

[7]   I also heard from Prof. Zumrud Dadaşzadə in Baku on Jun. 5th, 2011 that she knew of a contemporary Armenian *ašuł* from Urmia region in the Western Azerbaijan Province, Northwestern Iran, who had studied with an Azeri master.

[8]   Aşıq Pəri is often labeled as the first woman *aşıq*. She was from Karabakh and died in 1834 (Axundov et al., 1985: 118). However, in an article of Anna Oldfield Senarslan an even earlier name appears: Aşıq Zərnigar from Derbent, who was the wife of *aşıq* Valəh (Oldfield Senarslan, 2007: 2). But this name is otherwise unknown. Levonyan also reported the names of several nineteenth-century female Armenian *ašuł*s such as Maro Naxiǰevancʻi, Varso Łarsecʻi, and Tʻamar Erevancʻi, on which, see Levonyan, 1944: 44. I cannot find any biographical reference to them.

ԱՇՈՒՂՆԵՐԸ ՄՐՋԱՐԱՆՈՒՄ   Նկար Գ․ ԲՐՈՒՏՅԱՆԻ

Figure 1: *Ašuł* in a coffee house (Levonyan, 1944: 19)

the available sources, there seems to have been no restriction on what or where they performed (Oldfield Senarslan, 2007: 2–3). In contrast, even in the mid-twentieth century in Eastern Turkey and Iranian Azerbaijan the concept of a female *âşık* was still strenuously rejected by locals. Significantly, all six female *âşık*s listed by Artun were born after the 1920s in the Adana, Eskişehir, Çorum, and Sivas provinces, with only the last emanating from inland Anatolia (Artun, 2011: 480–488). For the sole case from the Sivas province, it is not clear whether the Âşık Şahturna is of Alevi-Bektaşi family background (Artun, 2011: 483–484). This is important as in that community there are fewer restrictions on women's activities. According to Başgöz, since the term *âşık* denotes a person in the throes of passionate love, it would be considered a disgrace for a Muslim woman to become an *âşık* before marriage, but even a married *âşık* would expose herself to serious pressure from men.

> Only after the 1960 Turkish constitution was ratified guaranteeing human rights and civil liberties to all citizens, did women *âşık*s, mainly from Alevi groups, begin to join *âşık* organizations and participate in concert tours with male *âşık*s. Yet even after this, there are no reports of a single woman *âşık* narrating *hikaye* (Başgöz, 2008: 208–209).

Until WWI, bards from a Sufi background propagating their religious beliefs by way of bardic performance were not rare. However, subsequently radical changes in both Soviet domains and the Turkish Republic significantly reduced their numbers. At the same time, *hikaye* story telling, or in some cases secular *âşık/aşıq* performance in general is opposed by conservative Muslim clerics.[9]

Origin and Etymology

As constituted in the sixteenth century, this tradition is characterized by a Turkic matrix. However, the term *ašuł/âşık/aşıq* derives from the Arabic form *ʿāshiq* ("lover"), the Armenian form *ašuł* emerging from a Turkic intermediary.[10] İlhan Başgöz adduces an important source, which provides grounds for speculating on the possibility of a secular Arab prefiguration of the later bardic tradition. This is found in the *Kitāb al-Fihrist*, composed in 987 CE by the Arab bibliographer Ibn al-Nadīm (ca. 935–990/1). The eighth chapter of the work deals with "the names of passionate lovers during the pre-Islamic period and the period of Islam about whose historical traditions there were books". According to his explanation, these "passionate lovers (*ʿushshāq* in Arabic, the plural of *ʿāshiq*)" refer to "tribal minstrels called *ʿāshiq*", who performed "the life stories, legendary or real (or a mixture of both), of the Arab minstrels" (Başgöz, 2008: 7–8). Though this tradition was in circulation in the pre-Islamic and early Islamic periods, this far no record of it has been found postdating Ibn al-Nadīm in the tenth century, while the current bardic tradition originates in the sixteenth century. Despite the time gap, this new approach raises important issues regarding the origin of the tradition, which merits further investigation.

In his monograph *Hikâye*, Başgöz also contextualizes the *ašuł/âşık/aşıq* genre within the development of earlier romance, epic- and story-telling traditions in the Near East. In addition to the Arabic *maddāḥ*[11] and Persian *naqqāl* traditions, another important trajectory is sketched by bards of the Parthian *gōsān* type widely disseminated in the Persian and Armenian realms in the Late Antique period and beyond.[12] In the Armenian sphere the parallel term *gusan* is attested into the fifteenth century,[13] at which point certain practitioners of the art are referred to by the Turkic form *ozan*, which was later used to refer to the *âşık* as well.[14] De-

---

[9]   As reported by Başgöz, in the 1960s, some conservative *mullah*s in Tabriz were still opposed to the *aşıq*s' singing and storytelling (1998a: 27).

[10] The Armenian consonant *ł* renders Oghuz Turkic q in loan words. For this consonantal correspondence, see Pisowicz, 1995: 95–110.

[11] Başgöz has not treated the *maddāḥ* story-telling tradition among Ottoman Turks in the book in general, on which, see *Encyclopedia of Islam*, "New edition" (2nd edition), (951–953). Leiden: Brill 1979–1985, vol. V, 1986.

[12] For the Parthian *gusan* tradition, see Boyce, 1957: 10–45.

[13] It is difficult to provide first-hand material on this issue. However, since Aṙakʿel Siwnecʿi used *awzan=ozan* in his treaties rather than *gusan*, one might conjecture that the latter term was not in circulation at that time. See Cowe, 1995: 43.

[14] Fuad Köprülü, "Ozan", included in *Edebiyat araştırmaları*, Ankara: Türk Tarih Kurumu Basımevi, 1966, p. 144.

spite certain linguistic problems with the reconstruction, attempts have been made to establish etymological connections between the two terms (Baxč'inyan, 1987: 105 and Başgöz, 2001: 234).

Since bardic storytelling (*hikâye*) consists of prose narration interspersed with rhymed songs, it is useful to examine earlier examples of such techniques already extant in the Near East. These include *The Arabian Nights* and the related Armenian *Kafa* tradition, which flourished from around the thirteenth to the seventeenth centuries (Simonyan, 1975). These traditions may afford more plausible and immediate connections with the bardic tradition than those often highlighted but of more distant origin.

Previous scholarship tended to identify the *ašuł/ âşık/ aşıq* bard as an offspring of the Central Asian Turkic minstrel tradition (Köprülü, 1966: 131–144; Başgöz, 2001: 229–235)[15] associating this with the epic tradition of that region, and ultimately, Shamanism.[16] Here, too, Başgöz has weighed in on the debate, arguing against the suggested parallels between shamans and *âşık*s (Başgöz, 2008: 94–95). According to him, the *âşık* does not share the same or similar character traits to troubled individuals, as has been postulated for shamans. Nor does the *âşık*'s dream or selection of his profession parallel the shaman's initiatory dreams and ceremony to cure mental illness. Another essential aspect underexplored by proponents of a Central Asian origin is that in much of the literature supporting this view, the storytelling aspect of the tradition, as opposed to the very different style of epic declamation, lacks a comprehensive treatment (Başgöz, 2008: 3–13).

In this connection, some scholars actually applied the term "*âşık* traditions" to storytelling among the various Turkic peoples in general, as, for example, the Kazakh and Kyrgyz *aqyn*.[17] Yet this categorization is questionable, since, even if these traditions share a common origin with the *âşık/ aşıq* tradition, if we accept the arguments regarding Shamanism and epic, they nevertheless mapped out their own distinct route of development over several centuries and do not necessarily maintain many common religious, thematic, prosodic, or musicological features. Hence, there is no documentation on the Kazakh and Kyrgyz *aqyns*, for example, engaging in the performance of prose narrative rather than singing or chanting to instrumental accompaniment. Moreover, the content of their narratives is predominantly epic, while in the *âşık/ aşıq* bardic tradition the themes are overwhelmingly romantic (Chadwick and Zhirmunsky, 2010: 316).

---

[15] It should be mentioned that the word *ozan* survived quite tenaciously into the eighteenth century, since famous âşık Karacaoğlan was called an *ozan* in a song from 1707. See Öztelli, 1971: XIX. It is also found in some modern Turkish dialects, as reflected in Başgöz's article. Another reference worth mentioning is that the Turkish term *ozan* even appeared in Armenian sources in the form of *awzan*, on which see Cowe, 1995: 43. For the critical edition of the Armenian text, see Xač'arean, 1982: 84.

[16] See Fuad Köprülü, "Bahši", included in *Edebiyat araştırmaları*, pp. 145–156, Başgöz, 2008, *passim*, and Qasımlı, 2003, *passim*.

[17] An example of such broad definition can be found in Artun, 2011: 26–29.

Most scholars agree now that the *ašuł/âşık/aşıq* tradition established itself by the sixteenth century when records of such bards begin to appear.[18] To support this view, both Boratav and Başgöz have formed their respective arguments on this formation. Boratav's approach is very innovative. He bases his argumentation on the evolution of poetic forms. According to him, an important support is the significant circulation of the 11-syllable line *koşma*, which is enormously popular among *âşık*s, at the turn of the sixteenth century, though it is rarely recorded in the early period.[19]

Returning to issues of nomenclature, there is a widespread view associating the application of the term *ašuł/âşık/aşıq* to bards within the Muslim Sufi mystical tradition.[20] After the rise of Sufism, the term's reference to Sufi practitioners was transferred to bards, since according to Sufi mystical philosophy they are lovers, whose love is God. This usage continues today among various Sufi orders. Even for secular bards the title *Hak âşık/Həqq aşıq* "God's lover"[21] or *Hak Aşığı* "God-inspired lover-poet"[22] is bestowed on those virtuosi, as had been used among Sufi *âşık/aşıq*s to address themselves (Başgöz, 2008: 9).

The nineteenth-century growth of nationalism in the Ottoman and Tsarist Russian domains and its twentieth-century developments in the Turkish Republic and USSR have spurred a widespread movement among Armenians, Turks, and Azerbaijanis alike to replace the lingering foreign connotations of the Arabic term *ašuł/âşık/aşıq* with "native" terms in their own languages pertaining to earlier bardic traditions. In the Armenian case, the alternative is *gusan*, while in Turkey and Azerbaijan that of *ozan* as well as *saz şair* (*saz*[23] poet), *halk şair* (folk poet) and less frequently, *müğənni* (singer), *el şair* (folk singer), etc. Ironically, the term *gusan* is ultimately Parthian; while the forms *şair, müğənni* etc. are Arabic still.

The bardic tradition used to be found over a vast geographic expanse mostly inhabited by the Oghuz Turks, roughly from the Balkans to Iran,[24] however, the focus of this study will be primarily Anatolia and Southern Caucasia and, to a less degree, Iranian Azerbaijan, due to the availability of materials and their historical importance.[25]

---

[18] As reflected in Köprülü, 1966; Günay, 1999; Artun, 2011; Sahakyan, 1961; Qasımlı, 2003; all holding this view.

[19] "La littérature des 'aşïq" in Jean Deny et al. Ed., *Philologiae Turcicae Fundamenta*, vol. 2, Wiesbaden: Aquis Mattiacis Apud Franciscum Steiner, 1964, pp. 138–139.

[20] For example, Başgöz, 2008, *passim*.

[21] For the Turkish title, see Başgöz, 2008: 9 and, for the Azeri one, see Qasımlı, 2003: 89–117.

[22] For this title, see Başgöz, 2008: 197.

[23] The *saz* is the most important musical instrument in the bardic tradition.

[24] From Zhirmunsky's description (Chadwick and Zhirmunsky, 2010: 316), it seems that the Turkmens have traditions of romance-telling parallel to the Turks and Azeris. Artun also has a very brief description of the "Turkmen *âşık* tradition" in Artun, 2011: 26–27.

[25] It also briefly covers Algiers, once the major base of Ottoman navy in West Mediterranean, and Georgia where bardic tradition had a tiny branch will be mentioned only when necessary. For a brief reference, see Hacılar, 2011: 40–44; Üstünyer, 2009: 137–149.

ԳԵՂՋՈՒԿ ԱՇՈՒՂԸ ՔԱՂԱՔՈՒՄ   Նկար Դ. ԲՐՈՒՏՅԱՆԻ

Figure 2: *Ašuł* in a town (Levonyan, 1944: 33)

An Overview of the History of the Bardic Tradition in the Target Region

It is regrettable that biographical materials regarding bards tend to be rather sparse, particularly for the sixteenth to eighteenth centuries, so that the main source for data on them is the text of their songs. In this they differ from elevated poets, whose biographies can be found in *tezkire* collections (memorandum, memoir) in Turkish or the lives (*varkʻ*) and manuscript colophons of ecclesiastics, who largely filled the ranks of Early Modern Armenian literati. Another complicating factor is that several bards share the same professional name. Thus, there may be at least two Turkish *âşıks* from different centuries and different locations known by the name Karacaoğlan.[26] Evidence includes anecdotes circulating in the area where a bard flourished and references in later bards' narratives or songs about their illustrious predecessors, such songs comprising the tiny subgenre of bardic songs called *şairname* (record of poets) in Turkish.[27] Other materials include tangible objects related to them, such as tombstones, manuscripts,

---

[26] There are different opinions about how many Karacaoğlans there may have been. See Öztelli, 1971: XIII-XXIII, which argues for the single authorship of the songs in the collection. See also Günay, 1999: 185–214, where two different *âşık* Karacaoğlans from different centuries and origin are differentiated.

[27] The same term is also used in the sense of *tezkire* as well. According to Artun, the first *şairname*s date back to the seventeenth century (Artun, 2011: 303).

etc. In contrast, evidence for the development of the bardic tradition in the nineteenth and twentieth centuries is much more profuse, and often serves as the only basis for reconstructing aspects of the earlier period. The overview of the tradition that follows loosely narrates the history of the genre by century without intending any rigid application of that timeframe.

1500–1600

This century is generally regarded by scholars as the era when the bardic tradition ultimately took shape.[28] The Ottoman navy and army as well as Sufi *tekkes* are the main institutions from this period that preserve the works of contemporary Turkish *âşık*s. Much of the naval material derives from Algiers, the Ottoman navy's major base in the West.[29] From the scarce record of these early *âşık*s, we learn that they served in the Ottoman navy and were regularly required to perform to improve the sailors' morale.[30] Information also exists about bardic activity in Anatolia and Azerbaijan. Several of the Turkic *âşık/aşıq*s there have explicit military affiliations, as can be seen from their works, either as soldiers or officers in the Ottoman army or Celâli rebels,[31] who were Alevites with Shiite affinities and hence hostile to the former group. A second strain of *âşık*s in these regions bore strong links to Sufism, e.g. Pir Sultan Abdal in Anatolia, who was an Alevi;[32] and Aşıq Qurbani from the Safavid sphere, who is said to have been at the court of Safavid Shah Ismail for a while and has songs in fervent praise of Shah Ismail Khaṭā'ī.[33] Later, such famous early *âşık*s, as well as Shah Khaṭā'ī, were to become the subject of *âşık* songs and heroic or romantic tales, though much of the data in these works is fictional.[34] From the sixteenth century onwards, the center for *aşıq* activity in Iran was Tabriz, center of the Azerbaijan re-

---

[28] Various titles, for example, Köprülü, 1962–1965: 39 and Artun, 2011: 273–274.

[29] In Köprülü's collection, 5 out of 11 *âşık*s from this period were navy *âşık*s. See Köprülü, 1962–1965: 59–64.

[30] Ibid.

[31] The Celâlî rebellions were a series of Alevi resistance movements against the Ottoman authorities in Anatolia in the sixteenth and seventeenth centuries, of which the first broke out in 1519 under the leadership of Celâl, an Alevi preacher. See Türkiye Diyanet Vakfı, İslâm Ansiklopedisi Genel Müdürlüğü: *Türkiye Diyanet Vakfı İslâm Ansiklopedisi*, Üsküdar, Istanbul, vol. 7, 1993, pp. 252–257.

[32] Very little is known about his life, except stories and his poetry, in which he always turns out to be an Alevi, participating in the Alevi revolt against the Ottoman Empire under the influence and instigation of the Safavids. See Artun, 2011: 286–289.

[33] Very little is known about his life. Though he was probably born in a village called Diri, its exact location is still not very clear. Qəzənfər Kazımov, his editor, claims it should be in what is now the Azerbaijani Republic, while others argue for a location currently in Iranian Azerbaijan. See Kazımov, 1990: 4–20; Axundov, Saim Sakaoğlu et al., 1985, vol.1: 1. For the fervent paean for Shah Ismail Khaṭā'ī, see: Kazımov, 1990: 53.

[34] For the plots of these stories, see Appendix A: Plot outlines of fifty *hikaye* romances, Başgöz, 2008 217–285.

gion, an early Safavid power base, and an important longstanding center of international trade. The first Armenian *ašuł*, Nahapet Kʻučʻak,[35] from Xaṙakunis in the Lake Van area also flourished in this century, of whose Turkish compositions about ten songs in standard *ašuł* meters are transmitted, treating themes common in Armenian *ašuł* literature.[36] Apart from Nahapet Kʻučʻak we also hear of the activities of other contemporary Armenian bards like *ašuł* Mesihi.[37]

1600–1700

Fuad Köprülü designated the seventeenth century as the "golden age" of the Turkish *âşık* tradition (Köprülü, 1966: 209) granted the emergence of exponents from a large geographical range and more diversified background. These included at least two of the most prolific and most accomplished pre-nineteenth century Turkish bards, Âşık Gevheri[38] and Âşık Ömer[39] who adopted not only the *ʿarūḍ* quantitative meters but also the style of the *divan* literature tradition and became the most prolific and successful among their peers. Sources for *ašuł/ aşıq*s in the Iranian domain, however, are relatively few. Two famous Azerbaijani *aşıq*s flourished in this century: Abbas Tufarğanlı[40] and Sarı Aşıq.[41] This century also witnessed the appearance of Łul Egaz[42] and Łul Arzuni,[43] the first Armenian *ašuł*s from the town of New Julfa across the river from the Safavid capital of Isfahan, where they were born in the 1650s. They are also the first extant *ašuł*s composing in the Armenian language, which thrived in the context of the cosmopolitan atmosphere associated with the international trade network created by

---

[35] See Bardakjian, 2000: 428–430 and, for the text of the songs, Ōnnik Ēganyan, "Nahapet Kʻučʻaki hayataṙ tʻurkeren tałerě", *Banber Matenadarani* (5), 1960, pp. 465–481.

[36] His tombstone used to be found in the graveyard of S. Tʻeodoros Monastery in his home village Xaṙakunis, which bore his name and the year of death: 1592. See Nairi Zaryan's account in Hrant Tʻamrazyan ed., *Nahapet Kʻučʻaki banastełcakan ašxarhě*, Yerevan: Erevani Petakan Hamalsarani Hratarakčʻutʻyun, 2001, pp. 117–118.

[37] One of exceptions is *ašuł* Mesihi, on whom, see Köprülü: "Turk Edebiyatinin Ermeni Edebiyati üzerindeki Tesirleri", in *Edebiyat araştırmaları*, 1966, pp. 263–264.

[38] Little is certain about him apart from data in some of his songs, such as one welcoming the Crimean Khan Selim Giray I to Constantinople, which was written in 1100 A. H./1688–1689 C. E.. See Elçin, 1984: 11–19 and Artun, 2011: 311–312.

[39] Little is certain about him except that he thrived in this century. This situation is true even in the most comprehensive collection of his works. See Ergün, 1936: 5–14. An brief updated description can be found in Artun, 2011: 305–307.

[40] Little is known about his life except his birthplace, the village of Tufarğan (close to Tabriz), as reflected in his professional name. See Dadaşzadə, 1973: 3.

[41] Little is known about his life except that his tomestone was discovered in Karabakh in 1927. See further Axundov, Sakaoğlu et al., 1985, vol. 1: 41.

[42] Born in the 1650s, little is sure about his life, except that he was circuiting among the Armenian villages around Isfahan with his musical instrument, the chongur; and his tombstone was in the Armenian cemetery there, erected in 1734. See Eremean, 1930: 2–3.

[43] He was a contemporary of Łul Egaz. But he spent much of his life in Kolkata, India. See Eremean, 1930: 12–13.

the wealthy Armenian *khoja*s.[44] Meanwhile, in the Ottoman Empire, Armenian *ašuł*s like Vartan and Civan composed songs in Turkish. Unfortunately, records for them are even more meager than those concerning Iranian Armenian bards (Köprülü, 1962–1965: 399, 446–454).

1700–1820s

Here it is appropriate to extend the period to the 1820s to include two watershed events, the annihilation of the Janissaries in Constantinople in 1826 and the completion of the Russian annexation of the Southern Caucasia, marked by the treaty of Turkmenchay of 1828, both of which exerted an important influence on the development of the subsequent traditions.

This period tends to be regarded as a stagnant period for the Turkish *âşık* tradition by modern Turkish scholars (Artun, 2011: 324). Although *âşık*s appeared from every social background as in the previous century, and more of their names and works have come down to us thanks to their inclusion from this point in *tezkire*s or *şairname*s, none were as prolific or accomplished as Karacaoğlan, Gevheri, or Ömer. Another noteworthy phenomenon is the expanded influence of classical Persian and Turkish poetry on contemporary Turkish *âşık*s expressed in the use of tropes, allusions, and other literary devices along with the *ʿarūḍ* quantitative prosody alongside syllabic prosody.

Across the border in the Iranian sphere of Azerbaijan and South Caucasia, the Azeri *aşıq* tradition echoes the Ottoman. Famous new *aşıq*s, for example, Xəstə Qasim[45] appeared in this century, whose life became a theme for later *aşıq* songs, like Qurbani or Abbas Tufarğanlı in previous centuries. However, their number is less than in the previous century.

The situation is quite different in the case of Armenians. Not only do we have more records of Armenian *ašuł*s than Turkish *âşık*s and Azeri *aşıq*s , but we also observe that they span a much larger geographical are from Constantinople to the Armenian Plateau, then on to Isfahan and its surrounding Armenian communities, as well as Tiflis, the three capital cities functioning as centers of Armenian *ašuł* activities. Moreover, Armenian *ašuł*s have left a more multilingual corpus of composition now embracing not only Turkish and Armenian, but also Georgian and (in very rare cases) Persian. Similarly, the background of those Armenian *ašuł*s is much diversified. Apart from those with an affiliation to the Armenian Apostolic Chrisitans, a few were followers of the Alevi-Bektaşi Sufi order, or at least held a syncretic creed uniting elements of Christianity and

---

[44] For their works, see Eremean, 1921; Eremean, 1930; Sahakyan, 1961: 71–103.
[45] Like the famous Azeri *aşıq*s mentioned earlier, there is little known about his life except that his hometown is Tikmədaş not far from Tabriz. His tomestone is also found in the cemetery there. See İsmayılov et al., 2010: 3–4.

Alevism.[46] Probably partly due to the sheer number of Armenian *ašuł*s known to us from this century, their compositions comprise more topics in more diversified styles as well. Many Armenian *ašuł*s from this century seem to have secured their places in modern publications of Armenian literature, e.g. Yart'un-Ōłli,[47] Nałaš Yovnat'an,[48] Šamč'i Melk'ō,[49] and finally, Sayat'-Nova.

1820s–1920s

The bardic tradition in this period reflects the change witnessed in the political, military, and cultural history of the region. These changes were connected to the introduction of much more powerful Western influence, and to Russian expansion and the incorporation of Southern Caucasia area, though the pace of change varied.

The demise of the Ottoman navy, the loss of Maghreb and the disbandment of the Janissaries and ensuing military reorganization led to a rapid decline of military *âşık*s. In contrast, bardic associations in Constantinople and Alek'sandrapol[50] formed themselves into professional organizations with a guild structure. Meanwhile, a number of bardic centers were established in various areas, many of which continued into the next century, as observed from the records adduced in twentieth-century monographs. Another striking development is that especially in the Russian sphere, under the impact of nationalism, Armenian *ašuł*s established an Armenian "national" *ašuł* tradition distinguished by the promotion of Armenian language in their compositions, gradually leading to a

---

46 The *Bektaşi*s like the *Mevlevi*s are quite open to people of all confessions. Therefore, participation in their activities cannot be used as an exclusive proof of participants' religious belief.

47 Born as Yovhannēs Yarut'iwnean in the 1760s in a peasant family in the village of Asadabad in the Č'armahal district of Isfahan province, he went to the village school, then learned the *ašuł* art from *ašuł* Łul Yovhannēs (c. 1740–1834, the death date is according to his tombstone in the Armenian cemetery in New Julfa: Aug. 16, 1840. See Eremean, 1929: 7–8), and superseded his master. For a better education, he went to Ejmiacin for some years during his wandering, and claimed that he received divine revelation as a qualified *ašuł* from S. Karapet (St. John the Predecessor) during his pilgrimage to the S. Karapet Monastery in Muş, which tradition would be explained further later. He died in 1840, and his tombstone is found in the cemetery of Mamuk'a village, Č'armahal. See Eremean, 1946: 7–14.

48 Born in the village of Šoṙot', Agulis, Nakhichevan in 1661, he was invited to Tiflis by Vakhtang VI, king of Kartli, as court singer and painter between 1703–1712, but returned to Agulis at an unknown time for unknown reasons. He died before Oct. 28, 1722, since his son composed an elegy him at his tomb on that day. See Mnac'akanyan and Nazaryan, 1951: V–VII.

49 Little is sure about his life. He might have been born in the 1750s and died after 1821. He called himself as from Tiflis, was an eyewitness to Agha Muhammad Khan's conquest and destruction of Tiflis, when his father Bežan was killed and presented "serfs" to Ejmiacin in 1801. See Melik'set'-Bek, 1958: 5–15.

50 Now Gyumri, Armenia. See Levonyan, 1944: 20–22 and Köprülü, 1962–1965: 526–527.

reduction in the use of Turkic dialects.[51] Another characteristic of this period was
the inauguration of modern scholarly bardic studies.

Though some Turkish scholars view the period as a second "golden age" of the
Turkish *âşık* art (Yardımcı, 1998: 98); others consider it the beginning of its decline
(Artun, 2011: 333). Moved by personal taste, the consecutive sultans from Selim
III (r.1789–1807) to Abdülaziz (r. 1861–1876), including Mahmud II (r. 1808–
1839), extended patronage to several secular *âşık*s in Constantinople for a good
time in this period. Sultan Mahmud II established a formal organization for *âşık*s
in Constantinople (Köprülü, 1962–1965: 527 and Artun, 2011: 333). However, certain scholars maintain that after the reign of these sultans the *âşık* tradition began
to lose its importance in cities (Artun, 2011: 333). Moreover, although the *âşık* art
aroused more interest from learned circles in the Tanzimat era (1839–1876), the
coffee house in the capital that used to be part of a Janissary monopoly until the
latter's disbandment in 1826 and dominated by *âşık* performance, evolved into the
semâî kahvehane (cabaret coffee house). People from other backgrounds, especially
traditional fire fighters[52] and hoodlums gained the monopoly of these venues (Artun, ibid.). Songs composed by the two groups of city dwellers were made up of
manis and *semâîs*,[53] in contrast to the *âşık*s' more diversified repertoire. This led to
the collapse of *âşık* song genres, and might be regarded as a prefiguration of the
general decline of the *âşık* tradition in the Ottoman Empire and future Turkish Republic. During the reign of Sultan Abdülhamid II (1876–1908), *alafranka*, or West-
ern-fashioned music was provided in *semâî kahvehane*s as well, which might be regarded as a sign of the further decline of traditional *âşık* performances. After Sultan
Abdülhamid II's deposition in 1908, these *semâî kahvehane*s began to decline as
well as part of a process, which came to an end at around 1920. Scholars from this
period like Rıza Tevfik,[54] Ziya Gökalp[55] and Fuad Köprülü, who were often writers
and social activists simultaneously, paid much attention to the *âşık*s and their art.
Under the strong influence of nationalism, and dissatisfied with divan literature,
which in form and language bore the ubiquitous influence of classical Arabic and
Persian literatures, these nineteenth-century Turkish intellectuals attempted to create a new national literature in an idiom closer to the language of the people. In
this regard, *âşık* literature naturally attracted them.[56]

---

51   See Ramazanov, 1976. I was also informed personally by scholars in Baku about a con-
      temporary Iranian Armenian *aşuł* from the Urmia region still composing in Azeri. Azerbai-
      jani National Academy of Sciences, Jun. 5, 2011.
52   These people, called *tulumbacı* or "pump man" in Turkish, were not modern fire fighters,
      but rather belonged to a tradition developed locally.
53   Two genres of *âşık* songs.
54   (1869–1949), later with the surname Bölükbaşı, Turkish scholar, politician, philosopher
      and leader of a sect of the *Bektaşi* community.
55   (1876–1924), Turkish scholar, writer, thinker and political activist, one of the first advocates
      for Turkish nationalism.
56   Köprülü, 1966: 225 and Boratav's contribution to *Philologiae Turcicae Fundamenta*, vol. 2,
      1964, pp. 143–144.

Azerbaijan and Southern Caucasia, both Iranian until the Russo-Persian wars, now bifurcated. The territory belonging to modern Iran is badly served by accessible historical data, while material published in Soviet Azerbaijan and now the independent Republic of Azerbaijan only sporadically covers the situation in Iran.[57] As a result, it is largely omitted from my study. Even for Russian Transcaucasia, available sources are too sparse to create a connected narrative.[58] Judging from the few references I have assembled, artistically it seems it remained on the old track, though with innovations and expansion in contents, and a certain exposure to elevated literature as well (Namazov, 1983: 85). Trends in the development of the Armenian *ašuł* tradition in the Russian Empire domain pursued a path parallel to that among the Azerbaijanis, but embraced more innovative or modernizing steps. This can be regarded as a result of the greater employment of Armenian language[59] and *ašuł* involvement in enlightening or nationalist trends, in which the key figure was Ašuł Ĵivani.[60] Among those *ašuł*s employing Turkic, the most accomplished figure was K'ešiš-Ōłli/Keşişoğlu (1804–1872), a blind *ašuł* from Tiflis, who was later brought to Sultan Mahmud II's court to perform in Constantinople.[61]

From the 1920s Onwards

In general, this period witnessed a decline of the tradition over the whole region. Western (including Russian/Soviet) influence and globalization after WWII comprehensively transformed conditions in the area. Modern media, such as publications, sound recordings, radio, film, television and internet, assisted in spreading the bardic tradition and making it more accessible, but also disseminated more modern cultural forms which thus competed for consumers' time and attention. Consequently, the bardic tradition, whose aesthetic structures were fixed in past centuries, is only one of numerous traditional art forms now

---

[57] It seems the situation is getting improved in the post-Soviet period, together with the enhanced Azeri-Iranian cultural exchange. News covering Iran on the website of Union of Azerbaijani *Aşıq*s (to be explained later in this section) can be found in ascending frequency on their website: http://azab.az/xeber/?do=cat&category=xeber , on which the latest updates are about the establishment of Union of Iranian *Aşıq*s in October 2015.

[58] For further details, see Araslı, 1960: 84–95.

[59] The Armenian *ašuł*s from Širin on began to discard Arabic, Persian, or Turkish loanwords from their compositions. They also started to translate and publish in Armenian stories that till then circulated in Turkic. See: *Hay nor grakanut'yan patmut'yun*, relevant chapters: Hasmik Sahakyan, "Ašułakan poezia" in vol. 1, Yerevan, 1962, pp. 269–271; Š. Grigoryan, "Ašułakan poezia" in vol. 4, Yerevan, 1972, pp. 697–698; as well as Levonyan, 1963: 121–123.

[60] See: Grigoryan's chapter in: *Hay nor grakanut'yan patmut'yun*, vol. 4, 1972, p. 702; and Levonyan, 1963: 137–145.

[61] He was born as Davit' and changed his professional name at least twice. See Lewonean, 1892: 26–27 and Xač'ik Amirean, 1989: 180–181.

gradually disappearing,[62] first from major city centers, then regional centers, and ultimately from the rural areas. Although writers of the literate tradition initially drew from oral traditions in structuring their plots, especially in the formative period of national literature, its older aesthetics and ethics, based on a more traditional social background, differs radically from contemporary trends under the impact of the West. Consequently, this period is marked by the introduction of various measures to preserve the traditions on the part of governments or other political entities, alongside academic efforts. Nevertheless, although these efforts may succeed in propping up the tradition, the continued process of decline is inevitable.

In Turkey, the decline of the *âşık* tradition in Constantinople/Istanbul, which had begun in the nineteenth century, was completed around 1920 (Artun, 2011: 41), and was then followed by the disappearance of *âşık*s from traditional ambiences, first in other major cities in Western Turkey and finally in Eastern Turkey over a sixty-year process up to the 1980s (Başgöz, 2008: 214–216). Of course *âşık*s are still around, some being honored by the government as distinguished artists and the recipients of financial support.[63] Actually, politicians in Turkey representing a whole spectrum of political views have connections with *âşık*s. For example, the *âşık* festival celebrated in Konya annually in October from 1965 onwards was originally organized by *Konya Âşıklar Derneği* (the Society of *âşık*s in Konya), an organization for politically more conservative *âşık*s, established by conservative political parties and individuals.[64]

In Soviet Azerbaijan and the now independent Republic of Azerbaijan, the *aşıq* tradition has received more sustained attention from the government (as well as the Communist Party in the Soviet era).[65] As is obvious, oversight, especially in the Soviet era, can never be divorced from political concerns. Besides the promotion of the *aşıq* tradition as part of Azerbaijani culture, the potential of propaganda through this art form has never been ignored. With all its positive and negative connotations, Azerbaijani *aşıq* art has at least benefited from the financial support and a steady source for its record, study, performance, inheritance and publication. *Aşıq*s were absorbed into artists' organizations, including the union of writers. Some of them won greater fame, while others were overlooked or even suppressed for political reasons.[66] The *aşıq* tradition entered the

---

[62] For example, Iranian *naqqāli* and other story-telling traditions in the Middle East.

[63] For example, Âşık Veysel. See Başgöz, 2008: 97.

[64] Ibid.

[65] Unfortunately, since the source for Iranian Azeri *aşıq*s in this period is still poor, it is omitted once again as in the last part. For relevant articles, see Başgöz, 1998: 24–42; and Albright, 1976: 220–247.

[66] An example of the suppressed *aşıq* might be Aşıq Mirzə Bilal (1872–1937), who was a representative for the first Qurultay of Soviet *aşıq*s, but arrested during the Great Purge, and executed as an "enemy of the people." He was only rehabilitted in 1993. See the website of Union of Azerbaijani Aşıqs: http://azab.az/qurban/68-aedq-mirzjj-bilal.html, as retrieved

curriculum of the Azerbaijan State University of Culture and Arts, the Azerbaijan National Conservatory, and a number of schools, while research on it has been carried out in the Azerbaijan National Academy of Sciences and other institutions.[67] A special museum dedicated to the Azerbaijani *aşıq* tradition was established in Tovuz, a regional town in Western Azerbaijan, where the tradition has been very active and is still alive. Congresses (in Azeri: *qurultay*) of Azerbaijani *aşıq*s have been held since 1928, of which the last in the Soviet period was held in 1984. Such congresses were convened under the Party's organization with the participation of all Soviet republics with an *aşıq* tradition.[68] From the Stalinist era onwards, Azerbaijani *aşıq*s adopted the Soviet tunic as performance attire alongside traditional costumes, which has established itself into the present.[69] This epitomizes the maintenance of many Soviet institutions and practices in the Azerbaijani Republic until today. Now international *aşıq* conferences and contests are held in Azerbaijan, with participants from Iran, Turkey, and other countries. In 2009, Azerbaijani *aşıq* art was officially registered by UNESCO as an item of intangible world heritage.[70]

The situation in Armenia bears certain similarities with that in Azerbaijan due to parallel conditions under the Tsarist Russian and Soviet rule. Since Jivani's death no new *ašuł* has appeared of his caliber. The improvisation tradition among Armenian *ašuł*s virtually came to an end with the passing of Havasi (1896–1979), the last *ašuł* born in the nineteenth century. Likewise, while the *ašuł* tradition entered the curriculum of the Komitas State Conservatory of Yerevan alongside the positive aspects of instruction and research on the tradition, the conservatory's primary formative influence from Western art music mediated by Russian music has led to the loss of an appreciation of the Near Eastern microtonic system on the part of graduates taught within the confines of the Western well-tempered major and minor scales. *Ašuł* ensembles, again probably modeled after Western orchestral structures, were created in the Soviet period. These ensembles still enjoy immense popularity that involve groups featuring several performers on the same traditional instruments, e.g., *tar, saz, santur, kamancha,*

---

on Sept. 4, 2015. Başgöz also reports an Azerbaijani *aşıq* fled to Turkey during WWII for political asylum, though the exact reason is unspecified. See Başgöz, 2008: 75.

[67] Adapted from the Republic of Azerbaijan's nomination for "The Art of Azerbaijani *Ashiqs*" to UNESCO as intangible cultural heritage: *Nomination for inscription on the Representative List in 2009 (Reference No. 00253)*, Convention for the safeguarding of the intangible cultural heritage, Intergovernmental Committee for the Safeguarding of the Intangible Cultural Heritage, 4th Session, Abu Dhabi, UAE, Sept. 28 – Oct. 2, 2009: http://www.unesco.org/culture/ich/doc/download.php?versionID=29485 as retrieved on Oct. 13, 2015.

[68] For details can see: Namazov, 1983: 154; Akman, 2008: 20.

[69] As reflected from the post-Soviet publications in Azerbaijani Republic still, available from the website of Union of Azerbaijani Aşıqs, *passim*.

[70] As on UNESCO website: http://www.unesco.org/culture/ich/index.php?lg=en&pg=000 11&RL=00253 as retrieved on Sept. 4, 2015.

Figure 3: Countryside *Ašuł* (Levonyan, 1944: 31)

kamani, tav kamani and *dap* to accompany *ašuł* songs.[71] This in contrast to the practice in Soviet Azerbaijan, where *aşıq*s still perform in traditional small-scale groups. But after the collapse of the Soviet Union, due to the severe financial stress in the Armenian Republic, it turned out to be difficult for such practices to continue. Joint efforts are still being made to further promote the Armenian *ašuł* tradition, such as performances in both Armenia and abroad, saving songs from oblivion, and the revival of improvisation. Important scholars and musicians are working on these initiatives, as for example T'ovma Połosyan, who is the professor of Armenian musical folklore studies at the Komitas State Conservatory of Yerevan since 1987, the founder and director of the Sayat-Nova Ašuł Ensemble since 1992, the founder of the Jivani School of Ašuł Art since 1997, and the founder and chairman of the Armenian Ašuł Association since 1997.[72] The revival efforts also benefit from the support of figures like Vahagn Hovnanian, a famous diaspora Armenian entrepreneur and philanthropist, who established and funded an annual *ašuł* competition named after Sayat'-Nova in 2000.[73]

---

[71] A list of the instruments in the ensemble can be found on the introductory page to the Sayat-Nova Minstrel Song Ensemble at http://sayat-nova.org/sayat-nova-ashough-ensemble/, as retrieved on Sept. 4, 2015.

[72] His introduction on http://sayat-nova.org/artistic-director/, as retrieved on Sept. 29, 2015.

[73] He passed away at the end of August, 2015. See http://www.1tv.am/en/news/2015/08/31/Vahagn-Hovnanian/22100, as retrieved on Sept. 29, 2015.

Bardic Organizations

This aspect of the tradition has received much less discussion and attention. Reports on bardic organizations before WWI are scattered and usually brief. Garegin Levonyan provided the most in-depth coverage based on the Armenian *ašuł* organization in Alek'sandrapol. The trade union[74] there was characterized by its statutes, with an administrative body elected by general vote, under the leadership of an *ustabaši*. The organization had a treasury funded by its members' monthly dues for money-lending. In addition to receiving the local *ustabaši's* consent, *ašuł*s from outside were required to pay the equivalent of three months' member's dues to the treasury to perform in the city (Levonyan, 1944: 22). This structure betrays all the features and norms of a guild (*hamk'arut'yun* in Armenian) as constituted at that time in the Near East.

Related to bardic organizations is the issue of bardic jargons only raised by Levonyan (Levonyan, 1963: 197–199). According to him, there was a kind of secret language among Armenian *ašuł*s known as *t'ars lezun* in Armenian.[75] Its main feature was the metathesis of letters in content words. For example, *ōr* (day) becomes *ro*, *ser* (love) *res*, *luys* (light) *suyl*, *sirun* (handsome) *risun*, *xanum* (woman) *nuxam*, *manušak* (violet) *šanumak*, *mxit'arank'* (consolation) *xmit'arank'*, etc. Structural words, reflexive affixes, and syntax were unaffected. Levonyan gives a detailed description of it but no indication of its origin. One might speculate that such a practice was not unique among Armenian *ašuł*s, but in broader circulation among bards from other regions. Clearly Levonyan, being the son of Jivani, the most famous and accomplished Armenian *ašuł* at the turn of the twentieth century, was in a unique position to discuss such phenomena, thus gaining access to much insider information inaccessible for scholars in general.

Köprülü reports that Sultan Mahmud II established a formal organization for *âşık*s in Constantinople as one of the *lonca*s, or guilds of artisans, whose head was an *âşık* chosen by the government from the *âşık*s gathering in a coffee house in the neighborhood of Tavukpazarı, the largest place in the city for *âşık*s to gather, who bore the title of *âşık kâhyası*, or "*âşık* housekeeper". Another official with the title *reis-i âşıkan/âşıklar reisi* (head of the *âşık*s) was employed by the government to control local *âşık*s and to use them for propaganda.[76]

Available sources for bardic organizations in the twentieth century are even scarcer. Başgöz indicates that an organization called *Âşıklar Derneği* (Society of

---

[74]   This is the literal translation of Levonyan's term *arhestakc'akan miut'yun*.

[75]   This term *t'ars* of Turkish origin should mean "opposite". See Hrač'ya Ačaṙyan, *Hayeren armatakan baṙaran*, vol. II, Erevani Hamalsarani Hratarakč'ut'yun, Yerevan, 1963, p. 162, under the entry *t'arsel*.

[76]   Köprülü, 1962 –1965: 526–527. He had more detailed description about the situation in an article "Âşık fasılları" (*İkdam*, Apr. 25th 1914), which is part of his series "Saz şâirleri" in a newspaper unavailable to me. Some parts of this article are quoted from Günay, 1999: 32–34.

âşıks) existed in Turkey in years 1961–1971, which was "supported politically and organizationally by the Turkish Labor Party, and turned into a vigorous protest movement, and shut down after the 1971 military coup"(Başgöz, 2008: 97). Similarly, the *Konya Âşıklar Derneği* (Society of *âşıks* in Konya) referred to above was established by Fevzi Halıcı in 1964 with support from conservative political powers (Başgöz: ibid.).

In Azerbaijan it seems no official organization for *aşıqs* existed before the Union of Azerbaijani *Aşıqs* (Azerbaijani: *Azərbaycan Aşıqlar Birliyi*) was established in 1983 under the Ministry of Culture (Oldfield Senarslan, 2007: 19) since the three prior congresses were convened by other institutions, e.g. the Central Executive Committee of the AzSSR or the Azerbaijani Writers' Union (Namazov, 1983: 154–184). Judging from fragmentary reports, it seems that the Union of Azerbaijani *Aşıqs* functioned by and large like the writers' unions and similar organizations during the Soviet period. It continued into the Post-Soviet period.[77] As for the situation in Armenia, it seems a separate *ašuɫs*' union might not even have existed in the Soviet period, since Tʻovma Poɫosyan became the founder and first chairman of this organization only in 1997, as mentioned before.

In Place of a Conclusion

As mostly a historical introduction, there is quite little to conclude theoretically from this chapter. However, I hope that my juxtaposition of up-to-date information from different parts of Anatolia and Southern Caucasia may be helpful in building a more complete understanding of the bardic tradition in the whole area, rather than studying the situations in each country in isolation.

Bibliography

Abovean, Xačʻatur (1948). Verkʻ Hayastani. *X. Abovyan: Erkeri liakatar žoɫovacu.* Vol. 3, Yerevan: HSSṘ GA Hratarakčʻutʻyun.

Academy of Sciences, Armenian Soviet Socialist Republic (Ed.) (1962–1979). *Hay nor grakanutʻyan patmutʻyun.* 5 volumes. Yerevan: Haykakan SSR GA Hrataraкčʻutʻyun.

Ačaṙyan, Hračʻya (1971–1979). *Hayeren armatakan baṙaran.* Yerevan: Erevani Hamalsarani Hrataraкčʻutʻyun.

Akman, Eyüp (2008). Stalin sonrası Azerbaycan'da âşık edebiyatı ve âşık kurultayları. *Türkbilig.* Vol. 15, 13–23.

Albright, Charlotte F. (1976). The *Azerbaijani Ashiq* and his Performance of a *Dastan. Iranian Studies.* Vol. 9, No. 4, 220–247.

---

[77] See their website: www.azab.az, as retrieved on Sept. 4, 2015.

Amirean, Xačʻik (1989). *Tʻurkʻalezu Hay ašułner, (Ōsmanyan kaysrutʻiwn, 16-20rd darer)*, J. Kasbarian. Paris: Aulnay-sous-Bois.

Axundov, əhliman et al. (Ed. in Azerbaijani); Sakaoğlu, Saim et al. (Ed. in Turkish) (1985–1986). *Azerbaycan âşıkları ve el şiirleri*. 2 volumes, Istanbul: Halk Kültürü.

Araslı, Həmid (1960). *Aşıq yaradıcılığı*. Baku: Birləşmis̡ Nəşriyatı.

Artun, Erman (2011). *Âşıklık geleneği ve âşık edebiyatı*. Istanbul: Karaman Kitabevi.

Bardakjian, Kevork (2000). *A Reference Guide to Modern Armenian Literature, 1500–1920: with an Introductory History*. Detroit, MI: Wayne State University Press.

Baxčʻinyan, Henrik (1987). *Sayatʻ-Nova: kyankʻĕ ev gorcĕ*. Yerevan: Erevani petakan hamalsarani Hratarakčʻutʻyun.

Başgöz, İlhan (1998). *Turkish folklore and oral literature: selected essays of İlhan Başgöz*, In Kemal Silay (Ed.). Bloomington, IN: Indiana University Turkish Studies.

— (1998a). Turkish *Hikâye*-telling tradition in Azerbaijan, Iran. In Kemal Silay (Ed.). *Turkish Folklore and Oral Literature*. Bloomington, IN: Indiana University Turkish Studies.

— (2001). From Gosan to Ozan. *Turcica*. Vol. 38: 229–235.

— (2008). *Hikâye: Turkish Folk Romance as Performance Art*, Bloomington: Indiana University Press, IN.

Boyce, Mary (1957). The Parthian *gōsān* and Iranian Minstrel Tradition. *JRAS*, 10–45.

Chadwick, Nora K. and Zhirmunsky, Viktor (2010). *Oral epics of Central Asia*, Cambridge, UK: Cambridge University Press.

Cowe, S. Peter (1995). Models for the Interpretation of Medieval Armenian Poetry. In J.J.S. Weitenberg (Ed.). *New Approaches to Medieval Armenian Language and Culture* (29–45). Amsterdam: Rodopi.

Dadaşzadə, Araz (1973). *Abbas Tufarğanlı: 72 şeʼr*. Baku: Gənclik.

Deny, Jean et al. (Ed.) (1964). *Philologiae Turcicae Fundamenta*. Wiesbaden: Aquis Mattiacis Apud Franciscum Steiner.

Ēganyan, Ōnnik (1960). Nahapet Kʻučʻaki hayataṙ tʻurkeren taɫerĕ. *Banber Matenadarani*, 5, 465–481.

Elçin, Şükrü (1984). *Gevherî Divānı*. Ankara: Ankara Üniversitesi Basımevi.

Encyclopedia of Islam, "New edition" (2nd edition) (1979–1985, Vol. V, 1986). , Leiden: Brill.

Eremean, Aram (1929). *Ašuł Łul Yovhannēs*. Venice: S. Łazar.

— *Ašuł Yartʻun Ōłli*, 1st ed. (1920/1946). Tparan Surb Amenapʻrkičʻ Vankʻi. New Julfa, Iran; 2nd ed. Karō Ašułean, Tehran.

— (1930). *Parskahay ašułner*. Tiflis.

— (1921). *Parskahay ašułner: A. Baɫēr Ōłli, B. Łul Arzuni, G. Łul Sargis Šriškancʻi, D. Miskin Stepʻan*. New Julfa, Iran: Tparan Surb Amenapʻrkičʻ Vankʻi..

Ergün, Sadeddin Nüzhet (1936). *Âşık Ömer, Hayatı ve Şiirleri*. Semih Lüfi Mat-
baasıve Kitap Evi.

Günay, Umay (1999). *Türkiye'de Âşık Tarzı Şiiri Geleneği ve Rüya Motifi*. 3rd ed..
Ankara: Akçağ.

Hacılar, Valeh (2011). *Türkçe söyleyen Gürcü* Âşık-şairleri. *Bizim Ahıska*. Vol. 10,
40–44.

İsmayılov, Hüseyn et al. (2010). *Xəstə Qasim*. Baku: Nurlan.

Kazımov, Qəzənfər (1990). *Qurbani*. Baku: Bakı Universiteti Nəşriyyatı.

Köprülü, Fuad (1962–1965). *Türk Sazşairleri*. 5 Volumes. Ankara: Güven Basımevi.

— (1966). *Edebiyat Araştırmaları*. Ankara: Türk Tarih Kurumu Basımevi.

Levonyan, Garegin (1892). *Hay ašułner*, Hratarakut'iwn "Širak" Gravačaṙanoc'i,
Tparan Gēorg S. Sanoyeanc'i. Alexandrapol (The author's family name was
still spelt as Lewonean then).

— (1944). *Ašułnerĕ ev nranc' arvestĕ*. Yerevan: Haypethrat.

— (1963). *Erker*. Yerevan: Haypethrat.

Melik'set'-Bek, Levon (1958). *Šamč'i-Melk'on ev nra hayeren xałerĕ*. Yerevan:
Haykakan SSṚ GA Hratarakč'ut'yun.

Mnac'akanyan, Asatur; Nazaryan, Šušanik (1951). *Nałaš Hovnat'an: banasteł-
cut'yunner*. Yerevan: Haykakan SSR GA Hratarakč'ut'yun.

Namazov, Qara (1983). *Azərbaycan aşıq sənəti*. Baku: Yazıcı.

Oldfield Senarslan, Anna (2007).'It's time to drink blood like its sherbet': Azerbaijani women ashiqs and the transformation of tradition". *Congrès des Musi-
ques dans le Monde d'Islam*.

Öztelli, Cahit (1971). *Karacaoğlan, Bütün Şiirleri*. Istanbul: Milliyet Yayınları.

Pisowicz, Andrzej (1995). How did New Persian and Arabic words penetrate the
Middle Armenian vocabulary? Remarks on the material of Kostandin
Erznkac'i's poetry. In J.J.S. Weitenberg (Ed.). *New Approaches to Medieval Ar-
menian Language and Culture*, Rodopi, 95–110.

Qasımlı, Məhərrəm (2003). *Ozan aşıq sənəti*. Baku: Uğur.

Ramazanov, Yusif (1976). *Azərbaycan dilində yazıb-yaradan erməni aşıqları: XIX əsr*.
Baku: Elm.

Sahakyan, Hasmik (1961). *Hay ašułner XVII-XVIII dd.*. Yerevan: Haykakan SSṚ
GA Hratarakč'ut'yun.

Silay, Kemal (Ed.) (1998). *Turkish Folklore and Oral Literature*. Bloomington, IN:
Indiana University Turkish Studies.

Simonyan, Hasmik (1975). *Hay miǰnadaryan kafaner (X-XVI dd.)*. Yerevan:
Haykakan SSH GA Hratarakč'utyun.

T'amrazyan, Hrant (Ed.) (2001). *Nahapet K'uč'aki banastełcakan ašxarhĕ*. Yerevan:
Erevani Petakan Hamalsarani Hratarakč'ut'yun.

Taylor, John Edward (translator) (1854). *Transcaucasia: Sketches of the Nations and
Races between the Black Sea and the Caspian*. London: Chapman and Hall.

Türkiye Diyanet Vakfı, İslâm Ansiklopedisi Genel Müdürlüğü (Eds.) (1988–2008). *Türkiye Diyanet Vakfı İslâm Ansiklopedisi*. Istanbul: Üsküdar.

Üstünyer, İlyas (2009). Tradition of the Ashugh poetry and Ashughs in Georgia. *IBSU Scientific Journal*, Vol. 1(3), 137–149.

Von Haxthausen, Baron August and Taylor, John Edward (trans.) (1982). The Armenian Way of Life. *Ararat*, Vol. XXII, No. 4, 11–12.

Xač'arean, L. G. (L. K. Khacheryan as the author himself realizes in English) (1982). *Aṙak'el Siwnec'i (1350-1422 t't'): YAłags k'erakanut'ean hamaṙawt lucmunk'*: Los Angeles, CA.

Yardımcı, Mehmet (1998). *Başlangıcından günümüze halk şiiri, âşık şiiri, tekke şiiri*. Ankara: Ürün Yayınları.

The Legacy of Sounds in Turkey: *Âşıks* and *Dengbêjs*

Canser Kardaş

For more than a century, research on *âşık* literature has been conducted in Turkey by the efforts of the state, foundations, associations and individuals. These studies have promoted the tradition in every way and have made important contributions to its development. The same, however, is not true for the *dengbêj* tradition. There have been many obstacles to researching the subject. Undoubtedly, the most important obstacle has been the authority itself. There are heavy economic and political burdens on the performers of the tradition and these heavy conditions also apply to the researchers.

The present study does not focus solely on the tradition of *dengbêj* but rather is a comparative discussion of the traditions of *âşık* and *dengbêj*, which exist in the same geography. My observations on the *âşık* tradition are based on previous studies. The majority of the practical aspects of the *dengbêj* tradition, on the other hand, are based on my own field research conducted at different times. Between the years 2008 and 2017, I have travelled to cities such as Muş, Diyarbakır, Batman, Şırnak, Siirt and Mardin more than once and conducted interviews with different *dengbêj*s, primarily with Salihê Şirnexî, Seyidxanê Boyaxçî, Şemsedinê Gimgimî, Mistafayê Boti, Şakirê Kopî, Hanîfeya Şırnexi, Kurdêya Spêrtî, Dengbêj Mehmet Bakan, Salihê Qubînî and Seit Elikî. I have interviewed *dengbêj*s either in *dengbêj* houses established by local governments or individually at different places.

Concepts of Âşık *and* Dengbêj

As is the case in societies in which oral culture is widespread, different names are used in *âşık* and *dengbêj* traditions depending on the region. With the advance of mass communication, these names are being standardized. Several names have been used for *âşık*s in the past. Depending on time and region, they have been called *baksı, ozan, âşık, saz şairi, kalem şairi, halk şairi, badeli âşık, halk ozanı, hak aşığı, halk aşığı, aşuğ, meydan şairi, sazlı ozan,* and *çöğür şairi.* The most widespread and commonly used term today, however, is "*âşık*".

The names used for *dengbêj*s are *stranbêj, deyrbaz, stranvan, goranîbêj, çîrokbêj, klambêj, klamxan [klamhan], kasidebêj,* and *mitirb/mirtib.*[1] Even though there are

---

[1]   It was seen that *dengbêj*s such as Salihê Şirnaxî, Seyidxanê Boyaxçi, Salihê Qubînî, Seid Elikî, M. Emînê Muşî, and Şakirê Kopî do not agree on the distinctions in these concepts.

nuances in definition among these terms, all of them are used to denote oral narration. The word *dengbêj* has become more widespread than the others. This is the reason why many *dengbêj*s use the word "*dengbêj*" as a title in front of their names. Despite these different names in both traditions, the terms "*âşık*" and "*dengbêj*" are now standardized both in terms of meaning and widespreadness in usage.

A Brief Look at the History of the Traditions

When the *âşık* tradition is considered, some scholars argue that it started to emerge in the thirteenth century (Alptekin-Sakaoğlu, 2006: 17–22) whereas others maintain the sixteenth century as the starting point, by indicating that the *âşık* tradition emerged as a result of the *kahvehane* (coffee house) culture in the Ottoman geography (Çobanoğlu, 2007: 34). As there is not enough surviving written evidence dated to before the sixteenth century and as there is no information on *âşık*s in *tezkire*s (biographical compendia), our knowledge is limited. There are written sources such as *şairname*s, *cönk*s and *mecmua*s that provide information about *âşık*s and their periods after the sixteenth century. Based on the written sources, the sixteenth century can be considered as the starting point during which the tradition was developed. In the seventeenth century, its heyday, the framework of the tradition was established. Even though there is an increase in the number of *âşık*s in the eighteenth century, they are not as qualified as those who lived in the seventeenth century. In the nineteenth century the tradition strengthens again with the emergence of important *âşık*s as well as *âşık* schools. In the final period of the Ottoman Empire, during the twentieth century, the tradition grew away from the urban areas and retreated to the countryside, going in decline. In the twentieth century, after the declaration of the Republic, with the support of *halkevleri* (community centers) and *köy enstitüleri* (village institutes), the tradition was revived and was introduced to new venues of performance. This century also saw great *âşık*s such as Âşık Veysel, who carried the tradition.

It is difficult to determine the beginning and the development of the *dengbêj* tradition across centuries. Even though there is no surviving written evidence, mentioning the relatively organized structure of the singer-poet network called "*gosan*" and arguing that *dengbêj*s are a continuation of these public narrators, Izady traces the origin of *dengbêj*s to the Parthian period (247 BCE–227 CE) (Iza-

---

Salihê Şirnexi calls one who is able to improvise *dengbêj*, and others *dengxweş* [one with a good voice]. Other *dengbêj*s accept that the terms *stranbêj* and dengbêj have the same meaning. All the *dengbêj*s who were interviewed consider *mitrib/mirtib* different (see Turgut in this volume).

dy, 2011: 428). In addition to the fact that there is not enough written evidence due to the oral nature of the tradition, the opposition to authority also prevented the uncovering of the history of the tradition. Despite all these difficulties, there is information on *dengbêjs* in seventeenth-century sources. All the well-known great *dengbêjs* are from the nineteenth century. The *dengbêj* tradition continued in a lively manner until the mid-twentieth century and different schools began to emerge within the tradition. Even though *dengbêjs* have been silent following this period, there still are great *dengbêjs* such as Reso and Şakiro.

As both traditions are oral, it is not possible to determine their exact point of origin. There have been powerful performers in different periods, who were able to carry the tradition by themselves, in both traditions. Different schools have developed in the seventeenth century in the *âşik* tradition, and in the twentieth century in the *dengbêj* tradition.

Resource for Oral History

The *âşik* tradition has an important place in transferring cultural elements. It especially provides significant information in understanding the emotions, ideas and position of societies resisting against authority. Lyrical forms of the *âşik* tradition such as *taşlama* (satire) and *destan* (epic) contain important data for oral history. In addition to information on customs and traditions, it is possible to find subjects such as settlement policies, difficulties during wartimes, and the treatment of governors to the public in *âşik* poetry. For example, oral history studies were conducted on *barak*s based on Âşik Mahgül's works (Ersoy, 2009). Similarly, one may obtain information on Afshars' resistance to the resettlement policies of the Ottoman Empire from Dadaloğlu's poetry.

Dengbêj tradition has a completely oral structure. As there is no established written Kurdish culture, the outputs of *dengbêjs* contain numerous historical elements. Because they recall historical events and transmit these to future generations, *dengbêjs* are important in transferring societal and cultural memory. Indeed, today many historical events are tried to be explained by analyses of the *kilam*s of *dengbêjs*.[2] It may seem ambitious, yet no historical document contains as much detail about Alikê Battê (=Ali Batı), who organized an uprising in the region of Midyat in 1918 as the *kilam*s by Miradê Kinê, Seide Hamo, M. Arif Cizîrî and Seid Cizîrî.

---

[2]   With regard to the Ağrı uprising that took place in the early years of the Republic, "*Ferzende Beg ve Gelîye Zîlan*" by Şakiro, "*Şerê Seyîdxanê Kerr, Nemînim, Şer Bişarê Seydo*" by Resoyê Gopala, "*Edo'ye Ezîzî, Elîcanê Emerê Eso*" by Nuroyê Agirî, "*Şerê Seyîdxanê Kerr*" by Hîseyne Farê, "*Biroyê Hesîkê Têllî*" by Keremê Kor, "*Kuştina Medenî*" by Nesoyê Agirî, "*Şex Zahîr*" by Ahmedê Agirî, and "*Seyîdxan û Elice*" by Evdilbarîye Panosî contain enough material to illuminate all the events that occurred.

Being oral culture, *âşık* and *dengbêj* traditions reflect the point of views and stances of the society as well as social memory. In this respect, oral history studies on works in both traditions that contain social events as their subject matter would yield important results.

Assuming a Pseudonym

As a rule, in the *âşık* tradition, each *âşık* uses a pseudonym. In choosing a pseudonym, concepts like ancestry (e.g. Dadaloğlu), faith, religious order (e.g. Kul Nesimi), hometown, talent, and appearance (e.g. Benli Ali) have been influential. Pseudonyms were usually given by the masters and as part of a ceremony (Durbilmez, 2004: 26).

The use of pseudonyms in the *dengbêj* tradition is slightly different than in that of *âşık*. Very few *dengbêj*s use their pseudonyms in the same way as it is used in the *âşık* tradition. In the *dengbêj* tradition, pseudonyms are essentially used to be known in daily life. Even though pseudonyms have a limited use in works, all *dengbêj*s have a pseudonym that they use in real life. Pseudonyms are usually taken by using "i-circumflex" ("î") (e.g. Ehmedê Bêrtî), based on the hometown (e.g. Salihê Kubînî), based on the tribe (e.g. Ehmedê Bêrtî), based on a member of the family (Miradê Kinê), by adding the letter "o" at the end of the name (e.g. Zahiro), or by mentioning a physical attribute (e.g. Keremê Kor). *Dengbêj*s are usually known by their pseudonyms (also known as "*nasnav*").

Pseudonyms are used in both *âşık* and *dengbêj* traditions. In *âşık* tradition, pseudonyms are used both to be known and to be remembered by future generations when the works are recited. In the *dengbêj* tradition, pseudonyms are mostly used to recognize the performer. Since the *dengbêj* tradition is oral and has not been written down, the transmission to later generations is difficult and the names of poets are often forgotten. Except for the works of Evdalê Zeynikê, who is considered one of the master of the *dengbêj* tradition, it is very rare to see pseudonyms in the surviving works. In both traditions, those who came from a master-apprentice relationship have received their pseudonyms from their masters. Since master-apprentice relationship has declined or became extinct today, however, performers determine their pseudonyms themselves in both traditions. The main difference in the use of pseudonyms is that *âşık*s consider the use of pseudonyms imperative in all of their outputs whereas *dengbêj*s use pseudonyms to be known, but rarely in their works.

Playing Instruments

The main instrument that is used in the *âşık* tradition is the *saz* (*bağlama*). Playing *saz* is considered one of the most important stages of the tradition and sets one apart from other *âşık*s. The *saz* is given such high regard that in some circles it is called "Quran with strings." It is considered important because it gives space for *âşıks* to think while performing, it provides harmony and rhyme, and it saves time as it provides meaning. Even though the *saz* is the main instrument used in the *âşık* tradition in Turkey, *âşıks* in the Black Sea region use *kemençe*.

On the other hand, improvisation without an instrument is essential in the *dengbêj* tradition. Today, most *dengbêjs* do not play an instrument. There are, however, *dengbêjs* with instruments in some regions (Nezan, 1996: 14). With the influence of *âşıks*, in some regions they play *saz*, around Mardin and Batman they play *kemaçe*, and in the uplands of the region of Eastern Anatolia they play wind instruments.

One of the major differences between *dengbêj* and *âşık* traditions is the use of instruments. Whereas playing *saz* is one of the most important aspects of the *âşık* tradition, performing without an instrument is essential in the *dengbêj* tradition. Due to the influence of Islam, playing an instrument was a taboo for a long time in both traditions. A common characteristic of both traditions, without any influence from one another, is the playing of bowed fiddles. That both *âşıks* in the region of the Northern Black Sea and some *dengbêjs* around Batman and Mardin play bowed fiddles is striking. It is well known that different instruments are used in the two traditions today.

Dream Leitmotiv

In order for a person to be accepted as an artist/bard in the folk tradition, it is necessary for him or her to pass through a series of stages and rituals that may be considered a sort of acknowledgement. One of the most common leitmotiv in the *âşık* tradition is to fall in love (become a lover/an *âşık*) in a dream by drinking wine. This happens as they drink the wine offered by a holy figure in a holy space while they are half awake and half asleep. Günay notes that the dream consists of the preparation period, the dream itself, the awakening and the first saying/song, and that with the dream leitmotiv, the *âşık* transforms from a simple person into an artist (Günay, 1999: 196). Some *âşıks* also fall in love with the beloved they see in the dream.

The dream leitmotiv is not widespread in the *dengbêj* tradition. Considered the greatest *dengbêj*, Evdalê Zeynikê, became a *dengbêj* after seeing a dream during a long period of sickness. This, however, has not become common for later *dengbêjs*; in fact, it is impossible today to find a *dengbêj* who became a *dengbêj* with a dream motif. *Mitirbs* (see Turgut in this volume), who are also considered as part of the *dengbêj* tradition, on the other hand, say that they have been trained by the Master of the Jinn (*Mîrê Cina*) in order to indicate that they have mastered the tradition. This phenomenon is narrated in different ways by different *mitirbs* but a common theme is that the performer sees in a dream how the Master of the Jinn or the Devil is peeing on his finger (Keskin, 2006: 44).

Performing the Masters' Repertoire

In the *âşık* tradition, *âşık*s generally first learn their masters' repertoire and then create their own works. In *âşık* gatherings, works by masters are performed in "*hatırlama / canlandırma* ("remembering/recreate") sessions. These could include works from masters of different eras, primarily by *âşık*s such as Karacaoğlan, Dadaloğlu, Köroğlu, and Emrah.

In the *dengbêj* tradition, on the other hand, *dengbêj*s also learn first a repertoire that is considered to belong to masters but these are in some ways also anonymous pieces of folk literature. These include such works as Memê Alan, Dewrêşê Evdî, Kela Dimdim, Evdalê Zeynikê. A *dengbêj* can produce their own work after learning those of the masters.

There are differences in performing the masters' repertoire in the *âşık* and *dengbêj* traditions. In the *âşık* tradition, the work performed is easily identified because of the use of the pseudonyms. In the *dengbêj* tradition, it is difficult to identify the owner of the work due to the lack of pseudonyms. Performing the masters' repertoire constitute an important step in artistry in both traditions.

Improvisation

Improvisation is the ability to perform depending on the circumstances/moment without any preparation. In oral cultures, one of the most important conditions of being a powerful storyteller/narrator is the talent to improvise. In every culture, the storyteller/*âşık* tries to improve his improvisation skills. This becomes a point of pride for the narrator.

In the *âşık* tradition, *âşık*s with strong improvisation skills are considered powerful. Due to their improvisation skills, many *âşık*s have considered themselves more talented than diwan poets. Indeed, it is not easy to get right both the syllabic meter and the rhyme. Therefore, *âşık*s with these skills are considered masters and receive much respect. Some *âşık*s prefer composing in advance and memorizing the work. The reason for this is that the *âşık* culture is simultaneously oral and written.

In the *dengbêj* tradition, in order for someone to be called a *dengbêj* their improvisation skills have to be very strong. Improvisation is perhaps the most important talent, after voice and memory. Those who are not able to improvize are called not *dengbêj* but "*stranbêj*". Since the *dengbêj* tradition is completely oral, the improvisation aspect has to be very strong. Therefore, a *dengbêj* may recite a work on any given subject in different ways each time. Those *dengbêj*s who are good in improvizing are able to easily produce a work on any event they witness or hear about. The reason for this is the fact that each *dengbêj* develops different templates/formulas. The framework of the narrative remains fixed but the events and people change. *Dengbêj*s are able to structure their narratives very easily within these frameworks. Thanks to their improvisation skills, *dengbêj*s cut their narratives short or keep them longer depending on the attention of their audiences.

The manner of improvising in both *âşık* and *dengbêj* traditions is similar. In both traditions, those with improvisation skills are considered powerful artists. The performance is wholly based on improvisation in the *dengbêj* tradition, whereas in *âşık* tradition many *âşık*s write and memorize their works. This shows that the *dengbêj* tradition continues only in oral culture but that the *âşık* tradition exists also in written culture in addition to oral culture.

Master-Apprentice Relationship

In the the *âşık* tradition, the masters' repertoire and traditional performance style are transmitted to future generations through a master-apprentice relationship. *Âşık*s who have a respectable place in society and who have good improvisation skills take up raising apprentices. Masters teach apprentices the customs of the performance, the instrument (*saz*), the system of melody types (*makam*), opening rhyme (*ayak açmak*), the sequence of the stories, the genres in the tradition, poetry duels, and improvisation. Apprentices follow their masters on matters such as style, language use, rhyme (*ayak*), melody and storytelling. *Âşık*s who are raised in this way form schools. For example, in the regions of Tokat-Kastamonu there is the Emrah school, in Sivas the Ruhsatî school, and in Kars the Âşık Şenlik school.

The master-apprentice relationship has a long history in the *dengbêj* tradition and is still ongoing today. The continuation of the *dengbêj* tradition is indeed dependent on a master-apprentice relationship. In order for a *dengbêj* to become a master, they need to learn the repertoire, the rules of the tradition and the customs as well as the styles. After learning all of these, their improvisation skills also have to be powerful. When all skills except for improvisation can only be attained from a master, it is difficult to imagine the tradition to continue without a master-apprentice relationship. For example, Şakiro was an apprentice of Reso, Reso of Evdalê Zeynikê. Today, many *dengbêj*s consider Şakiro as their master and begin performing by imitating him. There also are those who continue the *dengbêj* tradition, especially *mitirb*s, as a family occupation. They learn it from their family members such as their fathers, uncles and grandfathers. Mıradê Kinê's family of Gercüş and Mala Avdê's family of İdil in the Batman-Mardin region have had *dengbêj*s for generations and have turned this into a family occupation. There were also schools, though no longer active, which were called "*dengbêj* schools," that raised *dengbêj*s (Jwaideh, 1999: 47; Gündoğar, 2005: 163). In these schools, a master *dengbêj* would take up a few apprentices and make them start performing after an intensive training (of breathing techniques, forming a musical sentence, stories, describing communal and social events). Again, due to master-apprentice relationships, schools have been formed in the *dengbêj* tradition. For example, in the region called Serhat (including cities such as Erzurum, Ağrı,

Iğdır, Muş, etc.) there is the Evdalê Zeynikê school, and in Mardin-Batman region there is the Miradê Kinê school.

The most important common point of the *dengbêj* and *âşık* traditions is the master-apprentice relationship. It is due to the master-apprentice relationship that both traditions were able to preserve accumulation of knowledge over decades and to continue to exist until today. Master-apprentice relationships are similar in both *dengbêj* and *âşık* traditions. These relationships continued because of traditional schools or through family members. Strong *âşık*s and *dengbêj*s have formed schools with the apprentices they have raised. Masters are also similar in the ways they convey to their apprentices those events and stories that deeply influenced the society, small or large, and preserve the continuation of social memory.

Performance Places

The *âşık* tradition consists of the unity of the narrator, audience, text and performance venue. The main performance place for *âşık*s is coffee houses. *Âşık*s also perform at dîwans, village rooms, and houses as well as weddings, festivals, fairs, and ceremonies. Today, there are still *âşık* coffee houses in Erzurum, Kayseri, Sivas, Van, Kars, and Ağrı, but they are mostly of symbolic value. In addition to face-to-face communication, written and electronic means are also used.

In the *dengbêj* tradition, narrator, audience, venue and time of performance are essential. Performance venue has always been important in the *dengbêj* tradition and has evolved according to the changing conditions of times. In the past, *dengbêj*s used to perform in the councils of *mîr*s, pashas, *bey*s, aghas or villages. The nighttime gatherings in these venues are called "*şevbêrk*" or "*şevbuhêrk*." All matters pertaining to the society are discussed at *şevbêrk*s, ideas are exchanged and decisions taken. Additionally, *dengbêj*s perform there as well. There are certain rules about being, sitting and talking in the councils where *dengbêj*s perform. Today, "*Mala Dengbêjan*" (*Dengbêj* Houses)[3] that may be found in many cities are a refuge for *dengbêj*s, important centers for them to perform their arts. These venues are adorned with photographs of great *dengbêj*s and the material culture of the regions, thanks also to technological possibilities. On certain days of the week, councils are held in these venues. At these gatherings *dengbêj*s perform in traditional local outfits. Traditional principles are applied at the councils, and the performance is directed by a master *dengbêj*. These principles may be enumerated as follows: older *dengbêj*s begin the performance, if a *dengbêj*'s master is present

---

[3]   In many cities such as Diyarbakır, Van, Batman, Erzurum, and Hakkâri, venues that sometimes directly are called *dengbêj* houses are furbished to allow for *dengbêj*s to perform their art, providing in some ways a refuge for them. Councils are being organized in these venues at regular intervals and the traidition is being kept alive.

they do not start without their permission, no *dengbêj* will repeat a *stran* that has already been recited, a *stran* is never interrupted, however long it may be.

As *dengbêj* and *âşık* traditions are essentially oral, performances happen face to face. Coffee houses are the main venues of performance for *âşıks* and councils are for *dengbêjs*. Dîwans, village rooms, festivals, ceremonies, and *fasıls* are common venues for face-to-face communication. The *âşık* tradition historically existed in oral, written and electronic media. The *dengbêj* tradition, on the other hand uses oral and electronic media. Even today the *dengbêj* tradition is not very well acquainted with written media. Both traditions keep renewing themselves according to the times, no matter how much living conditions change, and continue to produce works that are consumed in oral, written and electronic form.

Classifications

It is possible to categorize *âşıks* and *dengbêjs* into different groups according to the conditions of the time, where they live and the structure of society in which they live. Even though it is difficult to determine where they were raised with clear borders, one can still look at elements such as the art, aesthetics, language and narrative techniques in their works.

Many researchers categorize *âşıks* in different groups, for example according to the places where they were raised. Boratav's categorization is the most accepted. According to him, one can distinguish between town-city (urban) *âşıks*, village *âşıks*, nomadic *âşıks*, and *âşıks* who recite religious-mystic poems (*âşıks* of dervish lodges). Urban *âşıks* are educated to some extent. Therefore, the diwan literature is dominant in their works. As they place emphasis on metaphors, style, and phonetic patterns they are called "*kalem şairi*," literally meaning "pen poet" that emphasizes their education. Village *âşıks* are those who live away from city centers and who perform their art at weddings, houses of *bey*s and aghas. Nomadic *âşıks* are usually those who used to migrate between summer and winter residences in the nineteenth century. These *âşıks* are the ones who mastered heroic themes in their works. *Âşıks* who recite religious-mystic poems are raised in dervish lodges and religious orders. These dervish poets narrate the principles of their orders in a simple language that would be understood by the public.

As the number of studies on *dengbêjs* are limited, the categorization also has been limited. Çelebi categorizes *dengbêjs* in three groups (Çelebi et al., 2008): public *dengbêjs*, *mîr-bey dengbêjs* and *mitirbs*. Even though this classification is correct, it is nevertheless insufficient. I think that the categorization should be as follows: village dengbêjs, agha-*mîr*-pasha *dengbêjs*, tribal *dengbêjs*, wandering *dengbêjs* and *dengbêjs* of a religious order (*qesîdebêjs*). Village *dengbêjs* are those who live in villages and choose customs and traditions of village life as a subject matter in their works. Tribal *dengbêjs* are those who belong to a tribe and perform works that are related to the protection and unity of that tribe. Agha-*mîr dengbêjs* are those who recite the battles, memories and history of their patrons to the next generations.[4] Şerafetin Elçi, Member of the Parliament from Şırnak, who recently passed away always had a *dengbêj* with him, namely Aşiq Selîm of Cizre (Kaya, 2012: 35). Travelling *dengbêj*s are different with respect to economic dependency. These *dengbêj*s earn their living by travelling and perform their art in return for money or food in those places they visit (Çelebi et al., 2008: 11). *Dengbêj*s of a religious order, as it might be guessed, are those who receive some form of religious education. These *dengbêj*s form a bridge between classical literature and the *dengbêj* tradition.

When the groups are considered, it is seen that there are not many differences between *âşık*s and *dengbêj*s. There are some urban *âşık*s who are raised in the city, but there are almost no urban *dengbêj*s. *Dengbêj*s who live in the city are those who moved to the city at a later age.

Female Performers

Women are not as comfortable with performing in the *âşık* tradition as men because of problems related to societal structures and religious concerns. Due to the socio-psychological structure of the society, female *âşık*s take pseudonyms by using terms such as "*kadın*" (woman), "*abla*" (sister), "*ana*" (mother) and "*hanım*" (madam). Şimşek lists the following as problems female *âşık*s face: the society acts as if this is immoral for women; their husbands do not allow them; and male *âşık*s do not allow females to attend their gatherings (Şimşek, 2007: 18). Güzide Ana, Seher Bacı, Adviye Anabacı, Emine Hatun, Şah Turna, Durşah Bacı and Sarıcakız are examples of female *âşık*s from different periods.

As voice is very important in the *dengbêj* tradition, women are considered to be advantageous. Due to their social status, it is difficult for women, however, to fulfill their responsibilities and perform as *dengbêj*s. Female *dengbêj*s do not use any pseudonyms relating to their societal roles. The use of pseudonyms is similar to that of male *dengbêj*s (see Schäfers in this volume). Their numbers are not known exactly as there are few studies on this topic; however, some female *dengbêj*s, who are not pressured by their families, now freely enter *dengbêj* councils thanks to the changing circumstances of our times and receive much respect by other *dengbêj*s. Gulê, Elmas Xan, Meryem Xan, Fatma İsa, Ayşe Şan, Sosika Simo, Feleknaz, Xelide Bertî, Gazin and Helime Şirnexî may be enumerated as examples of female *dengbêj*s.

Women in both *âşık* and *dengbêj* traditions face common problems: not being able to perform their occupation by travelling; not being able to take advantage of the master-apprentice relationship; motherly duties; not being able to get

---

4   Salihê Şirnaxî states that this is not the case in Botan region as it causes enmity against pashas or tribes, but that it continues in Serhat region.

permission from their spouses/families, and that being among men is considered sinful for a woman. In terms of pseudonyms, there are differences between female *âşık*s and *dengbêj*s. Whereas the pseudonyms of female *âşık*s are directly related to their social roles, this is not the case for female *dengbêj*s. Another difference lies in the fact that *dengbêj*s perform without an instrument which makes it easier for women, while the indisputable place of the *saz* in the *âşık* tradition makes it more difficult for women to become *âşık*s.

Armenian Âşıks (Aşuğs) *and* Dengbêjs

The *âşık* tradition, an important element of Turkish culture, is known as *"aşuğ"* among Armenians. There are many *aşuğ* names in *şairname*s (records of poets). Many *cönk*s (private lyric anthologies) were composed in Armenian and Arabic alphabets. The poems recorded in these books contain all elements of the *âşık* tradition and use syllabic meter and *aruz* prosody masterfully. Agahî, Âşıkî, Kul Agop, Cehdî, Kul Elfazî, Serunî and Vartan are among these *aşuğ*s, to name a few.

Many Armenians performed as part of the *dengbêj* tradition. Furthermore, some of these *dengbêj*s became very well established during the period in which they lived. Some Armenian scholars published *dengbêj* works in the Armenian alphabet (Bayrak, 2005:106). Karabetê Xaço, who is well known and respected among all Kurds, can be given as an example.

Frederic Macler provides the following information on Armenian musicians:

> An *aşuğ* [must be a *dengbêj*] who enters under the patronage of a Kurdish Bey used to adapt their music to Kurdish melodies, which has more of a pastoral tone. If the same artist entered under the patronage of a Turkish Pasha, they would then adapt it accordingly. Persian music was much more refined, and *aşuğ* once again would adapt their music in accordance with the culture and taste of their new patron. The most famous musicians under the patronage of sultans, shahs, *xwedîve*s [mîrs/noble families] were Armenian (Bayrak, 2005: 108).

Armenian scholar Arşak Çobanyan states that folk poetry is an element of interaction between peoples and culture: "*Armenian* aşuğs *gave back more than what they received from Muslims. Most of the Armenian* aşuğs *composed poetry in Turkish, Persian, and Kurdish. As a matter of fact, many famous Turkish and Kurdish poets are of Armenian descent.*" (Bayrak, 2005: 106). Çobanyan underlines that there was a cultural exchange due to Armenian bards contributing several elements from their religion and culture to Islamic societies.

In spite of coming from a different religion, there have been many Armenian masters in both *âşık* and *dengbêj* traditions. Thanks to these performers, who functioned as a bridge, there was cultural exchange. There have been more *aşuğ*s compared to Armenian *dengbêj*s, and these recorded their poetry in *cönk*s. Also, in both traditions, "Armenians" are an important motif in the works.

Genres and Forms

Studies have been carried out on the genres and forms of *âşık* literature for over a century; yet, there is no consensus. According to the general categorizations in *âşık* poetry, the accepted versions in terms of form are *mani* (one quatrain), *koşma* (ballad consisting of two to four quatrains), and *destan* (epic consisting of several quatrains), and in terms of genre are *güzelleme, yiğitleme, semaî, taşlama, destan* and *ağıt*.

Studies on genre and form in the *dengbêj* tradition recently have begun to be conducted. There is almost no study on form. The studies on genre, on the other hand, do not follow any methodology. It is also difficult to conduct vigorous studies as most of the works in the tradition have not been written down. In order to determine the genres and forms in the *dengbêj* tradition, melody, time of performance and subjects have to be classified first. It is not possible to talk about a standardized form in the *dengbêj* tradition. The stanzas of the works with a melody range from 2 to 9 lines and each stanza in a given work may have a different number of lines. Genres depend on the time of the performance and the melody. In different interviews, *dengbêj*s have stated this: "I perform the same *kilam* differently in the morning, at noon and in the evening. I also change the melody according to the audience."[5] The genres in the *dengbêj* tradition are: *kilam, lawik, şer, dîlok, lawij, heyranok, payizok, şeşbendî, belitê, şin* and *destan*. These genres and their different characteristics are provided in the table below:

Genre	Subject	Time of Performance	Manner of Narration	Structure	Form (Volume)
Şer	Heroes and their struggles	Council	Praise Epic	Unmetered	Unlimited, Not fixed
Lawik	Love, separation, affinity, beauty	Council	Glorification	Unmetered	Unlimited, Not fixed
Dîlok	Love, separation, affinity, beauty	Festivities Weddings	Glorification	Metrical	Couplets / Tercets / Quatrains
Heyranok	Love, nature and beauty of humans	Spring	Glorification	Unmetered	Unlimited

---

5   Interview with Dengbêj Seit Alîkî dated 6 June, 2011.

Genre	Subject	Time of Performance	Manner of Narration	Structure	Form (Volume)
Payîzok	Separation / natural life	Fall	Glorification	Unmetered	Unlimited
Şeşbendî	No restriction	Council	Counsel, Didactic	Metrical	Composed of sestets
Bêlîte	No restriction	Working, council	Glorification	Metrical	Composed of stanzas/very short lines
Destan	Heroism, love, natural disasters, etc.	Council	Counsel, Didactic, Heroic	Metrical	Stanzas are 2/3/4/5/6/7 lines
Şîn	Death, separation	Council, Morning place	Mourning	Unmetered	Unlimited

The characteristics of the *âşık* and *dengbêj* traditions may be described as follows:

- Even though debates continue, there is some sort of standardization of genres and forms in the *âşık* tradition. It is not possible to talk about any standardization of genre in the *dengbêj* tradition.
- Whereas the subject and the melody are important elements in determining genres in the *âşık* tradition, in the *dengbêj* tradition, in addition to the subject and the melody also the time of the performance is important.
- In the *âşık* tradition principally syllabic meter is used but *aruz* prosody is also used. In the *dengbêj* tradition only syllabic meter is used. Here, the length of the sentences is determined by the power of the breath; therefore, there is no standard meter.
- In terms of form, *âşık* tradition consists of *koşma*s. There is no fixed form in the *dengbêj* tradition.
- The genres that correspond exactly in *âşık* and *dengbêj* traditions are *destan*s (epics) and *ağıt*s (elegies).

Poetic Aesthetics

Form (volume), rhyme, measure, proverbs, idioms, reduplication and features of dialects may be considered as elements of harmony in poetry. Works of the *âşık* tradition may be in the form of verse, prose or prose poetry. The basic form of verses in *âşık* tradition is quatrain. In verse works, different types of rhymes, *radif*s and regular rhyme are used. Rhymes and *radif*s are among the indispensable elements for *âşık*s. The most appropriate and natural meter for the Turkish language is syllabic meter, however, some *âşık*s also have used *aruz* prosody. *Âşık*s have furthermore employed proverbs, idioms, and reduplications used in their own regions and elsewhere in order to strengthen their narratives, claims and counsels.

Works of the *dengbêj* tradition may be in the form of verse, prose or prose poetry. There is no standardized form for verse works. They can be in couplets, tercets or quatrains. Different types of rhymes and radifs may be found in *dengbêj* products; however, assonant/consonant rhyme (of a single sound) and perfect rhyme are more common. In almost all verse works, regular rhyme is used. Whereas some works such as *lawje* and *dîlok* use syllabic meter, other genres do not use any metre. The length of the lines changes according to the breath of the *dengbêj*s. *Dengbêj*s still utilize many idioms, proverbs, and reduplications that fell out of use in daily language and they use all kinds of local or general lexical patterns.

When the products of the *âşık* and *dengbêj* traditions are considered in terms of poetic harmony, it is seen that the use of different types of rhymes, regular rhyme, local dialects, proverbs, idioms, reduplications, and conventional word patterns are common. The consistent use of syllabic meter and the fact that verse products are made up of quatrains in the *âşık* tradition, set it apart from the *dengbêj* tradition. In *dengbêj* tradition most of the works are without metre and performed according to the breath of the *dengbêj*s.

Conclusion

Stating that "there should be in-depth studies conducted on bards, musicians and storytellers who have lived in Asia Minor, whether called *âşık*s, *aşuğ*s or *dengbêj*s," Duygulu in fact argues that these traditions are not disconnected from each other (Duygulu, 2001). The *Âşık* tradition has been and still is being studied in every aspect, whereas there are much less studies on *dengbêj* tradition.

Differences and commonalities between cultures have to be determined according to objective criteria in order for people who speak different languages to get to know each other, to communicate with each other, and in order to achieve a tolerant environment. Only when these differences and commonalities are known, tolerance, communication, and relationships develop among communities. Both traditions, *âşık*s and *dengbêj*s, have developed practices in accordance with their respective natures; yet, both were able to regenerate themselves according to time and place. As both traditions exist in the same geography, there have been some commonalities; nevertheless, the two traditions managed to continue their existence independently.

Translation from Turkish: Kıvılcım Yavuz

Bibliography

Alptekin, A. B.-Sakaoğlu S. (2006). *Türk Saz Şiiri Antolojisi (14-21. yüzyıllar)*. Ankara: Akçağ Yayınları.

Bayrak, M. (2005). *Alevi-Bektaşi Edebiyatında Ermeni Âşıklar*. Ankara: Özge Yayıncılık.

Çelebi, N. et al. (2008). Li Muzîka Kurdan a Kevneşopî Nêrîneke Giştî. *Zend*. Spring–Summer 2008.

Çobanoğlu, Ö. (2007). *Âşık Tarzı Edebiyat Geleneği ve İstanbul*. İstanbul: 3F Yayınları.

Durbilmez, B. (2004). *Taşpınarlı Halk Şairleri*. Kayseri: Bizim Gençlik Yayınları.

Duygulu, M. (2001). "Anadolu Ermeni Müziğinde Bölgesel Etkileşimler". *Uluslararası Anadolu İnançları Kongresi Bildirileri Kitabı*. Ankara: Ervak Yayınları.

Ersoy, Ruhi. (2009). *Sözlü Tarih Folklor İlişkisi Baraklar Örneği Disiplinler Arası Bir Yaklaşım Denemesi*. Ankara: Akçağ Yayınları.

Günay, U. (1999). *Âşık Tarzı Şiir Geleneği ve Rüya Motifi*. Ankara: Akçağ Yayınları.

Gündoğar, S. (2005). *Üç Kürt Ozanın Hikâyesi*. İstanbul: Elma Yayınları.

İzady, M. R. (2004). *Kürtler. Bir El Kitabı*. (Trans. Cemal Attila). İstanbul: Doz Yayınları.

Jwaideh, W. (1999). *Kürt Milliyetçiliğinin Tarihi*. İstanbul: İletişim Yayınları.

Karataş, T. (2001). *Ansiklopedik Edebiyat Terimleri Sözlüğü*. İstanbul: Perşembe.

Kardaş, C. (2017). *Aşığın Sazı Dengbêjin Sesi (Dengbêjlik ve Âşıklık üzerine Bir İnceleme)*. Ankara: Eğiten Kitap.

Kaya, H. (2012). *Doğu'nun Elçi'sinden Yüce Divana: Şerafettin Elçi*. İstanbul: Fanos Yayınları.

Keskin, N. (2006). *Mardin ve Çevresinde Bir Anlatım Biçimi Olarak Mıtırblık*. Unpublished master's thesis. University of Ankara. Institute of Social Sciences. Ankara.

Nezan, K. (1996). "Kürt Müziği Üzerine". *Kürt Müziği*. İstanbul: Avesta Yayınları.

Pamukciyan, K. (2002). *Ermeni Kaynaklarından Tarihe Katkılar-II/Ermeni Harfli Türkçe Metinler* (Ed. Osman Köker). İstanbul: Aras Yayıncılık.

Şimşek, E. (2007). "Âşıklık Geleneğinde Kadın Âşıkların Yeri ve Ayşe Çağlayan Örneği". *Somut Olmayan Kültürel Miras: Yaşayan Âşık Sanatı Sempozyumu*, 29–30 November, Ankara.

Uzun, M. (2009). *Dengbêjlerim*. İstanbul: İthaki Yayınları.

Imagining a New *Mitirb:*
A Text Analysis of a Singer-Poet Tradition
in Ṭûr 'Abdîn

Lokman Turgut

Introduction

The word *mitirb* is derived from the Arabic radicals طرب (T.R.B) meaning approximately "being in movement, being happy". The second and fourth forms of this radicals express the action of entertaining, giving pleasure, or pleasure provided by singing. The word مطرب (*mutrib*) means "musician" and is generally used to qualify a person playing an instrument and making music (Wehr, 1977: 503). In the Ṭûr 'Abdîn[1] area, the term *mitirb* has two meanings, or better put, two levels of identification. On the one hand, it denotes professional musicians, especially players of the spike fiddle *kemaçe*. On the other hand, it is used to refer collectively to the communities of which these musicians are members. As a community, *mitirb*s commanded very low social status in the area, intermarriage with them was taboo, and they could not become full members of tribes.

In the anthropological sense,[2] *mitirb*s are one of the two categories of peripatetic (migrants and non-propertied) musicians in the Ṭûr 'Abdîn area, in addition to the so-called *qereçî*-s.[3] They display a high degree of dependence on the exploitation of social resources (i.e. other people) for their sustenance and exploit these human resources via calculated patterns of social mobility. These musicians in the area generically did not (and probably could not) own land or livestock, and for their sustenance, they depended on the provision of various services and products to non-nomadic people (such as the agriculturalist Muslim Kurds, Êzîdîs, Suryanî Christians, and Mihalmî Arabs, and pastoralist Kurds), and hunting and gathering on a smaller scale. *Mitirb*s are Kurmanji speaking wereas Qereçî developed a language called Domanî, they call themselves Dom, and have myths about the origins of Doms. Both groups are Muslims.

---

[1] The Kurds name the region of Ṭûr 'Abdîn (Mountain or Plateau of God's servitors) "Tor". Tor is situated south of Bişêrî, it borders the region of Botan in the east and on the city of Mêrdîn in the West. Midyad forms the centre of the region. In any case the plateau located in east of Mêrdîn is accepted as Tor, see Turgut, 2002: 3.

[2] The information in the following paragraphs was obtained in cooperation with Argun Çakir, who also did field research in this area, and communicated during a personal communication on 16 August 2017.

[3] They are gypsy or gypsy-like groups performing amongst others music and epic-narratives but are socially one of the most disadvantaged and most discriminated groups, for more see Turgut, 2002: 24.

Professional musicianship led to a very important difference between *mitirb*s and *qereçîs*. As social status would govern most if not all relationships between individuals in the area, the extremely low social status of migrant musicians meant that they could never become respected members of society and would never get to engage with people of higher status other than as inferiors. For professional musicians, specifically for those who performed in gatherings in village guest rooms, as opposed to those who strictly played dance music, the situation was different. *Dîwanxane*, *dîwan* or *ode* (Guest room) musicians were in a uniquely advantageous position as musical entertainment was rare and highly desired. Their performances in *ode*-s, however, were not only conducive to direct economic gain in the form of gifts. *Ode* musicians were held in high esteem and the owners of *odes* did their best to treat them with sufficient hospitality and generosity. The reason behind that was not only these musicians' skills in musical performance: performers could speak ill of them and mock them in song in other *odes*, thus jeopardizing their reputation.

Mitirb performers' capacity to act as conduits for people's reputation stemmed from a unique license that they commanded, that is, they could praise or criticize people with impunity. It cannot be overstated that this was extraordinary for anyone especially for people who had such low social status as the migrant *mitirb*s. Their state of being unrestricted seemed to be used by performers mainly to maintain a respectable image in society and to secure various forms of alms and gifts from powerful and wealthy people.

In parts of Rojava[4] it is common to describe any musician as a *mitirb*. This gives traditional *mitirbs* in Qamişlo and surroundings the opportunity to rely on their art and reconstitute their formal status within society. However, in the Ṭûr 'Abdîn or the region where I did my fieldwork, the connotation of the word *mitirb* has pejorative meanings that are defined as an "inferior" social group. This pejorative use of the word *mitirb* has grown so strong that newer generations of *mitirb*-families prefer to refer to themselves as *hunermend* or as *dengbêj* and sometimes as *hozan*[5]. We observe the same among the *qereçî*, who perform the same art and repertoire as the *mitirb* in the same region. The main focus of this chapter, after having highlighted some of the different narrative traditions and their nomenclatures, will be the efforts made in the past by performers to ameliorate their social status.

A well quoted statement of Kurdish novelist Mehmet Uzun about *dengbêj*s (Kurdish singer-poets) asserts that the latter could enjoy high social respect, some of them at the rank of a tribal leader (Uzun, 1992: 31). This may have been the case for a traditional *dengbêj* who was a full member of his own tribal society, but

---

[4]   In this work regions with a Kurdish population majority in Syria are called in this way.

[5]   As the member of the family originally from Ṭûr 'Abdîn, living now in Germany, referring to themselves with the surname Hezexî, who called themselves as *Hozan* (Evdilkirîmê Hozan) or *Hunermend* (Mihemedê Hunermend), now both mostly use the word *dengbêj*.

what about professional or semi-professional performers/musicians such as *mitirb*s from Tor[6]? They are not considered full members of any tribe, but as the *mitirb* of a tribe. Their social status hinders them from becoming members of a tribe, even though there seem to have been some exceptions, as for example Ferho (2007) claimed that Miradê Kinê is a tribe's member[7]. In order to understand the dynamics at play here, it is important to know that the nomenclature of *dengbêj* has prevailed as the dominant term in the Kurmanji-Kurdish "tradition". Although *stranbêj* from Sinjar (Kr. Şingal) and *şair* from Hekarî are full members of their respective tribe, they never enjoyed the social respect a *dengbêj* could possibly attain, should the situation arise. The main focus of this chapter will be *mitirb* performances and their texts, created in the past. This has the downside of projecting today's reflections (mainly those of the author) to past performance situations; the environment of the *mitirbs* as it was in the past; and their continuing interaction between participants before and after the performance, in and outside of the performance room.

This article concerns some variants of the epic poems *Cembelî, Kurê Mîrê Hekariya* and *Kalo û Hemê Zerê*, from the Ṭûr 'Abdîn area performed by two *kemaçe* players Reşîdê Mala Mûsa (Reşîdê Omerî) and Bedranê Mala Alê, both *mitirbs*, who have both passed away around three decades ago.

Variants of the epic Cembelî are commonly performed in many areas across Kurdistan, but *Kalo û Hemê Zerê* is specific for the repertoire in Ṭûr 'Abdîn. The variant of Cembelî we will look at in this paper is distinguished from the others by its featuring a *mitirb* performer as its main protagonist. The central position of the *mitirb* performer in the Cembelî variant in question also distinguishes it from other epic poems from the area which feature *mitirb* characters. Another unique feature of this variant is that the *mitirb* protagonist is portrayed as advisor to the tribal chief, a distinguished warrior, hence embodying qualities and positions with which *mitirbs* were not often associated, if not actively excluded from. In the variants of *Kalo û Hemê Zerê* we have also *mitirb* characters, which are not protagonists but decisive in the course of events.

---

[6]   I am using this denomination for the region of Ṭûr 'Abdîn; it defines a plateau east of Mêrdin (Tr. Mardin), with the district Midyad (Tr. Midyat) in its centre.

[7]   In his discussion of the word *mitirb* in Wikipedia, author Medeni Ferho first tries to make us believe that the society indeed respected *mitirbs* and gave them their annual reward cordially. His main argument is that the denomination of *mitirb* was "originally" a positive loaded one which described "big artists [hunermendê mezin]. Later this became loaded negatively when gipsy families started to perform music using the same instruments and same repertoires [for his argumentation he used also the Arabic meaning of the word, which is explained in this text too]. He then argues that some *mitirb* families such as the *Kinê* family, which "can be compared to the family of Homer", lived in *Tor* and were/are respected.

Figure 1: Bedranê Mala Alê (in the center) with members of his own family in an unknown place in Ṭûr ʿAbdîn at the beginning of the 1980s.

In this paper, we will investigate the Cembelî variants in question and the way Ehmedê Mitirb is portrayed in it as a proposition for a new *mitirb* image to audiences (and through them to the whole society) through musical performance. We will first explain the social position of *mitirb*s and their communities in the past. By doing that, we will point to the potential motivations behind the proposition of a new *mitirb* image and how *mitirb* performers were in a unique position to make that proposition via musical performance.

Afterwards, we will look at other epic poems performed by *mitirb*s, which feature *mitirb* characters in order to show the way *mitirb* performers are represented in these performances and set the scene to show why the Cembelî variant performed by *mitirb*s is unique. Showing that *Kalo û Hemê Zerê* variants also introduce a decisive role to the *mitirb*s, we will demonstrate that these variants were probably an attempt of some *mitirb*-performers to introduce a new discourse about *mitirb*s' social status. Here we will also briefly discuss the unique features of the performance genre *şer*, which allowed these performers to make such a proposition through musical performance in the first place. Finally, we will analyse the text of Cembelî to discuss the proposed new image and speculate on the strategies used by the *mitirb* or *mitirb*s, who composed the variant, to make this proposal a realistic one, one which would be taken seriously by their audiences.

Nationalist Discourse and Preference of Dengbêjî Above Other Traditions

All of the above-mentioned performers have similarities but also differences in their repertoire, genres, performances and social classes. The *dengbêj* tradition (which traditionally was proper to the region of Serhat in North-Kurdistan[8], but found its way already relatively early to the regions of Diyarbekir and parts of Urfa), has a repertoire that can be divided into three main categories: Rebellions against the state, tribal conflicts, and love. It is important to say that with few exceptions, protagonists in the narratives performed by *dengbêj*s are usually real people known in their regions, and sometimes also known in neighbouring regions. We know that in the past some *dengbêj*s were travelling around to perform their art. As performers, *dengbêj*s were full members of their tribal society, but usually from humble origins or sometimes they just were poor. They could be of any age, but a performer was perceived as a *dengbêj* after his 20s, and those who were famous for their art and performances needed to have experience with performing at the *ode, diwan / diwanxane*: gatherings for (usually) members of a certain tribe or village. For the transmission of local and regional historical events *dengbêj*s were indispensable; they served as a central source of information on historical events. In that capacity, they can be seen as actors in creating local history, as they were authors of a large variety of epics/*kilam*s/songs about historical events and epics. This is probably the reason why *dengbêj*s are characterised, especially since four decades, as a "Kurdish national cultural" expression (see i.e. Aras, 2007). Although the tradition was not performed in all Kurmanji-speaking areas as the main performing art, and was in some regions not at all known in that form, it has been described as an authentic Kurdish tradition, prevalent in all Kurdish areas (see i.e. Uzun, 2006). Indeed, the tradition was mainly performed in the regions Serhed (or Serhad, Tr. Serhat)[9], neighbouring Xerzan, Di-

---

8   I am using this term for Kurdish regions in east and southeast Turkey.
9   It is a historical-geographical region, which is now politically part of Eastern Turkey. While the core of the region comprises of the cities Agirî (Tr. Ağrı), Qers (Tr. Kars) and Wan (Tr.

yarbekir and Urfa. It received praise for as being a "Kurdish tradition," as Uzun did, and also in academic works such as that of Canser Kardaş. He used the denomination *dengbêj* for all epic performers in Kurdistan, and called Miradê Kinê (see footnote 1) a dengbêj as well, even though he is a symbol of the *mitirb* tradition in Ṭûr 'Abdîn (see Kardaş, 2012: 387–399, and Kardaş in this volume).

Although nowadays most performers of Kurdish language who sing prose or poetry without accompaniment of instruments and even many of them with instrumental accompaniment choose to refer to themselves as *dengbêj*, in reality, their singing style; denominations used by locals to refer to them; or their position in the society, are or were different. The spread of the use of the word *dengbêj* has both practical and social-political reasons. One of the practical reasons is, without a doubt, Radio Yerevan's Kurdish broadcasting (Hamelink, 2016: 26). Performers who performed in Radio-Yerevan broadcasting were usually referred to as *dengbêj*. The radio programs made the nomenclature of this tradition known in most parts of Kurdistan. This had a huge impact on the earlier generations of Kurmanji-speaking Kurds, many of them recounting how they first listened to the Radio's broadcasting. As a result, people nowadays associate the word *dengbêj*, even if they traditionally did not know them, with something special, with a personal experience which gave them the joy and the feeling of being part of something bigger[10].

Radio Yerevan may have played a role in spreading the use of the word *dengbêj*, but this alone cannot explain why also other types of performers began to prefer to call themselves *dengbêj*. Nationalist discourse on the "Kurdish national cultural" practice/performance can provide a helpful starting point to understand what has happened over the last four decades. In the 1990s, we see that Kurdish singers were searching for "authentic expressions of Kurdish music," and apparently, they found their answer in the music performed by *dengbêj*s, as B. Siynem Ezgi Sarıtaş demonstrated through several interviews with Kurdish musicians (2010: 115–116).

This may explain partly why performers similar to *dengbêj*s, ethnically also Kurdish, adapted the same term for themselves in other parts of Kurdistan. For instance, in the regions of Hekarî and Botan, the main carriers of oral narratives are traditionally the *şair*. *Şair* means poet in Arabic, but also refers to poets of Kurdish oral tradition in the above-mentioned regions. They are not professional or semi-professional musicians which are called *mitirb, mirtib, aşiq, gewende[11]* or

---

Van), the cities Erzirom (Tr. Erzurum), Mûş (Tr. Muş), and Bedlîs (Tr. Bitlis) are also occasionally considered part of the region (See Çakir, 2012: 4–7).

[10] Interview with Hiseynê Zaxuranî (80 years old) from the region of Ṭûr 'Abdîn (25.02.2017) proves that he indeed do not know *dengbêj*s in his traditional environment but remembers those *"starnbêjs"* from earlier times when he used occasionally to listen to the Radio Yerevan.

[11] It is important to acknowledge that *gewende*s have in some regions the same social status as *qereçî*s which is lower than *mitirb*s' status. While *qereçî*s are considered to be from a differ-

begzade, depending on the region. These terms are used for musicians who are regarded as ethnically separate from "mainstream" Kurds, and usually play an instrument. Traditionally they are educated in mostly semi-formal social gatherings and they are talented to author and compose poems themselves, and to hand down the tradition (Turgut, 2011: 29–30). This very talent is the reason why they are called *şair*, which is also used for the great literate poets of the region Melayê Cizîrî and Feqiyê Teyran. *Şair*s need to be musically talented, and they need to have a good voice. They also need to be able to recognize and differentiate between different *maqam*s[12]. It is very rare that a young man (or today also a young woman) is accepted as a *şair*, which makes it likely that, in order to be generally approved as a *şair*, one needs to have a certain experience. As we can see with no instrumental accompaniment, performers being full member of their tribe, can easily relate themselves to *dengbêj*s.

We observe in the same region that, since ca. 30 years, the traditional *şair* as well as the new generation of musicians (who also perform from the repertoire of *şair*s), began to consider themselves as *dengbêj* and to present themselves as such. The tendency among *şair*s to describe themselves as *dengbêj* is apparently increasing, on the one hand because *dengbêj* are portrayed as a "purely Kurdish" tradition in nationalist discourse (see the above mentioned Siynem Ezgi Sarıtaş 2010), and on the other hand because *dengbêj* are associated with more positive values. This phenomenon should not be confused with the efforts of some *mitirb*s in the region of Ţûr 'Abdîn to escape their disadvantaged social status and to free themselves from the pejorative meanings of the term *mitirb*. Doing so, they prefer to replace this term by *hozan* (bard), *hunermend* (artist) or, increasingly, by using the label *dengbêj* (see Turgut, 2002: 24 and 2011: 30).

Mitirbs *Propose a New Portrait of the* Mitirb

*Mitirb*s seem to have been aiming at establishing or re-establishing their role as *mitirb* of a noble family or tribal chieftain. While it is probably easy to explain this phenomenon in the context of the nation-building process and its discursive context, it will be too simplistic to assume that the members of this group suddenly realized their socially disadvantaged status and began to make efforts to change it. It is true that the discourse of the "authentic Kurdish cultural" elements represents a good opportunity for some members of these groups to challenge their accustomed status: They may want to claim another status in the framework of the nation being built, for example as its bards, as its carriers of

---

ent ethnic origin, *mitirb*s are considered in a lesser degree as such, and they on the other hand are not considered to be memebers of a/the tribe (see Turgut, 2003: 23–24).

12   *Maqam* or *Meqam* (مقام) is the system of melodic modes used in traditional music in Near East. But it refers in our case to different melodic oral genres from Botan and Hekarî (see Turgut, 2011: 203).

history, and/or as being different and unique. These would be mainly an adaptation of arguments of promoters of Kurdish nationalist discourse. However, this will not be an essential part of the analysis in this study even it is mentioned for what it is worth.

The question raised here should be how we can follow the *mitirb's* efforts to elevate their social status in a (primarily) oral tradition? As unique as each of such processes is, it has similarities to other such processes in the present world and also in the history. Which means that we may find some better-documented similar processes in neighbouring societies or elsewhere in history. First, by studying some of the older texts, I looked if such processes also took place in the past. And in a very outstanding way we found them in some performances of epic-narratives telling a story that happened in neighbouring or even faraway regions, so different places than those where the performers actually originated from.

We observe in the performance of "Cembelî, son of the chieftain of Hekarî (*Cembelî kurê Mîrê Hekariya*)" (hereafter only Cembelî) that the performing *mitirb* emerges as one of the decisive characters, as one of the protagonists, in his own narrative. This is not the only but the most striking example. In the performance about the battle between Kalo and Hemê Zerê, *mitirb*s are decisive for the conflict development and play an important role at the start of the events. There are several questions we may ask to adequately analyse this phenomenon in the performances of *mitirb* in Ṭûr ʿAbdîn: which role do they have in the narratives, how do they stage themselves, is it in a historical context, and can the probable audience spatially trace them? The performance of Cembelî begins in both eco-types of the performances on which I will rely in my analysis with Ehmedê Mitirb (Ehmed the Mitirb) visiting the home of the prince or prince's son, and asks for provisions, because he has to serve his guests and has nothing left at home to do so adequately. The wife of the prince (or of prince's son) apparently humiliates him by not giving him the whole butter produced in the churn for that very morning and proposing just a part of it. Even though she is aware of the rage she causes by her behaviour, it seems that she does not need to fear the rage of Ehmedê Mitirb due to her high social status:

> Hêhêy, erê dibê "Xatûnê ezê kevime xopana keviya, ma ne zozanê Şerefdînê, bêxwedanê belekiyê berfêyo,
> Aûy! Xwedê teʿela kuleke li şeş kulê berda mala bavê te li alyê vê perdêyo,
> Minî sûnd xwariyê bi navê rebbê ʿalemê, daim miqatî rehma xwedêyo,
> Ti nedî mi [qasê niviş] kê sibêyo,
> Ezê lingê xwe bavême rikêba hespê şêyo,
> Bavême milê xwe darê kemaçêyo,
> Erê gidî gidyano, serê vê şeveqê têkevim nav êl û urbana ha têkevim binê Kerbelêyo,
> Şeş salê mi biqedê heta biqulibê sala heftêyo,
> Ezê bigerim her qul û berê li çolêyo,
> Erê heta yeke ji Fatima Salih Axa sipehîtir, jê comerttir, ji mala bavê malmestir, ezê ji mîrê xwe re

ênim zozanê belekiyê berfê lêkir bin konê 'amê, xopana binê vê perdêyo,
Erê li mi Ehmedê Mitirb *heram nivîna pîreka Pîr Fatêyo,*
Erê talya vê çît û perdê telaqê te bikî destê te, berê te bidî mala bavêyo lo lo oy oy ay şêrîna minê lê
lê lê lê hêyî heyê ax de raba kevok ferxîna minê hay lê lê"

"Oh, yes", he says, "My lady I will go to those ruined borders, is it not so that the summer pastures of Şerefdin should be lordless, blurred with snow
Ouch! Almighty God should inflict to your father's home a wound with a six-bullet revolver at the side of this tent-home,
I have all ready taken an oath on the name of the God of the world; I always await the mercy of God
If you do not give me [all the butter] of this morning,
I will put my foot on the stirrup of bay horse,
I will put this *kemaçe*-violine on my shoulders,
Yes on this beginning of morning, I will start to the search within the tribes and towns; I will enter the desert,
Till six years passes and seventh [year] begins,
I will look/search every hole and stone in the desert,
Till I have found someone more beautiful, more generous, from a more aristocrat fathers-home, I will take her [as bride] for my prince to the summer ranges blurred with snow, I will bring her under the public tent, under this ruined tent-home
Yes, the bed of the woman *Pîr Fatê* should be forbidden to Ehmedê Mitirb,
Yes, [so that the Prince] divorce you behind this curtains, dismiss you to yours father's home, oh my sweetheart, oh stand up my dove's fledgling" (Turgut, 2002: 97–98)

But as we see, the performer lets Ehmedê Mitirb say that he will let the prince divorce her, and find someone else for the prince, even if he has to look for her for years among tribes of the plain and desert. This threat is not taken seriously by Fatima Salih Axa, the prince's wife who is the daughter of a tribal leader. The *mitirb* is not threatening her to harm her reputation, which is what the community usually expected from a *mitirb*. From the very beginning there is a change of *mitirb's* mission in the narrative: he is an assistant to the prince, a judicious corrector, a social actor able to change the game, a challenger.

But it is not just usurpation of this role which makes this performance important. By means of the protagonist Ehmedê Mitirb, it is his ability to endure, his persistence to succeed with his efforts and indeed his sacrifices for his patron and his fighting skills, that allow him to be victorious in a duel for his master Prince Cembelî or Prince's son Cembelî. Another aspect which will be analyzed below is, that the "characteristics" of a *mitirb*, who very probably was known to the audience of this very performance, are repeatedly mentioned during the performance itself.

In this epic, Ehmedê Mitirb searches a long time for a woman more beautiful than Fatima Salih Axa, and finds her in the tent of Faris Beg. Her name is Binevşa Narîn, but she is promised to her cousin Ehmed (in the performances outside of Ţûr 'Abdîn, he is called Derwêş), who later challenged Cembelî to a duel. Ehmedê Mitirb replaces his master and defeats him but spares his life. As Cembelî returns to his tribe to make preparations for the wedding-procession, Ehmed, the cousin of Binevş, raids the tent of Faris Beg and marries Binevş for-

Figure 2: Bedranê Mala Alê on a video clip prepared for the youtube channel of Suleyman Dag www.youtube.com/watch?v=z_0WsVTA_Vg (published 26 October 2017)..

cibly. As a consequence, the tribe of Faris Beg leaves the area as the weaker side in the emerging conflict. Cembelî, when coming to take his bride, finds out that the tribe has left the area, and he takes an oath to find Binevşa Narîn. She meanwhile gives birth to a baby boy whom she insists to be called Cembelî too. After many years, Cembelî finally finds the pasture in which the tribe of Faris Beg, Ehmed and Binevşa Narîn settled. Without revealing his identity, he proposes to work as a shepherd for Ehmed, who accepts this. After one month at the pasture, Cembelî has the hope that Binevşa Narîn will come to the milking, who, after several failures of her servants and maids, decides to do the milking herself. She recognizes Cembelî when his silver poniard falls into the milking pail. Binevşa Narîn asks Cembelî to pretend to be ill, to take him to the settlement, and finalize their plan to elope together. They decide to do so in the night, and at the end, Ehmed, who will get his chance for a duel with Cembelî, follows them. Cembelî kills Ehmed during this very duel.

The core question I focus on in this paper is why there was the need to promote such a new role for a *mitirb*[13]? Was it an attempt to construct a new status or even identity for performers who are socially and politically disadvantaged? And how is this elevation of social status done in the performance? I regard the choice for performance as decisive for the construction of a new status to succeed in having the intended impact on the audience, on the respective community, and on the entire Kurmanji-speaking communities.

---

[13] I may admit, that there is a very small chance that such *mitirb* used to exist in the time of Kurdish chieftains until 19th century, but it is a very small chance and there is no evidence to persuade one to assume, it has happened ones that *mitirbs* were court artists/poets.

Before proceeding to the analysis, I think it is important to point to the work of Dwight Fletcher Reynolds (1995). His work addresses the performative realities of a group of oral poets of an epic tradition who were clearly considered as outsiders in the villages they are living in, or where they are rather living on the margins. He not only refutes the stereotypical image of a static folkloric poem and shows how even in seemingly conservative rural setting an epic tradition is open to constant reshaping and reinterpretation, but he also points out the interaction between poet, audience and heroes glorified in their epic as he describes in the preface of his book:

> The focus of this book is the intense tripartite relationship that obtains between the poets, their listeners, and the heroes of the Bani Hilal narrative. In examining the tradition from several different angles, I demonstrate that poets, heroes, and audience members perceive one another, interact with one another, and even rely on one another as social allies (or adversaries) in fascinating and highly significant ways, all of which contribute to the continual re-creation and propagation of the epic tradition. (1995: XIV)

He furthermore states that this process

> is not necessarily restricted to moments that we outsiders would recognize as moments of epic performance, but rather is one that takes place both inside and outside of the epic 'text.' Though it might at first seem surprising to consider the epic heroes as active participants in this exchange, they are deployed both by poets when singing and by audience members in the ensuing discussions, so that their characters as conceived and constructed by participants invariably leave their mark on the personal relationships and social tensions that are played out during epic performances. Major issues, including ethnic identification, Arabness, religious orientation, traditional codes of behaviour, manhood, womanhood, and the hierarchisation of social power, are woven into the texture of any modern performance of Sirat Bani Hilal. (Ibid.)

This relatively long citation will help to continue the analysis of the "text" of our performances we are looking at. That the performance is not limited to the moments considered by outsiders as the performance situation, and is indeed going on in daily life outside of the performance context, will enable us to see *mitirb* performers, and one of the heroes of the epic "text," the *mitirb* (here Ehmedê Mitirb) in a new light, especially concerning their ethnic identification and social status.

Homogenizing Performer Diversity

The ethnic identity of the *mitirb* is a complex, sensitive and highly ambiguous issue. Members of the tribes in the past and today, especially the Kurmanji-speaking population of the Ṭûr ʿAbdîn region and neighbouring areas, have evolved continuously during last six decades. This can be traced through the testimonies of the concerned community members.

While doing fieldwork in Rojava in 1982, Celîlê Celîl worked in the region which he describes as Mardin-Cizîr (1989: 12–13), with its centre in Qamişlo. Its population consisted of a slight majority of people originating from Ṭûr ʿAbdîn, or of members of the same tribal confederacy Hevêrkan. In this time period, he encountered the tradition of *mirtib*s and describes them as musicians who play different instruments, among other *kemaçe*, *def*, *tambûr* and *zurne*[14]. He adds that they sing during wedding feasts and other festivities. He calls them students of an "old tradition" called "oda" or "ode" which in this context means a room/place for community gatherings. A school of *mitirb*s were then, according to Celîl, given the room for performing several oral genres, mainly *şer*, *dîlok*, and *stran*[15]. We can already note that this institution *ode* does not anymore exist in the way it did in the past, and newly constructed occasions/situations to perform the above-mentioned genres are totally different from the relatively homogenous gatherings that existed once in the villages (when participants were primarily members of the same tribal confederacy).

Contrasting with these performance practices, we may mention the House of *Dengbêj*s built recently in several cities in the north of Kurdistan (in Turkey) to offer "traditional" performers the opportunity to perform on a daily basis. Next to publicly organized events, where several performers can perform their art, this place gives the performers the opportunity to gather, interact and perform also in less formal performance situations. Wendelmoet Hamelink tells about the House of *Dengbêj*s in Diyarbekir (Tr. Diyarbakır) that in 2008 there were 24 officially registered *dengbêj*s of the house and that those *dengbêj*s found the interest in their art rising with the establishment of the House of *dengbêj*s and they felt that their art was "reviving" (Hamelink 2016: 151). What is more important is, that this "reviving" has concerned only the tradition of *dengbêj*s, and not other traditions present in the region. This revival thus meant at the same time assimilation of all other traditions into the newly constructed performer identity *dengbêj*. As Hamelink states, after 2000s *dengbêj*s became more and more visible and the House of *Dengbêj*s made their presence more established: "In newspaper and magazines they were presented as the guardians of Kurdish culture." (Ibid.) And she adds to this that they were not accustomed to this newly established presence and tried to define an alternative space for themselves. Then follows, important for our topic, information about how *dengbêj*s were feeling about this

---

[14] *Kemaçe* is a bowed fiddle with three strings which is played with a bow. *Def* in this context used here, is also called *dahol*, it is a drum. *Zurne* or *zirne* is a double-reed wood wind instrument accompanied often by *def*. *Tembûr*, a long-necked lute, which's resonance box is made from mulberry tree's wood. The most used *Tembûr* among Kurds has seven strings.

[15] *Şer* is a genre of Kurdish oral literature, which is essentially an epic narrative of a war, tribal conflict or mostly tragic love story (in the region of Ṭûr ʿAbdîn it is the core of the repertoire of a *mitirb*); it is partly prose (not sang), partly poetic (sang). In the region of Ṭûr ʿAbdîn its performance is accompanied by *kemaçe*. In this context *dîlok*s are dance songs and *stran* will be the general term to describe German denomination *das Lied*.

public interest: "At the same time, even though they felt inspired by the new attention, there was among most *dengbêj*s also a strong sense of dissatisfaction with the lack of genuine interest among their audiences." (Hamelink 2016: 152) As a matter of course, the audience would have the same impression as the performer, namely that they are not 'real' *dengbêj*s, which indeed existed for them in the past or rather in their memories, memories reflecting totally different living and performance situations.

The problem here is not just the assimilation of all existing traditions into one which is considered truly Kurdish, but also inventing totally new performance environments, in which the expectations of all participants are differing: Performers hope to have performance situations in which they can perform and teach, that is in all similar traditions in Kurdistan and probably beyond, one of the main functions of a performance, and re-experience the same interaction with the audience they once had in their villages or in their respective tribal community; on the other hand, some parts of their new audience expect to experience something purely Kurdish, something they assume their parents or grandparents experienced in the past, the 'real Kurdish rural life.' They hope to re-experience what they experienced in entirely different circumstances and places in the past.

But how can these expectations be met if, from the start, the main composition of the performers and audience is changed, and the interaction between them is limited to a minimum? This is nearly impossible in a big city as Diyarbekir. So indeed, we can conclude that the expectations must change for both performers and audiences in order to enjoy the new performance style. Another newly constructed performance situation is television programmes that are broadcasted in nationwide or local TV channels, and internet platforms allowing the uploading and sharing of video and audio recordings. All of these newly created performing platforms and situations show that the tradition is changing and adapting to new environments (see Turgut, 2011: 227–228). At the same time, we are observing a homogenising of the tradition(s) which are all called *dengbêjî*, labelling only one type of performance as the "real" Kurdish cultural expression. It is then very natural that all other performers try to fit into this newly created style, which is difficult to fit in even for people from the *dengbêjî* tradition.

The pressure is so high, that even music groups of new generations have adopted the same idea of *dengbêjî* as the 'real Kurdish cultural expression'. The members of Group Avesta performing in Qoser (Tr. Kızıltepe) when asked what they consider as *dengbêjî*, or what a *dengbêj* performance looks like, replied as followed: "*Dengbêj*s from the past, those we see as an example to follow, when they were somewhere to perform, they could immediately describe this place with a *stran*. We think that *stranbêjî* (performing *stran*s) and *dengbêjî* are different. The first one is just singing old *stran*s and (*stran*s belonging to the tradition of) *dengbêj*s, one can call him *stranbêj*. And if someone is singing old *stran*s and is able to describe his epoch, one can call him *dengbêj*." (Ogur, 2017). This exhibits clearly the strong idea of relating *dengbêjî* with the "real Kurdish cultural expression", which also partly explains why today performers from different oral traditions in Kurdistan prefer to call themselves *dengbêj*. This brings us back to our argument that *mitirb*s nowadays feel a similar pressure to homogenize performer diversity, and that their attempts to do so can be seen as an opportunity to claim a new social status that is more respectable, namely as 'the Homer's of the rising Nation' (see Ferho, 2007 and Çiftçi, 2015: 110[16]).

A New Mitirb *Emerges as Protagonist*

In the past however, a *mitirb* had no other choice than to be a *mitirb*, which means that he was not a member of the tribe or larger community in the region of Ṭûr 'Abdîn. If he wanted a change in his social status, he apparently should first of all, invent a discourse allowing for such a change; if not, how would people accept without any reason to contemplate the possibility of such a change taking place? Reşîdê Omerî was a *mitirb* from the Ṭûr 'Abdîn area with close relations with the neighbouring Omeryan tribal confederacy, and thus Şerefxan Cizîrî (1999) called him Omerî (from the Omeryan). In his performance of Cembelî[17] we can see that the introduction of a new role for the *mitirb* in the terms discussed above did not lead to any changes in the social status of the performer in question. We can simultaneously observe that the *mitirb* as the performer and *mitirb* as the protagonist in the performance are clearly aware of what it means to be a *mitirb*. Another performer from the *mitirb* tradition, Bedranê Mala Alê (who is referred to also wrongly as Bedranê Mala Sivûk[18] and called usually Bedrano), expresses the same idea through the people present in Cembelî's *ode*[19]. When Ehmedê Mitirb tells him that he has found a woman more suitable for him, someone from the gathering reminds Cembelî some clichés commonly attributed to *mitirb*s:

> *Heçî mêrikê* mitirb *e, zilamê xatirê wî bigrê, gezek xwarina taze bidyê, xelateke taze lêkê, wallehî navê wa bigelekî bi însanetî li odê kurê camêra digerênin.*

---

[16] As introducing citation to his article about *dengbêj*s Çiftçi quote Yaşar Kemal saying "Evdalê Zeynikê [a well known *dengbêj* of 19th century] is Homer of Kurds".

[17] The performance was recorded and copied multiple times on the tapes; the presence of an audience could be heard. Reşîdo (as he was usually referred to) probably was invited in an *ode* in the 70s and the owner probably arranged to record the performance.

[18] In a personal communication on 10 Mai 2017, Argun Çakır corrected my earlier information about this appellation and proved that younger generations may wrongly have identified Bedrano (Bedranê Mala Alê) as being from the family of Sivûk, resulting in the appellation Bedranê Mala Sivûk.

[19] This performance can be found on youtube part one at https://www.youtube.com/watch?v=z_0WsVTA_Vg and part two on the https://www.youtube.com/watch?v=8IBGo1SO LXI (last accessed 4 May 2018). It may be much more recently compared to the performance of Reşîdê Omerî, given the quality of recording.

Figure 3: Reşîdo (Reşîdê Mala Mûsa, 4th person from the right) is performing in Çal (a village west of Nisêbîn), and his performance for an all-male audience is being recorded; probably in the late 1970s.

> With regard to a *mitirb* man, if someone respects him, if he offers him some good food, and gives him a good gift, then by God, they praise them for being gentlemen in the *odes* of respectable people. (Turgut, 2002: 64)

We clearly observe that the performing *mitirb* is very aware how a *mitirb* is considered to be in the larger society in which they perform their art. The fact that they are not considered members of tribes and are not seen as equals to the tribesman is as well included in the by *mitirb*s themselves introduced discourse about *mitirb*s in the performances available from Ṭûr 'Abdîn. For instance, in Reşîdê Omerî's performance of Cembelî, Ehmed, who is the cousin of Binevşa Narîn, responds to Ehmedê Mitirb, after the latter challenges the former to a duel: "*Taliya paşî, ti* mitirb *î, em 'eşîr in ji bavê me re belê kemayî ye*" (In the end you are a *mitirb*, we are tribal, it is shameful for our ancestors. (Turgut, 2002: 22)

Doing so, both Reşîdê Omerî and Bedranê Mala Alê, and the performers who may have introduced the protagonist Ehmedê Mitirb to the performance of the epic Cembelî, indeed challenge the idea of the exclusion of *mitirb*s. They are described as authentic as possible, so that they do not seem to be some outsider characters, but related to the performer himself. For instance, when Ehmedê Mitirb in his performance tries to force Binevşa Narîn to listen to him and the message he brought to her, he clearly expresses the actual power attributed to *mitirb*s, namely, that if they are not content with someone, they can give them a bad reputation:

> ...
> *Li devê vê perdê belekî, li kêleka te rûnênim, [...] lawika, li alyê çît û perdê ez nebêjim ji xatûna xwe re,*
> *Ezê navê te têkim koda kemaçê nava 'erfan û 'egîda, bav û berana bi pîsîtî gerênim bi xwe re,*
> *Erê ez nahêlim kes te bixwazê, erê heta ti pîr bibê di mala bavê xwe de lê lê lê hîwî lê hê lê hêwî lê hê lê lê lê ax de rabe kevok fexrîna minê hay lê.*

...

If I cannot sit down on your side in front of this lined curtain [separating rooms in a tent], [...] if I do not sing love songs for my lady from inside the curtain and the straw-walls [marking the outer borders of a tent],
I will put your name in the box of my *kemaçe* and take it with me, and spread your bad reputation among the wise and the brave, among the brave fathers and sons,
Yes, I will make sure that no one would want to marry you, yes so that you grow old in your father's house, oh, stand up my dove[20]! (Turgut, 2002: 65)

As a result of their ability to shame someone's reputation, but also because entertainment dictates it, *mitirb*s are allowed to perform relatively free and also in rooms usually closed to public or men; as Reşîdê Omerî says in his performance of Cembelî, "... *heçî mitirb in, ma'lûm e li nava her heft dewleta destûrdayî ne. Sohbet bi wa re gula ji me'r lazim e. Zilamê kêfçî ne. Sohbet bi wa re ye, gula civata ne. Xeberê xirab û hek yê qenc bin, kes nikarê ji wa bixeydê. ...*" (Regarding *mitirb*s, as it is known; they have permission in all seven states. Having a conversation with them is a rose we need. They are man of pleasure. Having a conversation with them is a rose of gatherings. Whether they [say] good words or bad words, no one can get mad at them . ...) (Turgut, 2002: 62)

We cannot assume that with the introduction of this discourse on the role of *mitirb*s, performers forget about their functions and focus only on the change or on the creation of the new *mitirb* in performance. As we have already demonstrated, the new *mitirb* introduced in the oral text of the performance is still the old one, but he wishes to command more respect, as a man of goodwill like other members of the tribe, as a man of courage able to challenge people to duels and as a loyal subject to his master and their tribe. That is why we retrieve all the important characteristics attributed to the *mitirb*s, and the issue of their payment is not at all neglected, as we observe in the performance of Bedranê Mala Alê, when he tells how Binevşa Narîn's father pays Ehmedê Mitirb for his performance:

> *Hê nûka dibê gelî camêra, dibê rabû çi kir bavê Binevşa Narîn, hêçê mêra? Qapûtekî servekirî avête nav milê wî, qundereke teberderzî kire lingê wî de, rahişte sê lib zêrê mahmûdî kire destê wî de*

> Just now, dear gentlemen, do you know what the father of Binevşa Narîn, the bravest among men did? He put an elegant coat on his shoulder, he put shoes of Tabriz on his feet, he took three pieces gold[21] and gave them to the *mitirb*. (Turgut, 2002: 63–64)

Where *Mitirb*s Change the Course of Events

In the performance of *Şerê Kalo û Hemê Zerê* (The battle between Kalo and Hemê Zerê) by Bedranê Mala Alê[22], we observe also that a pair of *mitirb*s are introduced

---

[20] It is a way of addressing a woman in praising her beauty.
[21] The word Mahmûdî used here informs us that those gold pieces are coined during the reign of Mahmoud II.

as elements to start the conflict between *Faris Axa*, the chief of the tribes of Hesenan and Heyderan, and his cousin *Ni'o Axa*. After the two *mitirbs* perform for
Ni'o Axa and are paid adequately, they also perform for the "ladies" of the *Ni'o
Axa*'s family, because they have seen his beautiful sister *Gewrê Xatûn* and insisted
to perform specifically for her and the other ladies of the house. They are afterwards paid adequately and go to perform for the chief of Hesenan and Heyderan, Faris Axa's tribes. He also awards them adequately, but they insist to perform for his three wives too. Although as *mitirb*s they are allowed to go into the
private family part of the tent, the three wives of Faris Axa are not interested in
their art and they make it clear that they do not respect the *mitirb*s. Consequently, the *mitirb*s, who are dissatisfied and feel humiliated, tell Faris Axa that
his wives are not suitable for a chief of tribes, and that they know a woman more
appropriate for him, and tell him about the sister of his cousin Ni'o Axa, Gewrê
Xatûn. That is how the conflict between the two cousins emerges, and Ni'o Axa
is subsequently forced to leave his land. The story ends with a battle, in which
Ni'o Axa's uncle Kalo kills the commander-in-chief of Faris Axa's tribal army
Hemê Zerê and Ni'o Axa manages to kill Faris Axa in a duel, which he agreed to
during the battle[23].

It seems to be a tradition to introduce a role to the *mitirb*s, which is decisive
for the course of events, but the role of *Ehmedê* Mitirb as an important protagonist in the performance of Cembelî is beyond usual, which leads us to an analysis of two different points. First, the performer attempts to restore his important
role within tribal life, as the one who provides entertainment to tribal leaders
and other members of the tribe, which constitutes important work and demands
respect. Secondly, the *mitirb*s elaborate on their role in their stories. They point
out that they are more than just ensuring entertainment, but can also form a potential threat if they are not treated respectfully. These two points can be observed in both performances. In Cembelî, however, we are confronted with a
strategy to introduce a new discourse, a strategy which allows *mitirb*s to become
powerful figures within the narrated epics, and allows at the same time the audience to receive it as a proposal to be discussed. In the introduction of this new
discourse, convincing the audience is the main objective of the performer. He
seems to have decided such a strategy, preferring communication and interaction
between participants of a given performance.

But *Ehmedê* Mitirb has a considerably more important position in the discourse on the new *mitirb* introduced in the performance of Cembelî: He is a

---

[22] This performance can be found on youtube part one on the https://www.youtube.com/
     watch?v=42sA3ELsA5M (accessed 16 April 2018) and part two on the https://www.you
     tube.com/watch?v=Wo6LJK_hyhA (accessed 16 April 2018). It is probably recorded in the
     late 70s or early 80s.
[23] The performance is uploaded in Youtube; see https://www.youtube.com/watch?v=m8Z
     JVhzoHV8 (accessed 16 April 2018)

mitirb who is the best adviser to a prince, he is as loyal as possible to his patron and he is an excellent warrior at the same time. That is why we have to deal with this level of discourse separately. It does not simply challenge the existing social status of *mitirb*s, by claiming more respect and less discrimination, but proposes a negotiation of their very social status in its entirety by portraying them as loyal members of tribes, even as advisers to tribal leaders and warriors ready to sacrifice themselves for these leaders, i.e. as true heroes. This proposal is creating just an idea, which is communicated during the performance situation, but continuing to affect participants beyond the performance situation, because the hero portrayed in the performance becomes a party of the interaction between performer and audience: The hero constitutes a new idea that shapes the perception of the audience. The audience can imagine that a *mitirb*, even though he is not in Ṭûr 'Abdîn and he does not exist at the moment of performance, can be more than a *mitirb* he knew until then: A *mitirb* can be a member of a tribe, he can be a tribal warrior and a tribal hero.

Introducing *mitirb*s as important actors in tribal life and as entertainers for tribal leaders and others in the tribe, seems to be a more established performance related convention. It clearly has its roots in the region prior to the emergence of national movements there. That is why it is legitimate to frame it in a pre-nationalist discourse, and understand it as a continuing interaction between performer and audience also beyond the "actual" performance situation at the time of the composition of the epic but also today with the involvement of more complex discursive elements. And it can not be excluded that *mitirb*s and other protagonist and characters in a performance, continue to have interaction with other participants, namely *mitirb*s and their audience, which extends beyond the 'actual' performance situation.

To illustrate this point, we should remember what we have already discussed with regard to the way audiences view *mitirb*s socially: Not as members of the tribe and not as equals; they are considered to be inferior to the other members of the community in question. However, at the same time they are conditioned to think that *mitirb*s should be awarded adequately for their performances. Introducing *mitirb*s who are comparable to the *mitirb*s they know, not wholly alienated and can easily be recognized is thus a suitable means for performers to communicate with their audiences on a subject they (or the performers as an institution) are willing to introduce, and therefore giving direction to the existing interaction too. However, it is not possible to interview people living in past situations, and we are mostly dependent on accounts of the past, i.e. recounts of both audiences and performers regarding past performances and the tradition of *şer*-epics and *mitirb*s. But at the same time, we have to bear in mind that they are subjective and affected both by the discursive realities of the present time as well as by modernity as a whole, both materially and mentally. That is why the performance text remains the most valuable resource for our analysis.

Claiming a New Social Status or a New Identity?

It is a pity that even academics do not distinguish between different performer identities called *mitirb*, and do not pay much attention to regional differences. Although the young academic Necat Keskin does distinguish between different performer types in Ṭûr ʿAbdîn, he does not go beyond the recognizing *mitirb*s as people playing *kemaçe* and says, "*… what makes a* mitirb *a 'mitirb' is their preoccupation with music and especially with the* kemaçe. *Thus this characteristic, which gradually became their identity, can be seen as a 'boundary' for* mitirb*s to describe themselves or for others to describe them as such*" (2015: 62–63).

The 'boundary' he points to is a kind of ethnic boundary, which, according to Barth, defines the group, and it is social and territorial, which he elaborates as follows: "*the ethnic boundary canalizes social life – it entails a frequently quite complex organization of behaviour and social relations.*" And this according to him "[*m*]*akes it possible to understand one final form of boundary maintenance whereby cultural units and boundaries persist. Entailed in ethnic boundary maintenance are also situations of social contact between persons of different cultures.*" (1998: 15). And indeed, what we observe in the case of the performances we analyse and the performer's general attempt to challenge their social status cannot be reduced to this and simply be interpreted as an attempt to reverse these boundaries or to annul them, so that they can be part of another identity or set new ethnic boundaries. In the performances we analysed, the denomination *mitirb* itself is not challenged, but the disadvantages related to it are. We can see this attempt, given the broader performance situations available recorded in form of CD, DVD, MP3 or online on several platforms, as an ongoing limited negotiation of new boundaries for the existent identity, which should at best enable them to be less disadvantaged or less discriminated against.

With the emergence of a nationalist discourse within the Kurdish communities, several performer groups, including some *mitirb*s, began to challenge the old denomination, and claim to be something else, i.e. bards of a nation performing its history and passing down its cultural values. This can be seen as a new strategy which they adopted to get rid of the disadvantages related to their ethnic-social status or identity. As explained above, attempts to elevate their social status began long before nationalist discourses gained prominence among the Kurmanji-speaking communities in Ṭûr ʿAbdîn. After nationalist discourses became predominant, their efforts to be recognized as full-members of a certain tribe, county or village continue to be of importance. This is because their main clientele is a local one, and even if they would succeed in establishing a new "identity" as belonging to a larger Kurdish ethnicity, they still have to convince their local audiences to accept their newly acquired status as equal members of the same community as their audiences. The main strategy in this regard has been to use attributes such as Hezexî (from Hezex) and the like to show their loyalty to a certain region or tribe.

However, in the performances we analysed, rather than referring to nationalist discourses, the main strategy was to introduce a discourse about the social and political role of *mitirb*s and their loyalty to tribes, thus recreating the conventional image of *mitirb*s while bestowing upon them new qualities, new roles and social-political importance beyond that of providing entertainment. These new qualities consist of passing down part of historical knowledge of the tribe or a certain region, and ensuring the conservation of a repertoire which can be used to maintain or reinforce existing tribal relations and the social-political tribal status quo. Another way in which they legitimate their claims for a new social status is by narrating from foreign spaces and times. By constructing a new role, identity and status outside their own locality, tribe or social context, they attempt to introduce such a new status as acceptable also in their own locality. Cembelî, the son of the prince of Hekarî, who lives in a relatively exotic context of time and space outside of the audiences' daily reality, is prospectively able to report to audiences in other places and times. In the performances from the Hekarî and Botan regions, neither do we have a *mitirb* character playing a similarly significant role in the course of events nor any other protagonist having a similar role as Ehmedê Mitirb in the performances from Ṭûr 'Abdîn. In the performance of Kalo and Hemê Zerê, the tribal units Hesenan and Heyderan are mentioned, and the lands they occupied in the Serhad region, both of which are hardly known in the Ṭûr 'Abdîn area. Given this, they first of all present a *mitirb*-image best received by communal or tribal leaders, who compensate them in the best way possible. Using clichés about *mitirb*s that are felt as being in their best interest, they are able to communicate with their audiences and negotiate these issues with them. Introducing attributes relating to an alternative social or ethnic identity and social status makes it possible for performers to negotiate also a new ethnic or rather social identity. These performances are partly available on social media, where they continue to interact with other members of the performer community beyond local boundaries. They are also in a complex relationship with nationalist discourses trying to elaborate and praise "truly" Kurdish cultural expressions.

In short, digital performances and the spread of these through social media platforms, continue to communicate the proposal of a new meaning for the existing denomination *mitirb*, enabling *mitirb*s as performers to promote a new social status for themselves as full members of a certain tribe, locality or ethnicity, for instance, as potential Ehmedê Mitirbs. On the other hand, the efforts to replace the denomination *mitirb* by terms such as *hunermend*, *hozan* or *dengbêj* are continuing on the broader level within Kurdish nationalist discourse. Even if the latter development would succeed, they will not be able to integrate in their own communities in the way they wish to if the immanent audience is not convinced to accept them as full members of their tribal or rural communities.

A very clear sign of a change in this respect would be the willingness to accept marriages between Kurdish women and *mitirb* men. Randomly asked the mem-

bers of a community from Ṭûr 'Abdîn living in Germany[24], we get a result showing that out of 17 people, 15 were against and only two were in favour of such a
marriage, and this is much telling about the continuing negotiation of the new
potential social status claimed by *mitirb*s in Ṭûr 'Abdîn. That some (in our not so
representative survey ca 12 % of respondents) were already in favour of such marriage or would not object to it, could possibly show that the nationalist discourse
as well as the discourse *mitirb*s themselves introduced, and the subsequent interaction taken place with the audiences, have had some impact on the communities.
Many people who were asked the question above, first replied "*ti behsa hunermendê
me dikê /* do you mean our artists?", which indeed clearly shows that this impact is
not limited to the 2 out of 17, but should be regarded as a general phenomenon.

Conclusion

In this paper, I focused on the *mitirb*s from Ṭûr 'Abdîn, who play the *kemaçe* and
those talented among them who were at the same time performer of the performance genre *şer*. We should be aware that the performance situations, performers and audiences, which have been the subject of this chapter, are situated
in the past. Thus, my analysis consists of today's reflections projected on past
performance situations, performers and audience. Since today there is an ongoing process of social recognition of performers denominated as *mitirb*s as those
analyzed in this chapter, the analysis of past performance contexts and performers' roles as they appear from the texts, and performers' motivations to introduce
new social roles, which can provide more insight into present-day developments.

We analysed by means of some performances probably composed and performed among others to introduce a new discourse about the social status of
*mitirb*s as performer. It is also important to point at the Kurdish nationalistic discourse and new phenomena impacting several performer groups including
*mitirb*s as a separated but at the same time interrelated later development. The
difference is, that while the second indeed affect the majoritarian group within
which *mitirb*s perform their art as well as *mitirb*s and is kind of identity building
process for both, the first one is part of an ongoing negotiation, interaction between mainly performers, audience and also characters or heroes in the performances in the actual performance situation and beyond.

The strategy to do so seems not to be randomly decided but rather well
planned and efficiently executed to have the impact it was supposed to have
through the interaction between participants during the performance situation

---

[24] Survey is conducted between 30 April 2017 and 5 May 2017, and participant are asked just
one question, with two possible answers namely yes or not to the question "Would you
agree to a possible marriage between your daughter or sister and a young man from a
mitirb family?" All 17 persons asked are living in Landkreis Gießen, 9 men and 8 women
from any age between 16 and 70 years old.

and beyond. In the introduced discourse the performer as he should be known by the audience and could be recognized through his description by the same audience during the performance is pictured, with all clichés associated to it, but put in another light that could be used in favour of *mitirb*s. And it is kind of proposed to accept another role for *mitirb*s have lived in the past (or may be still living) in another location. This role gives them the opportunity to be honoured and awarded for their art and performances adequately, to be respected socially and be less discriminated. If not they can act in a way, that they evoke a totally new situation for all participant in the respective narrative, provoke a turning point in the course of events depicted in the same narrative.

Choice for a far away location seems to be part of the strategy mentioned above to illustrate that in spatially different places a tribal leader could have a permanent *mitirb*, an entertainer for the highest instance ever in tribal society, for the prince. In our second example it is demonstrated that *mitirb*s moving around were in demand by tribal leaders and important families. And in both situations, in the case that they felt they were not treated with respect or were humiliated, they can change the course of events for all other participants in the narrative subject matter of respective performances. *Mitirb*s were presented as sort of powerful figures, and it is received by the audience as a proposal to be discussed. In this introduced new discourse convincing audience is the main objective of performer, decisive for him to decide such a strategy.

In one of the performances analysed in this paper, an entirely different portrait of a *mitirb* is proposed: imagining *mitirb* as a member of the tribe, as a warrior, as a hero. This may come as a very strange idea to audiences in Ṭûr 'Abdîn, but it is proposed and takes shape in their perception too as a possible reality in another place and time. This perception allows performers indeed to challenge their social status as a whole. Both subjects of this new introduced discourse are still affecting participants and are ongoing parallel to the nationalistic discourse as well as interconnected with it. Since Kurdish nationalistic discourse affect audience as well as performers. It has different results such as allowing or rather enabling an assimilation of all performer groups into *dengbêj* perceived largely as more respected and purely Kurdish, while influencing different audiences to perceive their respective performer groups in a new, more positive light. Both processes are still ongoing and affecting the perception of audiences and performers alike.

References

Aras, A. (2007). "Kilama Kurdî û Dengbêjiya Serhedê", *Kovara Bîr*, Nr. 7., http://kovarabir.com/315-2/ (last accessed 4 May 2018)

Barth, F. (1998). *Ethnic Groups and Boundaries: The Social Organization of Culture Difference*. Long Grove: Waveland Press, Inc.

Bedrano, Niho û Kalo, youtube, https://www.youtube.com/watch?v=42sA3EL sA5M (accessed 16 April 2018); https://www.youtube.com/watch?v=Wo6LJ K_hyhA (accessed 16 April 2018).

Bedrano, Sere Kalo u Heme Zere, youtube, https://www.youtube.com/watch?v= m8ZJVhzoHV8 (accessed 16 April 2018).

Celîl, C. (1989). *Zargotina Kurdê Sûrîyayê*. Upsala: Weşanên Jîna Nû (first published in 1985).

Cizîrî, Ş. (1999). *Kultur û Edebiyata Devkî*. Stockholm: Weşanên Nûdem.

Çakır, N. A. (2010). *An Investigation of the Singing Style of the Kurdish* Dengbêj *Reso*. Unpublished Master of Arts final project (Ethnomusicology). Centre for Advanced Studies in Music (MIAM), Istanbul Technical University.

Çiftçi, T. (2015). "Di Çarçoveya Çanda Devkî de di nav Civaka Kurdan de Dengbêj û Saziya Dengbêjiyê", *International Journal of Kurdish Studies*. Nr. 1. pp. 110–124.

Ferho, M. (2007). Gotûbêj: Mitirb, Şiroveya Medenî Ferho. Published on Kurmanji Wikipedia, https://ku.wikipedia.org/wiki/Got%C3%BBb%C3%AAj:Mitirb, (accessed 1 April 2017).

Hamelink, W. (2016). *The Sung Home: Narrative, Morality, and Kurdish Nation*. Leiden and Boston: Brill.

Kardaş, C. (2012). "Dengbêjlerde Toplumsal Belek Alîkê Battê Olayinin Dengbêjlere Yansima Şekli", in: *Uluslararasi Midyat Sempozyumu 7-9 Ekim 2011 – Sempozyum Bildirileri*. Mardin.

Keskin, N. (2015). "Ṭûr 'Abdîn'de bir Kimlik ve Anlatim Biçimi: Mitirb*lar* ve *Mitriblik*." In *Folklor Edebiyat*, vol. 21, Nr. 84. Cyprus International University. Lefkoşa, North Nicosia pp. 53–77.

Ogur, A. (2017). "Dengbêj Şahidê Serdema xwe ye". *Yeni Ozgur Politika*. 04.05.2017, Kurdish Pages 3.

Reynolds, D. F. (1995). "*Heroic Poets, Poetic Heroes: the Ethnography of Performance in a Arabic Oral Epic Tradition*". Ithaca: Cornell University Press.

Sarıtaş, B. S. E. (2010). *Articulation of Kurdish Identity through Politicized Music of Koms*. Unpublished Master thesis submitted to the Graduate School of Social Sciences of Middle East Technical University, http://www.academia.edu/13 585216/Articulation_of_Kurdish_identity_through_the_politicized_music_of_ koms (accessed 30 April 2017).

Turgut, L. (2002). *Cembelî fils du prince de Hekkarî et la Tradition des* Mitirb*s*. MA thesis, Institut National des Langues et Civilisations Orientales, Paris. http://www.uni-goettingen.de/de/138346.html (accessed 30 April 2017).

– (2011). *Mündliche Literatur der Kurden in den Regionen Botan und Hekarî*. Berlin: Logos Verlag.

Uzun, M. (1992). *Destpêka Edebiyata Kurdî*. Ankara: Weşanên Beybûn.

– (2006). Dengbêj*lerim*. Istanbul: İthaki Yayınları.

Wehr, H. (1977). *Arabisches Wörterbuch für die Schriftsprache der Gegenwart*. Beirut: Librairie du Liban.

Tracing Connections:
Kurdish Women Singers and the Ambiguities
of Owning Oral Tradition

Marlene Schäfers

While doing fieldwork with female Kurdish bards (*dengbêj*s) in the Eastern Anatolian region of Van in 2011/12, I was often struck by how my interlocutors could insist that a particular ballad (*kilam*) or folk song they knew belonged to them (*Ev ya min e!*) while at the same time explaining to me how the song in question had been sung by other people in the past, or how they had learned it from a particular relative or acquaintance, a radio broadcast or cassette tape. This volume focuses on the vibrancy of connection and exchange between different singer-poet traditions in Anatolia. My interlocutors, however, effectively disavowed certain connections as they asserted that a particular piece belonged to them (those connections, for example, that would regard the piece in question as part of an overarching, communally shared heritage) while simultaneously acknowledging others (including lines of genealogical transmission and apprenticeship). This paper seeks to unravel the ambiguous engagement with musical exchange and connection that comes to the fore in these instances. It does so by investigating how claims to ownership over musical traditions made by female *dengbêj*s work both with and against notions of collectively held cultural heritage as well as genealogical logics of tracing descent.

Simultaneously insisting on owning a folk song and acknowledging that same musical tradition to be practiced by others might seem paradoxical. In this chapter I argue, however, that such seemingly paradoxical statements are expressions of the friction that arises as different logics of reckoning relations rub against each other. In contemporary Turkish Kurdistan, we can observe how older genealogical ways of reckoning connections between the oral traditions practiced by *dengbêj*s are being reconfigured through the logics of cultural property. The latter find expression, I suggest, both in claims to individual ownership over particular cultural artefacts and in the notion of a collectively held, overarching Kurdish cultural heritage. *Dengbêj*s, in particular, have come to be heralded as amongst the most important protagonists of this heritage. I argue that this has introduced a dynamic of commodification into the field of *dengbêjî*, which has rendered questions of owner- and authorship of genealogically transmitted and often anonymous oral traditions a nexus of debate, anxiety, and controversy. Gender, I moreover suggest, is one central fault line around which these contestations unfold in the Kurdish context.

.

More broadly, my aim in this chapter is to shed light onto how the logics of cultural property, in tandem with discourses of cultural heritage and multiculturalism, have come to reconfigure how members of Turkey's Kurdish community conceive of, relate to and perform their "culture." At the same time I also want to offer some reflections on the politics and poetics of making (and breaking) connections, as the theme that unites contributions to this volume. Anthropologist Marilyn Strathern (1996a) has argued that asserting intellectual ownership relies on what she terms "cutting the network." Within the logics of property, Strathern holds, claiming ownership over a cultural product requires disavowing or "cutting" links to a potentially infinite number of relations that might have impacted the creation of a cultural artefact. Such acts of cutting are exercises as much in channelling forces of creativity as in forging communal genealogies by tracing roots and establishing descent. Cutting a network, in other words, always entails acts of inclusion and exclusion. As such, it is inherently political. Here, I seek to document how a number of Kurdish women singers are involved in the delicate work of handling relations – including cutting some, while acknowledging others – and with what effects. Needless to say, as researchers we are equally involved in seeing, establishing, and denying relations and might well want to pause over how this involves us in the fashioning of networks, genealogies, and communities.

Fantasies of Homogeneity

Before focusing in more detail on how the female *dengbêj*s I worked with engage in the forging and cutting of networks it will be useful to outline how *dengbêjî*, in the past a set of rather dispersed regional oral traditions, has come to be resignified as a central constituent of an ostensibly overarching Kurdish cultural heritage. Today, *dengbêj*s are routinely celebrated as perhaps the most paradigmatic representatives of authentic Kurdish culture and traditions. The intense interest in *dengbêj*s and their oral traditions is relatively recent, however, dating back only to the early 2000s.

To be sure, *dengbêj*s and their oral traditions had already been discovered by Ottoman-Kurdish intellectuals of the early twentieth century in their attempts at delineating a Kurdish culture that would befit the nation they hoped to forge (Fuccaro, 2003: 206–209; Strohmeier, 2003: 151–154; Yüksel, 2010: 239–267). Their initiatives to collect and document Kurdish oral traditions and folklore crucially drew upon *dengbêj*s' repertoires, though mainly for the insights these provided into the Kurdish language, whose documentation and standardization was deemed instrumental for the forging of Kurdish national unity (Yüksel, 2010: 65; see also Klein, 2000: 16–17). The Kurdish political movement that emerged in Turkey over the course of the 1970s, by contrast, was much less enthralled with the oral traditions of singer-poets who had formed an integral element of Kurdish feudal and tribal society. Staunchly socialist, the movement re-garded *dengbêj*s largely as symbols of the old order that the Kurdish people ought to overcome in the name of both social and political revolution (Scalbert-Yücel, 2009). The movement's cultural politics consequently encouraged protest music combining elements of Western rock music, socialist marches and Anatolian folk music rather than elderly men and women chanting (hi)stories of tribal warfare, blood feuds, and elopements (Aksoy, 2006; Blum and Hassanpour, 1996).

Beginning in the late 1990s and early 2000s this situation started to change as the result of several factors. One important element was the ideological reorien-tation of the PKK and the Kurdish movement more broadly after the arrest of Abdullah Öcalan in 1999, which entailed the embracement of a politics of iden-tity focusing on the attainment of cultural and linguistic rights for Kurds in Tur-key. This shift in the political arena coincided with a renewed interest in *dengbêjî* amongst Kurdish writers and intellectuals (Scalbert-Yücel, 2009). Central to the change in perception of *dengbêjî* has moreover been the role of Kurdish munici-palities and cultural institutions like the Mesopotamia Cultural Centres (*Navendên Çanda Mezopotamya*, NÇM), which have since the early 2000s increas-ingly promoted *dengbêjî* through festivals and concerts, the opening of so-called Dengbêj Houses (*Malên Dengbêjan*) and other institutionalized cultural activities (see also Watts, 2010: 142–160).

As a result, *dengbêj*s enjoy unprecedented popularity today. Television pro-grammes of various Kurdish and Turkish broadcasters regularly feature *dengbêjî* per-formances during entire evening shows, often in studio settings that seek to evoke the "authenticity" of the Kurdish village through artefacts like hand-woven carpets, clay pots, and oil lamps. *Dengbêjî* recordings also make up a sizeable proportion of the professionally distributed Kurdish music in Turkey and of the music that circu-lates outside the realm of copyright law, judging from the ubiquitous acoustic presence of *dengbêj*s' voices in both public and private spaces (cf. Reigle, 2013).

The revival of *dengbêjî* also has to be seen in the context of a global turn to-wards (multi)culturalist politics and the particular ways in which this has taken shape in Turkish Kurdistan. An important condition for the renewed interest in *dengbêjî* has thus been the turn to a politics of pluralism during the Justice and Development Party's (*Adalet ve Kalkınma Partisi*, AKP) first term in office (2002–2007), which granted greater cultural rights to Turkey's ethnic, religious, and lin-guistic minorities and eased restrictions on the public use of the Kurdish lan-guage. Arguably, however, this opening of the public sphere was tied to the im-perative to depoliticize cultural content. The state granted public visibility to its minoritarian subjects only under the condition that they would not question well-rehearsed narratives of national history and belonging or the country's terri-torial integrity (Karaca, 2011: 158; Tambar, 2014). In the particular case of *deng-bêjî* this has meant that the public performance of oral traditions that address legacies of state violence, displacement, and the ongoing war between Turkish

Figure 1: Dengbêj Gazin alongside male *dengbêj*s at the television studio of Van TV preparing for the recording of a *dengbêjî* programme. For the occasion, the studio is decorated to represent "authentic" Kurdish village life and features a large poster of *dengbêj* Meyrem Xan on the right. (Photo: Marlene Schäfers)

state forces and the Kurdistan Workers' Party (*Partiya Karkerên Kurdistanê*, PKK) are routinely censored and legally prosecuted as instances of "terrorist propaganda" (Schäfers, 2015). This means that minoritarian voices in Turkey are able to emerge into the public only so long as they stay within the bounds of innocuous folklore that bolster rather than threaten the state's image as the patron of benevolent tolerance.

As a result, Kurdish cultural production is sharply divided over adhering to or defying state-imposed notions of folklore, culture, and politics. Yet what remains remarkably constant across divisions is a strong investment by actors in the Kurdish cultural field in the notion of one overarching Kurdish cultural heritage. "Kurdish culture" thus constitutes an established field of debate and intervention. This culture, moreover, is regularly described as being at acute risk of disappearance due to decades of state-enforced denial and assimilation, which has prevented Kurdish cultural traditions from being lastingly recorded, documented, and archived. Much cultural activism today consequently focuses on conserving, promoting, and reviving Kurdish oral traditions in particular, as these are often regarded as the core of authentic Kurdish culture.

The idea that each ethnic or national community has its own distinctive culture is of course in many ways a distinctly modern one and, as scholars of heritage have pointed out, it has been central to the forging of the modern nation-state (Viejo-Rose, Isar, & Anheier, 2011). Having "a culture" constitutes a crucial condition for being recognized as a distinct community with a justified claim towards political representation. Important for the purposes of my argument here is to note how this reification of cultural traditions as the marker of ethnic or national identity also entails the erasure of local and regional differences within such traditions. Nicolas Elias's (2016) research on cultural festivals in Turkey's Black Sea region shows, for example, how subtle local variations in lyrics, performance style, or instrumentalisation easily fall victim to the organization of the culture industry which demands widely recognizable tunes that can be marketed as characteristic of an overarching ethnic or, in Elias's case, regional identity.

In this way, the notion of "a" Kurdish, Turkish, Greek or else "culture" effectively produces what I want to call a fantasy of ethnic or national homogeneity. Local or regional differences may feature in such fantasies as colourful illustrations of variation within the body politic yet largely remain reified as marketable markers of sub-national identity (cf. Öztürkmen, 2001: 140–141). The term *dengbêj* itself testifies to the processes of erasure that the forging of a national cultural heritage necessarily involves. Argun Çakır (2011: 52) writes that this term, originally confined to the region of Serhed[1] where it indicated singer-poets performing without musical accompaniment, has become an umbrella term that is today used to describe a wide variety of orally performed Kurdish traditions. Alternative regional terms to refer to singer-poets with repertoires or performance styles similar to the Serhedî *dengbêj*s, such as *stranbêj* or *şair*, on the other hand, have become increasingly marginalised. Given the prestige attached to the term *dengbêj* as the paradigmatic representative of authentic Kurdish tradition Çakır (2011: 52) reports that "some *şair* and *stranbêj* nowadays tend to drop these local performer designations, and call themselves *dengbêj*s."

Translated into a vocabulary of connections, we may say that the idea of a national cultural heritage acts as a mechanism that relates all individual cultural production directly to the overarching collective. This forms part of the dilemma that producers of ethnic art or world music face in global arenas, where they are recognized less for individual acts of artistic creativity than as representatives of an ethnic or national collective (Kosnick, 2007: 97). Inversely, this means that "culture" necessarily becomes the product of collective—and that is always also anonymous—creativity. Modern copyright law reflects this assumption when it ascribes all intellectual creation for which no individual author comes forward to the public domain, thereby declaring it by default property of the undifferenti-

---

[1]   The term Serhed refers to the mountainous regions that lie to the north of the Diyarbakır plain, an area that is roughly taken to include the contemporary provinces of Bingöl, Muş, Bitlis, Van, Ağrı, Iğdır, and Kars.

ated collective of "the people" (Goodman, 2002: 89–91). What gets disavowed in this way are local and regional traditions reckoned through genealogical lines of transmission which would trace specific cultural forms back through time to specific individuals or locations (cf. Glasser, 2016). In the past, the *dengbêj* tradition would have thrived on such genealogical reckoning of descent and pieces associated with particular master *dengbêj*s still testify to these dynamics (cf. Hamelink, 2016). Contemporary forms of political representation and a modern culture industry, however, dictate a bifurcation along the lines of property between individual artists who own particular cultural products and a "culture" owned by the anonymous collective of "the people."

Allegations of Theft

The elevation of *dengbêj*s to the paradigmatic producers and transmitters of an overarching Kurdish culture, then, has gone hand in hand with the introduction of a logic of culture as property into this field of cultural production. *Dengbêj*s, it should be noted here, are primarily understood as masters of the *kilam*, a genre at the intersection of epic and lamentation. Described by the ethnomusicologist Estelle Amy de la Bretèque (2012, 137–143) as "melodized speech," *kilam*s narrate non-fictional stories in a chant-like, recitative style. Many *kilam*s are transmitted from *dengbêj* to *dengbêj* over generations, while others are newly crafted in order recount contemporary events and experiences. Previously communally owned and transmitted, logics of cultural property reconfigure *kilam*s and similar oral traditions into objects that can be owned—either by individuals, or by collectives. Once objects can be owned, however, they may also be stolen. And indeed, while I did fieldwork I repeatedly witnessed anxieties about and allegations of theft, particularly on the part of the female *dengbêj*s I focused my research on. Such allegations provide valuable insight into the gendered contestations around *kilam*s as ownable property. Let me first, however, provide some more information about the gendered dimensions of *dengbêjî* as a field of cultural production and performance.

The majority of my fieldwork centered on Van's Women Dengbêj Association. This association, founded in 2011 upon the personal initiative of Dengbêj Gazin[2]—one of the few female *dengbêj*s to have entered the Kurdish music industry in Turkey—was the first and only of its kind in Turkish Kurdistan at the time of my field research. Conceived by Gazin as a space where female singers and musicians would be able to socialize and support each other, the association managed to gather more than a dozen women *dengbêj*s, singers and musicians. Apart from providing a space where these women could sing and make music without being

---

[2]   I anonymized all names of interlocutors except where individuals are publicly known under their own names. All translations are mine.

overheard by men, the association organized a number of concerts and arranged music classes for young girls and women. Shut down in the meantime, the significance of the association arguably lay in its attempt to organize Kurdish women singers publicly yet separately from men. Many of the women who came together at Van's Women Dengbêj Association had previously been part of the local NÇM, which had a special section for *dengbêj*s. Within this section, however, women were in the minority and, as Gazin told me, not taken seriously as singers by the male *dengbêj*s. The latter dominated public performances and relegated the women singers to the background.

The Women Dengbêj Association was founded in reaction to such experiences of gender-based discrimination at a Kurdish-run cultural institution. Yet these experiences also reflect long-standing practices widespread amongst Kurdish communities that have limited the ambit of women's voices to private and all-female domains. Particularly members of older generations often consider the audibility of women's (singing) voices in public shameful (*şerm*) and potentially compromising of family honour, and therefore seek to restrict it. While this perception is changing—not least due to the influence of the Kurdish movement and its emphasis on gender equality—it has rendered women's voices less audible in public. It is not that Kurdish women are deprived of voice, but that their voices tend to circulate in private spaces, secluded from being overheard by strangers. One result is that the tradition of *dengbêjî* as a form of public oral history telling has largely been dominated by men, a situation that persists as *dengbêjî* has become integrated into cultural politics and the music industry.

The main exceptions to this trend only seem to confirm the rule. Meyrem Xan and Ayşe Şan, for instance—two of the earliest female *dengbêj*s who had their voices recorded in the nascent Kurdish music industry of the early twentieth century and who enjoy extraordinary fame and popularity amongst Kurdish audiences today—both experienced severe conflicts with their families over their public singing. Born in 1904 and married to a member of the famous Bedîrkhan family of Kurdish politicians and intellectuals, Meyrem Xan was forced to choose between her aspirations for a music career and her marriage, since her husband rejected her singing in public. She eventually divorced and in the 1930s moved to Bagdad, where she recorded with the Kurdish section of British-run Radio Bagdad until her death in 1949. A generation later, the *dengbêj* Eyşe Şan was equally rejected by her family for engaging in public singing. Faced at the same time with Turkish state policies that censored Kurdish language and cultural expression, she was forced into exile after the 1971 coup d'état, first to Germany and later to Iraq, where she, too, realized recordings with Radio Bagdad. Both Meyrem Xan and Eyşe Şan's music reflects the emotional toll that familial rejection, exile, and loneliness had on them, and their *kilam*s were highly popular amongst the women I encountered in Van. Gazin in fact often likened herself to Eyşe Şan, noting how similar her own struggles were to those of the famous *dengbêj*.

And indeed, the stories of the women I got to know through Van's Women *Dengbêj* Association bore important similarities with those of Meyrem Xan and Eyşe Şan. Most of my interlocutors had grown up in rural areas, where they had married early, looked after large families, and engaged in hard agricultural labour. Now most of these women were beyond child-bearing age, meaning they enjoyed a more powerful position within their kinship networks, which made engaging in cultural activism a lot easier. Yet almost all had stories to tell of severe conflicts they had lived in the past—some of them involving physical violence—with (often male) family members, who sought to prevent them from singing in public. Gazin herself was only able to do so since her father-in-law, the dominant patriarch of the family, had passed away. Not coincidentally, the most active women at the association were either widowed or had husbands who were absent for long periods of time or sick. Others had managed to convince their families that the attribution of shame to the female voice was inappropriate and did not befit modern Kurdish society, in doing so heavily drawing upon arguments regarding female emancipation as propagated by the Kurdish movement.

Most of my interlocutors had acquired their knowledge of *dengbêjî* in childhood and adolescence through oral transmission from other *dengbêj*s (both male and female), radio broadcasts (particularly those of Radio Yerevan broadcasting from Armenia), and cassette tapes (often clandestine copies). The repertoire these women commanded was not radically different from that of male *dengbêj*s. In fact they often noted with pride that they knew the *kilam*s of legendary male master *dengbêj*s such as Şakiro, Reso, or Karapetê Xaço and were able to perform them just as well as their male colleagues. Despite this emphasis on gender equity in terms of repertoire and performance, I noted that the *kilam*s women composed themselves tended to focus on gendered themes, particularly gendered forms of suffering that Kurdish women regularly experience in their daily lives. Such *kilam*s included, for example, pieces expressing a newlywed woman's loneliness when separated from her natal family after marriage, grief over the premature death of a child, or sadness over a failed romantic engagement. In this context it is important to note that the genre of the *kilam* is closely related to that of funeral lamentations (*şîn*), with which it shares both textual and musical elements. Funeral lamentations, in turn, are generally performed by women, who are thus chiefly responsible for carrying out society's "work of pain" (Magrini, 2008).

Not only my interlocutors, but also male *dengbêj*s, cultural aficionados and musical practitioners repeatedly asserted that the genre of the *kilam* had developed out of funeral lamentations and that it was therefore a distinctly female genre. The women *dengbêj*s I worked with regularly invoked this idea to argue for the legitimacy of their quest to sing in public, and it is in these contexts that allegations of theft were brought forth. Asya, a woman in her forties originally from the region of Şirnex (Şırnak), for instance, once put it that way: "*Dengbêjî* comes from women, from Kurdish women. Women used to sing most. All *kilam*s that I know used to be sung by women. Women sang them but then men appropriated them. Men's voices came to be listened to by everybody, while the woman's voice remained secret. She could only sing at home, while putting her children to sleep, or outside where there were no men." Gazin similarly often complained about how men performed *kilam*s that they had unrightfully appropriated from women as if they were their own, thereby accruing fame, status, and—in a growing Kurdish music industry—even financial gains that should in fact belong to women.

The narrative of *dengbêjî* as an originally female preserve that was over the course of history appropriated by men also needs to be understood in the context of the Kurdish movement's own distinct historiography. According to the movement's account, Kurdish society in Neolithic Mesopotamia was matriarchally organized. This "original" period of matriarchy is seen as a golden age of natural socialism, during which hierarchical relations both inside and between communities were inexistent. The development of patriarchy, however, introduced the principle of hierarchy, which eventually led to the formation of the state and monotheist religions as the primary instruments of oppression. The demise of matriarchy thus connotes the fall of Kurdish society, its domination by patriarchal, feudal, and tribal structures and, in direct causal correlation, permanent political subordination (Açık, 2013: 119). Translated into the realm of *dengbêjî*, the narrative suggests that while this most authentic element of Kurdish culture was originally crafted and performed by women, with the "fall" of Kurdish society formerly powerful female *dengbêj*s were banned from the public, their voices branded as shameful and their works misappropriated by men.

Embedded within this broader historical narrative, the idea that men had stolen the art of *dengbêjî* from women was able to suggest that the restriction of women's voices through patriarchal notions of honour and shame constituted a historical mistake, as it were, and that women had all the right to take back what had unrightfully been taken away from them. Importantly, the *kilam*s that women alleged men had stolen from them were often pieces that were commonly known as *gelerî*, a term that literally means popular but has come to denote anonymous in the context of music production. These were pieces, in other words, which circulated anonymously, were often orally transmitted and constituted part of a widely shared repertoire of Kurdish oral traditions. Claiming that women and not men were the actual yet misrecognised creators of this repertoire of anonymous folklore consequently also meant claiming that women and not men were the real holders and transmitters of Kurdish culture and tradition. In this vein, Gazin several times referred to women *dengbêj*s as the hidden "treasuries" (*hazine*) of Kurdish culture, implying that these treasuries urgently needed to be tapped in order to salvage the heritage they contained, before it would succumb to the pressures of political suppression and assimilation.

What I want to draw attention to here is the way in which the narrative of theft destabilizes the notion of a collectively produced and owned Kurdish cultural heritage. As outlined above, once culture is defined as property, ownership becomes a central category through which struggles over cultural production are expressed. When ownership over cultural products for which no individual artist is identifiable is attributed to the anonymous collectivity of "the people," the question of who is to legitimately represent this amorphous entity inevitably becomes a matter of debate. Within this framework, women *dengbêjs*' allegations of theft may be read as illustrating what is at stake when the ownership of prestigious cultural products is handed over to the allegedly undifferentiated entity of the people. Their claim that women and not men are the true producers and transmitters of *dengbêjs*' repertoires break up this ostensibly homogenous entity, exposing the hierarchies and struggles that traverse it (cf. Goodman, 2002). Put otherwise, we may say that women's allegations of theft represent acts of cutting the network of alleged collective cultural production; acts that are, moreover, specifically targeted at cutting out men from this collectivity.

Cutting Relations and Channeling Returns

Apart from claiming collective ownership over Kurdish cultural heritage as women, some of my interlocutors also took up the second avenue that the culture as property logic offers, namely that of claiming individual ownership. During my fieldwork encounters, the women I interviewed often felt a need to highlight that a certain *kilam* or folk song they were telling me about "was theirs" (*-ya min e*). Yet such claims did not prevent them from acknowledging in the same breath the genealogies through which they had acquired their knowledge of these pieces. That is to say, they fully acknowledged that the pieces they claimed "were theirs" were also part of a broader repertoire of oral traditions widely shared throughout Kurdish geographies. Such instances represent, I suggest, ambiguous moments of concurrence and intersection between genealogical ways of claiming belonging and the logic of individual ownership that newer models of cultural property provide. Following Marilyn Strathern (1996b), we may conceptualize the latter as requiring individuals to perform acts of truncating relations between their own works and others in order to make claims to ownership legitimate. The repertoires that *dengbêjs* routinely perform, however, do not lend themselves easily to such truncating. Claims to individual ownership on the part of *dengbêjs*, I argue, therefore take the shape of a delicate labour of negotiation between acknowledging and disavowing connections.

What is it about *dengbêjs*' repertoires that renders acts of cutting in the name of individual ownership difficult? Here it is useful to distinguish between folk songs and *kilam*s that have been transmitted over long periods of time, usually orally, without attribution to a particular author (i.e. pieces that are deemed anonymous or *gelerî*) and "new" (for lack of a better word) *kilam*s which individual *dengbêjs* have crafted themselves in order to recount a particular event in the present or near past. The former lend themselves more easily to the kind of collective claims of ownership on the part of women that I describe above. These are pieces that are clearly inscribed in broader networks of oral and musical exchange and contact, which my interlocutors would take great pleasure to explore. I hence observed at several occasions how female *dengbêj*s who encountered each other at the Women *Dengbêj* Association, concerts, or other cultural events would compare and contrast at great length the different versions of folk songs and *kilam*s they knew. They would happily spend hours performing for each other the same piece in different variations and debate in depth about which version might be the correct one.

Such conversations were marked by a sense that one or other version ought to be more "correct" or "true" (*rast*) to the "original" (*orijinal*) version of a piece, the latter presumably a sort of ur-version of a song at its moment of creation before it started its journey of oral transmission over the generations.[3] Most times such debates would end without resolution, with each woman proudly asserting that the way she knew the song in question was the correct one. This conviction of knowing a piece correctly (which might concern both textual and musical elements) would repeatedly translate into an assertion of belonging or ownership of the kind "This song is mine (*Ev ya min e*)!" The sense that a particular *kilam* or folk song "was theirs," then, entailed less a disavowal of the connections making up a branched-out and widely connected collective repertoire than the assertion of knowledge of "true" form and content. As such, claiming ownership entailed cutting out others from the true and correct knowledge of the intricacies of a widely dispersed repertoire.

The assertion of ownership over *kilam*s which some of my interlocutors had crafted themselves might appear a more straightforward matter by contrast. These were *kilam*s, after all, that recounted my interlocutors' personal experiences, thoughts and sorrows. Emerging out of women *dengbêj*s' attempts at giving testimony to personal experience by means of language and music, these were not the anonymously transmitted songs that circulate widely across Kurdistan but products of an identifiable individual's creativity. Yet as much as these pieces might have been "new" with regards to what they recounted (for example an event like the Van earthquakes of 2011, or a women's personal pain over having lost a loved one), the lyrical and musical form they took drew heavily upon a pool of poetic expressions and melodic elements widely shared across *kilam*s and other oral genres such as epics, fictional stories, or fairy tales.

---

[3]   The notion of the original deserves investigation in its own right. Suffice it to say that it appears linked to modern technologies of sound recording as these make it possible to permanently fix sound. In this way they allow producing unchanging "original" versions of songs that may subsequently become the standards for measuring correctness and for determining claims to ownership.

Take, for example, Gazin's *kilam* about the Van earthquakes of 2011, of which I reproduce a stanza below. In order to show the extent to which even "new" *kilam*s draw upon established textual themes, I have marked elements that can frequently be found in other *kilam*s and oral genres in bold.

Dewrane, dewrane, dewrane, dayê li min bûye dîsa dewrane	**These are bad times, bad times, bad times, mother once again these are bad times for me**
Berê vê payîzê min ê ji xwe re kirî kar û barê	Before this fall I occupied myself with craft and trades
*Vê zivistanê li ser serê me digeriya **ewrekî reş û tarî**, ewrê erdhejane*	This winter **a dark black cloud** hovered above us, the cloud of earthquakes
***Dema min ê bala xwe lê dida** Erdîşê Wanê, temame bi gundane*	**When I turned towards** Erdîş and Wan and all its villages[4]
Wele dîsa bûye fermane, fermana** erdhejane, **dayê dewrane	**Oh God, a verdict again, the verdict** of earthquakes, **mother these are bad times**
*Min ê bala xwe didayê xanî û malane, zarîn têtin zarokane, hewar têtin dayik û babane, qerîn têtin mamostane, **dayê li min bûye fermane***	**I turned towards** homes and houses, I heard the wailing of children, the cries of mothers and fathers, the shouts of teachers, **mother this is a verdict upon me**
Wê di min got dewrane, dewrane, dayê dîsa li min bûye fermane, fermana** erdhejane, **dayê dewrane	**I said these are bad times, bad times, mother once again a verdict upon me, the verdict** of earthquakes, **mother these are bad times**
*Wî di şûna axîn û nalînê wan name yaz kirine, xistine berîka wane, torbe tijî kirine bi kevirane, ji wan re şandine, dibê: 'Ev heqê wan Kurdan e.' **Dayê dewrane, dayê dewrane***	Instead of crying and wailing they sent letters, put them in their pockets, filled up bags with stones, and sent those to them, saying: 'This is what the Kurds deserve.' **Mother these are bad times, bad times**[5]
Wî de dewrane, dewrane, dewrane, dayê li min bûye fermane	**Bad times, bad times, bad times, mother once again a verdict upon me**

As the above illustrates, nearly half of the stanza's lyrics is composed of recurrent textual elements, these being mainly the poetic motifs that lend the account its emotional and affective impact. Their arrangement throughout the *kilam*, preceding and following sections that recount the events of the earthquake in more fac-

---

4   The first of the 2011 earthquakes' epicentre was in Erdîş/Erciş, a town situated in the province of Van.

5   The stanza makes reference to reports widely circulating on social media after the earthquakes, which claimed that volunteers had found letters with nationalist slogans, Turkish flags, and stones in packages that were sent as aid to Van's majority Kurdish earthquake victims.

tual terms, suggests that these motifs function quite literally like brackets which emotionally frame the account and in this way insert this personal—and in many ways highly political—testimony into a longstanding genealogy of tragic accounts transmitted by *dengbêj*s.

Even though Perihan had in a sense "borrowed" a large part of her *kilam*'s lyrics from a communal pool of textual motifs and set them to a well-known *meqam* (melody mode), she considered this *kilam* not only her own but also proceeded to legally instate that ownership by claiming copyright over the *kilam*. She had it registered under her name at the Professional Union of Owners of Musical Works (*Musiki Eseri Sahipleri Grubu Meslek Birliği*, MSG), one of Turkey's two principal institutions managing musicians' copyright claims, alongside a dozen other *kilam*s and folk songs she also considered her own. Gazin was the only female *dengbêj* amongst those I encountered who took this step. I nevertheless deem it important because it speaks of a readiness to cut networks much more radically than might have been the case in the past.

What is at stake, I suggest, is a potentially quite profound change in how connections are reckoned within a musical tradition such as *dengbêjî*. This is a tradition in which connections between musical works would in the past have been traced through personal and geographical genealogies. That is to say, *kilam*s would have been transmitted orally when *dengbêj*s encountered each other during the mainly male gatherings in the houses of village headmen or in the teahouses of Kurdish towns, when women sang songs together while herding livestock or engaged in housework, or yet again when they listened to the Kurdish broadcasting hours on Radio Yerevan, played cassette tapes with Kurdish music recordings that had been smuggled clandestinely across the Iraqi or Syrian borders, or tuned into one of the Kurdish satellite TV stations. Some of the *kilam*s transmitted in this way would be associated with particular personalities recognised either as these *kilam*s' authors or as their most important performers. Other *kilam*s or folk songs might be identified less with a specific personality than with a certain region. Inscribed in such personal and geographical genealogies, *kilam*s and folk songs were nevertheless free to circulate and open to communal use, that is, they were free to be performed by anybody skilled enough to do so. At the same time, this communal repertoire also constituted an important resource of "building blocks" for the assemblage of *kilam*s recounting previously untold events and experiences, as we saw in the case of Gazin's *kilam* above.

Registering certain *kilam*s as the personal property of individual artists through copyright arrangements will certainly not prevent ordinary Kurdish women and men from continuing to share and transmit oral traditions, even if these are legally speaking another's property. Yet what the readiness to appeal to copyright legislation speaks of, I believe, is a willingness to channel any returns that the circulation of such traditions might accrue—be it in the form of status, fame, or financial profit—much more adroitly towards the individual artist. The latter in

this way becomes the start and end point of circulation, in a logic rather different from the tracing of genealogical lines of alliance and descent that would dis-
tribute returns more broadly.

Indeed, the women I worked with were convinced that large profits could be
accrued in the music industry, and this conviction certainly constituted a key
motivation for Gazin to formally claim copyright. Yet this conviction came with
a sense of exclusion: considering themselves to be the real owners of Kurdish
cultural heritage they felt that others—successful male dengbêjs, for example, but
also male and female Kurdish pop singers whose success thrived on their adaptation of traditional folk songs for the popular music market—were making a profit
out of what actually belonged to them. Gazin herself was one of the few female
*dengbêj*s of her generation who had successfully entered the music industry and
she could proudly count a dozen albums featuring *kilam*s and folk songs as her
own. Her male producers, however, had never paid any royalties to her even
though some of her albums became bestsellers, taking advantage of the fact that
Gazin was illiterate, largely unfamiliar with the workings of the music industry,
and unaware of her own rights and entitlements when her producers first discovered her.

The context of an emerging music industry and the way in which it distributes
financial profits along relations of property rather than genealogical lines of
transmission thus represents a central mechanism in the carving up of communally owned, transmitted and utilized repertoires into domains of individual ownership. The latter necessarily relies on cutting or disavowing relations that could
potentially challenge the sovereignty of the individual artist over his or her work.
Yet as I have tried to show, this cutting of relations is an ambiguous, laborious
and above all contested process given that the repertoires which dengbêjs master
are not necessarily conducive to such cutting. *Kilam*s and folk songs are steeped
in a genealogical ethos that makes it difficult to disavow their shared character
and constant transformation through repeated performance.

Conclusion

The seemingly paradoxical statements with which I opened this chapter testify to
how women *dengbêj*s seek to negotiate the fragmented terrains of contemporary
Kurdish cultural production. Saturated with promises of authority, fame, and financial profit, these terrains are highly contested. Gender, as we have seen,
represents one of the key faultlines in ongoing struggles over promised returns.
Such struggles are centrally fuelled by a logic of culture as property and the ways
in which it validates as eligible owners of cultural products individual artists, on
the one hand, and anonymous collectives such as "the people," on the other
hand. Both these forms of ownership radically reconfigure—though each in different ways—how connections and exchange are reckoned within networks of cul-

tural production. While logics of individual authorship entail a cutting or arresting of genealogically reckoned relations of transmission, the notion of cultural heritage risks erasing local and regional variations in favour of an overarching popular or national culture.

But the capitalist logics of property inscribed in modern state institutions do not simply erase local and regional ways of reckoning relations of transmission and descent. What I am telling is hence not a linear story of the inevitable demise of tradition, a story that might be read with either nostalgia or triumphalism, depending on one's perspective. Rather, what I have tried to show is how women *dengbêj*s mobilize different logics of tracing connections in ways that are not always coherent or straightforward. Yet it is in and through the resulting friction, to use a term coined by anthropologist Anna Tsing (2004), that oral traditions are practiced in Turkish Kurdistan today.

Acknowledgements

Research for this article and writing were funded by fellowships from the German Academic Scholarship Foundation, Trinity Hall College, the Wiener-Anspach Foundation, the Orient Institute Istanbul and the Research Foundation Flanders. I wish to thank the editors of this volume for their generous comments and feedback on earlier versions of this article. I also thank my interlocutors and friends in Turkey, whose generosity and support have made this work possible.

References

Amy de la Bretèque, E. (2012) Voices of sorrow: melodized speech, laments, and heroic narratives among the Yezidis of Armenia. *Yearbook for Traditional Music*, 44, 129–48.

Açık, N. (2013). Re-defining the role of women within the Kurdish national movement in Turkey in the 1990s. In C. Gunes & W. Zeydanlioglu (Eds.). (2013). *The Kurdish Question in Turkey: New Perspectives on Violence, Representation and Reconciliation*, (114–135). Oxon: Routledge.

Aksoy, O. E. (2006). The Politicization of Kurdish folk songs in Turkey in the 1990s. [Electronic version] *Music and Anthropology: Journal of Musical Anthropology of the Mediterranean*, 11.

Blum, S., & Hassanpour, A. (1996). 'The morning of freedom rose up': Kurdish popular song and the exigencies of cultural survival. *Popular Music*, 15(3), 325–343.

Çakır, A. (2011). The Representation of the Dengbêj Tradition in Kurdish Contemporary Popular Discourse. (Unpublished M.A. thesis). University of Exeter, Exeter.

Elias, N. (2016). This is not a festival: transhumance-based economies on Turkey's upland pastures. *Nomadic Peoples*, 20, 265–286.

Fuccaro, N. (2003). Kurds and Kurdish nationalism in mandatory Syria: politics, culture and identity. In A. Vali (Ed.). (2003). *Essays on the Origins of Kurdish Nationalism*, (191–217). Costa Mesa: Mazda.

Glasser, J. (2016). *The Lost Paradise: Andalusi Music in Urban North Africa*. Chicago: University of Chicago Press.

Goodman, J. E. (2002). "Stealing our heritage?": women's folksongs, copyright law, and the public domain in Algeria. *Africa Today*, 49(1), 85–97.

Hamelink, W. (2016). *The Sung Home: Narrative, Morality, and the Kurdish Nation*. Leiden: Brill.

Karaca, B. (2011). Images delegitimized and discouraged: explicitly political art and the arbitrariness of the unspeakable. *New Perspectives on Turkey*, 45, 155–183.

Klein, J. (2000). Proverbial nationalism: proverbs in Kurdish nationalist discourse of the late Ottoman period. *The International Journal of Kurdish Studies*, 14(1/2), 7–26.

Kosnick, K. (2007). *Migrant Media: Turkish Broadcasting and Multicultural Politics in Berlin*. Bloomington: Indiana University Press.

Magrini, T. (2008) Women's "work of pain" in Christian Mediterranean Europe. [Electronic version] *Music & Anthropology: Journal of Musical Anthropology of the Mediterranean* 3.

Öztürkmen, A. (2001). Politics of national dance in Turkey: A historical reappraisal. *Yearbook for Traditional Music*, 33, 139–43.

Reigle, R. F. (2013). A brief history of Kurdish music recordings in Turkey. [Electronic version] *Hellenic Journal of Music, Education, and Culture*, 4(1).

Scalbert-Yücel, C. (2009). The invention of a tradition: Diyarbakır's dengbêj project. [Electronic version] *European Journal of Turkish Studies*, 10.

Schäfers, M. (2015). Being sick of politics: the production of dengbêjî as Kurdish cultural heritage in contemporary Turkey. [Electronic version] *European Journal of Turkish Studies*, 20.

Strathern, M. (1996a). Cutting the network. *Journal of the Royal Anthropological Institute*, 2(3), 517–535.

– (1996b). Potential property: intellectual rights and property in persons. *Social Anthropology*, 4(1), 17–32.

Strohmeier, M. (2003). *Crucial Images in the Presentation of a Kurdish National Identity: Heroes and Patriots, Traitors and Foes*. Leiden: Brill.

Tambar, K. (2014). *The Reckoning of Pluralism: Political Belonging and the Demands of History in Turkey*. Stanford: Stanford University Press.

Tsing, A. L. (2004). *Friction: An Ethnography of Global Connection*. Princeton: Princeton University Press.

Viejo-Rose, D., Isar, Y. R., & Anheier, H. K. (2011). Introduction. In H. Anheier & Y. R. Isar (Eds.). (2011). *Cultures and Globalization: Heritage, Memory and Identity*, (1–20). London: Sage Publications.

Watts, N. F. (2010). *Activists in Office: Kurdish Politics and Protest in Turkey*. Seattle: University of Washington Press.

Yüksel, M. (2010). *Dengbêj, Mullah, Intelligentsia: The Survival and Revival of the Kurdish-Kurmanji Language in the Middle East, 1925–1960*. (Unpublished doctoral dissertation). University of Chicago, Chicago.

Neither *Âşık* nor *Dengbêj* – The Lament Singers from Dersim (Tunceli)

Martin Greve

Until the late twentieth century, the most important literary and musical form in the region of Dersim (roughly today's province Tunceli) were laments. While also other songs used to be sung in this region, both the aesthetic emotional value and the large number of laments have led to a widespread equation of sung poetry in Dersim with laments, both in research literature and in the region itself.

Figure 1: Silo Qiz (b. 1918, official name Süleyman Doğan), singer-poet from Mulo, a village near the city of Tunceli. Photo: www.dersim37-38. org/silo-qiz-dersim-agidi-klama-dersim/ (accessed 18 May, 2018)

Within the culturescape of Anatolia, the lament singers from Dersim do not fit into the common narratives of singer-poets. In close proximity north of the region, the tradition of Turkish-speaking *âşık* is flourishing (Şenel, 1991). A great number of well-known singer-poets lived (and still live) in the region of Erzincan-Sivas, many of them Alevi (and some even of Dersim origin), including nation-wide famous singers such as Davut Sulari (1925–1985), Âşık Daimi (1932–1983), and Ali Ekber Çiçek (1935–2006). Northeast of Dersim, from Erzurum up to Kars, another style of *âşık* predominates, with mostly Sunni singer-poets, and a popular tradition of song duelling (*karşılama*; Özarslan, 2001; Erdener, 1995). Finally numerous *âşık*s lived west and southwest of Dersim in the region of Elazığ-Malatya.

The tradition of *dengbêj*, on the other hand, is wide-spread east of Dersim beginning in the neighboring province of Bingöl, as well as south-east of Dersim, in the region of Diyarbakır. Common language of the *dengbêj*s is Kurmanji. Even Zaza living in close contacts with Kurmanji speakers, obviously do not have their own *dengbêj* tradition; Zaza-speaking *dengbêj*s as in Kiğı (Bingöl), or Varto (north of Muş), often sing in Kurmanji. In Dersim, however, until at least the 1980s, the term *dengbêj* seems hardly to have been in use.

Ali Baran, Kurmanji speaking singer, b.1956, Hozat:

> *They never called my father* [Mahmut Baran, 1923–1975] *dengbêj. We did not use this word. Our people said:* kılam vat, kılam vana, kılamcı [he sang *kılam, he sings kılam, kılam-singer*] (Interview 17 November, 2015, Istanbul; Greve & Sahin, 2017)

Peter Bumke, anthropologist, talking about his fieldwork in the late 1970s in Kurmanji-speaking villages in Mazgirt-Darıkent:

> *(Question: Did the singers call themself* dengbêj?)
>
> *No. Yes. Sometimes they used this word, but they called their songs* kılaman. *They could refer to the singers as* kılaman, *those wo transmited them – sometimes with* saz, *sometimes without.* (Interview 16 June, 2015, Berlin)

Likewise, the Turkishs terms *âşık* or *ozan* probably only exceptionally were used among the Zaza-speaking people in Dersim, as for example for Âşık Yusuf Kemter Dede (1928–2015, born in Ovacık; see below). I do not know of any source that mentions the term *ozan* (or as *hozan*) as used in Dersim before the later twentieth century (e.g. for Ozan Serdar, b. 1955). In his memories (written in Turkish language), Nuri Dêrsimi (1892/93–1973) refers to his father Mılla İbrahim as *halk şairi* ("folk poet"; 1952/ 2014: 13). However, we do not know if (or to what extent) this term was used in Dersim itself.

Whereas in Dersim no general term exists for the singers of laments, their poets are called *sa* or *sayir* (literally: poet), reminding of the nominations as *şair* in some Kurmanji-speaking regions such as Botan and Hekarî/Hakkari (Turgut, 2010: 29). Only in regions east of Dersim, however, rather the term *dengbêj* was common (Çakır, 2011: 52). Similar to the practice among Kurdish singer-poets of several regions (Turgut, 2010: 29), also Kurmanji-speaking singers in Dersim (remarkably no Zaza-speaking singer) hence recently began to call themself *dengbêj*s, therewith adopting the recent spread of this term among Kurds.

At first sight, than, the tradition of singer-poets in Dersim might be seen as a phenomenon of transition between the larger traditions of *âşik*s and *dengbêj*s. A second conceivable model would interpret the tradition of the mostly Zaza-speaking singers in Dersim as an independent "Zaza tradition", parallel to both the "Turkish *âşik*s" and the "Kurmanji *dengbêj*".[1] In the present articles, however, I will argue that none of both models describes the situation in Dersim properly. The singer-poets in Dersim do not present a homogeneous style, nor a clear transition form *dengbêj* to *âşik*. In terms of performance practice and musical style Dersim rather gives us insights into the complex, inconsistent and highly creative singer-poet landscape before the emergence of nationalistic narratives, which only since the early twentieth century formed the perception of discrete and homogeneous "Turkish" and "Kurdish" folk music styles in Anatolia.

Sources

Today, hardly anything is known about music and music life in Dersim before 1937,[2] and even about the time after that, until the 1970s, we have very little information. Some rare recordings, made under unclear circumstances, and today stored in state or private archives (most of them closed for the public), preserve some older melodies and songs. Almost no written sources reliably report from music life in Dersim, no notations from the region (as for example Armenian notation) have been discovered yet.

Official Turkish folklorists of the early Republican time such as Muzaffer Sarısözen (1899–1963), Sadi Yaver Ataman (1906–1994), Halil Bedii Yönetken (1899–1968) and Mahmut Ragıb Gazimihal (1900–1961) several times visited neighboring provinces of Dersim, including Erzincan and Elazığ (1929, 1937), recording and transcribing hundreds of songs (Kaya, 2014; Elçi, 1997). Similar to other regions with mainly non-Turkish populations, as for example Bingöl, Şırnak or Hakkâri, also Dersim was mostly excluded from official research. Until 1937, Dersim was an almost autonomous region, protected by surrounding mountains and rivers, and for state officials and official researchers the access

---

[1] Between both traditions of course numerous transitions exist. Hande Saglam (2013: 96) for example mentions in Sivas Âşık Şentürk (Sivas, Zara), who sang *âşik* songs in Zaza; on the otherhand, a number of Kurdish *âşik*s sang in Kurmanji.

[2] Historically important, though unfortunately not investigated yet are memory books and transcriptions of folk music made among Armenian refugies and migrants from Dersim in France and America. Most well-known is the collection of Gomitas's student Mihran Toumajan (1972). In addition Hovhannes Acemyans small book on Armenian songs in the region of Çemişgezek need to be mentioned (1955).

was difficult. In the years 1937–1938 a large military operation of the Turkish army finally brought the region under complete control of the government (Bilmez, 2011). In official Turkish historiography this operation was described as a reaction to the so-called "Seyit Rıza Rebellion" (or "Dersim Rebellion"), while local memory refers to the events as "*tertele*", a Zaza word akin to "chaos". In fact the operation led to massacres on civilians. According to official reports, approximately 14 000 persons were killed, and 11 000 forced to move to western Turkey. A local researcher on oral history of the *tertele*, Cemal Taş (2016), estimates the real figures of victims about three times higher. As a result, a decimated and traumatized population remained in what became a regular province of the Republic of Turkey, which from 1936 on was renamed Tunceli instead of Dersim.

It was during these crucial years, that the first official collection of folk music in the region was conducted. At that time, M. Ferruh Arsunar (1908–65), an experienced folk music researcher, was based at the "People's House" (*Halkevi*) in Elazığ (Özcan, 2014; Emnalar, 1998, 41; Altınay, 2004: 99ff, 156–165). Beginning on 26 August 1936, Arsunar traveled through some south, central and western districts of Tunceli (Pertek, Hozat and Ovacık) and transcribed *deyiş*'s and folk songs. Due to the lack of a phonograph he did not record music but rather notated them on the spot. In 1937, Arsunar published two almost similar small booklets dealing with his fieldwork in Dersim (Arsunar, 1937a, 1937b). His articles on Dersim and Elazığ, which he published already one year earlier, clearly exhibit the nationalistic ideology of this period. All lyrics printed in these booklets are in Turkish. The languages Zaza, Kurmanji and Armenian (the latter might still have been spoken at that time by remaining Armenians) are not even mentioned. It is hence unclear if he included songs of the lament tradition or not.

In 1944, seven years after Arsunar, another group of folklorists, now in charge of the State Conservatory Ankara, and including Muzaffer Sarısözen, Halil Bedii Yönetken and Rıza Yetişen collected in total 293 songs from Elazığ, Tunceli, Bingöl and Muş (Elçi, 1997: 61–64; Yönetken, 2006: 106–109). This time, the researchers recorded the songs on a phonograph. Unfortunately, similar to most officially recorded collections, the recordings are still closed for research, only undocumented copies are spread unofficially among musicians and musicologists. Also Sarısözen published all songs exclusively in Turkish. Transcriptions based on the recordings made in 1944 were published several times later.[3] However, in an interview with Mesut Özcan, Sılo Qız (Süleyman Doğan) confirmed

---

[3]   For a list of the recording see Elçi, 1997: 128ff. In 2012, the province government of Tunceli published the book Folk Music from Tunceli (*Tunceli Halk Müziği*, Turhan & Kantar, 2012) edited by Salih Turhan, folk music collector and member of the Ankara State Choir for Turkish Folk Music of the Ministery for Culture and Turizm. The songs in this volume include only Turkish lyrics, most were collected by Sarısözen and other collectors. Özcan, 2003.

that some of the recordings where made in Zaza. *"The song which Sarısözen mentioned as Seyit Şah Haydar's song for example, was a lament which Sılemano Qız created as his son Sa Heyder died in the army. The song is entirely in Zaza.* (Özcan, 2003: 57).[4]

After 1944 no further official music collections were ever conducted in Dersim (Özcan 2003). At that time the entrance to the province of Tunceli was still restricted. In 1947, however, when the ban ended, the efforts for the creation of a national Turkish music repertoire had already diminished. In 1952, the "Peoples Houses" were closed.

Beginning in the late 1960s, with the availability of mobile tape recorders, and even more of mobile cassette recorders, a growing number of private, local folklorists, researchers and collectors began to record proverbs, tales, oral history and songs.[5] Some published their findings in the first journals in Zaza, which were published in this time, including *Hêvi*, *Berhem* or *Piya* (Selcan, 1998). Most of these collectors had no academic background, they collected what seemed to be of cultural value. Noteworthy most of these researchers were based in Europe and recorded during their regular trips home.[6]

Hıdır Dulkadir, collector:

> *Ibrahim Gök came from Germany for holidays. He brought with him a tape recorder from "Grundig". He called me: Come with me, let's go to your uncle Hasan Arslan [Hesê Kêk]. He took the tape recorder over his shoulders and together we went to his house in the neighborhood of Şejeru. This was in 1967... In an amateurish way we recorded his voice on tape. The voices that are on the market today belong to these days.* (Dulkadir, 2011: 22; similarly Kıllı, 2008)

Ozan Serdar, singer, b. 1955, central Tunceli:

> *In this time, everyone had a tape recorder and recorded. We liked that. We encountered a tape recorder in every village and every house we went to. In this way we saw that our voice spread in Dersim.* (Interview October 29, 2015, Bonn, Germany)

The first private collectors recorded non-Turkish songs without any kind of official support by the Turkish state under difficult conditions. In particular after the coup d'etat on 12 September, 1980, when the use of non-Turkish songs was forbidden, researchers secretly recorded songs under great personal risk. In addition, during the 1990s, fights between the Turkish army and the PKK in Dersim esca-

---

[4] Özcan, 2003: 57, 63; cf. Elçi, 1997: 270; Zaza lyrics in Özcan, 2002: 433.
[5] Private collectors active in Dersim include Zılfi Selcan (Berlin, today Tunceli), Musa Canpolat (Stuttgart, today Tunceli), Munzur Cömerd, Daimi Cengiz (Duisburg), Hawar Tornêcengi (Frankfurt), Munzur Çem (Berlin), Cemal Taş (Istanbul), Metin Kahraman (Pülümür / Istanbul), Mesut Özcan (Ankara, today Tunceli), Seyfi Mûxûndi (Konya), Mehmet Yıldırım (today Istanbul), and many others.
[6] Several reasons might explain the pioneering role of researchers from the diaspora. First, some "guestworkers" in Germany (or elsewhere) where able to bring together the money for a tape recorder earlier than those in Tunceli, where the economical situation was still difficult. In addition, the longing for a lost home might have motivated expatriates to record at least songs from there. Finally discourses of Zaza or Dersim identities forbidden in Turkey were first discussed in Europe, and only later in Turkey (Greve & Şahin, 2018).

lated; in 1994 a great number of villages where evacuated and destroyed by the Turkish army. Research in this region hence was dangerous. From 1976 until 1979, as the first foreign researcher in Dersim, the German ethnologist Peter Bumke stayed several times for months in Mazgirt-Muxundi/Darıkent and recorded laments, which he mainly used as sources for local history (Bumke, 1979).

Consequently, the first anthologies of lyrics of traditional laments from Dersim were published as late as 1992 (Düzgün, 1992).[7] Its first and largest part contains laments on the massacres of 1937/38. In 2002, a much larger collection was published in two volumes by Mesut Özcan. In 2011, Hıdır Dulkadir (living in Duisburg, Germany) published a booklet on some selected poets (in particular on his elder relative Hesê Kêk), based on historical recordings made in 1967/68. The book from Daimi Cengiz (2010, also based in Duisburg) on the famous singer-poet Sej Qaji presented a large collection of Sey Qajis poems, together with a description of the long search for songs, family members of the poet and his pupils.[8] Until today two CDs and one book including three CDs with recordings of lament singers have been published. The earliest, "Elders sing songs from Dersim" (*Yaşlılar Dersim Türküleri Söylüyor*, Lızge Müzik) was released by Metin and Kemal Kahraman in 2002. Only one year later the less well documented CD *"Kurdish Bards. Traditional Music from Dersim"* was released by the Austrian label *Extraplatte*, edited by Mehmet Emir, including recordings of Zeynel Kahraman, Mursaê Sılêmani and Hıdır Akgün. In addition a number of historical recordings were spread among musicians from Dersim and on the internet. For example Alaverdi (Ali Çawdar, 1921–1983), who in his lifetime never produced any official cassette, gained fame among musicians after his death, and a number of his private recordings became widely known in Dersim.

Lyrics and Poets

Unfortunately no research has been published yet on the literary form, language and aesthetic of the lyrics. Already the terminology of this rapidly disappearing tradition is unclear. Several words in Zaza language are in use inconsistently, including *lawıke / lawuka*, *hewa* or *kılam*, which all have the (unspecified) meaning "air", "song". The term *hewa* is related to the Turkish word *hava*, similarly meaning

---

[7] Other, smaller collections of songs lyrics from Dersim of this time include Uşên, 1992; Çem, 1993.

[8] While several Turkish *âşık*s of other Turkish regions published their own lyrics, I never came across any similar publication by a folksinger from Dersim. The only comparable book was edited by singer Mikail Aslan, also based in Germany, who remarkably edited not only his own lyrics but also their melodies in western notation (Aslan 2012). The collection also includes some notated songs either from field collections (without clear information about circumstances of collections) or other composers (as recorded on of Mikail Aslans CDs), e.g. Ahmet Aslan (*Nî Adîrî*), Âşık Daimi (*Oy meleme*), Zeynel Kahraman (*Sevê*) and Firik Dede (*Efendim Efendim*).

"air", as in *uzun hava*, "long melody", which is a general term for free metered vocal forms. The term *kılam* on the other hand, is widely used in Kurmanji, probably originating from the Arabic "*kelam*" which means "word" (Çaçan, 2013: 25). The songs of the *dengbêj*s as sung east and southeast of Dersim are generally called *kılam*, while the similar term *kalâm* or *kelam* is furthermore used for, for example, religious hymns of the *Ahl-e Haqq / Yaresan* in Iran (and Iraq) (Hooshmandrad, 2014; 2013). The Zaza word *şiwari / şuar* is mainly used for lamentations as improvised by women at funerals in Dersim, but only rarely refers to poetic laments.

Although most laments were sung in Zaza, in Mazgirt and in the south of Dersim also Kurmanji was used for laments. The most well-known Kurmanji singer was Mahmut Baran (1923–1975), a member of the Kurmanji-speaking *ocak* family Ağuçan, who lived in the village Bargini (Karabakır) between Hozat and Pertek. Mahmut Baran also sung in Zaza. Already his father Mehmet Baran is known to have been a singer, and at present Mahmut Baran's son Ali Baran (b. 1956) is one of the few remaining singers of more or less traditional songs.

Different from *âşık* songs and similar to the *kılam*s of the *dengbêj*s, laments in Dersim are not structured in stanzas with a fixed number of syllables but rather use changing numers of lines of different length in free meter. Hence, neither the fixed rhymes of *âşık* poetry are used nor the traditional *âruz* prosody (Düzgün, 1992: 51). Free rhymes, however, are used frequently, in several existing rhyme schemes. As Düzgün (1992: 50f) pointed out, many Zaza words end on vowels, which simplifies the formation of rhyms.

Again different from *âşık*s, neither *dengbêj* nor the singer-poets of Dersim mention their own name in their lyrics. Consequently, today the poets of many laments are unknown. Only locally some historical poets from Dersim are still remembered, including Sey Qaji (?1871–1936), Sa Heyder (d. 1917?), Hesê Kêk (1889–1974), Hesenê Gaj (1889–1982), Sey Weliyê Kupikey (Sey Weli Kemaneci) (1900/05–1980) and Apê Keko (Keko Demirkıran, 1915–1992). A great number of songs has been transmitted anonymously. Due to the exclusively oral transmission, songs obviously could change over time. From some famous songs, including *Sılo Feqir*, *Welat Welat*, *Sah Haydar* or *Setero*, recordings exist of different singers, such as Alaverdi, Sılo Qız, Said Bakşi, İbrahim Güler, Hıdır Malkoç, Mehmet Çapan and İsmaile İmami, often in sligthly different versions.[9]

Similar to other singer-poet traditions, also in Dersim, lyrics and music form one unity, and every lyric is connected with its own melody (Düzgün, 1992: 45).

---

[9] Variants of several laments in Çem, 2003; Özcan, 2002, the well-known lament *Çuxure* (name of a village near todays Tunceli) one by Hesê Fate, another one by Silo Qiz (Özcan, 2002: 93ff); sometimes even different versions of the same singer-poet exist (Özcan, 2002: 27); e.g. *Hewa Wuşene Tornê Hesê Seyd*, in two variants by Silo Qiz (Özcan, 2002: 221ff); *Hewa Xılvêş* (from Sey Qaji) two different variants sung by Silo Qiz, one recorded by Musut Özcan, one by Mehmet Yıldırım (Özcan, 2002: 365ff)

Sait Bakşi:

> *(To what extend is the singer free in his interpretation? Can you change anything?)*
> *Now for this music, for a given work there is one music, an instrumental form. We definitely have*
> *to play that. Except for that, no other instruments can be used anyway.*
> *(That means the way you sing Sey Qajis* kılams *is one hundred percent like he sang them?)*
> *Exactly my friend. And it has to be like that.* (Interview 2 December, 2015, Istanbul)

In the same interview, Sait Bakşi referred to "melody" with the term *makam*, similar to the use of this term in Anatolian folk music (Şenel, 2007: 52; Neubauer, 1971):

> *(How many* makams *do you know?)*
> *Well as* makams, *every song has its own* makam. *You have to remain in the same* makam, *and*
> *with that I mean the same measure (*ölçü*). In every song there is one* makam. *So in one* makam
> *you can not adopt a second song.*

The spread of this term at least in northern Dersim (similar to the region further north of it) deserves particular research.

On the other hand, in practice, singers seem to have had some degree of artistic freedom in their interpretation of older songs.

Hıdır Akgül:

> *There are very old songs, which I heard from ear to ear, and I liked them. A man sings five* kılam,
> *the music of these five* kılam *is the same. I said to myself: 'It can't be like that. So if the music of a*
> *given* kılam *is like this, it must be changed a bit.' So I arranged this music, I gave it a form. So it*
> *became more beautiful, the people liked it.* (Interview 27 December, 2015, Ovacık)

Looking at the lyrics, striking in almost all types of songs and laments in Dersim is the strong presence of Alevi elements. Whatever the content tells, the names of spiritual persons, places (*ziyaret*s) or other Alevi topics are frequently mentioned (Özcan, 2002: 25). Since by far most *dengbêj* are Sunni, nothing comparable can be found in their songs. In the lyrics of Alevi *âşık*s, however, Alevi references are common, and the same holds for *âşık*s of Sunni or Christian origin (see also Hande Sağlam in this volume).

Probably all laments (as all other song types) in Dersim are based on true incidents rather than on invented stories or general religious or natural issues. In this aspect, the Kurdish *dengbêj* tradition is again comparable, which songs similarly mostly deal with historical events and which protagonists are known persons (at least known by name; Hamelink, 2016, Çaçan, 2013). Different from the *dengbêj* tradition, however, most songs in Dersim deal with personal issues. Only few praise tribal leaders or other historic heroes. Some laments are created about the death of close relatives of the poet, or they lament the poet's own fate. As Hıdır Çavdar, son of the singer-poet Alaverdi told me in an interview, his father created his first lament when he became blind.[10] Sılo Qız sung laments about the death of two of his sons (lament *Sahheyder*), and similarly Hesê Kêk about two of his sons

---

10   Interview in Tunceli on May 28, 2015; lyrics of this lament in Özcan, 2008: 190.

after their death (Dulkadir, 2011: 41–51; Özcan, 2002: 372ff). Mehmet Örtün created two laments for his father, the singer-poet Hesenê Gaj, after the latter died in 1982 (Özcan, 2008: 106ff). In 1986, Qemero Areiz (Kamer Demir, b. 1934 in Karvan-Morarike, Nazimiye) created a lament about his deceased son, Ali Demir (www.youtube.com/watch?v=Avpb9r2mzds, accessed 7 November 2017).

While songs, including laments, in Dersim could be made at any time by anybody, some persons became known as gifted poets, being remembered even long after their death. Less gifted villagers, in fact virtually everyone (depending on financial means), could order personal songs from locally well-known poets.

Hıdır Çavdar, son of the poet-singer Alaverdi (1921–1983), central Dersim:

For example the son of someone here goes to the army, steps on a mine and dies. My late father would immediately make a song about him, and record the composition on a cassette. The man would take it and go, and he would listen to it for years. [...] For example, a man shaked a walnut tree, fell down and died. So they come to my father and told him what happened: 'so and so, my son went to the garden like this, climbed on a walnut tree and shaking it he fell down and died.' My father of course made a lament of 5–10 verses, and the man listened to it from time to time. [...] On whatever comes into one's mind, whatever happens, he definitely made a new song.

Most songs are laments on individuals who were killed violently, in fights with the Ottoman or Turkish army respectively, in fights between local tribes (*aşiret*) or (less frequent) as a result of accidents (avalanches, persons drowned etc.).[11] By far most of the laments still remembered today deal with the massacres of 1938. On some particular events of this period even several laments have been made, as for example "*Setero*" by Memed Çapan and Silo Qiz (Özcan, 2008: 23).[12] The lyrics tell the circumstances leading to a person's death and thereby turn the pain into a narrative. The personal memories of incidents and people killed hence became more public as they were shared with others, spread over the region, and therewith kept memories alive over a longer time. However, instead of describing exactly what happened, songs transform events into a poetic form, which can be memorized better. Due to the poetical form, the actual story the lament is dealing with does not always become clearly understandable. As historical sources, laments hence require further knowledge on the circumstances of their production. Cemal Taş for example, conducted in-depth interviews with numerous witnesses of 1937/38, which he published in several books and articles.[13] Recently

---

[11] The genre of laments, Turkish *ağıt* (in addition to several other names), is known in a large range of literal and musical styles all over Anatolia. Naskali, 2011; Başgöz, 2008; Bayrak, 1996; Boratav, 1996, 1986; Özdemir, 1994; Esen, 1982.

[12] Other example include "*Çuxure*" by Hesê Fate and Silo Qiz; "*Sonde Sonde*", one anonymous, one song by Hesê Fate and Silo Qiz (Özcan, 2002: 118ff); "*Hewa Zegeriye*" (a village in Nazimiye) by Mehmet Kılıç / Mehmet Coşkun, another one by Silo Qiz. Also on the massacre of "*Lac deresi*" two different laments are known (Dulkdair, 2011: 75ff, 96ff).

[13] Dalkılıç, 2015; Saltık & Taş, 2016. For oral history of Dersim see Bilmez et.al. In fact many Anatolian folk songs obviously may ground on a concrete event, without, however, narrating it in a comprehensible way. This transformation from historical facts to poems and

Nilüfer Saltık and Cemal Taş published an encompassing collection of laments on 1938 including numerous historical documents, interviews on oral history, lyrics with comments and three CDs with the original recordings of the laments (Saltık & Taş, 2016).

Older songs by formerly known or unknown poets were thus transmitted orally and are therefore about incidents that happened long ago, and which otherwise would have been forgotten.

Peter Bumke, ethnologist, speaking on villages in Mazgirt / Darıkent in the 1970s:

> *Partly these where events which had happened in the immediate surroundings, in the villages of Hacı Yusuf or in Karasakal, or the violent death of a boy in the nearby Perisu river. There was also a story which took place in Bingöl, in Varto, but almost always it used to be Alevi-Kurdish regions. [...] Some of the songs must have been quite old. [...] At the same time I did my standard ethnology work, that is record genealogies. [...] At a certain point I found that people talked about a certain Süley, some three or four generations ago, who came up in both a genealogy and one song. In this way I could find out some things about conflicts that happened around the 1880s, and about the persons in the genealogies, hence the great-great-great-grandfather of someone of the village.*

Only some few songs known today go back before 1900, printed exceptions include the songs *Hewa Kalax* and *Hewa Ağdat* which tell stories that happened during a struggle between tribes in 1850–1860.[14] Sa Heyder is known to have been killed during the first World War. Furthermore, some surviving songs of Sey Qaji deal with World War I.[15] In many cases, the age of the laments and the names of the poets are unknown. This loss of older laments might also explain the lack of Armenian poets known in Dersim, and the small amount of Armenians mentioned in the lyrics, although many Armenians used to live in this region, according to oral history in good terms with their Alevi neighbors. If any Armenian singer-poets might have sung in either Armenian or Zaza in the Dersim singer-poet tradition, their songs where forgotten just as almost all other songs created before 1915.[16]

We may conclude that the laments of Dersim are mostly younger than many songs of *dengbêj*, which often refer to the late nineteenth century, as an idealized, past social and political world: „*they speak of caravans, horse riders, past tribal alliances and other features that no longer exist.*" (Hamelink, 2016: 62; Çaçan, 2013). Songs of *âşık* might even be older, several going back centuries ago.

---

      songs is hardly studied in Turkey. Often stories are told in addition to particular folk
      songs, even sometime in different variants.
[14] Dulkadir, 2011: 61–65; Özcan, 2002: 250ff. Similarly *Hewa Mudırê Heyderiye u Bedê Hey-
      deriye* remained from mid nineteenth century, Özcan, 2002: 278ff; *Hewa Xelil Bey* tells a
      story which happened around 1900 (Özcan, 2002: 260ff).
[15] Dalkılıç, 2015: 98f; some more songs of this period in Özcan, 2002; *Herbê Cihani, Hewa
      Domonê Sowşenê Kali, Guli Beg* (Düzgün, 1992: 115ff; 157ff; 205ff).
[16] As a rare exception, Daimi Cengiz collected a lament on the massacres of Armenians in
      1915, from a certain Selvi Hanım in the village of Sey Qaji, said to be from Hese Mexsi
      (personal communication, 21 August, 2017). Cengiz 2015. Bayrak, 2005.

Only few laments created later than 1938 are included in anthologies, as for example *Hewa Qore* (*Lawıka Xıdır*) or e.g. *Avasê mı* telling a story from the Korean war (1950–1953), where some soldiers form Dersim have been sent to (Düzgün, 1992: 207f; Özcan, 2002: 153f); or *Sayidê Mı*, a lament on Dr. Sait Kırmızıtoprak, leader of the Turkish Kurdistan Demokrat Party, who was killed in 1971 (Özcan, 2003: 208f).

In her master thesis completed in 2010, Aylin Demir describes another related tradition of Dersim, that is lamentations improvised privately by women. No standard terminology refers to these laments, which do not have any fixed literary or musical form. The women rather claim to "sing on her own" during the daily work, and only when they are alone. These spontaneous lamentations could be sung in either Zaza, Kurmanji or even in Turkish–weeping in Dersim (just as everywhere) normally happens in one's mother tongue. Actually these secretly sung lamentations remind one of those which are improvised during funerals, although they are less emotional. The number of syllables per line is again free, reaching from seven to fifteen. Remarkably, political or historical topics such as 1938 are not mentioned here, but rather issues of the women's personal lives, such as forced marriages (at an early age), former unhappy love affairs, general discontent, loneliness, poverty, or the pain of a lost child. Again, Alevi spiritual figures or places of pilgrimage such as Düzgün Baba, Hızır or Munzur Baba are mentioned regularly.

Kemal Kahraman, singer from Pülümür, northern Dersim.

My mother sang, what we in Zaza used to call "lorlaene". […] You speak and sing spontaneously. You sing in a simple melody but at the same time you tell a story of your own. Your attitude, your situation. But they do that more often while working. Whenever my mother did that I cried. I was a child. I never wanted her to do that. This used to happen to my mother at home. For me, my mother was a thousand year old woman. […] It was done over long tones, in a form without clear ending. […]

(So she tells from her own life?)

Yes, it could be about anything. "My son went away, if he only could have stayed" for example. Ok? "How beautiful he looked when he left", something like that. Her mother died about 40 years ago. But until today she could sing something like "my mother was so beautiful", or "my fate is so bad" and so on. […] You know the melody is in fact static. Everyone sings with the same melody. (Interview March 5, 2014, Berlin)

Estelle Amy de la Bretéque (2012) found similar female vocal forms, to which she referred as "melodized speech", spread in a wide region including Azerbaijan, Yezidi in Armenia, and Kurds in Istanbul and Diyarbakir.

Always associated with feelings of loss and self-sacrifice, melodized speech resembles a chant: an indefinite number of syllables and words are uttered on a limited range of notes. This monotonous or singsong intonation in speech is a liminal form between music and language and considered locally not as song but as speech.[17]

Different from many laments, the women do not achieve catharsis, they do not expect any relief (2016: 52).

The main difference between the melodized speeches of men and women, therefore, seems to revolve around the degree of involvement by the speakers in the utterance. Women melodize mainly what they see as their own "black" destinies (or those of their children and brothers), while men relate stories of tragic heroes whom they have in most cases never met. (2016: 51)

In terms of musical style, however, female lamentations in Dersim do not differ substantially from the laments by men as described before.

Local researchers such as Mesut Özcan (2002) and Mustafa Düzgün (1992) suppose funeral lamentations sung by women to be the origin of the *kılam*s. "*Laments as performed by lament singers are similar in content and form to the laments as sung by women*" (Özcan, 2002:17).

When someone dies, the women call for a woman with a 'burning' voice [sesi yanık bir kadın] *and ask her to come to the funeral. They say: 'Come and sing some laments and let's cry.' These women who sing laments upon the deceased, the şin-şiwan (lamentations) singers are no poets, and after the funeral is done, their work ends. It is not the task of women with burning voices to make songs. A poet will take part at the funeral of a friend just like anyone, but in general he will not sing songs at the funeral. If he makes a song for someone, he will go home and prepare, and sometimes several years after the deadly incident he will make a song and sing it. However, before singing his song the poet will gather information on the deceased, on his friends and enemies, the reason and the way of his dying, the situation of his family, his mother and father, and on his wife and children. Then he will take his* saz *or violin and sing his song*" (Düzgün, 1992: 46)

Noteworthy, a similar wide-spread narrative attributes the origin of *dengbêj* songs to lamentations as sung by women during funerals (see Schäfers in this volume; Hamelink, 2016). However, since no research on funeral lamentations sung by women in Dersim has been conducted yet, this theory can neither be confirmed nor rejected. The melodies of laments sung by Kurdish-Alevi women in Maraş-Elbistan and Koçgiri (hence in a linear distance of 300 and 200 km respectively) as recorded by Besê Aslan (CD, 2011) and Ayfer Düzdaş (CD, 2012), remind one of those of the *kılam*s in Dersim. In this context, (music) historical connections with Dersim would deserve further research. Interviews conducted with singers in Tunceli by the present writer, however, clearly demonstrate that at least during the last fifty years *kılam*s where created without any connection to lamentations of women (Greve & Şahin, 2018).

---

[17] 2016: 29. According to Amy de la Bretéque, the melodies are characterized by groups of three or four sonic plateaus, "*each plateau contains syllables uttered flowing fast within a single breath over one or two notes*" (2016: 47), partly accompanied by beating on knees, or a series of plateaus and a descending path" (p.48), sometimes "*large vibratos on word-ending vowels*" (an element which is also known from most *dengbêj* styles).

As mentioned before, while most songs from Dersim were laments, a much smaller amount of songs tell different stories including love affaires (Özcan, 1995).

Hıdır Akgül, singer, b. 1957, Ovacık:

> *For example someone said: „There is a girl I am in love with. Make a piece on her."*
> *We talked a bit like that, I immediately began, played and sung while he recorded it.[18]*

In particular Sa Heyder (d. 1917?), is known as a poet of love songs (of which some few survived in the repertoires of Silo Qiz, Sait Bakşi and others).

While also songs of *âşık*s and *dengbêj*s might include *ağıt*s (Artun, 2014: 186ff), the amount of songs dealing with death in Dersim is significantly higher. The outstanding importance of deads in the literature and music from Dersim might be explained by Alevism (which dominates the society of Dersim) with its general emphasis on suffering and dead. As generally known in *cem*s vocal forms such as *mersiye* lament on the death of Ali and Hüseyin and intend to arouse commiseration for them.

A second explanation is more speculative. Due to the lack of sources (in particular of field recordings) the question about a possible influence of the massacres of 1937/38 in Dersim on the tradition cannot be proved. Among the oldest *kılam*s the proportion of laments is obviously lower. Arsunar in 1937, does not mention laments explicitly, but rather states *"with exceptions folk songs from Tunceli deal with heroism, while also there are many songs on love and nature."* (Arsuner, 1937 b: 10). Probably only after 1938 the number of laments increased and gained a higher proportion among the *kılam*s. In this time almost no topic was used for songs except laments. Before the traumatic events, *kılam* (and similar terms) might have been a much more general tradition of epic and even love songs. With the massacres the psychological and social demands for laments possibly changed the tradition.

Performance Practice

Our knowledge on the singers is again limited. Some of the singers of historical recordings obviously were locally well-known in their time, others not. In Dersim, obviously everyone could sing *kılam*s, on private occasions, before their relatives, friends or neighbors. However, singers with an extraordinary good voice and strong memory could regionally become well-known, either for their poems, or their voice (even if they would not create poems themselves, such as Sait Bakşi), in most cases, however, for both together. After the 1970s, private recordings spread the fame of individual singers, after the 1980s recordings were

---

[18]   Interview 27 December, 2015, Ovacık. Similarly Özcan Kahraman, grandson of the singer
      Zeynel Kahraman, 1930–2012, interview 27 May, 2015, Hozat.

produced professionally on commercial audio cassettes or later on CDs. Well-known singers of the late twentieth century include Sılo Qız (Süleyman Doğan, b. 1908), Mahmut Baran (1923–1975), Alaverdi (Ali Çavdar, 1925/6–1983), Seyfi Doğanay (1940–2005), Mehmet Çapan (d. 1945), Hozan Serdar (d. 1955) and others. Similar to singer-poets in other parts of Anatolia, most sang both their own songs and those of former poets.

Most of these semi-professional singers had additional jobs.

Ali Baran, singer, son of Mahmut Baran, Hozat:

> *In my first memories, Mahmut Baran was a blacksmith. He learned that during his military service. Later he sold cows to slaughterhouses and the army in Hozat. Again later he did smuggling of tobacco. But do not misunderstand smuggling: he sold tobacco.* (Interview 17 November, 2015, Istanbul)

Several late poet-singers from Dersim were known to have been blind, hence seriously handicapped regarding rural work, including Sej Qaji (?1871–1936), Alaverdi (1921–1983), Hüseyin Doğanay (1940–2005), Âşık Yusuf Kemter Dede (1928–2015, Ovacık), Mehmet Erdoğmuş (b. 1947, Çemişgezek)—just as several *âşık* (most well-known Âşık Veysel[19]) and *dengbêj* (including Evdalê Zeynikê or Hesen Cizrawî; Ceren, 2014). Some singers were members of *ocak* families, including the Barans (*ocak* Ağuiçen), Sey Qaji or Sey Weliyê Kupikey (both Bava Mansur), or Weliyê Wuşenê Yimami (1889–1958), Bava Bulisk, Hesenê Şıxali (b. ca. 1920) and Pir Ahmet Taş (1918–2008), who were members of the Kureyşan *ocak* (Dulkadir, 2011: 74ff). Hüseyin Doğanay's grandfather Baba Kazım was a *pir* of the Dervis Cemal *ocak*, but also played violine and *cura* (short long-necked lute). Similar to other singer-poet traditions, also in Dersim only few female poets are known from the past—and hardly any today.[20] In her time, Wakıle, the sister of Hese Fate was a well-known poet.[21] Similarly most protagonists of the laments where men, as were most of the singers.

Sait Baksi, singer, Nazimiye:

> *There are female poets in Dersim. One of them is Xıme [a daughter of Sey Qaji]. She is one. Before her in a village in Tunceli, Dersim there was someone called Maa Sıle Suri, hence mother of Süyleymane Süle Sür. Someone who was called 'red Süleyman'; his mother. Aliye Hese*

---

[19] Also Âşık Fehmi Gür, 1914–1982, Arapgir; Artun 2014: 437.

[20] In the tradition of *âşık*s women seem to be slightly more active. Hande Sağlams (2013: 226ff) found 32 female *âşık* in the province of Sivas, of whom only five also played *bağlama*, while the others used to be accompanied on a lute by close relative men. Though there where Kurdish female singers (such as Meryem Xan (1904–1949), Eyşe Şan), Wendelmoet Hamelink wrote, "*the material I collected is predominantely a male repertoire in which men generally are much more present than women.*" (Hamelink, 2016: 64). See also Schäfers in this volume.

[21] Furthermore, a recording of the wife of Zeynel Kahraman, Fadime, was published privately on Facebook https://www.facebook.com/Mameki.Dersim/videos/455163121357602/ (last accessed 4 May 2018); Another recording of the mother of Ali Baran, *Besi Baran* recorded on Roj TV in 2002 was published at www.youtube.com/watch?v=j_FhtQgONkk; Interview with Ali Baran, 17 November, 2015, Istanbul.

Kur was a singer, from the Demanan tribe, also his wife sang. She was a poet. Also in the village Çukur there is a female poet called Vakıle. In this aspect, Dersim is extremely rich and full. (Interview December 2, 2015, Istanbul)

In general, no formal education existed for the singers, however, in some cases singing and poetry was transmitted within families, as for example in the Baran familie who had singers over three generations (Mehmet, Mahmut and Ali Baran). Sey Qajis grandson Ismaili Imam and his daughter Xime also sang (Interview Sait Bakşi, 2 December, 2015, Istanbul; Cengiz 2010). Hüseyin Doğanay's grandfather Baba Kazım played violin and *thembur* and was a singer, too, such as again Hüseyin Doğanays nephew Seyfi Doğanay and the latter's daughter Eda Doğanay. Also the father of Bava Bulisk played *thembur* (short long-necked lute). Eventually Silo Qiz's family is said to have been of singer-poets since seven generations, his father was the (in his time) well-known singer Hasan Doğan. Almost all family members of Zeynel Kahraman later became musicians, though not professional, and today, his grandson Özcan Kahraman is a *saz*-maker.

Also villages with well-known singers could become informal centers for the tradition of singer-poets.

Sait Bakşi:

In this time [of my childhood] in our village lived many important singer-poets. There were good singers and poets. Of course, I only saw them as elderly people. In particular in our central village Cıvrak, there was a singer called Apo Hüseyini Kalmen. This poet sang all works from the late Sey Qaji, whom he had known and listened to from childhood on. He always played and sang. He played thembur. *In this time a* thembur *was rare, it could not be find in every house. There was one in the house of one of our relatives there. Every now and then I went there and played. [...] Of course the man we called Hüseyin Kalmem or Ap Huseni impressed me a lot. I remained under his influence. In addition there was a nephew of him, Mehmet Aslan, who also sang very good. The tradition continued. Besides, there was a person called Sa Gal, he just sang, he also was a good* dengbêj *but he did not play* thembur. *[...] I can say about our village that it was a singers' village (ozanlar köyü). Let's stay with Sey Qaji... Ap Huseni Kalmem, İsmaili İmami, İmami Sey Qaji, Humare, who was the daughter of Sey Qaji, Saydel Arik, who was called Saydere Say Gal, or Yusuf Güler, who was called Yusufe Cerg. All of them were educated in Civarik. Mehmet Aslan is the nephew of Uncle Hüseyin. As I told you, I can call our village Civarik a singers' village.* (Interview 2 December, 2015, Istanbul)

Similarly under the influence of Hese Kêk, the village Kortu (today: Meşeyolu, between Tunceli center and Nazimiye), hosted several singer-poets, including Kekil Arslan (Kêkê Durş, 1333–1987), Musa Yılmaz (1933–2004) and Mustafa Dulkadir (1915–1989) (Dulkadir, 2011)

Ozan Serdar, singer:

I learned by heart as much as I could (…). In our region there was an elderly poet called Sılo Qız. He came frequently to our village. Our villages are near to each other, not very far. For example I learned almost all the songs I heard from him by heart. It came so far that since my youth I can't stand without singing. (Interview 29 October, 2015, Bonn, Germany)

Transmission from master to regular pupils (as it was common practice within the *âşık* tradition) is documented only in some few cases from Dersim. We know that the eminent singer-poet Sey Qaji had two pupils, that is Memedo Derğ'in (d. 1938) and Bava Bulisk (1328/1912–1989). Others just learned by their own, for example we don't know about any teachers of Alaverdi.

Likewise, our knowledge on the performance practice of earlier periods is limited. Most recordings do not inform us about where and why the singers normally used to sing. Most recordings were made on the wish of researchers, most contain several songs directly after another, often even without any break, making it difficult to find the end of one, and the beginning of the next *kilam*. Obviously no clearly established situation existed, where songs were expected to be sung. Nothing indicates the existence of anything comparable to *âşık* cafés (such as in Kars, Erzurum or Sivas; Kaya, 1994; Sağlam, 2013) in Dersim. Similarly, at least in the 20th century in Dersim, no *divan* houses or regular gatherings of rich *ağa*s existed, who regulary engaged *dengbêj*s. As Mehmet Yıldırım (2013: 63) points out, „in inner Dersim, the institution of *ağa* [influential landowners] such as in other parts of Anatolia was never an issue".[22]

Ali Baran proudly distances his tradition from the *dengbêj*s, referening to a common stereotype of Kurdish singers:

> *These* dengbêj *[…] sang songs at the table of tribal leaders (ağa). They sang only songs which praise the tribe and his leader. Why? Because it was him who gave them bread. They did not sing anything for the people who opposed the pashas and ağas or on the suppressed farmers. Not all of them but the most* dengbêjs *were like that. But they told about the massacres of Ottomans, Iranians and Arabs, even about wares between tribes.* Dengbêj *hence means living history. Mahmut Baran was not like that. Mahmut Baran made independent songs by himself, he was nobody's* dengbêj. *He was a singer* (ozan) *of his own people. He spoke about the massacre of Dersim, love, seperation and living abroad* (gurbet). (Interview 17 November, 2015, Istanbul)

In most cases, hence, the performances in Dersim remained completely private. The tradition of public singer contests, such as among *âşık*s in particular in the region of Kars-Erzurum spread at least as westward as to Sivas, is called *atışma* or *karşılama, atışma* or *tartışma* (and according to Erdener (1995) was adopted from Azerbaijan).[23] Among *dengbêj*s this practice is unknown, and I never came across any indication of comparable performances in Dersim.

Most important setting for the singing of laments were the long winter days and evenings in the villages. Until the late twentieth century, hence before the

---

[22] In his memories, Nuri Dersimi (1892/93–1973) mentions that his father Mılla İbrahim, who was a singer and played both violin and „*tambur*" (i.e. *thembur*) served as secretary (hence not primarily as a singer-poet) for Seyid İbrahim Ağa (Hozat) (Dêrsimi, 1952 / 1997: 13).

[23] According to Hande Sağlam this particular performance was practiced in Sivas common practice in some coffee shops among Sünni *âşık*s, while Alevi *âşık*s regarded this practice as not being part of their own tradition. In the villages of Sivas it therefore does not exist.

modernisation of infrastructure (better streets, public transportation, radio, television and internet), each winter, mountain villages in Dersim were buried under snow for several months. Often, even neighboring houses could only be reached by digging tunnels through the snow. During the long, lonely and dark winter nights, no distraction existed except for telling each other stories and singing *kılam*s, the longer the better.

Sait Bakşi:

> For example, when this man, Apo Hüşen [...] came, everyone was curious, went to him and we gathered. When he came as a guest, they sat together, talked, and sang. And then the friends, people from around came to him, and when they said: "Uncle, sing for us!", he took the thembur in his hands and began. So, in this way there was the tradition. (Interview 2 December, 2015, Istanbul)

Singers such as Sey Qaji and Bava Bulisk, both members of respected *ocak* families only sang privately, while other singers such as Alaverdi, Mahmut Baran (though also member of an *ocak*, that is the Sarısaltuk), Sılo Qız, Zeynel Kahraman or Hıdır Akgül regularly sung at weddings.[24]

The Sound

The most characteristic element of the laments is the often melancholic sound of the singer's voices. Well-known singers such as Alaverdi, Hüseyin Doğanay or Sait Bakşi, but also many unknown local amateur singers share the expression of heavy and sad emotions, enforced by the almost always descending melodies. Even endnotes of longer phrases are sung relaxed without pressed voices or vibrato. Only later singers such as Hüseyin Doğanay or Ozan Serdar adopted a soft vibrato throughout the melody.

Not all singers, however, used this soft singing style. Hese Kêk (Hese Fate) for example had a unique high and powerful voice with strong vibrato, as well as (though less developed) the singer Ali Doğan, whom Mesut Özcan recorded in in central Dersim in 1992 (audio cassette MÖ 24). Also Silo Qiz's characteristic sharp and high voice, sounds less sad than others. Likewise, the absolute pitches of the singers vary considerably.

In terms of musical structure, recordings made from the 1970s on show a remarkably wide spectrum. Most widespread in central Dersim obviously were descending melodic patterns within an ambitus of a third or fifth, sometimes with characteristic short intermediate leaps to the upper fifth or octave. The fourth is often (though not always) missing, which reminds us of Arsunars (1937) theory of pentatonicism in Dersim. The second degree is often emphasized (e.g. record-

---

[24]   Interview with Zeynel Kahramans grandson Özcan Kahraman in Hozat, 27 May 2015; Interview with Ali Baran, November 17, 2015, Istanbul. While his grandfather was a dervish and his father a singer, Sılo Qız began already in his youth to sing *kılam*s on weddings.

ings with Alaverdi, Silo Qiz or Sait Bakşi).[25] In most laments, short melodic patterns are repeated without substantial changes, and only the different length of the text lines leads to variants, such as the frequent change to double tempo for short passages. Within this general melodic structure, mainly changes of rhythm, tempo, the sound of voice and the absolute pitch lead to individual and recognizable songs. In some laments, however, these melodic patterns are enlarged to descending melodic sequences with an overall ambitus of a sixth or more, which is reminiscent of melodies of *âşık*s. Some songs, in particular from Hozat display wide melodies, almost like *uzun hava* songs as being sung north and west of Dersim (Erzurum, Erzincan, Sivas). The most frequently used *makam* (melodic mode)—just as in most *âşık* songs of the region Sivas-Erzincan—is *hüseyni*.

A second performance type is nearer to recitation. While some recordings contain rhythmic speech (e.g. by Hese Fate or Ismailê Imami), in some cases the lament is presented almost spoken. Often singers even change between both styles (singing and speaking) or remain somewhere in between, as for example Silo Qiz, or Ibrahim Güler (audio cassette MÖ 70), Nazimiye, who sang several songs of Sey Qaji. Qemero Areiz (b. 1934, Karvan-Morarike, Nazimiye; official name Kamer Demir) sang/spoke with the accompaniment of a bağlama with an unforced, unaccented voice, though with a wide pitch range.

Likewise, most songs of *dengbêj*s are near to recitation. The long stanzas of the *dengbêj*s are normally recited in long recurring melodic patterns, however, different for the laments in Dersim mostly closed by long, vigorously and consciously shaped tones, typically with long and strong vibrato. Also, for *dengbêj* the sound of the voice is of major importance, yet with a clear aesthetic preference of powerful voices.

Finally, some rare recordings from Dersim contain a form of story-telling which is reminiscent of the tradition of *destan* (epics).[26]

In Dersim, laments were regularly sung without any instrumental accompaniment, often simply because no instrument is available in every village—or no one to play it. At least most semi-professional singers, however, preferred to accompany their voice with an instrument. Today in Dersim, the violin (of Western origin) is seen as the most traditional instrument for the accompaniment of *kılam*s, played upright like the Back Sea *kemençe* rather than held horizontally on the neck such as in Western music (see figures 1 & 2). Main factor for this important role of the violin might be the person of Silo Qız (Süleyman Doğan, b. 1908?), who over the later twentieth century was the most well-known folk poet

---

[25] Similarly Zılfê Şıxê (1926–1992, official name Zülfü Hasbeyoğlu), lived in the village Kimsor, Nazımiye (Özcan, 2008: 351).

[26] E.g. *Memê Alan destani* by Silo Qiz recorded in 2002 by Mesut Özcan (MÖ 8 A 1), or a recording by Seyfi Muxundi (MÖ 4 A) of Seyit Süleymanê Axce (1912–1995; Kupik / Gelincik, Mazgirt), in this case with a basic accompaniment by a bağlama (Başgöz, 2008; Kahraman, 2013; Özcan, 2008: 352).

Figure 2: Hıdır Malkoç (1924–2017), Tunceli 2015. Photo: Martin Greve

in Dersim.[27] In addition to Sılo Qız, further recordings of violinists include Sey Weliyê Kupikey'in (Sey Weli Kemaneci, official name Veli Yılmaz, 1900/05–1980), Mahmut Baran (1923–1975, Bargini), Hıdır Malkoç (1924–2017) and Ali Bava Bedri (b. 1927 in Arphepug; official name Riza Caglayan).[28] According to oral history, also in other districts of Dersim, including Pülümür, Ovacik and

---

27 Cf. the documentary *Sairê Dersimî Silo Qiz* by Bülent Boral, 2011.

28 Recordings from Bava Bedri on Saltık & Taş 2016, CD 1, track 10, and on CD *Yaşlılar Dersim Türküleri Söylüyor*, Lızge, 1997, Tr. 10). Sılo Qız and Hıdır Malkoç used to life in the very same village, that is Mulo, near Tunceli center (Satun, 2014, 23), Sey Weliyê Kupikey lived in the village Kupik / Gelincik, which belongs to Muxundi / Darıkent in the district of Mazgirt (south eastern Dersim; Muxundi 2011). The latter singer used to sing Kurmanji, the other two Zaza.

Figure 3: The Euphrates College orchestra before 1910 (Source: Hapet Pilibbosian, Ed., Yeprad College Memorial, 1878–1915, Boston, 1942 (in Armenian), Tachjian 2012), www.houshamad yan.org/mapottomanempire/vilayetofmamuratulazizharput/harputkaza/education-and-sport/ schools-part-i.html (accessed 18 May, 2018).

Hozat, violins were played. As Özcan Kahraman told, his grandfather, Zeynel Kahraman (1930–2012) played both, violin and *cura*, his violin is said to have had only three strings, hence similar to a *cura* (Interview May 27, 2015, Hozat). Most violinists mainly play drones (long notes) as accompaniment to the voice, only adding short melodic phrases between sung lines.

It is unclear when, from where, and how, the Western violin found its way to the mountains of Dersim. I could not find any written or iconographic source which could enlighten its local prehistory. At least three theories concerning the origin of the violin in Dersim are conceivable. On the one hand the instrument might have been introduced by Armenians from Harput (Elazığ), where in the late nineteenth century several Armenian school orchestras of Western style are well documented (see figure 3).

According to Sungurluoğlu, until 1915, most instrumentalists in Elazığ were Armenians:

But in this aspect in Harput Armenians supplied superiority. Turks were leading in singing, they with instruments. In every Armenian house there was a violin, a kanun *and a piano or harmonium.* (Sungurluoğlu, 1968: 14).

Ali Baran:

My grandfather Mahmut Baran played saz, *and he played violin. Later I saw the violin he had played. It was a bit big, the Armenians called it "bıraça". As you know also the Germans call it "bıraça" [Bratsche, i.e. viola]. Because he was tall, a massive man. [...]*

(From where might the violin have come to Dersim?)
Many people have asked that to me. I heard it like this: at that time our people had close relations
with Armenians. The Armenians had close relations with Russians, and with Syria and Iraq. For
example they talked about Bagdad and Aleppo, and only little about Istanbul. Most of their trad-
ing they did with Aleppo.
(Were there Armenians in your village?)
In the villages near to our village there were many Armenians. (Interview 17 November, 2015,
Istanbul)[29]

This second theory, the import of the violin by Russian soldiers during World War I, is much less likely considering the short time of direct contact and the fact that tribes from Dersim fought against the Russian army. Following both theories, the practice of playing the violin upright, than, probably developed in Dersim. As Ali Baran remembered from his father, in the village of Bargini (Karabakır)–only 50 km from Elazığ with his Western educated Armenian musicians, the violin was still played in Western technique.

Finally, the violin might have simply replaced an older tradition of bowed fiddles as it still remains in Koçgiri, which is situated west of Dersim. The photograph on the cover of this book depicts Âşık Revani (1898–1968, sitting, second from left, official name Kurtveli Bozkurt), who lived in the village Mamaş near Kangal in the province Sivas, west of Dersim. Revani in 1931 played violin in a technique similar to that in Dersim.

Today, the violin in Dersim is played again almost exclusively with western technique.

Hüseyin İnler, violin teacher Ovacık:

Also my father used to play violin, he played it upright. He said to me: 'Don't play like this, the
way I play is primitive. Play modern, learn it in a school. I did not have the means, I couldn't learn
it, it came to me like this.' (Interview May 14, 2013, Tunceli)

Another instrument used frequently to accompany laments is the small long-necked lute *thembur* (Turkish: *dede sazı, cura sazı, ruzba*), which in Dersim also was regularly played during Alevi *cem* rituals. The *thembur* was played by hands, hence without plectrum. Just as the violin, also the *thembur* mainly provides drones during the vocal passages, in between the lines short patterns are repeated, as also *âşık* singers regularly use them. Obviously only few singers (at least before the 1980s) played developed melodies on their instruments, in particular Zeynel Kahraman (Hozat) who displayed remarkable virtuosity on his three-stringed *cura*. In general, however, we may conclude that for laments, instruments mainly served as a kind of sound background for the voice, rather than gaining any musical character by their own.

---

[29]   As mentioned before, also Nuri Dersimis father Mılla İbrahim around 1900 played violin in the village Ağzunik, close to Ali Barans village Bargini, hence again only a few kilometers north of Harput (Dêrsimi, 1952 / 1997: 13).

Figure 4: Imam Özmen (right), grandson of Sey Qaji holding his grandfathers *thembur*; together with Daimi Cengiz, 1988 (Photo: Cengiz, 2010: 525).

Since about the 1980s, most musicians left the small *thembur* for the larger *bağlama*. Singers including Hüseyin Doğanay or Sait Bakşi hence mainly played *bağlama*. And many musicians adopted the playing technique of the Arif Sağ school (who was born in Aşkale, northeast of Dersim), as for example Hıdır Akgül or Yılmaz Çelik (both from Ovacık). Hardly any other instrument than the *bağlama* was used for the accompaniment of the laments, only Mahmut Baran sometimes played *cümbüş*, which he had brought from Istanbul.

Recent studio productions, however, beginning with Ozan Serdar and Ali Baran, continued by younger singers including Metin Kemal Kahraman, Mikail Aslan, or Ahmet Aslan, further use instruments such as the guitar, *mey*, *kaval*, *zurna*, percussion, violin (in Turkish-Western style), flute, clarinet, saxophone and others, similar to the contemporary practice in professional Turkish folk music.

Regional and Individual Musical Styles

Due to the lack of research, the regional scope of the tradition described here as well as its supra-regional interrelations due to individual travels and migration can hardly be estimated.[30] In particular traditions in the larger Dersim region, including Koçgiri, Tercan, Kemah, Kemaliye (Ağın), Kiğı, Bingöl and Varto-Hınıs deserve detailed fieldwork and comparative analysis with central Dersim. Unfortunately, even the stylistic scope within Dersim is largely unclear. For a stylistic map of laments in Dersim, a linguistic analysis of the used dialects would be necessary. Available recordings do not cover the whole area of Dersim equally, in particular very little research has been conducted (and recordings been made) in Pertek and Çemişgezek in southern and southwestern Dersim.

In fact before 1937, Dersim was divided in territories of a great number of tribes (*aşiret*s), between which relations fluctuated, and combats regularly took place. As Nuri Dêrsimi points out in his memoire: "*In Dersim there are 60 tribes and between the tribes there is no communication and no sincere relation*" (1952/1997: 105). The fact that moving within Dersim seems to have been possibly only to a limited degree (with the exception of Alevi leaders, *pir*s) might have led to the establishment of regional musical / literary styles. Since 1938, however, and hence over the full period documented by the sources, singer-poets could travel at least throughout the province of Tunceli (and even beyond). Silo Qiz for example (born in central Dersim) performed also in Erzincan, Pülümür, Hozat and Mazgirt; Hüseyin Doğanay sang in Hınıs/ Varto, later he went up to Erzincan, Denizli, Aydın, Kayseri, Maraş and Europe (CD *Kılamê Dêrsımi*, 2004). Consequently, also songs spread over different regions, and laments, both on 1937/38 and older ones, found their way into the repertoire of singers all over Dersim.

As far as we can see at present, at least in the second half of the twentieth century, the tradition in Dersim was not standardized but rather open to both individual creativity and influence from outside. Recordings, made since the 1970s show an unexpected musical variety, including varied individual styles. The main region for this tradition of laments was central Dersim, from today's Nazımiye over Tunceli until Hozat and Ovacık. Well-known singer-poets include:

— Sey Qaji (1860–1936), Civarik, Nazımiye.
— Sa Heyder (d. 1917?), Galia Mıku village, Kırmızıköprü (Yıldırım, 2005; Akar, 2017; Dalkılıç 2015: 169–178).
— Weliyê Wuşenê Yimami (1305/1889–1958), Halvoriye, central Dersim (Beltan 2013).

---

[30] Singer-poets of Dersim origin, such as Âşık Nesimi Çimen (Kayseri-Maraş), Âşık Sadık Doğanay (Çorum), or Cafer Tan (Kayseri, Sarız), who were born and lived outside of this region are not discussed in the present article. In these cases later musical influences are difficult to seperate from a possible ongoing musical tradition from Dersim.

- Hesê Fate (1313/1898–1973/4, also known as Hesê Kêk, official name Hasan Arslan); Kortu (Meşeyolu), central Dersim (Kıllı, 2000; Dulkadır, 2011: 11).
- Silo Qiz (b. 1918, official name Süleyman Doğan), Mulo, near Tunceli.
- Alaverdi (1921–1983, official name Ali Çavdar); todays city of Tunceli.
- Zılfê Şıxê (1926–1992, official name Zülfü Hasbeyoğlu), village Kimsor, Nazımiye (Özcan 2008: 351).
- Hesenê Şıxali (official name Hasan Özcan), central district.
- Qemero Areiz (b. 1934, official name Kamer Demir), Karvan-Morarike, Nazimiye.

From Ovacık, in particular laments from Hesenê Gaj (1307/1892–1982), who was born in the village Örtünük (Yoncalı), have survived. In the collection of Mesut Özcan, recordings of both Hesenê Gaj himself and his son Ahmet Şan can be found. At present Hıdır Akgül (b. 1957, village Kozluca; Satun, 2014: 22) is known for a rich and characteristic personal style. The most well-known past poet-singers from Hozat are Zeynel Kahraman (1930–2012), Hüseyin Doğanay (1940–2005) and Mahmut Baran (1923–1975). Some laments from Hozat, and partly also in Ovacık, exhibit similarities with *âşık* songs (sometimes even with *uzun hava*-styles), as for example sung by Zeynel Kahraman. Also a certain Haydar Uçar, whom Mesut Özcan recorded in 1979 in Ovacik, sang songs with an unusual wide ambitus. Also Mahmut Baran had an individual musical style, which might have been influenced by Kurdish singers further south of Dersim up to Diyarbakir.

Two recordings of songs (accompanied by *bağlama* and reminiscent of Alevi *âşık* songs) which are said to have been performed by the well-known political activist Nuri Dêrsimi (born 1890 in Ağzunik / Akpınar, Hozat; died 1973 in Syria), are available on youtube,[31] posted by Ali Baran, who was born in a neighboring village. In his notes to the recording, Ali Baran informs us that the recordings were made by a friend called Alixasi.[32] However, a musical evaluation of these undated recordings is difficult. Nuri Dêrsimi studied in Istanbul, later lived in Elazığ, and on the eve of the massacres of 1937/38, he escaped to Syria. He hence might have heard (and was influenced by) a number of other regional musical styles.

Unfortunately, I had only limited access to laments from northern Dersim, most probably the archive of Metin and Kemal Kahraman offers more recordings.[33] Recordings from the district of Mazgirt, in the south-east of Dersim display different, seemingly individual performance styles, often near to the recitation style of central Dersim. Recorded singers include:

---

[31] "*Dağlar dağlar*" (www.youtube.com/watch?v=KY5CDNRCL2c, last accessed 4 May 2018); Kieser, 1997; Dêrsimi, 1952/1997; Düzgün, 1992: 363ff.

[32] http://www.baranvakfi.org/?p=346 (accessed 8 September 2014).

[33] For lyrics collected in Pülümür see Dalkılıç, 2015: 99ff; 152f; Çem, 2003.

- Sey Weliyê Kupikey (1900/05–1980; Sey Weli Kemaneci, official name: Veli Yılmaz), Kupik / Gelincik, eastern Mazgirt, Kurmanci (Mûxûndî, 2011; Özcan, 2008: 46ff).
- (Apê) Keko (?1915–1992; Keko Demirkıran), Goman / Yaşaroğlu, eastern Mazgirt; Kurmancı (Özcan, 2008: 214ff, 349; Mûxûndi, 2001).
- Ali Barut (?1900–1938), Lodek, eastern Mazgirt (Özcan, 2008: 50, 351)
- Seyit Süleymanê Axce (1912–1995; Seyit Süleyman Şahin); Kupik / Gelincik, Mazgirt (Kahraman, 2013; Özcan, 2008: 352).
- Seyiz Süleymanê Ana Nur – Seyit Sılemanê Qurqurik (recorded by Seyfi Muxundi, MÖ 11 A).

Transition to Dêngbej *and* Âşık

The widespread practice of lament songs in Dersim, of singing without instrumental accompaniment, is reminiscent of *dengbêj*s. Due to the lack of serious research, however, a direct comparison with related Kurdish traditions is at present impossible. Unfortunately no musicological analysis of *dengbêj* songs has been published yet. On the *dengbêj* tradition in Bingöl, close to Dersim and hence most interesting for a comparison, almost nothing has been published at all (except for the anthology of lyrics edited by Karasu, 2007). In particular, the musical relationship of *kılam*s from Mazgirt and Nazımiye and those in Western Bingöl needs to be researched in detail.

The most obvious difference between the performance style in Dersim and that of the *dengbêj*s is the vocal technique and the resulting timbre of the voice. The strong vibrato, typical for most *dengbêj*s, for example does not exist on any historical or recent recording from Dersim. Here, the voices generally display a soft and melancholic character, which is clearly different form vocal styles as used by *dengbêj*s.

However, several singers display individual combinations of or transitions between different vocal styles.[34] Mome Kule for example, recorded in the late 1970s by Peter Bumke in Rîcik (Geçitveren), eastern Mazgirt, sings with the accompaniment of a *bağlama*, while his vocal style is near to that of *dengbêj* including the strong tones at the end of phrases sung with growing vibrato.[35] Kekê Fati, on the other hand, who in the same time lived in the neighboring village Kârdere (Sülüntaş), sang without instrumental accompaniment, but in melodic patterns typical for central Dersim, and with a soft and melancholic voice. (Apê) Keko

---

[34] Wendelmoet Hamelink (2016: 25) found *âşık*s who were influenced by *dengbêj*s (or vice vers), also in other regions, including Adıyaman, who used to accompany themself on a *bağlama*. Transitions between *âşık*s and *dengbêj*s might also exist in Koçgiri.

[35] Mome Kule (Mahmut Çetin, Ricik, Muxundi-Mazgirt), ca. 1978; recording: Peter Bumke, www.youtube.com/watch?v=5rlAVnKI4k4) (accessed 24 August 2017).

Figure 5: Dawudê Memedi (b. 1922, official name Davut Tekin), village Çala Heru, recorded by Cemal Taş in 2016 (Photo: Saltık & Taş,
2016: 316). Noteworthy the singer holds his left hand to his ear while
singing, a gesture common for *denbêj*s, but unusual in central Dersim—
and impossible for singers who accompany themself by an instrument. Although Dawudê Memedi sang with a strong voice, he only
rarely used (soft) vibrato, while the developed melody is more reminiscent of songs of *âşık*s (CD 2, Tr. 9).

(?1915–1992, Keko Demirkıran), from the village Goman (Yaşaroğlu) again in
eastern Mazgirt, sang in Kurmanji, like the before mentioned singers. He accompanied himself with a lute, using a high voice and clear vibrato, but sometimes
changed to a recitation style during the song, which than reminds us of *dengbêj*s
(Mûxûndi, 2001; Özcan, 2008: 214ff, 349; MÖ 12 with a recording made by
Seyfi Muxundi in 1987).

Figure 6: Ahmet Sarıgül (from the documentary of Nuray Canerik, n.d.)

In the northern region of Dersim, on the other hand, several singers sung and still sing in the style of *âşık*s. Here the *bağlama* clearly dominates as the accompanying instrument, reminiscent of the performance practice of *âşık*s.[36] Some singer-poets, singing in Turkish, can entirely be regarded as traditional *âşık*s. Several *âşık*s from Erzincan are known to be of Dersim origin. Pir Kaltuk / Kaltık Mehmet, for example, grandfather of the famous Davut Sulari (official name Davut Ağbaba, 1925–1985) moved with his tribe from Pülümür (northern Dersim), originally from Nazımiye, to Çayırlı (Mans) in the district of Tercan (province Erzincan), where Davut Sulari was born. Davut Sulari travelled for his *dede* duties (he was a member of the Kureyşan *ocak*) to his *talip*s in Erzincan and around, while at the same time he gave concerts as an *âşık* and released records (Özdemir, 2017: 95ff).

In the northern part of Dersim singers show almost the same musical style as *âşık*s in Erzincan, even if singing in Zaza. In these cases both, voice technique and melodies differ substantially from central Dersim singers such as Alaverdi or

---

[36] Also the case of Âşık Mahzuni Şerif (1940–2002) demonstrates the affinity of Dersim musical tradition to that of the *âşık*s. Mahzuni's ancesters moved around 1800 from Hozat via Antakya to the village Berçenek in Afşin, Elbistan (Dalkılıç, 2015: 52), from here Mahzuni became one of the most well-known *âşık* of his generation.

Sılo Qız. Ahmet Sarıgül (1937–2015) for example, lived in Kırmızıköprü, a village south of Pülümür. After having stayed in exile in Samsun, the family returned to Dersim in 1952 (Taş, 2009). His most important musical influence was Davut Sulari. In 1955 he began to give concerts. Over 40 years he lived in Istanbul. Numerous musicians sung his songs, including Sezgin Çoşkun, Yılmaz Çelik, Hıdır Akgün, Enver Çelik, Ozan Rençber, Metin-Kemal Karaman, Nilüfer Akbal.

Further singers of the *âşık* tradition in Dersim include:

- Âşık Kemter Yusuf Dede (1928–2015) from Ovacık, who sang in the style of *âşık*s, and played short necked *bağlama*. From 1938–47 he was sent to forced exile to Balıkesir, later he returned to Erzincan (Ceren, 2014).
- Âşık Zamani (b. 1948), village Kuşluca in Ovacık.[37]
- Mehmet Erdoğmuş (b. 1947), Çemişgezek. Kurmanji, but sings in Turkish, influenced by Âşık Mahzuni (Ceren, 2014: 250).
- Ali Cemal Çetinkaya (b. 1941) Akpazar, close to Elazığ.[38]

The use of long-necked lutes by both *âşık*s and contemporary singers in Dersim is another common musical element. Introductory formulas as well as the repetitive strikes of the final tone used by *âşık*s north of Dersim reminds us of the singers in Dersim. Besides, the melodies of *âşık* songs exhibit a wider range of melody types, in addition to the existence of different regional styles.[39] Alevi *âşık*s from Sivas-Erzincan, in particular during performances of *semah*s and *deyiş*s, are known for a particular strike plectrum technique called "*âşık*s style" (*aşıklama tavrı*"), over all strings from below up (Sağlam, 2013: 155, 165ff) which was also used by *bağlama* players from Dersim (although I never heard this technique on historical recordings of *thembur*s from Dersim).

Hıdır Akgül accompanies himself on a short-necked *bağlama*, and his playing technique reminds us of that of Erzincan. Even some songs of Hüseyin Doğanay (Hozat) are reminiscent of melodies of *âşık*s. Today the only active female *âşık* is Şavaklı Ayşe (b. 1979), who lives in the village of Celedor (Bulgurtepe), in the district of Pertek. Again some singer-poets from Dersim are in between styles, as for example Usênê Pardiye (b. 1935, official name Hüseyin Celik), recorded in 2008 in Adaköy 2008 by Cemal Taş (CD 1, Tr 12). Accompanied by a short necked *bağlama*, he changes between recitation, narrow melodic patterns as typi-

---

[37] https://asik-zamani.de.tl/Ozan-Zamani-ile-bir-S.oe.yle%26%23351%3Bi.htm (accessed 5 October 2017).

[38] Naçari, 1995: 44f; http://ayhanaydin.info/soylesiler/ozanlar/773-as-k-ali-cemal-cetinkaya (accessed 5 November 2017).

[39] Reinhard & de Oliveira Pinto 1989; Şenel, 1991: *Âşık* melodies might be *uzun hava* or *kırık hava*, hence metrical free or with meter, resitatif; melodic patterns called *âşık havaları, âşık makamları, âşık hacavatları* and others in Kars-Erzurum; cf. Said Bakşi; several forms including *ağıt, baş-ayak, destan, divan, lebdeğmez, duvak kapma* and others.

cal for central Dersim, and long descending melodies over the range of an octave reminiscent of *âşık* songs.

Decline of the Tradition

Today, the tradition of laments and the numerous personal performance styles are in serious danger to get lost. Sılo Qız is about 108 years old, Said Bakşi, still active, recorded 13 CDs with his laments, financed by himself, but unfortunately they were never released officially (interview December 2, 2015, Istanbul). Sılo Qız hardly gave any concerts, not even during the annual Munzur Culture and Nature Festival in Tunceli. In Ovacık the poet-singer Hıdır Akgül is still creating and singing *kılam*s. In Germany the singers Ali Baran and Ozan Serdar for some time were active in Kurdish organisations, and later returned to traditional *kılam*s. Ozan Serdar (b. 1955, official name Zılfi Engin) was a founding member of the famous Kurdish music group *Koma Berxwedan*. On his recent album *Klasîkê Dersimî* 1 (*Lawik û Klamê Dersimî*), however, he sings *kılam*s from well-known Dersimian singer-poets including Alaverdi, Sılo Qız and Hüseyin Doğanay. In 2015, Ozan Serdar published a video with his interpretation of the well-known lament *Setero*. Initially, Silo Qız sings alone, and only later Serdar continues, hence giving a reference to the legendary singer from whom he once learned numerous laments.[40]

Since the late 20th century, new *kılam*s are hardly made and the majority of historical laments is lost. Mehmet Capan (in a style deeply influenced by Ruhi Su) sang many laments and transmitted the tradition at least partly to younger singers. Only few singers, such as the brothers Metin and Kemal Kahraman on their last (at present still unreleased) album focus on this repertoire, others only from time to time include new versions of old laments (Greve, 2014). As a rare exception, Kadır Doğan (b. 1969 in Soğukoluk, south Erzincan) recently released a CD with laments and religious songs (*beyt*) created anew by himself.[41] The youth in Dersim is rarely interested in the *kılam*s.

Several reasons might explain the decline of laments in Tunceli: Due to the depopulation of the villages, and the migration to larger Turkish cities and abroad, village life in Dersim almost came to an end, in particular during the winter. While in the past during the winter, snow cut off many villages, nowadays, modern snow-clearers keep most main streets open. Radio, later tv and today the internet provided new forms of entertainment, reducing the desire for common conversation, story-telling and singing.

---

[40]   www.youtube.com/watch?v=FEgNg2xcXO0 (accessed 7 November 2017).
[41]   CD Dersimli Kadır Dogan, *Zıkrê Jiaranê Dêrsim'i: Beyit û Şuari / Dersim Ziyaretlerinin Zikri: Nefesler ve Ağıtlar*, Arşiv Müzik, n.d.

Peter Bumke:

In these days these songs provoked the imagination of the people. They in fact relived it. In spite of the revived dengbêj *culture in Diyarbakir and elsewhere, I assume that due to television and other entertainment media this form of evoking pictures and events of the past has lost its fundamentals, the precondition of their perception. You would use the songs at the most as quotes or as fragments of memory, and thereby possibly keep them alive.* (Interview June 16, 2015, Berlin)

Furthermore, among younger generations the Zaza language gets more and more lost. While most youngsters in Tunceli at least still understand Zaza, it is only rarely used for daily conversations. Media such as radio and TV broadcasts in Turkish, in addition to school education, enforces Turkish, leaving Zaza only for internal family communication. All over Turkey, the market for non-Turkish folk songs is limited, and in order to address a larger number of listeners, musicians need to sing in Turkish. Finally, nowadays, together with the first generation of 1938, also the psychological need for laments, namely to find relief for the experienced terror, fades away, giving way to new forms of expression that fit contemporary issues. Laments nowadays are mostly sung as nostalgic relics of a lost past. In 2012, the left-wing singer Ferhat Tunc (of Dersim descent) for example, produced his album "Dersim" (Kirkelig Kulturverksted) which contained among others a new arrangement of the well-known lament *Cuxure* in the style of electronic ambient music.[42] The cover photo shows Seyid Rıza, and inside another historical photo of 1938 is printed. His next album "*Kobani*", however, was intended as a musical comment on the war of this north-Syrian Kurdish city against the ISIS. This politically topical CD contains exclusively songs in the style of Turkish left-wing political groups, rather than newly composed traditional laments on these tragic events.

The commercialization of music in Turkey, including of folk music, deeply changed this music. The emergence of commercial music production since the 1980s (Greve & Sahin 2018), enforced a much stronger awareness for sound, recording technique, instrumental accompaniment and vocal technique, as can be seen for example in the CDs of Ozan Serdar. The long traditional laments are too long for the mainstream music market, which generally prefers shorter songs. Likewise, weddings today, even in Tunceli, are much louder than ever before, and younger generation prefer to dance to the sound of small bands, including keyboard, amplified *bağlama* and singer, than to listen to traditional singers and sad, melancholic laments.

Naturally, most of these factors similarly affected other singer-poet traditions in Turkey. However, different from both *âşık*s and *dengbêj*s, the laments from Dersim never gained symbolic value for nationalist movements (Turkish or Kurd-

---

[42] By Weliyê Wusenê Yimami, recordings as performed by Qemere Areyizi in Saltık & Taş, 2016 CD2; CD *Yaşlılar Dersim Türküleri Söylüyor*, Tr. 3. Another contemporary version for example was recorded by Sena Dersimi (CD *Nêama*; Pel, 2015).

ish respectively), which could have led to a reinvention or revival of the tradition. *Âşık*s (as generally known) even benefited from the strong state support, though for the price of ideological loading, control and standardization. Âşık Veysel (1894–1975), for example, was only 14 years older than Sılo Qız (born in the village Şarkışla, Sivas). In 1931 during the folk poet festival in Sivas, he attracted attention for the first time, later he played and sung at Radio Istanbul, and taught *bağlama* and interpretation in several "Village Institutes" (*Köy Enstitüleri*). Âşık Veysel gave concerts all over Turkey, and eventually in 1963 was received by President Cemal Gürsel. His works became part of the repertoire of TRT, and today are considered as the most important classics of Turkish folk music (CD Kalan, 2001). His rise hence began at the very time of the massacres in Dersim, which Sılo Qız only survived because he could (and had to) entertain the soldiers (who killed his neighbors and relatives) with his violin (Saltık & Taş, 2016: 56). None of his songs in Zaza ever had a chance to be broadcasted or produced in Turkey.

The history of the *dengbêj* tradition during the twentieth century clearly reminds us of that of the singer-poets from Dersim. Similar to all non-Turkish musicians, also *dengbêj*s where widely discriminated. In particular after 1980, also this tradition was in danger of getting lost (Hamelink, 2016). Even the Kurdish movement initially criticized *dengbêj*s as singers for *ağa*s, *emir*s, and sheikhs, regarding them as part of the feudal and tribal system. Beginning in the 1990s, however, the Kurdish movement intensified its interest in cultural issues. Political music groups (*koma*s) appeared, and became interested in the tradition of the *dengbêj*s. In 1994 the Dicle Fırat Culture Center opened in Diyarbakır. In 2003 in Van, and in 2007 in in Diyarbakır, new *dengbêj* houses were founded. An encompassing research project on the tradition of *dengbêj*s ("*Dengbêj ve Dengbêjlik Geleneği Projesi*") was co-financed by the European Community, and the municipality of Diyarbakır (Hamelink, 2016; Scalbert Yücel, 2009). Though the importance of the *dengbêj*s for Kurdish nationalism never reached the level of the support for *âşık*s by Turkish nationalism, they still benefited from Kurdish festivals and television programs, which influenced and changed their performance practice (Hamelink, 2016). The singer-poets from Dersim, on the other hand, never obtained any comparable political support and influence from any kind of nationalism, and consequently no revival happened.[43] Only from time to time on memorial days of the massacres in 1938, laments are again sung, and obtain a politically symbolic meaning.

---

[43]   Another difference between Kurdish and Zaza singing is the fact that in Turkey much more speakers of Kurmanji live than of Zaza. Furthermore Zaza never benefited from international Kurdish broadcasting such as on Radio Yerevan.

Conclusion

The laments from Dersim might be described as a rural musical-poetical tradition within an Alevi community with a poorly developed feudal structure. Poems and performance practices show several similarities with other singer-poet traditions, such as *âşık*s (in particular those from Erzincan) and *dengbêj*s. The textual structure of the *laments* for example is much more reminiscent of the *kılam*s of *dengbêj*s than of the songs of *âşık*s, while the instrumental accompaniment is often close to that of *âşık*s. No consistent tradition developed in the villages of Dersim, but rather, if it concerns the instrumental accompaniment (violin, *bağlama*, *thembur*) or vocal techniques, a field for individual creativity existed, open for influences from outside. The case of Dersim, unaffected by the standardization of TRT and nationalistic discourses, hence offers us an impression of how the musical situation in Anatolia might have looked like before or without the impact of Turkish nationalism and state engineering: an inconsistent field of small regional and individual musical styles, mutually influencing each other.

Bibliography

Allison, Ch. (2001). *The Yezidi Oral Tradition in Iraqi Kurdistan*. Richmond, Surrey: Curzon Press.

Altınay, R. (2004). *Cumhuriyet Döneminde Türk Halk Müziği (Kitaplar, Makaleler, Nota Yayınları)*. Izmir: Meta Matbaacılık.

Amy de le Bretéque, E. (2012). Voices of Sorrow: Melodized Speech, Laments, and Heroic Narratives among the Yezidis of Armenia. *Yearbook for Traditional Music*, 44, 129–148.

— (2016). Self-Sacrifice, Womanhood, and Melodized Speech: Three Case Studies from the Caucasus and Anatolia. Asian Music, 47 (1), 29–63.

Arsunar, F. (1937a). *Anadolunun Pentatonik Melodileri Hakkında Birkaç Not*. Istanbul: Nümune Matbaası.

— (1937b). *Tunceli–Dersim Halk Türküleri ve Pentatonik*. Istanbul: Resimli Ay Matbaası.

Artun, E. (2014 / 2001). *Âşıklık Geleneği ve Âşık Edebiyatı*. Ankara: Akçağ Yayınları.

Aslan, M. (2012). *Repertuar. Kilame Cemi*. Istanbul: Tij Yayıncılık.

Başgöz, İ. (2008). *Hikâye. Turkish Folk Romance as Performance Art*. Bloomington: Indiana University.

Başgöz, İ. (2008). *Türkü*. Istanbul: Pan Yayıncılık.

Bayrak, M. (2005). *Alevi- Bektaşi Edebiyatında Ermeni Âşıkları (Aşuğlar)*. Ankara: Özge Yayınları.

— (1996). *Öyküleriyle Halk Anlatı Türküleri*. Ankara: Özge Yayınları.

Beltan, H. (2013). Saire Dêsımı Weliyê Wuşênê Imami. *Ma*, (1), 23–25, (2), 12–13.

Bilmez, B. et al. (Eds.). (2011). *Dersim '38'i Hatırlamak. Toplumsal Bellek, Kuşaklararası Aktarım ve Algı*. Istanbul: Tarih Vakfı Yurt Yayınları.

Boratav, P.N. (1986). *Anadolu Türküleri*. Ankara: Türkiye İş Bankası Kültür Yayınları.

– (1996). Giriş. Esen, A.S. *Anadolu Ağıtları*. Istanbul: İletişim.

Bumke, P. (1979). Kızılbaş-Kurden in Dersim (Tunceli, Türkei). Marginalität und Häresie. *Anthropos*, 74, 530–548.

Cengiz, D. (2010). *Dizeleriyle Tarihe Tanık Dersim Şairi Sey Qaji*, Istanbul: Horasan Yayınları.

– (2012). Doğaçlama Ustası: Wakıle. www.gomemis.com/portal/yazdir.asp?ID=245 (accessed 15 October 2013).

Ceren, D. (2014). *Kalbini Göz Kılanlar. Âmâ Yazar, Şair, Ozan, Dengbêj ve Müzisyenler Antolojisi*. Istanbul: Chiviyazıları Yayınaevi.

Çaçan , S. R. (2013). *The Dengbêjî Tradition among Kurdish Kurmanj Communities: Narrative and Performance during the late Nineteenth and Twentieth Centuries*, Master Thesis. Boğaziçi University.

Çakır, N. A. (2006). *An Investigation of the Singing Style of the Kurdish Serhed Dengbêj Reso*, Master Thesis. Istanbul Technical University.

Çem, M. (1993). *Taye Kiliame Dersimi*. Stockholm.

– (2003). *Hewara Dêrsimî*. Istanbul: Weşanen Deng.

Dalkılıç, H. (2015). *Dêrsim'in Anadolu'daki Statüsü*. Istanbul: Kalkedon Yayınları.

Demir, A. (2010). *Oral Poetry and Weeping in the Case of Dersimli Women*, Master Thesis. Ankara: Middle East Technical University.

Dêrsimi, N. (1952 / 1997). *Hatıratım*. Istanbul: Doz Basım.

Dulkadir, H. (2011). *"Pepugê Des u Di Kowu". Dersim Sözlü Halk Edebıyatından Örnekler*. Ankara: Kalan Yayınları.

Düzgün, M. (1992). *Taê Lawıkê Dersımi/Dersim Türküleri*. Ankara: Berhem Yayınları.

Elçi, A. C. (1997). *Muzaffer Sarısözen (Hayatı, Eserleri ve Çalışmaları)*. Ankara: T.C. Kültür Bakanlığı Yayınları.

Emnalar, A. (1998). *Tüm Yönleriyle Türk Halk Müziği ve Nazariyatı*. Izmir: Ege Üniversitesi Basımevi.

Erdener, Y. (1995). *The Song Contests of Turkish Ministrels. Improvised Poetry Sung To Traditional Music*. New York: Garland Publishing.

Esen, A. Ş. (1982). *Anadolu Ağıtları*. Istanbul: Türkiye İş Bankası Yayınları.

Greve, M. (2014). Collecting and Reconstructing the Music of Dersim. Effects of oral history research on recent music production. *Power and Democracy: The Many Voices for Oral History*. Barcelona.

Greve, M. & Şahin, Ö. (2018). *Yeni Dersim Saundu Oluşumu*. Istanbul: Tarih Vakfı Yayınları.

Hamelink, W. (2016). *The Sung Home. Narrative, Morality, and the Kurdish Nation*. Leiden: Brill.

Hooshmandrad, P. (2004). *Performing the Belief: Sacred Musical Practice of the Kurdish Ahl-e Haqq of Guran*. Ph.D. Thesis, Berkeley.

Kahraman, M. (2001). Zeynel Kahraman: 'İşte Abi Manzara Böyle Geçti'. *Munzur*, 7, 83–87.

Kahraman, K. (2013). Seyid Süleyman Şahin Biografisi. *Alevilerin Sesi*, 9, 39.

Karadeniz, B. (2017). Davut Sulari'nin Şiiri ve Müziği Üzerine. Unpublished manuscript.

Karasu, D. et al. (Eds.). (2007). *Bingöl Dengbêjleri*. Istanbul: Pêrî Yayınları.

Kaya, C. V. (2014), *Ankara Devlet Konservatuvarı'nın Halk Müziği Alan Araştırmaları Kataloğu*. (unpublished Master Thesis). İstanbul Teknik Üniversitesi, İstanbul.

Kaya, D. (1994). *Sivas'ta Âşıklık Geleneği ve Âşık Ruhsatî*. Sivas: Cumhuriyet Üniversitesi Yayınları.

Kıllı, H. (2000). Hesê Kêk (1889–1974). *Munzur*, 3 (3).

– (2008). Saan Ağa (1901–1937). *Munzur*, 29, (3), 51–61.

Mûxûndî, S. (2001). Dersim'in Unutulmuş Ozanlarından Keko (Keko Demirkiran), *Munzur*, 21, (1), 4–10.

– (2011). İki Portre: Sey Weliyê Kupikey (Sey Weli Kemaneci) ve Ela Tere. *Munzur*, 35, 15–24.

Naskali, E. G. (Ed.). (2011). *Ağıt Kitabı*. Istanbul: Kitabevi Yayınları.

Neubauer, E. (1971). Drei "Makamen" des Âşık Divânî. *Orbis Musicae*, 1, (1), 39–56.

Orhan, Y. A. (1999). *Âşık Daimi. Hayatı ve Eserleri*. Istanbul: Can Yayınları.

Özarslan, M. (2001). *Erzurum Âşıklık Geleneği*. Ankara: Akçağ Yayınları.

Özcan, M. (2014). Cumhuriyet'in Türkçe 'Dersim Türküleri' (1936–1944). Boztuğ, A. et al. (Ed.), *2. Uluslararası Dersim Sempozyumu*, Tunceli, Tunceli Üniversitesi, pp. 736–753.

Özcan, M. (1995). *Dersim Aşk Türküleri*. Istanbul: Kaynak Yayınları.

– (2003). *Kürdün Gelini. Notalarıyla Tunceli Halk Türküleri ve Oyun Havaları*. Ankara: Kalan Yayınları.

– (2008). *Öyküleriyle Dersim Ağıtları*. Ankara: Kalan Yayınları.

Özdemir, A. Z. (1994). *Öyküleriyle Ağıtlar*. Ankara: T.C. Kültür Bakanlığı.

Özdemir, U. (2017). *Senden Gayrı Âşık mı Yoktur. 20. Yüzyıl Âşık Portreleri*. Istanbul: Kolektif.

Reinhard, U. & de Oliveira Pinto, T. (1989). *Sänger und Poeten mit der Laute. Türkische Aşık und Ozan*. Berlin: Museum für Völkerkunde (=Veröffentlichungen des Museums für Völkerkunde Berlin. Neue Folge 47).

Sağlam, H. (2013). *Die Âşık-Tradition in Sivas. Eine Untersuchung über alevitische und sunnitische Besonderheiten der Asik-Tradition in Sivas*, Ph.D. Thesis. Universität für Musik und Darstellende Künste Wien.

Saltık, N. & Taş, C. (Eds.). (2016). *Tertele. Ebe Şûara Tertelê 38i / Ağıtların Diliyle Dersim '38 / Dersim '38 In The Language of Lamanents*. Istanbul: Z / Kalan Müzik.

Satun, B. (2014). *Tunceli Yöresinde yapılan bir Derleme Çalışması ve Mahalli Sanatçı olarak Hıdır Malkoç, Zeynel Batar ve Hıdır Akgül*. Thesis. Sakarya Üniversitesi.

Scalbert Yücel, C. (2009). The Invention of a Tradition: Diyarbakırs's Dengbêj Project. *European Journal of Turkish Studies*, 10, http://ejts//revues.org/index 4055.html.

Selcan, Z. (1998). *Grammatik der Zaza-Sprache. Nord-Dialekt (Dersim-Dialekt)*. Berlin: Wissenschaft-und-Technik-Verlag.

Sungurluoğlu, İ. (1961). *Harput Yollarında*. Ankara: Elazığ Kültür ve Tanıtma Vakfı Yayınları, No: 2 (3).

Şenel, S. (1991). Aşık Mûsikisi. *Islâm Ansiklopedisi*. Istanbul: Türkiye Diyanet Vakfı Yayınları, 3, 553–556.

– (1999). Cumhuriyet Dönemi'nde Türk Halk Müziği Araştırmaları. *Folklor/Edebiyat*, 1, (17), 99–128.

– (2007). *Kastamonu'da Âşık Fasılları*. Kastamonu: Kastamonu Valiliği.

Tachjian, V. (2012). Harput (kaza) – Schools (Part I). Translator: Melkonian, A. http://www.houshamadyan.org/en/mapottomanempire/vilayetofmamuratulaz izharput/harputkaza/education-and-sport/schools-part-i.html; See also http:// www.genocide-museum.am/eng/online_exhibition_11.php (accessed 7August 2017)

Taş, C. (2009). Dersim'in keşfedilmemiş bir hazinesi: Ahmet Sarıgül. *Dersim, Kültür ve Etnografya Dergisi*, 8, (10), 18–23. (https://dersimzaza.worldpress. com/2011/10/06/dersim'in-kesfedilmemis-bir-hazinesi-ahmet-sarigül (last accessed 13 December 2014).

– (2013). Sairê Saira Sey Qaji. *Ma*, 2, 3–10.

Toumajan, M. (1972). *Hayreni Yerg ou Ban*. Yerevan.

Turgut, L. (2010). *Mündliche Literatur der Kurden in den Regionen Botan und Hekarî*. Berlin: Logos.

Turhan, S. & Kantar, H. (2012). *Tunceli Halk Müziği*. Tunceli: Tunceli Valiliği.

Turhan, S. & Taşbilek, Ş. (2009). *Elazığ-Harput Havaları*. Ankara: Elazığ Belediyesi Kültür Yayınları.

Uşên, H. (1992). *Lawıkê Dêrsımi*. Gulane.

Yıldırım, M. (2008). Kadınlarımız, Ağıtlarımız: Ohi Baskını ve Zegeriye Ağıdı. *Munzur*, 27–28, 1–2.

Yıldırım, M. (2005). Dersim'in (en) Büyük Sevda Şairi: Sa Heyder (Sah Haydar). *Munzur 23*, 3–4.

Yıldırım, M. (2005). Bir Ozan ve Bir Aşk Hikâyesi: Memê Pit'in hayatı ve Ivê Avas ile Fidê'nin aşkı. *Munzur*, 22, 28–31.

Yıldırım, Yıldız, *Cultural Memory in Post 1937–1938 Dersim Laments: Reflections on Trauma and Violence*, Yüksek lisans tezi, İstanbul Teknik Üniversitesi, 2013.

Yönetken, H. B. (2006). *Derleme Notları, 1. Kitap. Anadolu'da Geleneksel Müzik Yaşamı Üzerine Notlar, 1937–1952.* Ankara: Sun Yayınları.

Cds / Videos

Aslan, B. (2011). *Ocax û Xwelî- Zêmarên Kurdên Elewî/Ocak ve Kül - Kürt Alevi Ağıtları*, Istanbul: Kalan Müzik.

Âşık Veysel (2001). Istanbul: Kalan Müzik.

Nuray Canerık (n. d.), *Ahmet Sarıgül*, documentary

Dersimi, S. (2015). *Nêama*. Pel Records.

Doğan, K. (c. 2016). *Zıkrê Jiaranê Dêrsim'i: Beyit û Şuari / Dersim Ziyaretlerinin Zikri: Nefesler ve Ağıtlar.* Arşiv Müzik.

Düzdaş, A. (2012). *Şinen Qoçgırıye*, Istanbul: Kom Müzik.

Emir, M. (1997). *Kurdish Bards. Traditional Music from Dersim.* Wien: Extraplatte.

Kahraman, M.& K. (1997). *Yaşlılar Dersim Türküleri Söylüzor.* Lızge Müzik.

Hooshmandrad, P. (2013). *Ritual Music of Gurân.* Mahoor.

Ozan Serdar (2017). *Klasîkê Dersimî* 1 (*Lawik û Klamê Dersimî*). Mir Müzik.

Tunç, F. (2012). *Dersim.* Oslo: Kirkelig Kulturverksted.

– (2016). *Kobani.* Oslo: Kirkelig Kulturverksted.

Textual Characteristics of Alevi and Sunni *Âşık*s in Sivas/Turkey

Hande Sağlam

Introduction

*Âşık*s play a very important role in their communities, not only as musicians and poets but also as mediators of history. Through their songs and lyrics, they transmit to the younger generations their history, ethical, political and religious issues. At the same time, they are an essential part of numerous rituals, such as religious ceremonies, weddings and festivals. Consequently, they are one of the most significant mediators of the collective memory of their communities.

The most important regions of the *âşık* tradition in Turkey are Eastern and Central Anatolia. During my fieldwork in Sivas, which I conducted between 2003 and 2006 during my PhD project, the local *âşık*s told me that the most important provinces of the Anatolian *âşık* tradition are Kars, Erzurum and Sivas. This information is also confirmed by the relevant literature (Heziyeva, 2010; Yaldızkaya, 2016) The *âşık*s from Kars are almost exclusively Sunni. They are known for their tradition of *atışma*; a song duel which is held among two or more *âşık*s and based on primarily lyrical but also musical improvisation. These *atışma*s mostly take place in coffee houses in the provinces or at festivals and weddings. The *âşık*s of Erzurum are partly Sunni, partly Alevi.[1] Here again, the *atışma* plays a central role, mostly among Sunni *âşık*s. In Sivas, we find a completely different social structure among *âşık*s. Through my observations during my fieldwork on *âşık*s from Sivas I noticed that most of the Anatolian *âşık*s come from the province of Sivas. Relevant literature on this topic also supports this assertion (Manafi, 1995; Bekki, 2004; Karahasan, 2003; Yıldırım, 2014 et. al.). In contrast to other provinces, in Sivas we can find *âşık*s with these two different religious identifications, and they have very intensive conflicts and confrontations with each other concerning their religious differences.[2]

---

[1] To describe the difference between these two confessions would go beyond the scope of this work. For more information: see Kaplan, 2004; Karakaya-Stump, 2016, and Nasr, 2007.

[2] This article is based on the results of my dissertation, which was written on the differences between Alevi and Sunni *âşık*s in Sivas. These differences between Alevi and Sunni *âşık*s has a very significant influence on their own communities. To analyse these differences help us to understand not only their musical and poetic characteristics and goals, but also the memory and history of these two communities in order to understand their backgrounds, social struggles and also their conflicts with each other. For more information, see Sağlam, 2013.

According to official Turkish sources, almost 99% of the Turkish populations are Muslims and about 80% of them are Sunnis. There is no official government data about the Islamic confessions in Turkey. According to a report by the US Secretary of Democracy and Human Rights which deals with religion freedom (Report on International Religious Freedom, 2016), there are around 77.5 percent Hanafi, and around 25–31 percent of the population are Alevi. However, it should be noted that this information is based on estimates in other sources.

During my fieldwork in Sivas I was told by the locals and by government officials that today around 60% of the population in the province of Sivas is Sunni, and the rest, 40%, is Alevi. This population pattern leads to a different hierarchical structure than in many other provinces in Turkey and causes a different balance and social power relationship, which leads to complicated confrontations.

Because of the repression of Alevis since 14th century they have not been allowed to practice their religion legitimately (Kaplan, 2004: 137–139). This is why the Alevi doctrine was almost only orally transmitted to the next generation. Religious ceremonies were held by *dedes* and *zakirs* and were always accompanied by the *saz* (*bağlama*). The lyrics of the *deyiş* (hymns) which were sung in these ceremonies served as the central transmitting "methodology" of their history. Until the 20th century there was little secondary literature on Alevi culture. In her recent book, Karakaya-Stump analyzes these partly newly-discovered sources (Karakaya-Stump, 2017: 3–7; 17; 67).[3] However, these secondary sources on Alevis, which are very important and valuable from a historical point of view, cannot be considered as a method of transmitting their religious practice to the younger generation of the community. In addition, the artistic and aesthetic aspects of transmission through music and lyrics have a different meaning and value for Alevi communities.

Many Sunni and Shia believers view the Alevi religious community with a certain scepticism and distance, and in many cases they reject it, which leads to a degradation of the social status of Alevis as a minority group in Turkey. That the Alevis reject many of the essential rituals of Sunni and Shia Islam is only a part for this behaviour: such as not going on pilgrimages to Mecca, not praying five times a day, not fasting during the month of Ramadan (instead there is a twelve-day fast in mourning for the sons of Ali, Hasan and Hüseyin, during which no meat may be eaten and no clear water may be drunk). The liberal attitudes in their own community, like not wearing a headscarf, equal rights for women and men, and having no restrictions on alcohol are other social freedoms which resulted in conservative Sunni and Shia communities giving them a "marginalized identity" (Silver, 1994), which led them into an endless cycle of discrimination.

---

[3]   For more information: see Bal, 1997; İnce, 2012; and Karakaya-Stump, 2016.

Due to what is for many non-Alevi Muslims their unorthodox approach to Islam, Alevis repeatedly experience disapproval, and therefore they concealed their religious identity until into the 1980s. This spared most of the Alevis the related negative social, political and economic consequences. However, it should be noted that there is also contempt for Sunnis on the part of Alevis. Most of the Alevis (especially in the region of Sivas) consider themselves and their culture to be progressive and modern—unlike that of the Sunnis, who they consider to be backward. The role of women is frequently taken as an example of this. Many Alevis present women as being treated as the equals of men, and are neither excluded from any Alevi ceremonies nor viewed as being different from men.

The Alevi religious community is undoubtedly demonised by followers of a political grouping which wants to interpret Islam in a more anti-secular and more rigidly, radical Sunni way. For this reason, Alevis have increasingly suffered more problems in society in the past 15 years because they—among other things—are viewed as followers of Kemalism and secularism.[4] Already during Ottoman rule there was no place for their tradition and their ceremonies. Secularism after the Kemalist reforms gave them a little more freedom, but only after the late 1970s were they able to practise their belief freely and without repression or interference. Even in secular times, however, they were never an officially recognised religious grouping, but after the establishment of the Republic they were at least viewed as citizens with equal rights. Nevertheless, this was and is only the case for Turkish Alevis. Those Alevis who consider themselves Kurds have remained exposed to difficulties in various contexts (predominantly for ethnic reasons) to this day.

This article article will analyse one *semah* of the Alevi *âşık* Mahmut Erdal and one folk song by the Sunni *âşık* Sefil Selimi in order to show the differences, similarities and characteristics which are the result of the different religious identifications of these two communities. These analyses will also help us to understand the social and political conditions of the two communities who live alongside each other, not only in Sivas but also in many other provinces of Turkey and in the diaspora.

Oral Transmission of History – Folk Songs and Deyiş s

These two different interpretations of Islam led to considerable differences in the social development of these two groups, which is also observable in the musical expressions of *âşık*s, especially at a textual but also at a musical level. For centu-

---

4   In the meantime, Kemalism and laicism have almost the same meaning in Turkey. For left-wing and liberal Turks laicism is an essential ingredient, a cornerstone of their understanding of democracy. And this cornerstone has been in great danger since the 1990s. In this context, Kemalism should not be viewed as nationalist hero-worshipping but as a symbol of liberation from anti-secularity, a symbol of secularism and laicism.

ries, the Alevis were not allowed to practice their religion in public and were not allowed to pass on their religion in written form to the next generations. Music was the ideal element to teach the philosophy of their religion to the younger generations. For Alevis, there is no such thing as a religious ceremony without music. This is why music has a very essential and different role for Alevis than it does for Sunnis and Shiʿis. It is obvious that the *cem* (the religious ceremony of the Alevis) and *semah* (the religious ceremonial performance/whirling of the Alevis) have contributed greatly to this fact. The *cem* ceremony is led by a *saz* accompaniment. The *semah* is also accompanied by the *saz*. Accompanying a whirling performance significantly changes the musical/rhythmic precision of Alevi musicians. For Sunni *âşık*s this aspect (accompanying a ceremony and movements) does not exist. Nevertheless, describing both their musical and textual attributes would greatly extend the range of this paper. Therefore, I will concentrate solely on the textual attributes here.

Although the two religious groups use similar genres of poetry, in the case of *âşık* songs it is relatively easy to differentiate on the basis of the lyrics whether they were written by Sunnis or Alevis. The difference is not of a formal kind, but in the content and above all in the selection of words. In the case of Alevi songs, it is also possible to a certain extent to establish whether the song has been censored. Alevi musicians have frequently mentioned to me that until into the 1990s they had to censor their lyrics themselves in order to be able to perform them in public. For this reason, there are several versions of some songs which not only have differing melodies, but also different lyrics, and are sometimes completely different.

I would like to mention Ursula Reinhard here, who discusses these changes of lyrics and meaning:

> In the song variations of older masters, there are frequent changes of words (…). For example, the old form *eydür* (meaning says or speaks) is sometimes misunderstood, which leads to the fact that in the verses in which the poets call themselves by their own name, one can find *Pir Sultan iyidir* (Pir Sultan is good – Pir Sultan is fine) instead of *Pir Sultan eydür*. *Ser* (head) sometimes becomes *serin* (cool), *dest* (hand) becomes *testi* (jug). In this way, meanings can be distorted (…) They are sometimes deformed to such an extent by village folk singers and untrained folk singers that they are hardly recognisable. Nevertheless, they retain their persuasiveness and authenticity for Turkish believers. Contents are sometimes deliberately changed by folk singers. In this way, even religious songs can become love songs and vice-versa. (Reinhard, 1989: 188)

I partly agree with this verdict; however, Ursual Reinhard does not go into the issue of religious conflict and repression here, which was the motivation for many changes. First of all, I would like to point out that a large number of Turkish and Ottoman words have double or triple meanings. *Âşık*s frequently use plays on words with words which sound the same but have different meanings and are described in the literature as *cınas*. A very famous example is: *Bâki kalan bu kubbede* *hoş bir sedâdır*.[5] This is a very good and well-known *cınas* from Turkish literary history. The meaning is as follows: "What remains forever under this dome is a delicate sound" (in this context dome refers to the world). The second meaning of this sentence is "Bâki (the name of the poet and means eternal or permanent) is the one who leaves behind a delicate sound in this dome". This linguistic phenomenon is hardly mentioned at all in Ursula Reinhard's text analysis, leading to the fact that in her translations usually only one meaning of a word is found.

In addition, it is not a coincidence that Ursula Reinhard very often quotes poems by Pir Sultan Abdal when referring to the issue of word changes. The latter is namely one of the most important figures in Alevism. At the time when Reinhard was concluding her research in Anatolia, Alevism was still a hidden and almost forbidden religious tradition, which is why certain key words in the lyrics were avoided at public events. Among these were the names and words *Pir Sultan Abdal, Ali, pir, cem, can, semah, dost* and *Şah İsmail*, which were exclusively used in connection with Alevi values. The poets deliberately avoided using these "provocative" words and replaced them with alternatives. They were and are then passed on in this form in order to create a song tradition with a double meaning: internal and external. This gave the artist an extraordinary ability to write lyrics. Nevertheless, the original versions remained, because they were passed on secretly, while in public only the "censored" versions were heard. Ursula Reinhard interprets these changes either as misunderstandings on the part of the *âşık*s or sees them as modifications of old words which were no longer in use and were replaced by new or Turkish terms. I can only agree with these claims to a certain extent. Personally, when I started my research into *âşık* culture, I was amazed by the tremendous linguistic knowledge of the *âşık*s. They were extremely proficient, particularly in their respective dialects. Sometimes I had to accept the fact that my Turkish was insufficient to understand them. Particularly those *âşık*s who had learned their trade via a classical master-pupil relationship had to extend their vocabulary during their training, read a great deal and think about the opportunities which were offered by language. For example, they had to master specific terms depending on their own religious tradition, and they had to be familiar with a vocabulary that was unknown to most Turkish speakers. This is one of the reasons why I must exclude a lack of linguistic ability as a motive for the changes.

In addition, Turkish music scholars (cf. Tüfekçi, 1992) are familiar with the fact that *âşık*s hardly ever perform their poems twice in exactly the same way. They repeatedly insert small changes, sometimes deliberately and sometimes unconsciously, which however seldom lead to a significant change in meaning. The same applies to the melodies. Since 2003 I have recorded many different ver-

---

5   Bâkî (Mahmud Abdülhaki 1526–1600) is one of the famous Ottoman poets and one of the greatest contributors to Ottoman literature. This passage is from his poem "*Zülf-i siyâhı sâye-i perr-i*".

Picture 1: Mahmud Erdal, Istanbul 2005. Photo: Hande Sağlam

sions of numerous *semah*s at different fieldwork sessions. Some other versions also appear as examples in, for example, Ursual Reinhard's book (Reinhard 1989) and *TRT Nota Arşivi* (TRT folk music archive).[6] None of these *semah* versions are performed in an identical way. This non-repeatability of the melody, for which evidence can be found in many folk music traditions, also applies to the lyrics in the *âşık* tradition. My opinion here is that when the contents are not changed, the changes in these lyrics are only of a coincidental and mostly spontaneous nature. Nida Tüfekçi also confirmed this phenomenon in his essay (Tüfekçi, 1992: 232–233).

As an example I will analyse a very well-known *semah* by Mahmut Erdal in order to go into more detail.

This *semah* (called *Gine Dertli Dertli* or *Turnalar Semahı*) was sung for the first time by Mahmut Erdal to Nida Tüfekçi in 1957, recorded by Nida Tüfekçi[7] in 1970 and archived in 1977 at the *TRT Nota Arşivi*.

---

6   For more details see: http://www.trtnotaarsivi.com/thm_detay.php?repno=1603&ad=G%
    DDNE%20DERTL%DD%20DERTL%DD%20%DDN%DDL%DDYORSUN (last accessed
    18 April 2018)
7   Nida Tüfekçi (1929–1993) was, along with Muzaffer Sarısözen (1899–1963), one of the
    most significant folk music researchers of Turkish music history. Together with Muzaffer

TRT MÜZİK DAİRESİ YAYINLARI
THM REPERTUAR SIRA No: 1603
İNCELEME TARİHİ :   26_9_1977

YÖRESİ (Region)
DİVRİK

KİMDEN ALINDIĞI (Sung by)
MAHMUT ERDAL

SÜRESİ : ♪ = 152

GİNE DERTLİ İNİLİYORSUN

DERLEYEN (Collector)
NİDA TÜFEKÇİ

(date of recording)
DERLEME TARİHİ
14_1_1970

(Transcription)
NOTAYA ALAN
NİDA TÜFEKÇİ

Picture 2: Excerpt of the transcription of the semah. Source: TRT Müzik Dairesi Yayınları (Publication of TRT-Music Department).

Through this *semah* we can get a more profound view of the strategies for the transmission of Alevi philosophy by Alevi *âşık*s. Furthermore a more in-depth analysis of the following *semah* makes it possible to explain certain changes in the lyrics: the selection of words and the religious affiliation of the author.

1. Changed version by Mahmut Erdal (recorded and transcribed by Nida Tüfekçi for the TRT Archive)		2. Original version (transcribed by Hande Sağlam according to explanations by Hüseyin Fırtına and Mahmut Erdal)	
Gine dertli dertli iniliyorsun,	Why are you sighing so sadly again,	*Yine dertli dertli iniliyorsun,*	Why are you sighing so sadly again,
Sarı durnam sinem yaralandı mı?[8]	My crane, is your heart hurt?	*Allı durnam sinem yaralandı mı?*	My crane, is your heart hurt?
Hiç el değmeden de iniliyorsun.	You sigh without being touched.	*Hiç el değmeden de iniliyorsun.*	You sigh without being touched.
Sarı durnam sinem yaralandı mı?	My crane, is your heart hurt?	*Sarı durnam sinem yaralandı mı?*	My crane, is your heart hurt?
Yoksa ciğerlerin parelendi mi.	Was your heart torn apart, perhaps?	*Yoksa ciğerlerin parelendi mi?*	Was your heart torn apart, perhaps?

Sarısözen he collected many folk songs and dances and archived them at the TRT (Turkish Radio Television). Tüfekçi transcribed most of these songs.

8   The poet uses the word *turna* (crane) to refer to his *saz* here.

Yoksa sana ya düzen mi düzdüler,	Were you betrayed?	*Yoksa sana ya düzen mi düzdüler?*	Were you betrayed?
Perdelerin tel tel edip üzdüler.	Did they make you unhappy by separating your frets from each other?	------------	------------
Tellerini sırmadan mı süzdüler?	Did they inlay silver thread on your strings?	*Perdelerin sırmadan mı süzdüler?*	Did they inlay silver thread on your frets?
Allı da durnam, telli de durnam, Sinen de yarelendi mi.	My red crane, my maiden crane, Is your heart hurt?	*Allı da durnam, telli de durnam, sinen yaralandı mı?*	My red crane, my maiden crane Is your heart hurt?
Yoksa ciğerlerin parelendi mi?	Or is your heart torn apart?	*Yoksa ciğerlerin parelendi mi?*	Or is your heart torn apart?
Havayı ey deli gönül havayı Ay doğmadan şavkı dutmuş ovayı	The air, the lowland plain shimmered before the moon rose, you mad lover.	*Bahar seli gibi akıp çağlarlar*	They flow and race like a spring stream.
Türkmen kızı gater etmiş mayayı	A Turkmen girl attached the camel to the caravan.	*Ötüb öttü dertli sinem dağlara*	My sad soul cried out to the mountains.
Çekip gider bir gözleri sürmeli	The one with made-up eyes will leave this place.[9]	*Üstadını buldurayım ağlama*	Do not cry, I will help you find your master.
-------	----------	*Allı durnam, telli durnam, Sinen yaralandı mı?*	My red crane, my maiden crane Is your heart hurt?
		Yoksa ciğerlerin parelendi mi?	Was your heart torn apart, perhaps?
Kuru kütük yanmayınca tüter mi?	Does the block of wood smoke when it isn't burning?	*Yas mı tuttun, giyinmişsin kareler?*	You're wearing black, have you been in mourning?
Ak gerdanda çifte benler biter mi?	Are there double birthmarks growing on the white neck?	*Senin derdin açar bana yareler?*	Your worries hurt me too.
Vakti gelmeyince bülbül öter mi?	Is the nightingale tweeting prematurely?	*Esiri der nedir derde çareler?*[10]	"What solutions are there for these worries?" says Esiri
Ötüp gider bir gözleri sürmeli	Only the one with made-up eyes tweets and leaves.	*Allı durnam, telli durnam, Sinen yaralandı mı?*	My red crane, my maiden crane, was your heart hurt?
		Yoksa ciğerlerin parelendi mi?	Was your heart torn apart, perhaps?

---

[9] 'The one with made-up eyes' is frequently used in Alevi literature as a synonym for the Alevis themselves, especially for the Prophet Ali. Nevertheless, it is almost only understood by insiders.

[10] Esiri was a poet from the 19th century. This particular *semah* has a few verses from the poet Esiri. For more information, see: http://www.turkuler.com/ozan/esiri.asp

Dere kenarında yerler hurmayı	They eat dates by the stream.	*Oda Pir Sultan'ım açılır güller*	I am Pir Sultan, the roses bloom in the fire.
Kılavuz ederler telli durnayı	The little crane becomes the leader.	*Dostlar cem olunca söyleşir diller*	The friends talk when the community gathers to meet.
Ak göğsün üstünde ilik düğmeyi	After he opened the button on the white breast.	*Güzelin duyunca yeniler derler*	When they hear about beauty they are inspired.
Çözüp gider bir gözleri sürmeli.	The one with made-up eyes goes away.	*Allı da durnam, telli de durnam, Sinen yaralandı mı?*	My red crane, my maiden crane Is your heart hurt?
Karac'oğlan der ki geçti ne fayda,	Karac'oğlan says that it is over, without any benefit,	*Yoksa ciğerlerin parelendi mi?*	Was your heart torn apart, perhaps?
Bir vefa kalmadı ok ile yayda.	Bow and arrow are no longer faithful.		

(Transcription and free translation of the poems by Hande Sağlam)

In both versions, many codes related to Alevism can be found. The coding is so strong that in the first version Mahmut Erdal only had to leave out *Pir Sultan*, *dostlar* and *cem*, because they were the only ones which were perceived by the majority as Alevi-sounding. Nevertheless, the entire poem is enriched with terms which - to the trained eye - convey Alevi content.

Gine dertli dertli iniliyorsun,	Why are you sighing so sadly again,
Sarı durnam sinem yaralandı mı?	My crane, is your heart hurt?
Hiç el değmeden de iniliyorsun.	You sigh without being touched,
Sarı durnam sinem yaralandı mı?	My crane, is your heart hurt?
Yoksa ciğerlerin parelendi mi?	Was your heart torn apart, perhaps?
Yoksa sana ya düzen mi düzdüler,	Were you tricked?
Perdelerin tel tel edip üzdüler.	Did they make you unhappy, by separating your frets from each other?
Tellerini sırmadan mı süzdüler	Did they inlay silver thread on your strings?
Allı da durnam, telli de durnam,	My red crane, my maiden crane,
sinen de yarelendi mi.	Is your heart perhaps hurt?
Yoksa ciğerlerin parelendi mi?	Was your heart torn apart?

In the first part shown above we can see very intense symbolisation. The impression arises that this is a conversation with a person. However, in reality the poet is addressing his *saz* and his sorrow. The sorrow of Alevism is expressed here by a personified tortured *saz* which makes a sound without having been touched. This sorrow is the centrepiece of the poem. In order to preserve the ambiguity, the *saz* is never mentioned, because otherwise it would be simple to interpret the lyrics, which could be used as evidence that Alevism is being referred to here. In this version, however, the possible interpretations are vague and create the impression that this is a love song.

Havayı ey deli gönül havayı	The air, the lowland plain shimmered before
Ay doğmadan şavkı dutmuş ovayı	the moon rose, you mad lover.
Türkmen kızı gater etmiş mayayı	A Turkmen girl attached the camel to the caravan.
Çekip gider bir gözleri sürmeli	The one with made-up eyes will leave this place.
Kuru kütük yanmayınca tüter mi?	Does the block of wood smoke when it isn't burning?
Ak gerdanda çifte benler biter mi?	Are there double birthmarks growing on the pale neck?
Vakti gelmeyince bülbül öter mi?	Is the nightingale tweeting prematurely?
Ötüp gider bir gözleri sürmeli	Only the one with made-up eyes tweets and leaves.
Dere kenarında yerler hurmayı	They eat dates by the stream.
Kılavuz ederler telli durnayı	The little crane becomes the leader.
Ak göğsün üstünde ilik düğmeyi	After he opened the button on the white breast.
Çözüp gider bir gözleri sürmeli.	The one with made-up eyes goes away.
Karac'oğlan der ki geçti ne fayda,	Karac'oğlan says that it is over, without any benefit,
Bir vefa kalmadı ok ile yayda.	Bow and arrow are no longer faithful.

This part is significantly different in the first and second versions. In an interview, Mahmut Erdal confirmed my supposition that he had changed a lot in his version (version 1 here) so that in spite of this transformation the delicate content between the lines would remain recognisable.[11]

The expression "the one with made-up eyes" is used in popular literature as a synonym for a beloved woman, but when one knows that this expression also refers to the Alevis (especially the Prophet Ali), the entire meaning of the lyrics changes. Mentioning the Turkmen girl is another pointer towards Alevism, because the majority of the Alevis assume that they descended from Turkmens. In this part of the poem, "*Türkmen kızı katar etmiş mayayı*" would be understood by the average person from Turkey as "the Turkmen girl adds yeast". However, if we

---

11 Interview with Mahmut Erdal, Istanbul 2005.

understand *katar* not as adding something, but as a caravan (a *cinas*), and the word *maya* not as yeast but as a young camel (another *cinas*), the meaning changes completely:

Türkmen kızı gater etmiş mayayı	A Turkmen girl is preparing the dough
Çekip gider bir gözleri sürmeli	And then the one with eye liner will leave this place

Or

Türkmen kızı katar etmiş mayayı	A Turkmen girl brought the camel to the caravan.
Çekip gider bir gözleri sürmeli	The Alevi will leave this place

These subtexts are, however, unknown to most Turkish-speaking people, and the entire significance of the verses is therefore only understood by a few people ("The Turkmen girl has incorporated the camel into the caravan. The Alevi will leave this place"). What is meant here is that the caravan has been prepared for the withdrawal of the Alevis, because they are leaving the Ottomans behind and want to travel/flee to Şah İsmail. Knowing that the poem was written by Pir Sultan Abdal (1480–1550), we can understand its content better by considering the situation at the time he was alive. In his time the wars broke out between the Ottoman Sultan Selim I and the Safavid Şah İsmail, in which the Anatolian Turkmens were on the side of Şah İsmail. To summarise the content of the poem briefly, it is about the Anatolian Turkmens who had lost the war and wanted to withdraw to Şah İsmail's land, but were unable to do so because they were pursued by soldiers under the leadership of Yavuz Sultan Selim and then killed. This is why the crane (the *saz*) is sighing.

As we can observe here, the last three verses have been subject to considerable revision and are different. The affected words are *Pir Sultan*, *dost* and *cem*. So why did Mahmut Erdal change so many details if only three words stood out? According to his own statement, the purpose of the changes was so that the deeper meaning of the poem would not be lost. In addition, Mahmut Erdal also stated that these modifications arose spontaneously during the recording. Using the name of Karac'oğlan (Karacaoğlan), which he has inserted at the end of the lyrics, is a *mahlas* (pseudonym) which perfectly underlines the ostensible identity of the lyrics as a love poem, because Karacaoğlan was a poet who was famous for his love poems.

In many of the existing literature sources about the *âşık* tradition, this poem is mentioned as one of those written by the Sunni *âşık* Karacaoğlan, although the lyrics are those of a *semah*, and this is a custom which is exclusive to Alevism. With regard to the secret and subliminal transmission of Alevi culture, the lyrics above are an ideal and–in my view–successful example. The complexity of the lyrics can easily be recognised here and the motivation for the changes made can be understood–both of these remain hidden to outsiders. The poem was originally written in the 16th century and uses a well-concealed secret language as a reaction to the oppression taking place at the time. In the present we can find lyrics which are obviously addressed only to Alevis. There are many examples of such poems, of which I would like to mention one by the Sunni *âşık* Sefil Selimî, because it appears to me to be very important. He was one of the few Sunni *âşık*s in Sivas who had a close relationship with and knowledge of Alevi philosophy. In this poet he tries to describe his situation as a sympathiser of the Alevis:

Kimse Bana Yaren Olmaz	**Nobody can become my friend**
Kimse bana yaren olmaz yar olmaz	Nobody can become my friend or lover,
Mertlik hırkasını giydim giyeli	Since I've been wearing the bravery vest.
Dünya bomboş olsa bana yer kalmaz.	Even if the world were empty, there would have been no place for me.
İnsana muhabbet duydum duyalı	Since I discovered a love of humanity.
İmanım hükümdar, benliğim esir	My belief is my ruler, my existence is slavery.
Ehl-i beyti[12] sevdim dediler kusur	People thought it was wrong that I loved the family of Mohammed.
Kimi korkak dedi kimi de cesur	Some people thought I was cowardly, some thought I was courageous
Kurt ile koyunu yaydım yayalı	Since I set the wolf and the lamb free.
Ardımdan vuranlar yüzüme güler	My friends laughed in my face:
Kestiği az gibi parçalar böler	He shares the little he has
Herkes kılıcımı boynumda biler	Everyone sharpens their sword on my neck,
Başımı meydana koydum koyalı	Since I sold myself.
"Bu Kızılbaş olmuş, yunmaz" diyorlar	They say: "He has become Kızılbaş, and is no longer clean."[13]
"Kestiği haramdır, yenmez" diyorlar	They say: "What he slaughters is haram, you can't eat it"[14]
"Camiye mescide konmaz" diyorlar,	They say: "You can't let him into the mosque."

---

[12] *Ehl-i Beyit* means the family of the Islamic prophet Muhammed. In Shia Islam, most of the Sufi lodges and in Alevi doctrine, *Ehl-i Beyit* has a central role. They believe that the family of Muhammed are also the successors of Islam.

[13] Kızılbaş originally meant Alevis. However, the meaning of the word became pejorative over time, and it is now predominantly used as an insult by Sunnis who dislike Alevis.

[14] An object or persons described as *haram* is considered unclean in a religious sense and must not be eaten or touched.

İmam Şah Hüseyn'e uydum uyalı	[And all this] since I started agreeing with Imam Şah Hüseyin,
Çoğu bende kağıt hüccet arıyor	Many look to me for proof.
Hal bilmeyen dip dedemi soruyor	Those who do not understand ask about my ancestors.
Dostlar ölümüme karar veriyor	Friends decide that I should die,
Sefil Selimî 'yem dedim diyeli	Since I starting saying that I am Sefil Selimî.

Sung by the Âşık Kadimî during fieldwork in Sivas in 2004. Recording, transcription and free translation by Hande Sağlam.

The Sunni *âşık* from Sivas Sefil Selimî describes here how he has been discriminated by his own society since he started recognising, respecting and even supporting the beliefs and philosophy of the Alevis. It is noticeable that he uses many Alevi terms, and that he directly addresses Alevism in the lyrics (e.g. Ehl-i Beyt, İmam Şah Hüseyin and Kızılbaş). This is not frequently encountered among Alevi *âşık*s, because due to the centuries of repression they have developed a different way of expressing themselves.

Since the 1990s the Alevis have acquired somewhat more space and freedom concerning their religious activities. Unfortunately the situation is turning backwards again now leading to massive discrimination against Alevis. This insecure and fragile freedom has, however, not been reflected in their poetry and hidden sacred codes. And connected to this are certain aesthetics in their form of expression which they do not want to leave behind.

Conclusion: Parallel Societies

As is well known, poetry and lyrics are the fundamental artistic tools of *âşık*s. They transmit their points of view, religious statements and socio-political criticism through their lyrics. This is a means of artistic communication with each other and with their communities. For me, the goal of this paper was to consider the differences in the writings of Alevi and Sunni *âşık*s, and to ask the question as to why these two communities, which have lived alongside each other for several centuries, still differ so much with regard to their views about the function of their art. I also wanted to reveal the extent of the influence at an artistic level of religious differences, and of repression and conflicts. As I have shown using these two examples (one Alevi, one Sunni), the extraordinarily elegant and creative expressiveness of the two *âşık*s overcome repression and prohibition, and pass on their veiled messages to those who are able and willing to understand them. In this way they also prove once again that art can be deployed as the best weapon against discrimination and suppression.

This article has tried to highlight the artistic differences of two Islamic religious groups, who are living in the same province. As far as I know the lyrical and musical differences between these two communities have not yet been analyzed from an ethnomusicological point of view. To look beyond these differences was the goal of this article.

That the regional elements in their folk music and folk literature play the primary role rather than ethnic and religious elements is a well-known phenomenon in ethnomusicology (Sağlam, 2007). However, in Sivas we can observe an exceptional structure: although Alevis and Sunnis from Sivas live in one place, they live separate lives and have very limited contact to each other. This manifests itself on the poetic and musical level of their respective musical styles and leads to clear differentiations. Exploring the background of these differences seemed to me to be an appropriate way to present the Alevi elements in the *âşık* tradition, and through this analysis we can also better understand the relationship between the Alevi and Sunni communities. It also illustrates their role, difficulties and status in society as the majority (Sunni) and minority (Alevi) communities.

> It seems that fostering one's own traditions, especially musical ones, often compensates minorities for a lack of acceptance and integration; it is a retreat into their own world. (Hemetek, 2001: 159)

My research on music and minorities in Turkey and in Austria has confirmed Ursula Hemetek's statement. The special role of art, especially music within Alevis in Turkey, and especially in Sivas, proves that minorities use their cultural good as a way of communicating with each other, and in many cases this is a concealed way.

There are two main reasons that cause artistic differences between minorities and majorities:

1. Power structures: the official discrimination of Alevism during the Ottoman Empire and unofficial oppression in the Turkish Republic (until now).
2. Mutual exclusion due to different interpretations of religious and social behavior.

These two concepts led to the discourses on "parallel societies" between two communities who are located in the same territory but live separately. They began to show their differences in the use of other words, and the minorities want to express their mostly forbidden ideas, rules and ideologies in various indirect ways (for example through artistic tools). This inescapable solution has a lot of influence on their artistic worlds. In this particular case I observed that only in very rare situations did the *âşık*s use elements of "other" religions or refer to the *âşık*s of other religions as masters. An exception is the Sunni *âşık* Sefil Selimi, who was also recognized by Alevis; and another is the Alevite Âşık Veysel, whom the Sunnis also regarded as a master.

These article provided examples of how Alevi content is conveyed through a lyrical code. The Alevis in particular used this kind of enciphering in order to keep their identity secret and in order to transmit the contents of their faith in an unadulterated way. A reluctance to use written transmission gave oral transmission methods a key role: lyrics with musical accompaniment. In both of the *âşık* groups transmission is mainly oral, but they differ in their motivations.

For Alevis, the transmission of religion secretly is in the foreground. Ethical and political perspectives of Alevism are other elements which we can find in their lyrics. In contrast, ethics and politics only play a marginal role in Sunni texts. For the Sunni *âşık*s, the focus is on the art itself and the individual interpretation and improvisation ability of lyrics. Their vocal competitions–song duels (referred to as *atışma* in Turkish)–on the stage or in coffee houses are the most important activities of Sunni *âşık*s.

The comparisons made in the course of this paper do not intend to offer any assessments. They are merely descriptions of the status quo of the region. A judgmental representation of the artistic abilities of these two religious groups was also not my goal and was far from being my mission.

An artistic critique can only be carried out by those who actively perform this art; namely the *âşık*s themselves. My task is also not to disclose the secret transmission methods of the Alevi people. I only want to open a door in order to show and understand the deep, sophisticated and artistically very difficult expressions of these musicians. Understanding the transmission strategies of the Alevis as minorities is also necessary in order to emphasize the problems, difficulties and oppression of religious minorities.

References

Bal, H. (1997). *Sosyolojik Açıdan Alevi-Sünni Bütünleşmesi ve Farklılaşması*. Istanbul: Ant Yayınları.

Başgöz, I. (2014). *İzahlı Türk Şiiri Antolojisi*. Istanbul: Pan Yayıncılık.

Bekki, S. (2004). *Baş Yastıkta Göz Yolda, Sivas Türküleri*. Istanbul: Sivas Kitaplığı.

Duygulu, M. (1997). *Alevi-Bektaşi Müziğinde Deyişler*. Istanbul: Sistem Ofset.

Erdal, M. (2002). *Bir Ozanın Kaleminden* [from a poet's pen]. Çamşık/Sivas: Çamşık Hüseyin Abdal Derneği Yayınları, Çamşık Halk Kültürü Serisi.

İnce, B. (2012). *Citizenship and Identity in Turkey – From Atatürk's Republic to the Present Day*. London, New York: I.B. Tauris.

Hemetek U. (2001). *Mosaik der Klänge - Musik der ethnischen und religiösen Minderheiten in Österreich*. Wien: Böhlau Verlag.

Heziyeva, S, (2010). *Kars Âşıklık Geleneği ve Badeli Âşık*. A.Ü Türkiyat Araştırmaları Enstitüsü Dergisi (TEAD), 44, 211–255.

Kaplan, I. (2004). *Das Alevitentum – Eine Glaube- und Lebensgemeinschaft in Deutschland*. Köln: Alevitische Gemeinde Deutschland e. V.

Karahasan, T. & Karahasan, F.Y. (2003). *Âşık, Ozan ve Türküleri ile Köşe Bucak Anadolu*. Trabzon: Yörem Musiki.

Karakaya-Stump, A. (2016). *Vefailik, Bektaşilik, Kızılbaşlık. Alevi Kaynaklarını, Tarihini ve Tarihyazımını Yeniden Düşünmek*. Istanbul: Istanbul Bilgi Üniversitesi Yayınları.

Kaya, D. (2000). Kendi Dilinden Âşık Sefil Selimî. *Milli Folklor Dergisi*, year 11, No 44. Retrieved from millifolklor.com/PdfViewer.aspx?Sayi=44&Sayfa=61 (last accessed 20 January 2018), 62–67.

Korkmaz, E. (2003). *Alevilik-Bektâşilik Terimleri Sözlüğü*. Istanbul: Kaynak Yayınları.

Köprülü, M. F. (1930/2004). *Saz Şairleri*. Ankara: Akçağ Yayınları.

Nasr, V. (2007). *The Shia Revival: How Conflicts within Islam Will Shape the Future*. New York: W.W. Norton & Co.

Reinhard, U. & de Oliveira Pinto, T. (1989). *Sänger und Poeten mit der Laute, türkische Âşık und Ozan*. Berlin: Dietrich Reimer Verlag.

Sağlam, H. (2006). "Musical Identity of Ethnic Groups in the Sivas Region". In N. Ceribašić & E. Haskell Roč (Ed.) (2006). *Shared Musics and Minority Identities. Papres from Third Meeting of the "Music and Minorities" Study Group of ICTM*. Institute of Ethnology and Folklore Research – Cultural-Artistic Society (157–169).

Sağlam, H. (2013). *Die Âşık-Tradition in Sivas - Eine Untersuchung über alevitische und sunnitische Besonderheiten der Âşık-Tradition in Sivas*. Unpublished doctoral dissertation. Vienna:University of Music and Performing Arts.

Silver, H. (1994). "Social Exclusion and Social Solidarity: Three Paradigms". *International Labour Review*, 133 (5–6), 531–578.

Tüfekçi, N. (1992). „Âşıklarda Müzik". In S. Turan (Ed.). *Türk Halk Müziğinde Çeşitli Görüşler*. (227–243). Ankara: T.C. Kültür Bakanlığı.

Yıldırım, N. (2014). *Türk Saz Şairleri Antolojisi*. Istanbul: Etkileşim Yayınları

Documentary Film

In Sivas Wachsen die Dichter. (1995). Documentary Film. Director: Said Manafi. Script: Said Manafi and Werner Bauer. Austria. Österreichisches Bundesinstitut für den Wissenschaftlichen Film

Online Sources:

http://www.trtnotaarsivi.com/thm_detay.php?repno=1603&ad=G%DDNE%20D
  ERTL%DD%20DERTL%DD%20%DDN%DDL%DDYORSUN (accessed 18
  April 2018)

http://www.turkuler.com/ozan/esiri.asp (accessed 11 February 2018).

Bureau of Democracy, Human Rights and Labor. (2016). International Religious
  Freedom Report for 2016. Retrieved from: https://www.state.gov/j/drl/rls/irf/
  religiousfreedom/index.htm?year=2016&dlid=268876#wrapper (accessed 22 January 2018).

Yaldızkaya, Ömer Faruk. (2016). Emirdağlı Âşık Yoksul Derviş. http://www.turku
  ler.com/yazi/emirdagliasik.asp (accessed 15 March 2018)

Hakikatçi Âşıklık:
Historical and Musical Traces
of a Religious Movement

Ulaş Özdemir

For communities living inside the borders of the Ottoman Empire, the nineteenth century constitutes one of the most significant historical periods with irremediable social, cultural and political changes. On the one hand, Ottoman efforts to become part of Europe and on the other hand its unsteady policies on the issues of nationhood, identity, and religion with regard to the changes all over the world left their mark on this century. Selim Deringil summarizes the condition of the Ottoman Empire in the nineteenth century (Deringil, 1999: 3, 4):

> In more ways than one, the Ottoman Empire falls between the cracks of the fault lines that determined world politics in the nineteenth century, and this continues to determine the way the history of imperialism is written today. On the one hand, even at the turn of the century, it was still a force to be reckoned with and, unlike the Indian princely states or African colonized peoples, it was one which could not be pushed aside. On the other hand, it was the 'Sick man of Europe' whose demise was expected at any moment. It was heavily penetrated by Western economic interests, and suffered from chronic financial crises. It continued to lose territory in Europe, yet by the mid-nineteenth century it had the third largest navy in the world, and in the last quarter of the century, much to the alarm of the British, it actually succeeded in extending its influence along the Arabian Gulf. The central point about this was that the sultan and his staff at the Sublime Porte controlled their own fate. Operating under severe constraints, to be sure, they were nonetheless able to carve out a critical space for *manoeuvre* in an increasingly hostile environment. This produced the basic dynamic which determined the relationship between the Ottoman statesman and his Western colleague.

The nineteenth century also marked the beginning of a new era for Alevi, Bektashi and Kizilbash communities, with whom the Ottoman Empire had problems throughout the centuries. The abolition of Bektashi *tekke*s (lodge) and the Janissaries by Mahmut II in 1826 affected, directly or indirectly, a number of incidents these communities would go through until the Republican era.[1] During this period, centuries-long differences among Alevi communities on maintaining their faith became affected by the interaction between communities belonging to different *sürek*s (practice). Especially, after Hamdullah Çelebi's exile to Amasya, occasional appearances of the Babagan branch in Eastern Anatolia, in

---

[1] For studies on the abolition of Bektashi *tekke*s in 1826 and more generally the Bektashi in the nineteenth century see Soyyer (2005), Maden (2012, 2013). Also for details on the lives of Hacı Bektaş Çelebis from Hamdullah Çelebi, who was exiled to Amasya in 1826, to the War of Independence see Ulusoy (1986, 92–104).

addition to the Çelebi impact in the region, constitutes an important development in terms of the interaction between these branches and the *ocak*s (hearth) influential in the Eastern provinces.

From a religious perspective, another important aspect of the nineteenth century is the declaration of the Tanzimat Edict, which brought forth military, administrative and legal reforms, and the Reform Edict, which aimed for equal citizenship between Muslims and non-Muslims by resolving the *millet* (nation) system. The Ottomans, however, interpreted the "freedom of religion" principle in these edicts as "freedom of defending their religion" (Deringil, 1999: 115). It also provided the legal foundation for proselytization for the missionaries who had started working on the Ottoman soil. Deringil, stating that missionary activities presented the most dangerous threat against the legitimacy of the Ottoman Empire in the long run, describes this case as an ideological war between Christians and Muslims that challenged the very foundations of the Ottoman legitimacy (Deringil, 1999: 115). Alevis fell within a small front in this war.

Alevis and Protestant Missionaries

Starting with the second half of the nineteenth century, there is a significant amount of literature about different Alevi communities, from the Balkans to the hinterland of Iran—primarily about the ones in Anatolia, penned by Western travelers, bureaucrats, researchers and especially missionaries.[2] In this literature, missionary reports present the most interesting case both for the academic interest they have received so far and the information—be it true or false—they include.[3] American Board of Commissioners for Foreign Missions (ABCFM), an American Protestant missionary organization which started its activities in Anatolia in 1820, becomes the most actively involved organization to work with Alevis in the following years with the opening of its first office in Istanbul in 1831.[4] Hans-Lukas Kieser summarizes the relationship between the Alevis and the Protestants as such (Kieser, 2010: 52–53):

> The relationship between the Protestant missionaries and the Alevis began shortly after the establishment of the Protestant *millet* in 1850. It was one of mutual sympathy, some

---

[2]   For a collection on Alevis and Kurds by Western travelers, bureacrauts and missionaries see Bayrak (1997). For a comprehensive and critical examination of Westerners', and especially missionaries', texts on Alevis see Dressler (2013, 31–77).

[3]   Missionary reports, despite their biases and factual errors, include ethnographically and historically rich information about the Kizilbash-Alevi communities at that time (Dressler, 2013, 31). For a critical examination of the information provided missionary reports and the story of Ali Gako mentioned in these reports see Karakaya-Stump (2015: 207–234). For another study on the relationship between Alevism and Christianity taking these reports as its starting point see Gezik (2016: 225–255).

[4]   For ABCFM's general activities report on its work in Anatolia until 1910 see Bliss (1910). Also for ABCFM's activities about Alevis see Kieser (2005: 102–116).

shared values, and common hope for a new age. The reality, however, fell far short of the great expectations. Missionary enthusiasm for this people and curiosity about them remained nevertheless constant.

Numerous arguments can be made to explain why the Alevis and Protestant missionaries established a relationship. Since the information we have generally comes from the commentary on missionaries' reports, the issue cannot be explained by a single factor. According to one argument, for instance, the affiliation between Alevis and Christians had more of a political nature rather than a religious one; this stemmed from the fact that both groups lived under the control of Sunni Ottomans and hence shared common problems (Gezik, 2016: 244). According to another opinion, religious affinity has also contributed to this relationship (Akpınar et al., 2010: 318):

> It is possible that the Alevis were curious about and interested in the Protestant missionaries and they had a "sympathetic relationship." Some possible reasons include the fact that in the Alevi faith system, all religions are sacred and there are no biases against other religions; that Protestant missionaries created an appeal by building schools, hospitals and workshops that people needed; and that some Alevis expected a kind of "political protection" through their view of "Protestantism as a way out of the discrimination they have faced for centuries."

Regardless of the reasons for the affinity between the Alevis and the Protestant missionaries, this relationship was especially affected by the policy of including Alevis in "*ümmet*" (religious community) during Abdulhamit's reign and this situation, while bringing certain sanctions against missionaries, also led to creation of the necessary precautions for the Islamization mission (Akpınar et al., 2010: 318). Thus, this relationship seems to weaken towards the end of the nineteenth century (Dressler, 2013: 44):

> It certainly appears that at least some of the Kızılbaş, and more strongly those of the eastern provinces, considered conversion to Protestantism to be a move that promised a brighter future—provided that they could secure the support of the missionaries and foreign powers to receive official recognition as part of the Protestant *millet*. The material prospects that came along with the missionaries, such as the establishment of schools and access to the missions' hospitals, clearly were very attractive to many Kızılbaş. With the Ottomans making clear their rejection of the Kızılbashes' conversion, the latter's inclination toward Protestantism -which had been documented so meticulously by ABCFM missionaries in the second half of the 1850s- appears to have declined considerably.

Some Ottoman archival reports belonging to the 1890s and early 1900s mention the conversion to Protestantism and the tendency to proselytization among the Alevis living in the region from Central Anatolia to Dersim (Irmak, 2010: 255). Nevertheless, missionary activities in the Ottoman Empire during the nineteenth century, in general, achieved little and a relatively small number of Muslims converted to Christianity (Deringil, 1999: 134). In this period, those who converted to Protestantism or had relations with Protestants are started to be called

Prot, Purot, Prut, Purut, Prudi or Prodan.[5] We can see the missionaries' strongest influence on Anatolian Alevis in the traces of a religious movement known as "*Hakikatçi*" or "*Hakikatli*" even today.

The Vanguards of Hakikatçilik: *Araboğulları*

The story of *Hakikatçilik*, an extant religious movement influencing Alevi communities living in different regions, starts with Şeyh Süleyman and his son Veyis, known as Araboğulları.[6] Oral and written sources differ in their descriptions of Süleyman and Veyis as brothers or father-and-son.[7] The Araboğulları, *seyit*s (descendant of Hz. Ali) affiliated with the *ocak* of Baba Mansur located in Muhundu (Darıkent) village of Mazgirt, Dersim, for reasons unknown to us, moved to Mescit village of Kangal, Sivas where *ocak talip*s (disciple) lived.[8] Süleyman Metin, a grandchild of Araboğulları, conveys how Süleyman and Veyis from the Baba Mansur *ocak* took up the name "Araboğlu" (Coşkun, 2014: 137):

> These *dede*s from the Baba Mansur Ocak set out to follow the requirements of *Hakikat Kapısı* of "Dört Kapı, Kırk Makam," the basis of Alevi-Bektashi philosophy. They are reported to the *kadı* [Muslim judge] in Kangal, with the complaint that "they are trying to form a state against the *Devlet-i Âli*. They are even disregarding the border in their

---

[5] Ayfer Karakaya-Stump claims that there is no information available whether "*pençeci Kızılbaşlar*" were given the name Protestant or anything similar (Karakaya-Stump, 2015, 231). However, J.G. Taylor, the British consulate who recounts his meeting with Ali Gako in 1866—the main figure of Karakaya-Stump's article—mentions that Gako is known as "Prot Ali Ağa" in the region (Taylor, 1868, 317). Also, various names—*prut, purot, prudi*—mentioned in several sources cited in this article and in use since the nineteenth century prove this point. However, these names, up until today, are used in derogatory terms at times (Baran, 2011: 155; Özcan, 2001: 2, 45; Okan, 2016: 100).

[6] For three novels that take oral narratives as a starting point to tell what happened to Araboğulları and those living around them see Çiltas (1993, 1999, 2000).

[7] Even though some sources, starting with the testimony of Araboğulları's grandchildren, state that Süleyman and Veyis were brothers (even *müsahip*s (companion)) (Metin, 2014: 72; Baran, 2011: 146; Türkyılmaz, 2009: 258) the missionary reports clearly assert that they were father and son, and Süleyman was a well-respected *şeyh* (sheikh) (Jewett, 1858: 111–113; Winchester, 1861: 72–73; Herrick, 1866: 68–69). The only name in the reports as the *şeyh*'s son is Veyis. However, the reports do not provide any information about the pseudonym "Araboğlu." In the region and among their followers, both of them are called "Araboğlu" or "Araboğulları" (Baran, 2011: 146). In this article, "Araboğulları" will be used when needed.

[8] Araboğulları, after Muhundu, moved to Kelkit, then Zara and then Kangal (Baran, 2011: 151–152; Coşkun, 2014: 137). It is argued that Araboğulları left Baba Mansur *ocak* because of the *Tarikatçi* ve *Hakikatçi* dichotomy among Koçgiri clans in the second half of the nineteenth century and started their own organization, and since Baba Mansur *dede*s (elder) generally continued to be *Tarikatçi*, Araboğulları left Zara—where Baba Mansur followers lived—and moved to Mescit village of Kangal. However, there is not enough information on this matter (Gezik, 2013: 56–57). Araboğulları's house and graves are still in Mescit village (see Figure 1). The common grave of Süleyman and Veyis, which they desired to be plain and simple, has turned into a visiting point in the region (see Figure 2).

fields." The *kadı* orders them to be taken into custody and sends soldiers to the village. The soldiers cannot put the handcuffs on Şeyh Süleyman and his brother Veyis. Every time, the lock of the cuff fails. Once they arrive in Kangal, the *kadı* gets angry and asks why they are not handcuffed. The soldiers tell that the lock failed to work. This time the *kadı* tries but he fails as well. These two brothers are immediately sent to prison. Even though it is July, a very strong hail storm begins. The Ağa of Kangal comes to visit these two brothers. The door to the cell is open. Behind it, there is an Arab with a black headdress. After people learn about this incident, they start believing that the brothers are protected by this Arab and they come to be known "Araboğlu." After being tried with capital punishment in Sivas, they are sent to exile to Küçük Söbeçimen village, Sarız, Kayseri for seven years. Once Şeyh Süleyman and his brother Veyis return from their seven-year exile, all villagers and the *talip*s belonging to this *ocak* show more respect and affection due to the past events.

So far, no record has been found about the abovementioned trial. However, the problems between Araboğulları and the Ağa of Kangal are frequently mentioned in oral narratives. Thus, we can surmise that the trial might have been a verbal confrontation due to some sort of animosity, if not a court case in front of an official *kadı*. Furthermore, that the oral memory about the mythology of the name "Araboğlu" constantly references the same incident implies a rather strong hostility.

Süleyman and Veyis, who are understood to gradually gain power around Kangal and whose position as a "*şeyh*" becomes more accepted, appear in the Protestant missionaries' reports working in the region since the 1850s.[9] We are not exactly sure if the Araboğulları approached Protestants with sympathy because, as mentioned above, they regarded "Protestantism as a way out of the centuries-long discrimination" and had "political protection" in mind. Yet, what the Araboğulları went through after this relationship had a long-lasting impact on communities connected to them. Hans-Lukas Kieser interprets the Araboğulları's relationship with the missionaries (Kieser, 2005: 111–112):

> Towards the end of 1850s, the Harput, Sivas and Divriği offices started to send Kurdish- and Armenian- speaking teachers to not only Christian villages but also Alevi villages. In Sivas, Baron Krikore, a Muslim (Alevi?) *mühtedi* (convert) from Antep, was put in charge. Krikore had attended Bebek Divinity School of the American Mission in Istanbul for a few months. He arrived in Sivas in July 1857 and started visiting the Kizilbash in the same fall. With the Sivas missionary Oliver Winchester and a Kurd who attended Protestant services in Sivas, they went to visit Şeyh Süleyman, "the accepted leader of the Protestant Kurds with whom Krikore had established a relationship." Süleyman's son Veyis became friends with the missionaries and wanted to attend the mission school in Istanbul.

---

9   The question of why Süleyman, a *seyit* belonging to Baba Mansur *ocak*, is regarded as a "*şeyh*" rather than a "*dede*" emerges as an important detail. That Araboğulları's followers in the later periods also mention *Hakikatçilik* as "*şeyhlik*" indicates that this matter requires further research.

Figure 1: The *muhabbet* (gathering) room of the house of the Araboğulları in the village Mescit where they met the Protestant missionaries
(photo by Mahir Polat, 2015).

The report sent by the missionaries in 1858 conveys that Şeyh Süleyman and
those around him were persecuted and hence forced to go into exile. It is emphasized that Baron Krikore, who was in touch with them, had met with the
governor of the region and asked him to grant permission for their return. Also,
in Krikore's words, it is stated that Veyis, around the age of twenty-five, is very
intelligent, wants to go to Bebek[10], and—especially mentioned that—he is probably the only literate youth in the region (Jewett, 1858: 111–113). The report from
1861 notes that the missionaries went to visit the Şeyh on a day when he was not

---

[10] The Bebek School in Istanbul, the first institution of formal secondary education founded
      by the American missionaries on the Ottoman soil, gains the status of divinity school for
      good in 1856. The Bebek School moves to Merzifon in 1860 (Kocabaşoğlu, 1989: 81–85).
      For a comprehensive study on missionary schools in Anatolia see Kocabaşoğlu (1989).

at home, they were welcomed by the Şeyh's wife and son, and after Şeyh's arrival they read the Bible with him and conversed all night. The report conveys that fifty families from the region had converted to Protestantism yet they were expecting an educator, and that an aide was arranged to be sent to the Şeyh for a few months. As a last word, the Şeyh's son is mentioned as guiding the missionaries as they left the region (Winchester, 1861: 72–73).

The American missionaries visited the Şeyh's house again in 1866 in the village Mescit–which they reported as almost all were Protestant. In this report, the Şeyh's brother and children are described as intelligent yet almost all of them illiterate, and these people, while Muslim in name, are reported to be "pagan," practicing religion around their Şeyh. The report also recounts that they accepted the Bible brought by Armenian Protestants decades ago; yet, some households who accepted it had been attacked by other Kurds. The report also includes that these people were disappointed in the help they received from the missionaries; the Şeyh asked whether they could help his sons to be exempted from the military service, and in response he was told this can only happen when they deserve to be defined as Protestants (Herrick, 1866: 68–69).

It can be argued that the reason why Kizilbash chose Protestantism had more to do with their own appeals for reform rather than the teachings of Reformation (Kieser, 2010: 116). For instance, the dismissal of *tarık*–an important ritualistic object in the *cem* ceremony (Alevi, Bektashi, Kizilbash worship) which was regarded as a continuation of paganism and pantheism in the missionaries' reports–constitutes one of the most important reforms (Perry, 1880: 185). *Tarık*, also known as *"erkan," "evliya,"* and *"dest-çûp"* is a stick regarded sacred and used in the *cem* rituals of the *ocak*s connected to the *Dedegan sürek*. In the *cem*s of communities affiliated with Çelebi *sürek*, who is believed to be the son of Hacı Bektaş Veli, *pençe*, which means *"pençe-i âli abâ,"* and *"beşli"* representing the Ehl-i Beyt, is used. The dismissal of *tarık* in the rituals of Araboğulları, the leader of the fifty families mentioned in the missionary reports, is also related to similar discussions seen in Ağuçan *ocak* and other *ocak*s later on.[11] Also the aforementioned distinction between *"Tarikatçı"* and *"Hakikatçı"* seems to be related to this. An important detail for our discussion is that those who left the *tarık* for *pençe* are

---

11 The *tarık-pençe* issue, a source of discussion as well as a paper topic in itself, is an important issue mentioned by a number of researchers working on Alevi, Bektashi and Kizilbash since the early twentieth century (Yörükân, 2002: 468, 469; Gölpınarlı, 1977: 323–326; Dersimi, 1997: 109–112; Onarlı, 2001: 190–193; Koca, 2000; Munzuroğlu, 2000). For two articles where the issue of *"Kiştim marı,"* first mentioned by Nuri Dersimi, is discussed within this context see Özgül (2001); Yıldırım (2012). Also on the use of *tarık* stick as a ritual object during the Safavids see Morton (1993). As it can be seen from these studies, this issue goes way back than the nineteenth century and has several important details awaiting further examination.

called *"purut"* or *"dönük."*[12] However, it is not clear whether this naming has to do with the Alevis and Araboğulları who established a relationship with Protestants in the second half of 1800s or whether it was used as a more general term. Additionally, the question of whether those who opted for *pençe* in lieu of *tarık* before Araboğulları are also described as *"purut"* still awaits a response.[13]

While there are 20 reports about the Kizilbash in the missionary records of 1855–1861, there are only 6 reports in the period of 1861–1880 (Karakaya-Stump, 2015: 228). This situation points to the fact that the missionaries entered a new phase in their relationship with the Kizilbash, and the Kizilbash's request for protection did not meet with the desired response. Yet, these reports did not give a clear indication of whether Protestants lost their hope with the Kizilbash, and if so, when this happened. Even though there are no written records of what happened to Araboğulları during this period and in its aftermath, the oral narratives note that they were exiled to Sarız, Kayseri.[14] That there is still a rather large group of Araboğulları followers around Sarız shows, even partially, factuality of this narrative. However, this is regarded as more of a "self-imposed exile" rather than a "formal, enforced exile" since Sarız, relatively close to Mescit, is a well-known area by Araboğulları with *talip*s around.[15] According to oral narratives, Araboğulları, after spending seven years in Sarız, returned to Mescit. Yet, our knowledge about their life in Mescit afterwards and how they maintained their relationship with the Sarız region is limited. According to oral narratives, Veyis died in 1908 and Süleyman died in 1909 in Mescit (Baran, 2011: 159).[16]

---

[12] Abdülbaki Gölpınarlı asserts that during the time of Ahmet Cemalettin Çelebi the Kizilbash were divided into two: those who remained faithful to the *ocaks* and those who became faithful to the Bektashis; those following the Bektashis named the others "purut," and those remaining faithful to the *ocaks* called those following the Çelebis "dönük" (1977: 349; 1998: 81). Yusuf Ziya Yörükân presents similar commentary (Yörükân, 2002: 469). There is no information about where the name "purut" originated in these commentaries.

[13] Araboğulları's dismissal of *tarık* does not prove that they entirely opted for *pençe* or devoted themselves to the Hacı Bektaş Lodge, the Çelebis (or the Babagans). Although their followers are generally seen to lean towards the Bektashi, the most important effect of the dismissal of *tarık* is that the *muhabbet*, which will replace the *cem* ritual in the *Hakikatçi* tradition, comes to the fore.

[14] The missionary report issued in February 1880 and sent from Maraş states that only two Christian converts from the Central Anatolia have been in exile for four years and the missionaries' hands are tied about this matter (Marden, 1880: 49). Another report from the same year but from Sivas recounts that fifty families from Kangal, the very place where Araboğulları lived, converted to Protestantism; however, these people's religion is under the influence of paganism/pantheism; they are very devoted to their *şeyh* and the two leaders of this group have been sent to exile (Perry, 1880: 185). We do not know if these people were Araboğulları; yet, this period coincides with the Araboğulları's exile to Sarız as mentioned in oral narratives.

[15] There are no documents about the exile in the Ottoman archives either. For a dissertation project discussing the Ottoman documents related to this subject see Türkyılmaz (2009: 224–271).

[16] Even though there are missionary reports and some Ottoman archival documents on Araboğulları, the oral narratives about *Hakikatçilik*, which followed Araboğulları and

Figure 2: The tomb of Şeyh Süleyman and Araboğlu Veyis, in the village Mescit (photo by Mahir Polat, 2015).

Hakikatçilik *as a Religious Movement*

The foundational steps the Araboğulları took during their exile in Sarız paved the way for their leadership in the movement that would later take the name "*Hakikatçilik.*" Şıh Mamo (1840–1921), from Kırkısrak village of Sarız, emerges as one of the most important figures to receive their blessing and take their faith system as a guide.[17] After Araboğulları's return to Mescit, *Hakikatçilik* spreads in "*İçtoroslar*" (Anti-Taurus hinterland) including the region of Kayseri-Maraş and–

gradually turned into a religious movement within Alevism, include some information which, at times, cannot be proven with documents. In this respect, the subject encompasses a wealth which still requires a detailed archival work and field study. Also, the memoirs, poems of the people involved in this movement and/or accounts by their relatives constitute a rather large corpus.

[17] Şıh Mamo's real name is Mehmet Akyol yet he is known as Mamki Kose in his own region. In 1906, German geographer and researcher Hugo Grothe visited Kırkısrak village where Şıh Mamo lived, narrated his observations, and included an interview he conducted with a bearded old man, approximately fifty years old, in his book (Grothe, 1912: 148–161). According to Mehmet Bayrak, this man who responded the questions in a whimsical manner is Şıh Mamo (Bayrak, 2006: 158). The term "*Şıh*" refers to "*şeyh*"in the region. Thus, the movement, in this region, is also called "*Şıhlık*" and the hamlet where Şıh Mamo lived is referred as "*Şıhlar Obası.*" For an article on Şıh Mamo see Ülger (2014b).

Figure 3: The tomb of Şıh Mamo (1840–1921), (Ülger, 2014b: 15).

partially—Malatya, not in the Sivas-Dersim region (Bayrak, 2006: 2015).[18] Thus, one can argue that the movement known as *Hakikatçilik* or *Hakikatliler* is born after the Araboğulları. It is widely known that everyone affiliated with this movement in the following years showed great respect to the Araboğulları, established an emotional bond with them, and visited the village Mescit.[19]

---

[18] The region referred as "Anti-Taurus," "*İçtoroslar*" or "*Orta* (Mid) *İçtoroslar*," in the sources is a wide area that coincides with the territory of Dulkadiroğlu Beyliği which controlled the region from the period of the *beylik*s until the mid-sixteenth century. This region covers a rather large area including Darende, Akçadağ, and Doğanşehir of Malatya; Besni and Gölbaşı of Adıyaman; Islahiye, Yavuzeli, and Araban of Antep; Kadirli, Kozan, Saimbeyli, Tufanbeyli and Bahçe of Adana; Sarız and, partially, Pınarbaşı of Kayseri; Gürün of Sivas (Bayrak, 2006: 13).

[19] For instance, Halil Öztoprak (1892–1967), the son-in-law of Şıh Mamo and one of the leading figures of *Hakikatçilik* in the twentieth century, visits Mescit village frequently. For a memory from one these journeys see Öztoprak (1994: 109–111). Öztoprak wrote his famous work "*Kur'an'da Hikmet Tarihte Hakikat ve Kur'an'da Hikmet İncil'de Hakikat*" (The Wisdom in the Qur'an The Truth in the History and The Wisdom in the Qur'an The Truth in the Bible) during a long stay in the *muhabbet* room at Araboğulları's house (narrated by Mahir Polat).

Although it is difficult to trace Araboğulları's relationship with Protestantism after the missionary reports, we can say that this relationship had an "enlightening" influence rather than that of a Christian one.[20] The emergence of *Hakikatçilik* as a religious movement is under the influence of the reforms within Alevism undertaken by the Araboğulları. That the Araboğulları, despite coming from a family with *dede*s, did not maintain *dedelik*, left behind the basic rituals (*cem, tarık*, etc.) of *dede ocak*s, and revealed a tendency—given the information we have, at least mentally—towards Bektashilik, determines the path of *Hakikatçi* tradition that would give shape to the later period. Moreover, the flexibility regarding marriage between a *dede* and *talip*; multiple *müsahiplik* (religious brotherhood); abolition of *hakullah* (donation); dismissal of *tarık* (ritual object); abolition of borders in villages; equal sharing of goods along with a number of other changes constitute Araboğulları's most notable legacy both during their own time and afterwards. Seydi Özcan summarizes the faith system of those belonging to this movement as impartial, egalitarian, solidarist, and tolerant (Özcan, 2011: 262).

In the words of Hamdullah Erbil, the grandson of Meluli (1892–1989)—one of the most important *âşık*s of *Hakikatçilik* in the twentieth century—Araboğulları, by giving up the position of *dede*, attempted to follow Bektashilik through the path of *hakikat* (Özpolat, Erbil, 2006, 32). Therefore, it is possible to interpret the issue of "*hakikat*" as both "enlightenment" in terms of faith and a goal that aims to reach the most difficult aspect of Alevi-Bektashi thought.[21] Also, in this perspective, the issue of Araboğulları's and then the *Hakikatçi*'s relationship with Bektashilik carries an "ideational" and "spiritual" leadership. Meluli talks about their relationship with Bektashilik (Özpolat & Erbil, 2006: 33):

We have never been to Bektashi *tekke*s, we do not perform at *tekke*s; however, we got together with mature, virtuous, perfect Bektashi *mürşit*s, performed together. We took les-

---

[20] It is not sufficient to explain the lives of Araboğulları and the following *Hakikatçilik* through "conversion" and "being influenced by the missionaries." There are still so many questions about, first of all, the issue of Araboğulları's "*hakikat*," the source of their religious and social leadership, whether this is a historical continuation of a different "*yol* (religious path)," and how we can trace this issue within the context of Alevism. Other issues for further examination include whether this movement developed outside the Baba Mansur *ocak*, what kind of responses it elicited from other *ocak*s, and whether it had any influence on Babagan and Çelebi *sürek*s other than the Dedegan *sürek*.

[21] The door of "*hakikat*," the last stage of the "*dört kapı, kırk makam*," (four doors, forty steps) the basic principle of Alevi-Bektashi faith, is the final step that has to be taken in order to reach the goal of becoming "kamil insan" (perfect human). On this subject, for more information from the *Buyruk*, one of the essential, written Alevi sources, see Aytekin (1958: 9–10, 29–31). For a comprehensive study where the concepts of *hakikat* and *hakikatlilik* are discussed from a philosophical point of view see Williams (2002). For another discussion about *hakikat* from comparative study of Derrida and İbni Arabi, see Almond (2004). Almond states that Ibni 'Arabi's intricate and hierarchical system is like Wittgensteinian ladder that one can be kicked away out from under one's feet after it has been climbed (Almond, 2004: 14). This is the same hierarchical system of Alevi-Bektashi *hakikat* belief.

Figure 4: Aziz Baba (1894–1969), (Özcan, 2001, cover).

sons from them, got inspiration from them. In fact, all the inspiration we have got is in humans, the divine inspiration lies in humans.

Özcan, describing Apeseyd (1860–1932)–father of Aziz (Özcan) Baba (1894–1969) who will play a significant role in the development of *Hakikatçilik* in the twentieth century–Kangallı Araboğlu and Akçadağlı Dümüklü Ali[22] as the three leaders of *Hakikatçilik*, notes that Apeseyd, who is in the business of cattle trade, met Araboğlu and Ali Dümüklü in his every visit to Sivas and Malatya (Özcan, 2009: 15). Özcan, in another study, states that, during the time of Apeseyd, Araboğlu was one of the two important figures in the regional Alevi community and the other was Şıh Mamo of the village Kırkısrak of Sarız, Kayseri; he also

---

[22] Dümüklü Ali, who can be regarded as the continuation of this movement in Malatya, Akçadağ region, is also known as Şeyh Ali. For detailed information on Dümüklü Ali, who attempted to follow a similar path to the *Hakikatçi* and was murdered during a military raid to his village in 1895, see Şahhüseyinoğlu (1993: 63–68).

mentions that Apeseyd and Şıh Mamo got together every once in a while (Öz-can, 2001: 58–59). Hence, Araboğulları's recognition in the region of Kayseri, Maraş and Malatya can be seen to have increased during their time. Later, the development of *Hakikatçilik* is founded on this ground.

Another movement, which relationship with Araboğulları, and its extent, is unbeknownst to us, emerged in Erzincan. Hüseyin Özcan, who comes from a family called "*purot*" or "*hırpani*" in Erzincan, regards this movement, "*Purotluk*," a "contemporary interpretation of Alevism," and states that the movement started in this region in the 1830s and went through three stages (Özcan, 2007: 99): Foundation and Formation (1830–1915); Development (1913–1960); Disin-tegration and Dissolution (from 1960 until today).[23] For Özcan, the leading rea-son for the development of this movement is the Anatolian Alevism's need to renew itself in accordance with the changes in the world in the nineteenth and twentieth centuries, and its resistance to zealotry (Özcan, 2007: 97).[24] Özcan's approach also points to the "enlightening" aspect of this movement. We observe a commonality between the *purot* movement in Erzincan and the *Hakikatçi* movements in Sivas-Kayseri-Maraş route with regard to their perspective toward Alevism and daily life: Examples include rejection of certain traditions such as the *dedelik* institution, *hakullah*, bride price, ostentatious ceremony and weddings. Furthermore, in terms of "enlightenment," the importance of education and commitment to literacy come to the foreground in all of these movements.

Despite its apparent contrast to the idea of enlightenment, the fact that schol-ars from the *Hakikatçi* tradition were curious about the Quran, and even the Bi-ble, and wrote about them reveals another remarkable point in terms of the in-terest in literacy. The most famous figure among those, Halil Öztoprak, conducted a comprehensive research on this subject with his work "*Kur'an'da Hikmet Tarihte Hakikat ve Kur'an'da Hikmet İncil'de Hakikat.*"[25] Also several other

---

[23]   1830s also happen to be the period when the American Protestant missionaries started their activities in Anatolia. Yet, we do not have any information about the Erzincan *purots*' relationship with the Protestant missionaries and Araboğulları, who lived nearby at that time. Moreover, the fact that the leaders who are regarded as the founders of *purot* move-ment had close relationships with Varna, Bulgaria hints that this issue may have a history older than the arrival of Protestant missionaries to Anatolia. In this respect, whether the purot or *Hakikatçilik* has a past going before 1830s and its expansion emerges as another important issue requiring further examination. For *purots*' relationshio with Varna see Öz-can (2007: 108–114). While it is beyond the limits of this study, an important sidenote re-lated to this subject: For American missionaries' activities in Bulgaria see Aydın (2008).

[24]   In the nineteenth century, another group called "*porit*" is known as Anşabacılar. This community was founded by a *dede* named Veli Baba, who had abandoned the Hubyar *ocak*. Anşabacılar has been prosecuted by the Ottomans and accused by the Hubyars as "infidel" or "heretic" (Okan, 2016: 100). As can be seen from this example, "*purotluk*" issue is a subject that needs to be investigated by itself in the nineteenth century.

[25]   Bayrak, criticizing the publications described as "religious folklore books" by some *Haki-katçis* such as Halil Öztoprak, remarks that these books are used as a tool of assimilation

Figure 5: Halil Öztoprak (1892–1967), (Öztoprak, 2006, cover).

authors working on the *Hakikatçi* in the following years, such as Ali Bektaş and Seydi Özcan, made references to these subjects. In addition, it is possible to see a profound idea of Sufism with references to the Quran in the poems of *Hakikatçi âşık*s such as Ali Haki and Haydari. Thus, we can construe the "enlightenment" approach not as an elimination of the religious aspects of Alevism, but rather as an attempt to draw on any idea that can reach the "*hakikat*" as aimed by Alevism and eliminating the normative aspects of the religion in the meanwhile.

The issues of education and literacy that gradually gained more significance during the development of *Hakikatçilik* are also influenced by the dynamics of the nineteenth century. Meluli, one of the important *âşık*s of *Hakikatçilik*, attended the Armenian school in Afşin as a child. Therefore, another outcome of the enlightenment which can be thought to have started with the *Hakikatçi*'s ini-

---

(Bayrak, 2016, 120–125). This criticism also concerns the current controversial Islamic debate on Alevism.

tial relationship with the American Protestant missionaries is the followers' relationship with other local groups, especially Armenians, in their own regions.[26] In this respect, the *Hakikatçi* can be regarded as the representatives of the late-Ottoman rural "Enlightenment" (Kieser, 2004: 355). The impact of the nineteenth century developments on the *Hakikatçi* revealed itself, on the one hand, as "enlightenment," and on the other hand, as oppression from the state (Kieser, 2004: 357):

> In the third quarter of the nineteenth century, in the period before Abdülhamid II, Alevi villages and tribes had already tried to access modern education and protection via the American missionaries. Under the influence of these missionaries' puritanism -a mixture of individual spirituality and Enlightenments ideals- tribal chiefs and others questioned the *dede* system and compelled a revision of religious practices. Some changes, aimed at eliminating "superstitious traditions", as reported in missionary documents, seem indeed to have been initiated at that time. But the attempt to escape a world where they were tolerated perhaps, but certainly discriminated against economically, via outside help was considered by the authorities as a threat to the existing order and repressed accordingly.

Well-versed *âşık*s who either grew up in this tradition or committed themselves to it at a young age and improved themselves on different levels enabled the development and dissemination of the *Hakikatçi* thought. *Hakikatçilik*, spreading to the different corners of Anatolia vis-à-vis these *âşık*s, circulated in Alevi, Bektashi and Kizilbash communities for years through other *dede*s, *âşık*s and *zakir*s (music performers in *cem* ritual). Another reason is the flexibility in the *Hakikatçi* movement's rituals and the emphasis on the gatherings where *âşık*s' lyrics come to the fore. The *Hakikatli* do not have *vaaz* (sermon), *secde* (prostration) and *semah* (Alevi ritual dance); prayer and rituals in the *cem* leave their place to *muhabbet*; *secde* and *niyaz* are replaced with *görüşme* (meeting) (Özcan, 2011: 270). *Muhabbet* is composed of the following sections: conversation about worldly problems, reading and discussion of religious and philosophical books, and reciting *deyiş*s (Alevi, Bektashi, Kizilbash poem) with *bağlama*s (Özcan, 2011: 270–271). *Görüşme* refers to the act of those who are on the path of sufism kissing each other's faces in an attempt to beseech Hakk's (truth) beauty (Özcan, 2011: 271–272). Thus, the *âşık*s growing up and performing in the *muhabbet* atmosphere have emerged as the most predominant power and bearer of this movement.[27]

---

[26] The relationship between the Alevi communities and Armenians in the nineteenth century, a subject deserving a thorough examination in itself, can present important clues about the context of this study as well. In this respect, there is a need for the examination of the written Armenian sources from this period.

[27] For more detailed information about the religious life, communal structure and subjects discussed in the *muhabbet meclisi* of the *Hakikatçis* see Özcan (2001: 44–45, 134–140).

Manifestation of Hakikat *Thought:* Hakikatçi Âşıks

The Kangal province of Sivas, where the Araboğulları were influential in the mid-nineteenth century, along with the Şarkışla and Divriği regions can be described as the homeland of the most important *âşık*s of the period. The impact of the Araboğulları's faith on the *âşık*s well-known in the region at that time requires an examination on its own. Many *âşık*s affiliated with different *ocak*s, and some of them belonging to Hacı Bektaş *dergah* (lodge) became known in this period. Several *âşık*s, for instance Sıtkı–originally from Tarsus but located in Şarkışla–İğdecikli Veli, Şarkışlalı Agahi and Kul Sabri, Divriğili Feryadi (Deli Derviş), are known with their poems and music spreading to all Anatolia not only during their own time but also afterwards.[28] Kul Sabri maintains a long-time friendship with Sıtkı, Agahi and Halimi (Aslanoglu, 1985: 104). Most of these *âşık*s have the greatest influence on the upbringing of another *âşık* from Şarkışla who will leave his mark on the twentieth century, Âşık Veysel (Aslanoğlu, 1973: 16–19). Also, it is possible to come across poems of the same *âşık*s in other performers' (continuing the *Hakikatçi* tradition), such as İbrahim Erdem, *muhabbet* and album repertoires in later periods.

The information we have about Agahi among these *âşık*s bears significance to disclose some of the relationships with regard to the dissemination of *Hakikatçilik* in the Maraş region after Sivas: the father of Agahi's *müsahip*, Rahim Ağa, is the most important *dede* of the Üryan Hızır Ocak in Alakilise (Eskiyurt) village of Gemerek, Sivas (Aslanoğlu, 1985: 13). Meluli also talks about this family who has moved from Persor village of Erzurum–one of the central villages affiliated with the Üryan Hızır Ocak–to Sivas in the mid-nineteenth century: Şıh Mamo, who enabled the dissemination of the *Hakikatçi* in Kayseri, Maraş and Malatya region after Araboğulları, had an influence on Meluli's maternal uncle Ali's passage to Bektashism. Yet, the person who actually raised him is Rahim Paşa–known as "*Hakikatçi Dede*" in his own circle–who was originally from Erzurum and moved to Sivas. Köse Ahmet Dede, Rahim Paşa's nephew, is one of the *dede*s visiting Kötüre village where Meluli lived (Özpolat, Erbil, 2006: 31).[29] Thus, as we trace the *Hakikatçi* tradition in the region from Sivas to Maraş, it is also possible, especially through the *âşık*s' relationship with one another or their interaction, to gain new knowledge about the mobility and circulation of Alevi communities.[30]

---

[28] In the nineteenth century, several important *âşık*s gained recognition in especially Kangal and Şarkışla provinces of Sivas. For a collected work on the *âşık*s of this period see Aslanoğlu (1985). For Ruhsati, one of the important *âşık*s of the same period and region, see Kaya (2013). For *âşıklık* tradition in the region of Emlek, which also includes Kangal, see Kaya (1999).

[29] I would like to thank Mahir Polat again for informing me of the use of "*paşa*" referring to "*ağa* or "*dede*" in the region where the Üryan Hızır Ocak is located.

[30] Another interesting point about Agahi is his close relationship with Halil Paşa, who was stationed in Sivas during 1894–1899 and then appointed as the Governor of Beirut

The emergence of strong *âşık*s within the *Hakikatçi* movement in different regions contributed to the circulation of the *Hakikatçi* thought across different geographies through the *deyiş*s performed by these *âşık*s. This circulation affected both the Alevi communities with different *sürek*s and the Sunni scholars in the region. Although the Araboğulları resided in Sivas, Kangal, the *âşık*s following their tradition were known to be born in Kayseri-Sarız, Malatya-Akçadağ and Maraş, and exhibited a rigorous mobility among these regions.[31] In this respect, most of the *âşık*s who would, later, maintain the *Hakikatçi* thought in their poetry and *muhabbet*s were born and grew up in the triangle among Kayseri, Maraş, and Malatya. These *âşık*s deeply influenced other Alevi *âşık*s who are not affiliated with the movement, and even the Sunni *âşık*s. For instance, Osman Dağlı (Maksudi, 1936–2007), who is known in the region, is one of them.

Those who belong to the *Hakikatçi* tradition following Araboğulları are usually known to live in villages with *talip*s from Baba Mansur and Ağuçan *ocak*s. In Mescit village where the Araboğulları lived, in addition to Turkish, Kurdish and Zaza are also spoken (Baran, 2011: 147). Kurdish is usually spoken in the villages located on the Anti-Taurus route where this movement is spread; however, almost all of the *âşık*s growing up in this movement—with the exception of a few works in Kurdish—wrote their poetry and books (*divan* or prose) in Turkish.[32] Ali Haki and Haydari, greatly influenced by sufism and *divan* poetry, employed both *aruz* and syllabic meter in their poems infused with Arabic and Persian idioms. However, the influential *âşık*s of later period such as Meluli, Mücrimi and İbreti preferred performing their poems in lucid Turkish and syllabic meter. These *âşık*s are also experts of satire, their subject matter ranging from the issues of Alevism to daily life.

(Aslanoğlu, 1985: 17). Halil Paşa, who is rumored to be Alevi or lean towards Alevism, is also mentioned within the context of Protestantism in the Ottoman archives. An archival document dated October 11, 1894 states that the Governor of Sivas supported the Bektashis, and the Kizilbashes, during their conscription, tried to refuse serving in the army saying, "We are Protestants." (BOA Y.PRK.UM. 30/85).

[31] For comprehensive collections on *Hakikatçi âşık*s see Bayrak (2006: 459–668; 2015; 2016: 237–428); Özcan (2009). Also, for independent publications about the *âşık*s: for the *divan* of Ali Haki (1889–1961), who also used the pseudonyms of Hicrani, Figani, Ednai, Gulami, Harhari and Visali, see Kömür (2007); for the *divan* of Haydari (1872–1942), see Kömür (2010); for Meluli (1892–1989) see Özpolat, Erbil (2006); Kieser (2004); for Mücrimi (1882–1970) see Özdemir (2007); for İbreti (1920–1976) see Vaktidolu (1996); for Mikail Aksoy (1930–1994) see Çiltaş (2002). For more information about Ali Haki and related *âşık*s, visit the web-site of a foundation under his name which was founded in London in 2015: Ali Haki Edna Vakfı, https://www.ahev.org.uk/ (accessed 28 December 2017).

[32] Apeseyd–who was influential in the development of *Hakikatçilik* during the time of Şıh Mamo–and his son Aziz Baba's tribe (Gini/Ginyan) and their villagers (Küçük Söbeçimen) speak Zaza (Dımili) language (Özcan, 2001: 44–45; 73).

Figure 6: From left to right, Ali Haki (1889–1961), (AHEV, 2017); Meluli Baba (1892–1989), (Özcan, 2009: 9); Mücrimi Baba (1882–1970), (Özdemir, 2007, cover).

There are also female *âşık*s, such as Afe Ana, Kör Fatma, Sâdıka Ana, Zeliha Ana (Fedakar), among *âşık*s who belong to the *Hakikatçi* tradition and come out of *muhabbet*s (Bayrak, 2015: 102–110, 164–177).[33] Afe Ana, whose poetry speaks of her devotion to Şıh Mamo, is especially, a powerful female *âşık* influencing a number younger generation *âşık*s such as Osman Dağlı (Maksudi) (Dağlı, 2004: 48). In the regions affiliated with *Hakikatçi* tradition, there is an unique accumulation of folk culture in addition to literature and music.[34]

In *âşık* literature, the traces of different *âşık*s who created their own style and school are known as "*âşık kolu*." Doğan Kaya encapsulates this concept as such: "*Kol* is a school where *âşık*s growing up in the master-apprentice tradition and professing their devotion to the master *âşık*–the focus of identity–maintain and continue the language, *ayak*s, tunes, themes, memories and stories of him" (Kaya, 2013: 98). Although whether *Hakikatçi âşık*s constituted a *kol* as such is open for discussion, *Hakikatçilik* clearly functioned as a "school" for these *âşık*s. The main characteristic of *Hakikatçi âşık*s is that the dissemination of an Alevi-oriented religious movement to a large territory mainly occurs through *âşık*s; yet, rather than a master-apprentice hierarchy, this relationship is mostly maintained

---

[33] Another important note about the female *âşık*s is the poems Meluli's granddaughter wrote under the pseudonym Latife. These poems include references to the men's world from the perspective of a female *ozan* and present a playful, joking style through as implied by the pseudonym ["*Latife*" means joke in old Turkish]. For these poems and commentary see Özpolat, Erbil (2006: 271–289, 449–450). We see a similar case in Alevi-Bektashi poetry tradition with Edip Harabi, who employed a female pseudonym and satirized men. For Harabi's poems written under female pseudonym see Gümüşoğlu (2008: 40–41, 214–215, 329).

[34] For two comprehensive studies on humor, elegies, and tombstones in the *Hakikatçi* Alevis of Binboğalar region (located centrally in Kırkısrak village, Sarız, Kayseri) see Ülger (2013, 2014a).

through close interactions and *muhabbet*s among *âşık*s from different regions. Araboğulları's ideational legacy and the folk myths about them as well as the *muhabbet*s of later leaders such as Şıh Mamo and Aziz Baba greatly figure in these *âşık*s' interaction with one another.

Starting with the 1930s, Aziz Baba's house in the village Küçük Söbeçimen, Sarız becomes the first place where the pieces of *âşık*s such as Ali Haki and then Meluli, Mücrimi and İbreti are performed in the *muhabbet* meetings (Özcan, 2009). Some of the important *bağlama* performers of this environment were Haydar Bayrak, Ali Sayılır, Hacı Bayrak and Ali Bektaş. While Ali Haki and Meluli did not perform with *bağlama*, İbreti played the *bağlama* masterfully. Bayrak recounts that, in the *Hakikatçi* meetings, works by *âşık*s such as Ali Haki and Haydari were performed during the 1930s and 1940s; from the 1950s on works by *âşık*s such as Meluli and Mücrimi started to attract more attention (Bayrak, 2016: 250). In the witness accounts of this period, playing the *saz* and reciting *deyiş*s, conversing about *hakikat* and bringing those principles to life constitute the main obligations (Özcan, 2001: 134–140; Bektaş, 2011: 27–29). In addition to these *âşık*s, Şükrü, Öztoprak, Şıh Hatayi who were born in the nineteenth century also wrote strong poems. İbrahim Erdem, Ademi, Firkati, Perişan Güzel, Perişan Ali, Kul Hasan, Kul Ahmet, Nesimi Çimen, İsmail İpek, Vicdani, Meçhuli, Emekçi, Maksudi, Hüdai and Mahzuni can also be listed as some of the *âşık*s born in the twentieth century, again raised in the Anti-Taurus region, and influenced by the *Hakikatçi âşık*s (Bayrak, 2016: 250).

Özcan states that, today, the *Hakikatçi*s only live in some of the villages of Sarız, Elbistan, Afşin, Pazarcık, Akçadağ, Kangal and Zara (Özcan, 2009: 171). These aforementioned regions include Sivas, Kangal and Zara region where the Araboğlu thought first started, and Kayseri, Sarız; Malatya, Akçadağ; Maraş, Elbistan, Afşin and Pazarcık where it spread later. Thus, what started in Sivas spread to and developed in Maraş and its environs until today. In this respect, it is no coincidence that most *âşık*s growing up in this tradition are from Maraş. Nonetheless, even though Araboğulları are from the Baba Mansur *ocak* it is possible to find the traces of Ağuçan and Sinemilli *ocak* (the Ağuçan *ocak* is their *mürşid* (mentor) in the areas influenced by *Hakikatçilik*.[35] Especially the Sinemilli

---

[35] As a side note related to the Ağuçan *ocak* and the *Hakikatçi*s, the story of Cafer Tan, who moved with his family from Karaca village of Hozat to İncemağara village of Sarız, Kayseri in 1904, is quite interesting: the most well-know figure of Cafer Tan's family is Gangozade Yusuf Ağa, the leader of the Karabal branch of Şeyh Hasanlılar tribe and a powerful political figure who held the *dedes* of Ağuçan *ocak* under his auspices. Yusuf Ağa is also mentioned in the missionary reports from the nineteenth century and in Nuri Dersimi's memoir. He founded a private medrese in his village and later sent the family members schooled in this medrese to the Aşiret Mektebi (Bayrak, 2006: 488). Tan's father İsmail Efendi is a well-known figure in the region and taught a number of *Hakikatçi*s, most importantly Aziz Baba, in Sarız province. Cafer Tan grew up with Aziz Baba in Sarız, and then participated in *muhabbet*s with the *Hakikatçi*s. Tan is, also, the father-in-law of famous ozan Nesimi Çimen. For the relationship between Tan and Aziz Baba see Özcan (2001:

Figure 7: Ali Sayılır (1918–1963) with his wife Emey Ana; İbreti Baba (1920–1976) on the right side (personal archive).

*dede*s from Maraş region with strong musical performance frequently employed the works of *Hakikatçi âşık*s such as Ali Haki, Haydari, Meluli and Mücrimi in their *cem*s and *muhabbet*s.[36]

Throughout the centuries, *âşık*s, *zakir*s, *dede*s and performers carried the musical culture of Alevi, Bektashi and Kizilbash communities, specifically with forms based on lyrics, across regions and placed it in circulation.[37] We observe that the *Hakikatçi* tradition also puts emphasis on a musical form based on lyrics. That the *cem* ritual left its place to *muhabbet meclisi* and there is no *semah* in this tradition led to the dismissal of musical and literary forms employed in the *cem*, such as *semah*, *miraçlama*, *tevhid*, forms by *Hakikatçi âşık*s. This outcome caused the musical structure to follow the lyrics solely. Since *âşık*s performing with the *dede sazı* or *cura* instruments of *bağlama* family, or virtuoso performers who are not *âşık*s paid utmost attention to recount all the lines of a poem, they strived to prioritize the lyrics over the *bağlama* in their performances. These works, focusing on sometimes satire and sometimes philosophical sufi themes, emerge through the performance of musical sentences generally influenced by the musical culture of the region and recited in the local *ağız* (idiom). For instance, we can state that the *bağlama* performance and the powerful vocal musical performance of the *âşık*s and *dede*s affiliated with Sinemilli *ocak* interacted with the

---

72). For the relationship between Tan and Mücrimi see Özdemir (2007: 13). For Tan's poems under the pseudonym Cafer see (Bayrak, 2006: 488–490).

[36] For an album compiling the Sinemilli *ocak dede*s' *deyiş*s see Özdemir (1998). Also, according to Bayrak, the *Hakikatçi* Alevism movement influenced the Dedegan Alevism in the region and moved it to a more society-oriented, humanist position (Bayrak, 2015: 85).

[37] For a discussion on the sources of Alevi music see Özdemir (2018).

*Hakikatçi âşık*s living in the same region. Nevertheless, some performers exhibited an original performance style unique to themselves. İbrahim Erdem comes first in the line of these performers. Erdem, who had been to the same meetings with the preceding *Hakikatçi*s and quite prolific during his lifetime, is the most important source to comprehend the *Hakikatçi âşık*s' approach to the lyrics and the *bağlama*.

The Last Generation in the Line of Hakikatçi Âşıklık Tradition: İbrahim Erdem

İbrahim Erdem (1925–2014), known as Erdem Baba, was born in the Darıca village of Kürecik, Akçadağ, Malatya.[38] He completed his military service in 1948. He moved to Mersin in 1953, to Tepebaşı village of Afşin in 1955 and then to Sarız in 1960. During 1969–1970, he worked in France. He relocated to Bielefeld, Germany in 1971. He worked as a street vendor in Mersin, as a farmer in Tepebaşı village and as a carpenter in Sarız; he then worked in factories in France and Germany before he retired in 1990 (Özcan, 2009: 42). After this date, Erdem started travelling between Turkey and Germany. After spending his last days bedridden, he passed away in Germany (Bayrak, 2016: 385).[39]

We do not have any information about İbrahim Erdem's relationship with music as a child; yet, it is safe to assume that he became involved with *bağlama* at a young age and was present in *muhabbet*s quite often. Erdem's meeting with Meluli, the figure who influenced him most from early on, constitutes an important point for the steps he would take in the path of *Hakikatçilik*. Erdem recounts his first visit to Meluli (Özpolat & Erbil, 2006: 42):

> Meluli was always the focus of our conversations from afar. First, we played and performed his poems. (…) we still do. When I, with Musa Hazar, visited him in the village in October 1952, I was twenty six years old. I still have very vivid memories of the beautiful conversations we had during our three-day visit. Those three days became the beginning of a new understanding and faith for me.

The time İbrahim Erdem met with Meluli also coincides with the period when he met with the most important figures, such as Aziz Baba, that enabled the development of *Hakikatçilik* in its later stages. The different settings he frequented during this time serve as a school where he not only matured in the *Hakikatçi muhabbet*s but also learned about the works of various *âşık*s. His move to Sarız in

---

[38] This region is also where the aforementioned Dümüklü Ali lives. Darıca and Dümüklü villages are part of Akçadağ. İbrahim Erdem is also known as İbik-i Kurçe in the region (Ülger, 2014: 13).

[39] As far as we learned from Demos Yayınları, a book about İbrahim Erdem's life and poetry is being prepared by researcher Mehmet Kömür and it will be published in 2018.

Figure 8: İbrahim Erdem (1925–2014), (photo archive of Kılavuz Bakır).

1960s also takes place at the same period.[40] He meets and befriends the contemporary *Hakikatçi*s such as Haydar Bayrak, Ali Haki, Halil Öztoprak, Musa Hazar,
Ali Sayılır, Haşimi and Bimar in the villages of Kırkısrak, Dallıkavak, Söbeçimen,

---

[40] Mehmet Kömür states a letter which he received from Belgian Jurg Marius—another missionary in the footsteps of the German missionary Hugo Grothe, who came to the Kırkısrak village in 1902. In this letter, Marius says that he arrived in Sarız in 1962. During this
visit, Marius met İbrahim Erdem and a special dialogue occurred in between. Marius tells
that these people whom he met in Sarız called themselves *ruhani* (spiritual). After living in
Sarız for a while, Marius fell in love with a girl, but he couldn't marry with her and after a
while he was detained in Ankara and deported from Turkey. For more details about Jurg
Marius and İbrahim Erdem's dialogue, see Kömür: http://www.alevinet.com/2017/
03/14/yabanci-misyonerlerin-gozunde-hakikatci-alevilik/ (accessed 28 December 2017).
This example is also interesting in terms of the missionary relationship that has continued
up to the present day which began with Araboğulları.

Sarız (Bayrak, 2006: 501). Özcan elaborates on the relationship between the difficulties in Erdem's life, his progress in the path of *Hakikatçilik* and the development of his repertoire (Özcan, 2009: 43):

> He performed the Alevi-Bektashi classics Derviş Ali, Dertli, Gedayi, Gevheri, Harabi, Hatayi, Kemteri, Kul Himmet, Kul Hüseyin, Nesimi, Pir Sultan Abdal, Seyrani, Sıtkı, Veli and Virani at first; local poets that he personally knew, such as Haşimi, Hicrani and Mücrimi, in the second phase; Meluli's *deyiş* as recommended by Aziz Baba in the third phase, and after 1970s he mostly performed his own works. His difficult life matured him. He was self-sacrificing. Despite spending almost all his youth abroad to provide for his crowded family and losing his son at an early age, he managed to keep the beauty of his heart and mind. He was expressing his sorrows through *saz* and *deyiş*; taunting God and fate; directing criticism to the social structure and corrupt order that ignored his talent and skills. He was a real representative of the *Hakikatli*. He was honest and straightforward; he was virtuous, suiting the meaning of his name. He had a wide repertoire of *deyiş*. He would respond to the conversation and questions in friends' *meclis* by reciting *deyiş* with his *saz*, making explanations in line with Hakk *âşık*s' principles.

In contrast to most of the *Hakikatçi âşık*s, Erdem recorded albums from the 1970s on and became known with his works in the music market; yet, instead of participating in concerts, programs etc., he did not leave the *muhabbet*s, and gained popularity in Anatolia and Europe with his albums circulating among people. Aziz Baba's son Seydi Özcan notes that İbrahim Erdem made his first album in 1975—only after Özcan's insistent demands—and made the second one almost a decade later; since these albums were recorded and circulated in Germany, Erdem did not gain considerable recognition in Turkey (Özcan, 2009: 43). However, considering that Erdem's works were included in the TRT repertoire and performed by different artists, he has clearly become more well-known. Here are his works included in the TRT repertoire:

Kime Kin Ettin de Giydin Allar*[41]*
TRT Rep. No: 2516, Examination Date: 21.06.1984
Region: Malatya
Source: İbrahim Erdem
Compiler: İbrahim Erdem, Yavuz Top
Notated by: Yavuz Top

Sabahdan Cemalin Seyran Eyledim*[42]*
TRT Rep. No: 2854, Examination Date: 31.10.1986
Region: Malatya
Source: İbrahim Erdem
Compiler, Notated by: Nazmiye Özgül

---

[41] Lyrics belong to the *Hakikatçi âşık* Ali Haki. Ali Haki wrote this piece under the pseudonym Hicrani.
[42] Lyrics belong to Pir Sultan Abdal.

Figure 9: TRT music notation of "*Kime Kin Ettin de Giydin Alları*" song.

Gine Vedalaştı Dildarı Yaren[43]
TRT Rep. No: 2856, Examination Date: 31.10.1986
Region: Malatya, Akçadağ, Bekir Uşağı
Source: İbrahim Erdem
Compiler, Notated by: Nazmiye Coşkun

Also, as evinced from the singles of İbrahim Erdem issued by Aşkın Plak in the 1970s, Erdem must have recorded these albums in Turkey before he moved to Germany. He released a few singles in Germany as well. On the singles', Erdem's name appears as Âşık İbrahim Erdem. These are the pieces performed in the singles are known today:[44]

IS-93: *Ne Kaçarsın Benden* / Player and Performer: Âşık İbrahim Erdem
IS-94: *Hikmeti Lokmana Sor* (*Mersiye*) / Player and Performer: Âşık İbrahim Erdem

IS-103: *Hacı Bektaş Gibi Sultanımız Var* / İbrahim Erdem
IS-104: *Gel Softa Bizlere Kem Gözle Bakma* / İbrahim Erdem

IS-105: *Tabip Sen Sorma Derdimi* / Lyrics: Mücrimi Baba / Music and Performer: Âşık İbrahim Erdem
IS-106: *Cihane Değişmem Yar Seni* / Âşık İbrahim Erdem

IS-107: *Gam Yeme Divane Gönül* / Lyrics: Osman Dağlı / Âşık İbrahim Erdem
IS-108: *Mübtelayım* / Âşık İbrahim Erdem

IS-207: *Yazıktır* / Compiler and Performer: Âşık İbrahim Erdem
IS-208: *Suçum Nedir* / Compiler and Performer: Âşık İbrahim Erdem

VS-104: *Tabip Sen Sorma Derdimi* / Âşık İbrahim Erdem
VS-105: *Kaçma Benden* / Âşık İbrahim Erdem

The lyrics in Erdem's single performances include the poems of *âşık*s with whom he met at *muhabbet*s or those who influenced him. These poems include the works by *Hakikatçi âşık*s like Mücrimi and Meluli as well as younger generation *âşık*s, like Maksudi, who followed their path. In some of the singles, Erdem's name appears under "music," and in some others, under "compiler." That we come across similar phrases in the folk music and *âşık* singles (and even in the

---

43 Lyrics by Haydari.
44 IS references are from Aşkın Plak label in Istanbul, VS references are from Türk Müzik label in Cologne. Besides these singles, I also have the recording of "*Kime Kin Ettin de Giydin Alları*" taken from a single. Therefore, the number of Erdem's singles are more than those given here.

Figure 10: İbrahim Erdem's "*Tabip Sen Sorma*" single from Aşkın Plak (personal archive).

TRT Folk Music Repertoire) issued in the same period points to the difficulty of pinpointing the accuracy of these terms.[45]

In his first album after the singles, "*Başı Pare Pare*," İbrahim Erdem performs the poems of Hasreti (Hamdullah Çelebi), Hicrani, Meluli, Fakir, Veli, Nesimi, Fevziya (Feyzullah Çelebi), and Genç Abdal in addition to his own works penned under the name Erdem.[46] In his second album "Erdem," he sings pieces from Sıtkı, Kul Hüseyin, Gevheri, Pir Sultan Abdal, Noksani and Ruhi. His third album "Erdem Baba – Deyişler," issued in Turkey in 1994, includes only Meluli poems with the exception of one poem from Dertli.[47] In all these three albums, there are works composed by Erdem. Erdem, in the recordings for this album,

---

[45] This issue still constitutes a point of friction in copyright discussions related to folk music in Turkey. For an article discussing the terms such as composition, compilation etc. in folk music see Uslu (2012).

[46] Since we have limited information about the issue dates of Erdem's albums, it is not possible to provide the albums' exact issue dates in Turkey and Germany.

[47] Erdem is the first and only person to introduce Meluli to an international audience (Özcan, 2009: 53).

Figure 11: İbrahim Erdem (Erdem Baba), (photo: archive of Kılavuz Bakır).

uses either a long-necked or *tambura*-sized *bağlama* tuned in *bağlama* tuning be-tween D – F sharp tonics.

İbrahim Erdem's process of obtaining the lyrics of "*Azm-i Rah Eyledi Gurbet Elleri*" – a song that he performs in his second album as well as in his *muhabbet*s, and later on performed by several other artists – and of composing it epitomizes the interaction and communication among the *Hakikatçi*s. Here is the original story of this song, whose lyrics were written by Âşık Sıtkı for his mürşid Ahmet Cemaleddin Çelebi (Özcan, 2009: 43, 44):

> Erdem produced high quality compositions. The most impressive and emotional is probably the one that starts with the line "*Azm-i rah eyledi gurbet elleri.*" Here is the story: At the beginning of the First World War, The Third Army fighting in the Caucasian Front retreats after defeat. Upon a call from Hacı Bektaş *Tekkesi Postnişini* Cemaleddin Efendi, whom the Palace appealed for help, volunteers from all Anatolia organize into "*Alevi alayları*" in Erzincan. Famous poet Sıtkı Baba, who joined one of these *alay*s as a captain from Hacı Bektaş *Tekkesi*, writes this *deyiş* on the occasion of Cemaleddin Efendi's return to Hacı Bektaş after inspecting the aforementioned *alay*s and making up-lifting speeches. He gives it to one of the volunteer cavalries, Abdullah Mehmet (my paternal uncle: S. Özcan), and after his discharge he gives it to his uncle-in-law Aziz Baba. The Haydar Bulut, Ali Sayılır and Musa Hazar trio takes the *deyiş* from Aziz Baba, and İbrahim Erdem takes it from the trio and composes it.

İbrahim Erdem, in his album and *muhabbet* performances, didn't prefer to per-form instruments like *dede sazı* and *ruzba*–played by *dede*s and *âşık*s around Malatya and Maraş where he lived for a long time. He preferred to play different sizes of *bağlama* with *tezene* (plectrum) instead of *pençe* or *şelpe* (hand stroke), the bare-hands performance style. Erdem, who paid particular attention to play each melody clearly, instead of *âşıklama*–the act of hitting all chords at the same time–uses musical sentences related to this performance style in all the pieces he composed. He refrains from fast-paced and rhythmic sentences. For example, in Erdem's compositions and performances, one come across less rhythmic phrases or repetitions common to musical forms performed within the *cem* such as *semah*, *miraçlama* or *tevhid*. Also, improvisational elements are quite rare in Erdem's performances. Erdem, in his different performances, attempted to perform the poems sung with a conventional musical sentence in the same way at all times. In other words, he does his best to remain faithful to the "music" of the poems. In his performance of *arasaz* (instrumental part), he strives to enforce the musical sentence in the lyrics by repeating it with the *bağlama*.

İbrahim Erdem shows great virtuosity in performing *mersiye* or *uzun hava*-formed, meterless or free style pieces. He maintains a calm and self-assured style in both his *bağlama* and vocal performance. Erdem's main performative characteristic, his principle of composing the poetry of *âşık*s from different periods and performing them in their entirety, can be observed in both his album and *muhabbet* recordings. Erdem, in all his album recordings, performs Turkish *deyiş*s. However, it has been noted that he, every now and then, performed *deyiş*s in Kurdish during *muhabbet*s.[48]

Conclusion

As far as we can gather from the available sources, an original religious movement, which would later take the name *Hakikatçi*s and goes back to the period when Şeyh Süleyman and his son Veyis–*seyit*s belonging to the Baba Mansur *ocak* which relocated to Sivas from Dersim–established a relationship with the Protestant missionaries, came into shape in the Anti-Taurus region during the second half of the nineteenth century. This movement not only led to great changes in the regional Alevi communities' performance of rituals and daily lives but also paved the way for the emergence of a significant cultural legacy. Several scholars coming out of this movement and taking up leadership positions in communities affiliated with the movement became instrumental in raising numerous *âşık*s and creating an ideational effect on *âşık*s not affiliated with the movement. This *âşık* generation, born in the late nineteenth century and produc-

---

[48] Bayrak, noting that he compiled two Kurdish *kılam*s from Erdem, conveys two quatrains from these poems (Bayrak, 2016, 385). Erdem, in a video recording of a *muhabbet* (03.10.2000), is seen as performing works in Kurdish (different than the ones compiled by Bayrak) from two *âşık*s with the pseudonyms Sevdalı and Kul Fakir.

ing a large number of works throughout the twentieth century, enabled the emergence of a highly invaluable tradition for both general folk literature and the Alevi-Bektashi literature.

Another important aspect of the *Hakikatçi âşık*s is their musical performance. In this tradition, where a lyrics-oriented music is performed through a musical style that follows the lyrics, there are several performers who play the *bağlama* and sing. These virtuoso *âşık*s who write and sing their own works also performed the works of other *Hakikatçi âşık*s. Various Alevi communities across Anatolia performed and circulated the works of these *âşık*s, who were in close contact with the *dede*s and *âşık*s from the Sinemilli *ocak* in their own regions.

While *âşık*s like Ali Haki, Haydari and Meluli, whom we can group under the first generation *ozan*s, did not play the *bağlama*, other figures like İbreti and Mücrimi played the *bağlama*. This generation also influenced the next generation of *âşık*s, such as Mahzuni, Perişan Ali, Perişan Güzel, Hüdai, Meçhuli, Emekçi, and led to the emergence of one of the most important sources for folk music in general, and Alevi music in particular, from 1960s on in Turkey. The most important works of popular music starting in the 1970s, "*Anadolu Pop*," also came from these young *âşık*s. Yet, these *âşık*s who entered the music market usually left the *Hakikatçilik* behind and produced new works, inspired by the *Hakikatçilik*, appealing to different communities. Therefore, *Hakikatçilik*, for these *âşık*s, brought forth a new opportunity to progress in the path of *âşıklık*.

With the exception of few, the *âşık*s who stayed away from the music market and embraced the *Hakikatçilik* as a life style did not make any singles or albums. İbrahim Erdem, whom we can describe as the last representative of this tradition, is the most important exception. Erdem, who recorded singles during the 1970s and later recorded a few albums in his original style, still did not want to become part of the music market; and instead of concerts and programs he preferred to perform in *muhabbet*s. In his own works, Erdem, who brought about a powerful musical expression of the *Hakikatçi* thought coming from the Araboğulları to today, interweaved the relationship between the lyrics and music through an emphasis on the former. Having close followers among the folk music audience thanks to his powerful voice and style, Erdem stands out as a noteworthy source for today's young Alevi musicians with his works, performance and stance.[49] In contrast to the Alevism emerging in the public space after the 1980s and its ever-renewed manifestations, Erdem, whose recordings passed from hand to hand, carried the *Hakikatçi* thought to the twenty first century with his constantly circulating works.

---

[49] For different audio and video recordings of *Hakikatçi âşık*s, visit two popular YouTube channels of their followers: Ol Adular Bize Meyhur Demişler, https://www.youtube.com/channel/UCkzNj5e723mGhFUsGMjDktw/videos (accessed 28. December 2017); Ata Durak, https://www.youtube.com/channel/UCf34VVJXi3oCHMoqfWot_sw/videos accessed 28. December 2017).

Acknowledgements

I am deeply grateful to my dear friend and colleague Mahir Polat, whose ideas served as a source of inspiration for me and who did not hesitate to share the field study data from his doctoral dissertation studies at Istanbul University.

References

Archival Sources

BOA, (Başbakanlık Osmanlı Arşivi [The Prime Minister's Ottoman Archives]), Y.PRK.UM. 30/85).

Books and Articles

AHEV (Ali Haki Edna Vakfı) (Ed.) (2017). *Ali Haki.* London: AHEV Yayınları.

Almond, Ian (2004). *Sufism and Deconstruction: A Comparative Study of Derrida and Ibn 'Arabi.* London: Routledge.

Akpınar, Alişan, Sezen Bilir, Serhat Bozkurt, Namık Kemal Dinç (2010). II. Abdülhamit Dönemi Raporlarında "Dersim Sorunu" ve Zihinsel Devamlılık. In Şükrü Aslan (Ed.). *Herkesin Bildiği Sır: Dersim,* (311–333). Istanbul: İletişim Yayınları.

Aslanoğlu, İbrahim (1973). Veysel'i Yetiştiren Çevre Şairleri. *Sivas Folkloru.* Vol.. 5, 16–19.

– (1985). *Söz Mülkünün Sultanları.* Istanbul: Erman Yayınevi.

Aydın, Mithat (2008). *Bulgarlar ve Ermeniler Arasında Amerikan Misyonerleri.* Istanbul: Yeditepe Yayınları.

Aytekin, Sefer (Ed.) (1958). *Buyruk.* Ankara: Emek Basım-Yayınevi.

Baran, Mamo (2011). *Koçgîrî: Kuzey-Batı Dersim.* 2. ed. Ankara: Seresur-Kızılbaş Yayınevi.

Bayrak, Mehmet (1997). *Alevilik ve Kürtler.* Ankara: Özge Yayınları.

– (2006). *İçtoroslar'da Alevi-Kürt Aşiretler.* Ankara: Özge Yayınları.

– (2015). *İç-Toroslar'da Oda Kültürü ve Kürtçe Edebiyat.* Ankara: Özge Yayınları.

– (2016). *Kürt Bâtıniliğinde Kutsal Metinler.* Ankara: Özge Yayınları.

Bektaş, Ali (2011). *Ehlibeyt-i Âl-i Resul'e Karşı İç Muhalefet: Alevilik ve Sünniliğin Ortaya Çıkışı.* Ankara.

Bliss, Edwin Elisha (1910). *Condensed Sketch of the Missions of the American Board in Asiatic Turkey.* Boston: American Board of Commissioners for Foreign Missions.

Coşkun, Hasan (2014). *Geleneksel Alevi Sosyal Örgütlenmesi "Sivas Kangal Türkmen Alevileri Örneği"*. Necmettin Erbakan University, Social Science Institute, Unpublished PhD. Konya.

Çiltaş, Süleyman (Bathasica Hektor) (1993). *Binboğalı Kökçüler*. Istanbul: Can Yayınları.

— (1999). *Binboğalı Son Kökçüler*. Istanbul: Can Yayınları.

— (2000). *Zöre Zöre*. Istanbul: Can Yayınları.

— (Ed.) (2002). *Dost Aşkıyla Yanan Bilir*. Istanbul: Can Yayınları.

Dağlı, Osman (Ozan Maksudi) (2004). *Ara Beni, "Kırk Yıllık Hasret Bitti", Şiirler*. Ankara: Alternatif Sanat.

Deringil, Selim (1999). *The Well-Protected Domains: Ideology and the Legitimation of Power in the Ottoman Empire 1876–1909*. London, New York: I.B.Tauris Publishers.

Dersimi, Nuri (1997). *Kürdistan Tarihinde Dersim*. Istanbul: Doz Yayınları.

Dressler, Markus (2013). *Writing Religion: The Making of Turkish Alevi Islam*. New York: Oxford University Press.

Gezik, Erdal (2013). Rayberler, Pirler ve Mürşidler: Alevi Ocak Örgütlenmesine Dair Saptamalar ve Sorular. In Erdal Gezik, Mesut Özcan (Eds.). *Alevi Ocakları ve Örgütlenmeleri*. Ankara: Kalan Yayınları.

— (2016). *Geçmiş ve Tarih Arasında Alevi Hafızasını Tanımlamak*. Istanbul: İletişim Yayınları.

Gölpınarlı, Abdülbâki (1977). *Tasavvuf'tan Dilimize Geçen Deyimler ve Atasözleri*. Istanbul: İnkilâp ve Aka Kitabevleri.

— (1998). İslam Ansiklopedisi "Kızılbaş Maddesi". *Folklora Doğru*. Vol. 63: 79–88.

Grothe, Hugo (1912). *Meine Vorderasienexpedition 1906 und 1907*. Vol. 2. Leipzig: Verlag von Karl W. Hiersemann.

Gümüşoğlu, Dursun (2008). *Ahmed Edîb Harâbî Dîvânı, Yaşamı ve Tüm Şiirleri*. 2. ed. Istanbul: Can Yayınları.

Herrick, Mr. (1866). Visit to the "Protestant Koords". *The Missionary Herald*. Vol. 62: 67–69.

Irmak, Hüseyin (2010). Osmanlı Belgelerinde Dersim'e Dair Bazı Örnekler. In Şükrü Aslan (Ed.). *Herkesin Bildiği Sır: Dersim*, (245–267). Istanbul: İletişim Yayınları.

Jewett, Dr. (1858). Sivas. *The Missionary Herald*. Vol. 54: 109–113.

Karakaya-Stump, Ayfer (2015). *Vefailik, Bektaşilik, Kızılbaşlık: Alevi Kaynaklarını, Tarihini ve Tarihyazımını Yeniden Düşünmek*. Istanbul: Bilgi Üniversitesi Yayınları.

Kaya, Doğan (1999). "Emlek Yöresinde Âşıklık Geleneği". *I. Emlek Yöresi ve Çevresi Halk Ozanları Sempozyumu, 16-17 Mayıs 1998*, (142–153). Ankara.

— (2013). *Âşık Ruhsatî*. 6. ed. Sivas: Sivas Belediyesi Kültür Hizmeti.

Kieser, Hans-Lukas (2004). Alevilik as Song and Dialogue: The Village Sage Melûli Baba (1892–1989). In David Shankland (Ed.). *Anthropology, Archaeology and Heritage in the Balkans and Anatolia or the Life and Times of F. W. Hasluck (1878–1920)*, (355–368). Istanbul: Isis. Vol. 1.

— (2005). Iskalanmış Barış: Doğu *Vilayetleri'nde Misyonerlik, Etnik Kimlik ve Devlet 1839-1938*. Translated by Atilla Dirim. Istanbul: İletişim Yayınları.

— (2010). *Nearest East: American Millenialism and Mission to the Middle East.* Philadelphia: Temple University Press.

Koca, Şevki (2000). Anadolu Kızılbaş Süreklerine Dair Etnolojik Tesbitler: Sofyan Sürekleri. *Cem Dergisi*. Vol. 103: 34–37.

Kocabaşoğlu, Uygar (1989). *Kendi Belgeleriyle Anadolu'daki Amerika: 19. Yüzyılda Osmanlı İmparatorluğu'ndaki Amarikan Misyoner Okulları*. Istanbul: Arba Yayınları.

Kömür, Mehmet (2007). *Ali Haki Edna Divanı. Hayatı, Yaşam Felsefesi, Şiirleri*. Istanbul: Demos Yayınları.

— (2010). *Haydarî Divanı. Hayatı, Yaşam Felsefesi, Şiirleri*. Istanbul: Demos Yayınları.

Maden, Fahri (2012). *Bektaşilerin Serencamı*. Istanbul: Kapı Yayınları.

— (2013). *Bektaşî Tekkelerinin Kapatılması (1826) ve Bektaşîliğin Yasaklı Yılları*. Ankara: Türk Tarih Kurumu Yayınları.

Marden, Henry (1880). Central Turkey. *The Missionary Herald*. Vol. 76: 44–50.

Morton, Alexander H. (1993). The Chūb-i Tarıq and Qizilbash Ritual in Safavid Persia. ed: Jean Calmard (Ed.). *Études Safavides*, (225–245). Paris, Teheran.

Munzuroğlu, Doğan (2000). Tarıq: İnsanın Kullandığı İlk Alete Tapması. *Munzur: Dersim Etnografya Dergisi*. Vol. 4: 76–90.

Okan, Nimet (2016). *Canların Cinsiyeti: Alevilik ve Kadın*. Istanbul: İletişim Yayınları.

Onarlı, İsmail (2001). *Şeyh Hasan Aşireti: Anayurt'tan Anadolu'ya*. Istanbul: Aydüşü Yayınları.

Özcan, Hüseyin (2007). *Aleviliğin Çağdaş Bir Yorumu Purotluk Üzerine Denemeler*. Izmir.

Özcan, Seydi (2001). *Şeman-Söbeçimen ve Aziz Baba Aleviliği*. Ankara.

— (2009). *Alevilik ve Hakikatliler*. Ankara.

— (2011). *Alevilik ve Sorunları*. Ankara.

Özdemir, Ulaş (1998). *Ummanda: Maraş Sinemilli Deyişleri*. Istanbul: Kalan Müzik.

— (2007). *Şu Diyâr-ı Gurbet Elde: Âşık Mücrimî'nin Yaşamı ve Şiirleri*. Istanbul: Pan Yayıncılık.

— (2018) (forthcoming). Between Debate and Sources: Defining Alevi Music. In Johannes Zimmermann, Benjamin Weineck (Eds.). *Text and Cultural Heritage:*

Sources on Alevism Between Philological Research and Theological Canonization. Heidelberg: Peter Lang.

Özgül, Vatan (2001). Kiştim Marı (Evliyası) ve Tarik-Pençe Kavgası. *Türk Kültürü ve Hacı Bektaş Veli Araştırma Dergisi*. Vol. 18: 33–44.

Özpolat, Latife, & Erbil, Hamdullah (2006). *Melûli Divanı ve Aleviliğin, Tasavvufun, Bektaşiliğin Tarihçesi*. 2. Ed. Istanbul: Demos Yayınları.

Öztoprak, Halil (2006). Kur'an'da Hikmet Tarihte Hakikat ve Kur'an'da Hikmet İncil'de Hakikat. 6. ed. Istanbul: Demos Yayınları.

Öztoprak, Haydar (1994). *Yazar Halil Öztoprak'ın Yaşam Çizgisi ve Yıktırılan Köyünün Acı Öyküsü*. (Special Edition).

Perry, Mr. (1880). The Kuzzlebash Koords. *The Missionary Herald*. Vol. 76: 184–185.

Soyyer, Yılmaz (2005). *19. Yüzyılda Bektaşîlik*. Izmir: Akademi Kitabevi.

Şahhüseyinoğlu, H. Nedim (1993). *Kürecik*. Ankara: Sanat Yapım Yayıncılık.

Taylor, J. G. (1868). Journal of a Tour in Armenia, Kurdistan, and Upper Mesopotamia, with Notes of Researches in the Deyrsim Dagh, in 1866. *Journal of the Royal Geographical Society of London*. Vol. 38: 281–361.

Türkyılmaz, Zeynep (2009). *Anxieties of Conversion: Missionaries, State and Heterodox Communities in the Late Ottoman Empire*. Unpublished PhD thesis. Los Angeles: University of California.

Ulusoy, A. Celâlettin (1986). *Hünkâr Hacı Bektaş Velî ve Alevî-Bektaşî Yolu*. 2. ed. Hacıbektaş.

Uslu, Recep (2012). Müzik Terimlerindeki Karmaşanın Akademik Çalışmalara Yansıması: Orijinal, Nazire, Çeşitleme, Varyant, Aranjman, Cover, İcra. *İdil Sanat ve Dil Dergisi*. Vol. 2: 144–165.

Ülger, Ali Haydar (2013). *Binboğalarda Duyguların Sesli ve Sessiz Tanıkları: Ağıtlar ve Mezar Taşları*. Ankara: Ürün Yayınları.

– (2014a). *Binboğa Kızılbaşları: Hakikatçi Alevilerde Mizah (Fıkralar)*. Ankara: Ürün Yayınları.

– (2014b). Şıx Mamo (Mamîk-i Kose) ve Binboğa Hakikatçileri. *Kızılbaş Dergisi*. Vol. 36: 10–14.

Vaktidolu, Adil Ali Atalay (Eds.) (1996). *Aşık İbreti. İlme Değer Verdim*. Istanbul: Can Yayınları.

Williams, Bernard (2002). *Hakikat ve Hakikatlilik: Soykütük Üzerine Bir İnceleme*. Translated by Ertürk Demirel. Istanbul: Ayrıntı Yayınları.

Winchester, Mr. (1861). Sivas. *The Missionary Herald*. Vol. 57: 70–73.

Yıldırım, Rıza (2012). Kiştim Marı: Dersim Yöresi Kızılbaş Ocaklarını Hacı Bektaş Evlâdına Bağlama Girişimi ve Sonuçları. *Tunceli Üniversitesi Sosyal Bilimler Dergisi*. Vol. 1: 1–21.

Yörükân, Yusuf Ziya (2002). *Anadolu'da Alevîler ve Tahtacılar*. Ed. By Turhan Yörükân. 2. ed. Ankara: Kültür Bakanlığı Yayınları.

Internet Sources:

Ali Haki Edna Vakfı, https://www.ahev.org.uk/ (accessed 28 December 2017).

Ata Durak. YouTube Channel, https://www.youtube.com/channel/UCf34VVJX
i3oCHMoqfWot_sw/videos (accessed 28 December 2017).

Kömür, Mehmet. "Yabancı Misyonerlerin Gözünde Hakikatçi Alevilik", http://
www.alevinet.com/2017/03/14/yabanci-misyonerlerin-gozunde-hakikatci-alevi
lik/ (accessed 28 December 2017).

Ol Adular Bize Meyhur Demişler. YouTube Channel, https://www.youtube.
com/channel/UCkzNj5e723mGhFUsGMjDktw/videos (accessed 28 December 2017).

A Genre of Oral Poetry, the Fann, in the Alawi Community in the Hatay (Antioch) Province of Turkey

Mahmut Ağbaht

1. Introduction

This study deals with the *fann*, a genre of oral poetry in the Alawi[1] community in the Hatay (Antioch) province of Turkey. These poems, *fanns*, are composed by people known as *finnāns* in the local vernacular and display a variety of themes. The analysis here is based mainly on eleven *fanns* taken from the raw recordings made for the documentary entitled *Finnên*,[2] and partly on the field research carried out by the author. After discussions of the social role regarding the *fanns*, their content and form, the eleven aforementioned *fanns* are themselves presented and transcribed with translation.

Hatay province is located in the southernmost part of Turkey, bordering Syria, with a population of more than 1,5 million. Arabic is spoken in Hatay by Alawis, Sunnis, Christians and Jews, of which the Alawis are the biggest Arabic-speaking group.[3] In Hatay, Arabic maintains its existence only as a vernacular.

---

[1] Often also called Nuṣayri or Nuṣayri-ʕalawi. Most of the people in the community prefer to be named as Alawi or Arab Alawi (Mertcan, 2013: 305–308). For an overview on terminology and identity see Procházka-Eisl & Procházka (2010: 19–23).

[2] The documentary was among the finalists for the TRT (*The national public broadcaster of Turkey*) Documentary Awards 2013, in the amateur category. It is available online with Turkish, English, and German subtitles, see Evecen (2012). The raw recordings made for the documentary consist of more than five hours of recordings, which were collected by Gökhan Evecen and Nihat Çay between 2010 and 2012. Note that the raw recordings were not collected for an academic purpose, therefore many questions that could have helped us to a better understanding of certain aspects of the tradition still remain to be asked. I am grateful to Nihat Çay and Gökhan Evecen for sharing with me all the raw recordings and also for helping me confirm some data regarding the interviewees. I am also thankful to Prof. Dr. Eleanor Coghill for her contributions in the conception of this chapter and her valuable help in reviewing the *fanns'* translations; also to Ana Iriarte Díez and Prof. Dr. Paul A. Yule for their guidance in stylistic matters. Prof. Dr. Werner Arnold, Prof. Dr. Stephan Procházka, and Dr. Andreas Fink were very generous with valuable comments. Any deficiencies are my own responsibility. I thank the DAAD for its support during the actual publication phase of my study.

[3] The majority of the population is Turkish Sunni, but nearly half of the population is of Arab origin, regardless of whether they still speak Arabic or not. The last census that included the language question was in 1965, so it is not possible to give an exact figure for the Arabic-speaking population in Hatay. Doğruel (2005: 31) estimates the number of Alawis in Hatay to be roughly 400,000. The Arabic dialects spoken in the province belong linguistically to the Syro-Palestinian group, and they consist of two main types: bedouin

Therefore, in contrast to the diglossic situation in the Arab countries, the Arabic spoken in Hatay has scarcely interacted with the standard variety of Arabic, but rather with Turkish, since Hatay became a part of Turkey in 1939. Almost all Arabs in Hatay are illiterate in Arabic. A few, mostly from a religious background, are able to read and write in Classical Arabic, with a limited knowledge of the grammar (see Arnold, 1998: 1–3; 2000: 357–359).

Although the Arabic dialects spoken in the province have been described linguistically,[4] to this date, no thorough academic work has been done on the oral literature of these dialects. Therefore, a description of a genre of oral poetry in these dialects is not only significant for the field of oral literature studies in the Arabic dialects in general, but also necessary since Arabic is in decline in the province.

2. Social Aspects of the Fann Tradition

The Arabic dialects spoken by the community possess two words roughly corresponding to English 'poet', namely *finnān* (pl. *finnānīn*) and *šāʕir* (pl. *šiʕʕār*). While *finnān*[5] refers to the person who composes a *fann*, a poem in the local vernacular, *šāʕir* refers to the person who writes a *šiʕr*[6] (pl. *šʕūra* or *ʔašʕār*), a poem in

---

and sedentary. While bedouin dialects are spoken only by Sunni communities, the sedentary ones are spoken by all the religious communities. For the characteristic features for each type see Arnold (1998: 6–8; 2000: 358–360).

[4] The main descriptive work on the Arabic dialects of Hatay is *Die arabischen Dialekte Antiochiens* (1998) by Werner Arnold.

[5] Although the word *finnān* is cognate with the word *fannān* (masc.), *fannāna* (fem.) 'artist' in Modern Standard Arabic (Wehr, 1979: 853), the dialects spoken in the community use the word *ṣanaččī* (masc.), *ṣanaččī* (fem.), a Turkish loanword to refer to an 'artist'. Note that the feminine form of the word *finnān* is not attested so far in the dialects of the community, which reflects the fact that all known *finnāns* are men. Barthélemy's definition of the word *fannán* (1935: 623) in the neighbouring dialects is similar: "auteur qui compose des chansons et les chante lui-même en public" (the author who composes songs and sings them himself in public).

[6] *Šiʕr* is mainly produced by shaykhs, the religious leaders of the Alawi community, who, unlike the majority of the Arab population of Hatay, are able to read and write classical Arabic, although their knowledge of grammar, acquired at home, may be limited. Abū al-Faḍl Muḥammad ibn al-Ḥasan al-Muntaǧab al-ʕāni (born in the 4th century, Islamic calendar) and al-Makzūn al-Sanǧāri (born in the 6th century, Islamic calendar) are iconic figures among Alawis. The community considers them to be among their greatest poets. Their poems were written in the classical poetic style. Later poets tried to imitate the poems of this era, but did not follow this style and introduced dialectal features (see Reyhani, 1997: 50–59). Nowadays in Hatay few shaykhs are able to write in the classical poetic style. The most famous of this small group is Mahmut Reyhani (1920–2015), who was known in the community not only as a *šāʕir* but also as a *naḥawi* 'grammarian'. See http://www. albabtainprize.org/encyclopedia/poet/1683.htm for an example of his poems, and Sönmez (2015: 46–48) for a reflection on his life.

Classical Arabic. A *šiʕr*, also called *qaṣīd* or *qaṣīdi* (pl. *qṣāyid*), has mainly religious content, and its use is usually restricted to private religious practices.[7]

In contrast, the *fann* (pl. *fnūn*) covers a variety of topics used in a broad range of contexts, and performed publicly. The manner of performance of the *fann* lies somewhere between song and speech, which reminds one of *sprechgesang* (as used by some German composers in early 20th century music) or *melodized speech*.[8] Both expressions, *ġinnaytu* 'I sung it' and *qiltu* 'I said it', are attested in relation to the *fann*.

Sometimes people in the community use the word *šāʕir* to refer to a *finnān*, or *šiʕr* to refer to a *fann*. The word *ġinnī* 'song' is also used in the meaning of *fann*. The word *finnān*, however, is never used to refer to a *šāʕir*. Likewise the words *fann* or *ġinnī* are never used to refer to a *šiʕr*. There are several common expressions which mean 'to compose a *fann*':

rattab fann/ġinnī	Lit. 'He arranged a *fann*/song.'
naṣab ġinnī/tizkār	Lit. 'He set up[9] a song/remembrance.'
naṣab/qāl/naẓam byāt	Lit. 'He set up/said/composed verses.'
ṭallaʕ fann/ġinnī	Lit. 'He took out a *fann*/song.'

Most of these expressions are attested in the sample itself, but some are taken from other *fanns*; the last one is attested mainly in everyday speech. On the other hand the common idioms which express 'to write a *šiʕr*' are:

katab šiʕr	Lit. 'He wrote a poem.'
naẓam šiʕr	Lit. 'He composed a poem.'

The verb *ṭallaʕ* 'to take out' is also used in relation to *šiʕr*. The expression *katab fann* 'he wrote a *fann*', however, is not attested. These semantic nuances are connected to the fact that *šiʕr* is a written poem, while a *fann* is an improvised oral poem. The degree of preparation for a given *fann* varies from pure spontaneity to one or two days of cogitation.

Usually the *finnāns* do not make written collections of their *fanns*, neither in manuscript nor in published form. One *finnān* has recounted that he wrote down his poems as they came to him, as well as others that he had heard, in an exercise book, but unfortunately this was lost. Some *fanns* have been included in anthologies of oral literature.[10]

---

7   There is one type of *šiʕr* that might be performed publicly, the *mirtī* (pl. *mirtīyāt*) 'elegiac poem'. *Mirtī* poems consist of praise for the deceased's faith and are mainly written for shaykhs and by shaykhs.

8   Amy de la Breteque (2016) described the vocal performance by senior women in the Caucasus and Anatolia as *melodized speech*.

9   The main use of this verb in the active form is in the phrase 'to pitch a tent'. See *The tent*, quatrain 2.

10 Yuşa Arış (2009; 2012; 2014; 2017a; 2017b) has published several anthologies on the oral literature of Arabic in Hatay, which include *fanns*. A few *fanns* were also documented in a

Finnāns were usually popular people who were involved in village life. They performed *fanns* on various occasions, such as at weddings (*ʕirs* pl. *ʕrūsi*),[11] group work in fields (*ʔarḍ* pl. *ʔarāḍi*), festivals (*ʕīd* pl. *ʕyād*), special celebrations (*ḥafli* pl. *ḥaflāt*), or in evening get-togethers (*sahra* pl. *sahrāt*). They could also be performed anywhere. At weddings the *finnāns* were usually accompanied by flutes (*šibbābi* pl. *šibbābāt*), drums (*ṭabᶦl* pl. *ṭbūl*) and darbukas (*dirbakki* pl. *dirbakkāt*). On other occasions they were not necessarily accompanied by instruments. *Finnāns* performed in weddings by invitation. *Finnān* İzzettin Günay/ʕizzu Badᶦr (c. 1920–2015) from Dursunlu/Darsūni village[12] told me the following:

> When I used to go to a wedding that I was invited to, I did not start to sing immediately. At the wedding the best place was reserved for me. The host came several times to request me to sing. But as soon as I started no one could stay in their seats. People clapped and danced the *dabki* for a whole hour. I was singing until the early hours of the morning. (Translated from Arabic)

The *fann* that was performed in the fields was named *raddī* 'response' (pl. *raddīyāt*). This name is derived from a special form of responsory performance. The *finnān* stood in the middle of the workers in the field and performed, while the workers would repeat each line after him as a chorus. The *finnān*'s role here was to help the workers concentrate on their work. Some informants who worked in the fields that were owned by landlords (*ʔāġa* pl. *ʔaġawāt*) or worked as seasonal workers do not have happy memories of this. One informant refused totally to speak about that time. Another reports:

---

local magazine *Yakto* (2008; 2009a; 2009b). Some *fanns* can also be found in Resul Bağı's master (2007) and PhD (2014) dissertations. All were excluded from this study for various reasons: for instance, the transcription system used is unclear, or the precise authorship or context is not given. Moreover in Bağı (2007; 2014) several key concepts are treated inadequately. For instance in (2007) the terms *fann*, *finnān*, *šiʕr*, and *šāʕir* were not mentioned. In (2014: 42, 49) the notions of *finnān* and *šāʕir* were presented as synonymous and the differences between them ignored. The very concept of *fann* was not identified. In addition to this, the author overgeneralizes with regard to the linguistic reality of the area, and calls the dialect spoken today 'broken Arabic' (*bozuk Arapça*). In fact the dialects spoken by the community in the three provinces (Adana, Mersin, and Hatay) differ somewhat from each other on various linguistical levels. The same holds for dialects spoken in rural and urban parts of the same province. The sociolinguistic situation, as regards the relative decline of Arabic, also varies from place to place. Information about the linguistic situation is available in the main academic works written on the dialects, i.e. Arnold (1998; 2000; 2002), Smith-Kocamahhul (2003), Jastrow (1983), and Procházka (1999; 2002a; 2002b), but these are not referred to.

11 The *fann* is, however, different from the *mḥāyḥāy* (or *mḥāha*), special four-line songs performed exclusively by women at weddings, as described by Procházka (2009) in his study on the Arabic dialect spoken by the Alawi community in Adana. See Rosenhouse (2000–2001) for a comparative study of women's wedding songs in the neighbouring dialects.

12 The names of the villages and the names of the interviewees are given both in their Turkish and their vernacular Arabic versions, where available. Note that they have not officially had village status since 2014, when the Metropolitan legislation (*Büyükşehir yasası*) went into effect and replaced them with official neighborhoods (*mahalle*).

My son! What I should tell you! No matter how far away the landlord was we had to sing loud enough [so he would hear us and know that we were concentrating on our work]. Thank goodness these hard days are gone. (Translated from Arabic)

Up until the last decades, the *finnāns* were not only the main providers of entertainment, but also the voices of public opinion. In fact, one could say that they played the role of local media. They reported all kinds of events, both important and trivial, in their poems, and expressed their opinions in an artistic yet also lively manner.

The *fann* tradition has been in decline over the last few decades and is scarcely a living tradition today.[13] Some *finnāns* remain, but they rarely perform in public any longer. There are several factors behind this decline. As documented for Antakya by Smith-Kocamahhul (2003), Arabic is in decline in Hatay due to the process of language shift from Arabic to Turkish. Naturally, this has affected the *finnān* tradition, as its potential audience has shrunk. Connected to the language shift is the fact that, nowadays, the local professional musicians (Turkish *müzisyen*) who are normally hired to play at weddings sing Turkish songs and perhaps some Arabic songs in the neighbouring dialects of Syria and Lebanon, rather than *fanns*.[14] Other factors in the decline of the *fann* tradition are associated with modernity and urbanization, for instance the use of modern equipment in agriculture that reduced the number of workers needed in the fields and forced many families in the villages to exchange their agriculture-based economy for other occupations.

The following two statements from two *finnāns* highlight some of the abovementioned facts:

Nowadays people follow songs which appear on television. Before, you would compose a *ginnī* 'song', another [person] would compose *miwwāls*, and another would also compose something. People were like that, not as they are today. […] [Even] when I went to my children's weddings I did not say a word unless I came across someone [I knew]. (Translated from Arabic)   Hasan Kültekin/Ḥasan Silmān

I have not said them [*fanns*] for quite a long time. No one asks for them [anymore]. (Translated from Arabic)   Salim Delioğlu/Salim Riḍwān id-Dāli

---

13 I attended several screenings of the documentary *Finnên* for the people of the community, both in Turkey (Antakya, Ankara, İzmir) and abroad (Aalen, Hannover) between 2013 and 2014. During these screenings I observed the enthusiastic and even vociferous reactions of the spectators from the older generation, which contrasted markedly with the less emotional reactions from the younger generation.

14 Some attempts to revive the tradition have been carried out, particularly by Nihat Çay, who is known for his song, *misʕūd*, which deals with people from the community who went to work in Saudi Arabia. He has also made a music album which includes some *fanns* (see Çay, 2010). Nevertheless, the tradition seems to be facing complete extinction. Cf. Prochâzka-Eisl & Prochâzka (2010: 67–68), Prochâzka (2009: 236–237), and Prochâzka (1999) on a dramatic decline in Arabic and in Arabic songs in Cilicia (Çukurova).

3. Formal Aspects

3.1. Rhyme Patterns

The number of quatrains appearing in the eleven *fanns* analyzed for the purpose
of this study–excluding any repetition–ranges between 3 and 21 per *fann*. The
first three lines of each quatrain share the same rhyme, while the fourth lines of
all the quatrains within a *fann* share one rhyme.[15] This leads us to identify them
as quatrains rather than couplets. The following model illustrates the main rhyming pattern found in *fanns*:

–b
–b
–b
–a

–c
–c
–c
–a

Only one *fann* out of the eleven, however, restricts itself exclusively to the main
rhyming pattern described above. All the others have between one and five quatrains which follow one or more other patterns. Five such patterns have been
identified:

1.	2.	3.	4.	5.
–a	–a	–b	–b	–b
–a	–a	–b	–b	–c
–a	–b	–a	–c	–b
–a	–a	–a	–a	–a

In two of them the first quatrain follows pattern 1. In another seven the first
quatrain follows pattern 2. The third pattern is attested only in one *fann* (*The cow*)
in its last three quatrains. In this *fann* there is not a single quatrain that follows
the main rhyme pattern: it uses only patterns 1 and 3.

---

[15] One of the *fanns* (*The schoolgirls*) exhibits two separate rhymes in the fourth lines of the
quatrains. The fourth line's rhyme, which in the first three quatrains is -*āt*, becomes -*ām* in
the fourth and fifth (the final) quatrains. In two other *fanns*, the fourth line's rhyme differs
slightly only in one quatrain: in one (*The Korean war*), -*ēn* becomes -*ēm* in the fourth quatrain, and in the other (*Politics*), -*āt* becomes -*āṭ* in the fifth quatrain. Afterwards it reverts to
-*ēn* and -*āt* respectively for the remainder of the quatrains.

3.2. The Metrical Structure

The following analysis is based on the quatrains transcribed for this study. The metrical structure of the *fanns* is syllabic, based mainly on seven syllables per line:

The workers, quatrain 18   *w̱ in* | *nā* | *ẓim* | *ḥā* | *za̱ l* | *ʾab* | *yāt*[16]

                                 ʿā | *le* | *ʾaḥ* | *mad* | *yā* | *sā* | *dāt*

                                 sal | *lim* | *tim* | *mo* | *w̱ id* | *day* | *yāt*

                                 rat | *tab* | *ḥal* | *ġin* | *nī* | *tis* | *kār*

Between the first two lines, or between the last two lines in a quatrain there is, however, often an extra syllable (marked in bold in the next example):

The Korean war, quatrain 4   *ḥaṭ* | *ṭū* | *nā* | *ǧiw* | *wa̱ l* | *bā* | *bū* | *ṟ*

                               ᶦw | *maš* | *šū* | *nā* | *ǧiw* | *wā* | *li̱ b* | *ḥūr*

                               qil | *na* | *yā* | *xē* | *ḏᶦr* | *das* | *tū* | *ṟ*

                               ᶦt | *raǧ* | *ǧiʿ* | *na̱ b* | *xē* | *ṟ ᶦw* | *sā* | *lām*

The attested syllables are CvC, Cv, Cv̄, and Cv̄C,[17] which appear to be the only syllables allowed. The last one may only be found at the end of the line.[18] Sometimes Cv̄ and Cv̄C syllables are realized extra-long for melodic reasons (notated here as Cv̄: and Cv̄:C). Some syllables may be lengthened or shortened in order to match one of the permitted syllables, to fit a rhyme or for melodic reasons. For instance, a final CvC syllable may be lengthened to Cv̄C or Cv̄:C, e.g.

The schoolgirls, quatrain 3   *̱ᶦw* | *biṭ* | *rā* | *nat* | *mā* | *lin* | *ʿā* | *tāb* (< *tab*)

The ox, quatrain 1   *ka* | *ṭᶦt* | *maṭ* | *rā* | *min* | *wič* | *čā:k* (< *čak*)

If a Cv̄C syllable is going to appear elsewhere in the line, then it is shortened to CvC, so as not to violate the rules, as in the following example:

The ox, quatrain 1   *la̱ ṣ* | *ṣir* (< *ṣīr*) | *mī* | *ṭᶦl* | *xuk* (< *xūk*) | *mal* | *ʿū:n*

Fashion, quatrain 2   *w̱ ir* | *riǧ* | *ǧal* (< *ǧāl*) | *ʾa̱ b* | *yit* | *naf* | *fās*

---

16   The following symbols are used for the transcription. Consonants: | *ʾ* [ʔ] | *b* | *t* | *ǧ* [dʒ] | *ḥ* [ħ] | *x* [x] | *d* | *r* | *z* | *s* | *š* [ʃ] | *ṣ* [s] | *ḍ* [đ] | *ṭ* [ŧ] | *ʿ* [ʕ] | *ġ* [ɣ] | *f* | *q* [q] | *k* | *l* | *m* | *n* | *h* | *w* | *y* [j] |. In the dialects spoken by the community, *č* [tʃ], *g* and *p* are only marginally phonemic. The old interdentals have shifted to the corresponding plosives: *t* [θ] > *t* or *s*, *d* [ð] > *d* or *z*, *ḍ* [ð̧] > *ḍ* or *ẓ* [z̧]. For more details see Arnold (1998: 33-38). Vowels: *a, i, u* (short), *ā, ē, ī, ū, ō* (long). The two vowels, *a* and *i*, are realised as [ɛ] and [i] in the environment of non-emphatic consonants, and as [a] and [ɪ] in the environment of emphatic consonants (Arnold, 1998: 46). The emphatic consonants are those realized with velarization *ṣ, ḍ, ṭ, ẓ, ḷ* [ɫ]. I did not present these aforementioned realizations of the vowels in the transcription.

17   The letter C is used to represent any consonant, likewise the letters v and v̄ are used to represent short and long vowels.

18   One exception has been found, where it is in the middle of a line (*Politics*, quatrain 2): *ᵉw* | *ʾaw* | *wil* | *sā* | *čim* | *yā̱ x* (< *yā ʾix*) | *wān*.

Original Cv syllables may be lengthened to Cv̄, which seems to be preferred to Cv, e.g.

A local hero, quatrain 2   *Ǧā* (< *Ǧa*) | *mil* | *Ḥā* | *yik* | *sab* | *ʕ‿il* | *ġāb*

The Korean war, quatrain 6   *‿w* | *šif* | *na‿d* | *dā* (< *da*) | *wal* | *maḥ* | *rū* | *rā*

The schoolgirls, quatrain 1   *‿ⁱb* | *bā* | *b‿iǧ* | *ǧi* (< *ǧi*) | *sⁱr* | *ʕa‿z* | *zay* | *nat*

Such lengthening to fit the syllabic structure of the metre may restore the Classical/Standard Arabic form:

The tent, quatrain 1   *ṣā* | *bit* | *nā* (< *na*) | *maṭ* | *ra‿g* | *bī* | *ri*

The schoolgirls, quatrain 4   *šū* | *bad* | *dī* (< *di*) | *ġan* | *nī* (< *ni*) | *tā* | *qūl*

Compare the same morphemes (marked in bold) in the following lines:

The tent, quatrain 1   *fik* | *kay* | **na‿w** | *riḥ* | **na** | *ʕa‿č* | *čā* | *dir*

The schoolgirls, quatrain 1   *lā* | *ġan* | *ni‿w* | *lā* | *qū* | *l‿ⁱb* | *yāt‿*

The lengthening of this restoration to (a further lengthening) Cv̄: is attested only at the end of the line:

The tent, quatrain 2   *xad* | *na‿t* | *taʕ* | *rī* | *qa‿w* | *riḥ* | *nā:* (< *na*)

CvC sometimes appears as a result of the resyllabification of final Cv with a consonant from the following word:

The ox, quatrain 1   *ʾaḷ* | *la‿y* | *ʕī* | *nak* | *ʾā* | *bu‿q* | *rūn* (< *ʾābu qrūn*)

In the following case, CvC arises out of the combination of a final consonant with the initial consonant from the following word, with an epenthetic vowel intervening between the two (marked in bold):

The schoolgirls, quatrain 5   *tiḥ* | *fiẓ* | *kī* | **n‿ⁱg** | *bar* | *w‿ⁱz* | *ġār‿*

Compare the following line where the same word (*tihfiẓkin*) does not undergo resyllabification:

The schoolgirls, quatrain 4   *ⁱw* | *tiḥ* | *fiẓ* | *kin* | *ṭū* | *l‿il* | *ʾay* | *yā:m*

Sometimes an epenthetic vowel is added in order to create an extra syllable and avoid CvCC, which would be a violation of the syllabic rules:

The Korean war, quatrain 1   *w‿il* | *qā* | *lⁱb* (< *qalb*) | *ʕan* | *now* | *ġif* | *lān*

The dialects spoken by the community in Hatay are known to have different types of pausal forms.[19] Pausal forms are variant forms of words found in speech

---

[19]   As documented by Arnold (1998: 43–44, 87–91, 226–227; 2010: 227–235). See also Ağbaht & Arnold (2014: 12–17) for the pausal forms attested in Dursunlu/Darsūni village, and Durand Zúñiga (2015) for a detailed analysis of pausal vowels in the dialect spoken in Tekebaşı/Ǧilli village.

at the end of intonational phrases: they involve changes in vowels and, occasionally, consonants. The following cases from the *fanns* are reminiscent of pausal forms, although they may be found also in contexts where, in non-sung speech, they would not be expected:[20]

-u > ow

A local hero, quatrain 3	*kil* | *l̬ il* | *ʕā* | *lam* | *ḥab* | *bī* | *tow* (< *tu*)
Fashion, quatrain 2	*bī* | *lib* | *s̬ il* | *mō* | *ḍa* | *zā* | *dow* (< *du*)
Fashion, quatrain 6	*w̬ⁱt* | *ʕow* (< *ʕu*) | *yā* | *nas* | *w̬ⁱq* | *šā* | *ʕow* (< *ʕu*)

Compare the final -u (marked in bold) in the following lines:

A local hero, quatrain 3	*tid* | *ʕī* | ***lu̬ b*** | *ṭū* | *l̬ il* | *ʕī* | *mⁱr*
Fashion, quatrain 1	*lib* | *s̬ il* | *mō* | *ḍa* | *zā* | ***du̬ k*** | *tīr*

-u > o

The tent, quatrain 3	*qil* | *til* | *lo* (< *lu*) | *ma̬ b* | *yit* | *ḥaw* | *wāš̬*
The wife, quatrain 2	*bad* | *do* (< *du*) | *yis* | *raḥ* | *bad* | *du̬ y* | *ṭir*

-i > -e

The workers, quatrain 1	*ʕa̬ l* | *le* (< *li*) | *ǧē* | *ri̬ ʕ* | *lay* | *na̬ w* | *ṣār*
The cow, quatrain 3	*mā* | *tit* | *mā* | *hī* | *yi̬ b* | *bā* | *le* (< *li*)

-i > -ē

The workers, quatrain 2	*ⁱs* | *kit* | *yā* | *wā* | *ḥid* | *ya̬ š* | *rī* | *kē̬* (< *ki*)
The Korean war, quatrain 1	*ta̬ n* | *ġan* | *nē* (< *ni*) | *w̬ⁱn* | *qaḍ* | *ḍi̬ ḥ* | *zāːn*
The Korean war, quatrain 4	*qil* | *na* | *yā* | *xē* (< *xi*) | *ḍⁱr* | *das* | *ṭū* | *r̬*
The wife, quatrain 2	*bad* | *du̬ y* | *ǧib* | *lē* (< *li*) | *k̬ⁱʕ* | *šā* | *fiːr*

Compare the last example with the same word in the following line (marked in bold):

The wife, quatrain 3	*bad* | *du̬ y* | ***ǧib*** | ***lik*** | *šaḥ* | *rū* | *rāt*

CiC > CeC

Fashion, quatrain 5	*baḷ* | *ḷa̬ s* | *tim* | *ʕu* | *ya̬ ḥ* | *bā* | *yeb* (< *yib*)

---

20 In addition to the above mentioned, the following cases are attested in the *fanns*: *bithimmu* > *bithimmow*, *ʕantar* > *ʕantor*, *ǧābitu* > *ǧābitow*, *rabbitu* > *rabbitow* (*A local hero*); *ʕimru* > *ʕimro*, *mkātib* > \| *t̬ⁱm* \| *kā* \| *tē* \| *b̬ⁱw* \|, *yqūlu* > *yqūlo* (*The schoolgirls*); *ḥabībi* > *ḥabībē*, *rabbi* > *rabbe*, *il-mayyi* > *il-mayye*, *bayyi* > *bayyē*, *lḥaqni* > *lḥaqne*, *xayyi* > *xayye*, *xayyē*, *qabʕit* > \| *qab* \| *ʕē* \| *t̬ ič* \|, *qilnālu* > *qilnālo* (*The tent*); *stimʕu* > *stimʕo*, *ǧiri* > \| *ǧē* \| *ri̬ ʕ* \|, *hīki* > *hīkē*, *hattiki* > *hattikē*, *rūḥu* > *rūḥo*, *ʕali* > *ʕāle*, *timmu* > *timmo* (*The workers*); *stimʕu* > *stimʕo*, *illi* > *ille*, *ʕannu* > *ʕannow* (*The Korean war*); *biʕawwiḍ* > \| *bī* \| *ʕaw* \| *wē* \| *ḍ̬ aḷ* \|, *il-ʕāli* > *il-ʕāle*, *qalbi* > *qalbe*, *qālu* > *qālo* (*The cow*); *maḥlāki* > *maḥlākē*, *šrāki* > *šrākē*, *ʔāfandi* > *ʔāfande*, *tiryāki* > *tiryākē*, *daxni* > *daxne* (*Smoking*); *maydūru* > *maydūro*, *rādu* > *rādow*, *wlādu* > *wlādow*, *ḥbāyib* > *ḥbāyeb*, *ġāyib* > *ġāyeb*, *ʔāġānib* > *ʔāġānēb*, *zdāġu* > *zdāgow*, *ʔabšāʕu* > *ʔabšāʕow*, *ḥālu* > *ḥālo*, *ḥamzi* > *ḥamze*, *timmu* > *timmo* (*Fashion*); *nṣib* > \| *la̬ n* \| *sē* \| *b̬ⁱb* \|, *miʕ* > \| *mē* \| *ʕ̬ ad* \| (*Politics*).

4. Stylistic Devices

Various stylistic devices can be identified as occurring repeatedly in the *fanns*. The verb *qāl* 'he said' appears three times at the beginning of a quatrain in two different *fanns*. In the first example, the performer, Besime, adds *qāl* at the beginning of the *fann* (*A local hero*). This could mean that she is referring to the *finnān* who composed the *fann*. However, in the second example, *finnān* Hasan Kültekin used *qāl* in his own *fann* (*The tent*), at the beginning of the first line of quatrain 2 and quatrain 4. In these cases, it is not clear who the subject of *qāl* is. In all the instances, this verb is never followed by a pause. This makes the first line of the quatrain one syllable longer than the rest. Further examples would be needed to reach a solid conclusion as far as the function of *qāl* is concerned.

Six out of the eleven *fanns* present introductory lines at the beginning of the *fann*. In three of them these lines request people to listen (Group 1 below) while two *fanns* have an expression where the *finnān* announces that he is about to perform (Group 2). Such introductions are followed by lines where the topic of the *fann* is introduced. Generally the introductory lines form part of a quatrain, but in one *fann* (*Politics*) they stand alone as a pair.

Group 1:

The workers	*baḷḷa stimʕo yā ḥiḍḍār*	Please listen, O audience!
	ʕa lle ğēri ʕlayna w ṣār	to what happened to us.
	ᵃw lākin šū ṭāliʕ bi l-ᵓid	Yet what we can do?
	hāda min ᵓaḷḷa mqaddār	This is God's will.
The Korean war	*baḷḷa stimʕo yā ᵓinsā:n*	Please listen, O people!
	ta nğannē w ⁱnqaḍḍi ḥzā:n	Let's sing and pour out our grief
	lā xābār ille ğānā:	about the news that has reached us
	w il-qālᵇ ʕannow ğiflān	of which the heart had been unaware.
Fashion	*baḷḷa stimʕūli yā nās*	Please listen to me, O people!
	ṭār il-ḥāya min ar-rās	People have no more shame.
	libs il-mōḍa zādu ktīr	In wearing fashion they have gone too far.
	ṣar maydūro kašf ir-rās	They have started walking around bareheaded.

Group 2:

The schoolgirls	*lā ğanni w lā qūl ⁱbyāt*	Let me sing and say verses
	ⁱb bāb iğ-ğisⁱr ʕa z-zaynat	for the beautiful girls at the Bridge Gate.
	niyyal min kān ⁱw min šāf	How happy is the one who has been there and seen them,
	ⁱbtiswā ʕimro w il-ḥāyāt	one might give one's life for this.
Politics	*min qīnī la nṣēb ⁱbyāt*	Let me dream up some verses
	ʕa l-xālᵇq w ad-dēmoqṛāt	about the *Halk* and *Demokrat* parties.

In one of the *fanns* (*A local hero*), the *finnān* begins with lines aimed at persuading people to listen, by highlighting the delightful effect of his poetry. This is the only example of self-praise attested among the *fanns* analysed:

yā ḥāwi ṭīb il-ʾafkār	O holder of the good thoughts
ᵗw xizlak min yaddi tiskār	take from my hand a remembrance.
la niẓmi ṣ-ṣāḥi yiskār	My composition makes the sober feel drunk
ᵗw yinxi la ṭābūr ʕaskar	and able to cope with a battalion.

Only three *fanns* mention the name of the *finnān* (in the third person). This appears in the last quatrain. It may be significant that all three of these *fanns* have introductory lines, as described above.

The workers	*w in-nāẓim hāza l-ʾabyāt*	And the composer of these verses
	ʕāle ʾaḥmad yā sādāt	is Ali Ahmad, O Sirs.
	sallim timmo w id-dayyāt	Well said and well done!
	rattab hal-ġinnī tiskār	He composed this song as a remembrance.
Fashion	*w in-nāẓim hāza l-ʾabyāt*	The one who composed these verses
	ḥamze ʾaḥmad bat li-wlād	is Hamza Ahmad from the Wlād family.
	sallim timmo w id-dayyāt	Well said and well done!
	rattab hal-ġinnī yā nās	He composed this song, O people.
Politics	*silman rīhāni w miḥyiddīn*	*Silmān Rīḥāni* and *Miḥyiddīn*
	naṣbūwa w yaḷḷah li-mʕīn	composed this, and God is their helper.
	ʾaḷḷā yilʕān it-tintaynˌ	May God damn them both:
	il-xālᵗq mēʕ ad-dēmoqṛāːt	the *Halk* and the *Demokrat* parties!

There is a considerable amount of repetition in the *fanns*, sometimes of a whole quatrain, sometimes of two lines. In four *fanns* quatrain 1 is repeated at the end of the *fann* (in two of them also elsewhere). In four *fanns* (one of them among the ones just mentioned) the first two lines of quatrain 1 are repeated later on. In two *fanns* (both of them among the ones mentioned) the first two lines of a quatrain are repeated immediately, then followed by the third and the fourth lines. In one *fann* (*Politics*), the repetition follows a certain pattern. The first two introductory lines (which form a pair, rather than a quatrain) are repeated after each quatrain (except after the last quatrain). A larger sample of *fanns* would need to be analysed to confirm the existence of a systematic repetition pattern.[21]

5. *Themes*

The *finnāns* deal with all kinds of themes, significant and trivial, in their poems. They range from accounts of events and social changes to the community's livelihood and daily life.

---

[21] We cannot assume that the *fanns*, as performed in the interviews, are as they were originally composed. Almost all the interviewees mentioned that they had forgotten several of *fanns* that they had known, or at least a part of a *fann*. It may also be that some content or the order of quatrains, including repetitions, has been altered.

Domestic livestock was an important part of the community's livelihood and two *fanns* in our sample deal with the family's animals (*The cow* and *The ox*). *The workers* and *The tent* are the other examples of *fanns* dealing with their livelihood, both of them dealing with the hardships of working in the fields. Events dealt with may be events of historical importance, such as the story of a local hero who became an outlaw (*A local hero*), the young people who left to fight in the Korean war (*The Korean war*), and a local political conflict (*Politics*), or of importance only to the *finnān* and his family, such as the death of their cow (*The cow*). Examples of *fanns* dealing with social changes are *The schoolgirls* (which also describes a historical event), *Smoking*, and *Fashion*. Only in *The schoolgirls* does the *finnān* describe the social change in a positive manner. Daily life is treated in one *fann* of the sample, namely *The wife*. Other *fanns* outside our sample also deal with subject of the *finnān's* wife.

6. The Fann*s of the Sample*

The sample on which this study is based is made up of eleven *fanns* taken from the raw recordings of the documentary. All eleven are presented here. Three (*The schoolgirls*, *The tent*, and *The wife*) are given in full, while for the others, only a selection of quatrains of particular interest are given. In the translations, I have tried to render the Arabic in idiomatic English, but have not attempted to make it rhyme, which would demand a freer translation further from the original meaning.

6.1. A Local Hero

The following is a *fann* which deals with a local hero known as Ǧamīl Ḥāyik, from a village in the district of Samandağı/is-Swaydī. Despite the passing of time, neither this *fann* nor its story, which took place towards the end of the French Mandate period (1918–1938), have been completely erased from the memories of the old generation. According to local narratives, one of the landlords in the area raped Ǧamīl's sister. Ǧamīl did not receive any help from the judicial authorities, so he shot the landlord. Being wanted as an outlaw, he settled in the mountains where he started living as a fugitive. People talked about him as a kindhearted, fair and honorable man. Sometimes people would even help him avoid being caught by the authorities, until one time the French gendarmerie finally cornered him and his brother in a house. Many gendarmes were killed in the clash and in the end the gendarmerie set fire to the house. Instead of surrendering, Ǧamīl killed his brother and himself (Özbay, 2017: 98–105).[22] Later on,

---

[22] The accounts given in the narratives vary in certain details from each other and from those in the very few written sources available. See Özbay (2008; 2009; 2017) for a presentation of some variants.

the community continued to celebrate his memory and he became a legend. This *fann* was then orally transmitted over the years, a fact that eventually led to the appearance of different variations of it. As stated by Özbay (2017: 109) this *fann*, whose composer is anonymous, became an epic in the community. The following are the first three quatrains of this *fann*:[23]

	qal	He said:
1	*yā ḥāwi ṭib il-ʾafkār*	O holder of the good thoughts
	ⁱw xizlak min yaddi tiskār	take from my hand a remembrance. [24]
	la niẓmi ṣ-ṣāḥi yiskār	My composition makes the sober feel drunk
	ⁱw yinxi la ṭābūr ʿaskar	and able to cope with a battalion.
2	*Ǧāmil Ḥāyik sabʿ il-ġāb*	*Ǧāmil Ḥāyik*, lion of the forests,
	ʾā bithimmow ḍarb ⁱṭwāb[25]	he fears not the cannon fire,
	ʾafras min Miršid w ⁱDyāb	more chivalrous than Murshid and Diyāb,[26]
	ⁱw ʾarġal mi z-zīr ⁱw ʿantor	more heroic than Zīr[27] and Antar.[28]
3	*tiḥyā ʾimm iǧ ǧābitow*	Long live the mother who gave birth to him!
	tiḥya blād ir rabbitow	Long live the land which raised him!
	kill il-ʿālam ḥabbitow	All the people loved him
	tidʿīlu b ṭūl il-ʿimⁱr	and prayed for him to live a long life.

6.2. The Schoolgirls

The following *fann* might be the first one composed after 1939 when Hatay province became a part of Turkey. The *fann* deals with a parade that took place in the city center. Many of the girls in the parade were wearing what was for the community rather eye-catching school uniforms. Some people used to come down from the villages just to see them, even if the walk would take hours. *Finnān* Slāmi Ṣayyūf (c. 1911–1986) composed a *fann* about this event, which he witnessed. His daughter, Nazire Zorlu/Naẓīra Ǧabbūri (1935–) from Değirmenbaşı/Nahⁱr li-gbir village, related (translated into English):

"When Turkey came, people would go to the Bridge Gate[29] to see the school children passing in rows. People used to find them interesting. [So], on this topic, he [my father] composed this *fann*:"

---

[23] As performed by Besime Kuş/Basīma Dannūra (born around 1935) in Mızraklı/Mišrāqī village.

[24] The word *tiskār* (< *tizkār*) 'remembrance' refers to the word *fann*.

[25] This line is missed by the informant and added from other informants.

[26] Both are heros from the Arab folk epic, *Sīrat Banī Hilāl*. See Reynolds (2006: 307–318).

[27] A pre-Islamic hero. See Procházka (2016) for a version of his story in Cilician Arabic.

[28] A pre-Islamic poetic hero, *ʿantar b. Šaddād*. See Kruk (2006: 292–306).

[29] There was a gate to the Roman bridge in the city center. Unfortunately the bridge was destroyed in 1970 (Okay, 2010: 9–14). Although the new bridge does not have a gate, the expression *bāb iǧ-ǧisⁱr* 'the bridge gate' is still used in the vernacular to refer to the bridge.

1	*lā ḡanni w lā qūl ⁱbyāt‸*	Let me sing and say verses
	ⁱb bāb iḡ-ḡisⁱr ʕa z-zaynat	for the beautiful girls at the Bridge Gate.
	niyyal min kān ⁱw min šāf‸	How happy is the one who has been there and seen them,
	ⁱbtiswā ʕimro w il-ḥāyāt	one might give ones life for this.
2	*ʾawwil ṣaff ⁱw tānī ṣaff‸*	The first row, the second row,
	il-bōnaṭ[30] bī baʕḍa btinḥaff	the hats touch one another,
	– The previous two lines are repeated. –	
	daqq ⁱsnūḡ ⁱw rāḡ ⁱw xaff	the sound of the brass band goes up and down,
	w il-ʾaznūd ⁱmšakkālāt	and the sleeves are rolled up.
3	*killayti[31] bnēt ⁱmkātēb‸[32]*	All of them are schoolgirls,
	ⁱw biṭrānat mālin ʕātāb	and they are spoiled - how can you blame them?
	– The previous two lines are repeated. –[33]	
	lōḥ ⁱḡrēhin mi r-rākāb‸	Their legs are uncovered from the knees down.
	ⁱyqūlo ya zmāni xiz hāt[34]	That is how it is: times change.[35]
	– Quatrain 1 is repeated –	
4	*šū baddi ḡanni tā qūl*	What shall I say when I sing?
	w iṣ-ṣālāt ⁱʕla r-rāsūl	Peace be upon the Messenger.[36]
	– The previous two lines are repeated. –	
	yā xiḍⁱr yā bu d-dastūr‸	O Khiḍr[37] father of the request.[38]
	ⁱw tiḥfiẓkin ṭūl il-ʾayyāːm	[May God] protect you whole life.
5	*tiḥfiẓkīn ⁱgbar w ⁱzḡār‸*	[May God] protect you, old and young,
	ⁱqwāḡa[39] w šibbān ⁱw ʾatfāl	elders, youths and children
	– The previous two lines are repeated. –	
	ʾⁱb ḥaqq ⁱmḥammād il-mixtar	for the sake of Muhammed, the chosen one
	nāṭaq bi l-mihdi w ⁱtkallām	who spoke in the cradle.
	– Quatrain 1 is repeated twice –	

---

30 Cf. French *bonnet* and Turkish *bone*.

31 < *killaytin*.

32 Sg. *maktab*. The word *madrasa* 'school' is not used in the dialects spoken by the community, in contrast to the neighbouring dialects. Cf. Barthélemy (1935: 703, 236) and Wehr (1979: 952, 321).

33 Some words are pronounced slightly differently in the repetiton, e.g. *bnāt*, *ʕatab*, also in the next repetitions, e.g. *ʕa z-zaynāt*, *qul*, *rāsul*, *ʾatfal*.

34 The *t* is not audible.

35 Lit. 'They say: O my time, take, give!'

36 The Prophet Muhammed.

37 Khiḍr is a holy person venerated in the Alawi community. See Procházka-Eisl & Procházka (2010: 128–130) for a discussion of his position in the community.

38 This is an epithet of Khiḍr. The word *dastūr* 'request' is used mainly in a religious sense.

39 Sg. *qūḡa* (masc.), *qūḡi* (fem.). Cf. Turkish *koca* 'husband', 'elderly'.

6.3. The Tent

People in the community used to go to the Adana and Mersin provinces as seasonal workers, in order to improve their living conditions. In each village someone would be in charge of recruiting workers and organizing their transportation. Known as *čāwīš*[40] *il-ʕamala* (pl. *čiwwāš*) 'foreman', he used to act as an intermediary between the peasantry and the landlords. The workers would be transported in trailers to the fields where they would stay in tents, together with all their family members. Children aged twelve and above could also work and receive *yawmī* 'a daily wage'.

A *finnān* from Küçük Karaçay/Nahr iz-Zġayyir village, Hasan Kültekin/Ḥasan Silmān (1926–2016), related that he had composed many *fanns* for all kinds of occasions in his life. He composed *fanns* about the work in the fields, and also performed them there. The following is one of these *fanns*, as performed by him:

1	*ʕa č-čādir*[41] *ya ḥabībē ʕa č-čādir*	To the tent, my dear, to the tent,
	fikkayna w riḥna ʕa č-čādir	we stopped work and went to the tent.
	ṣābitnā maṭra gbiri	We were caught up in a heavy rain shower.
	li-wlad ǧiwwāt ič-čādir	The children were in the tent.
	qal	He said:
2	*xadna t-taʕrīqa w riḥnā:*	We took the basket and left.
	yā rabbe la tfāriqna	O God, don't separate us!
	maʕa l-ʾāġa ʕillaqnā	We've got trouble with the landlord.
	w b il-ʾarḍ ᶦ*nṣabna č-čādir*	On the field we had pitched the tent.
3	*w* ᶦ*ltammu ʕlayna č-čiwwāš*	The foremen then gathered around us,
	w il-wēḥid minnin ġawwaš	and one of them yelled [at us].
	qiltillo ma byithawwāš	I said to him: It's impossible to go on picking,
	il-mayye fātit ʕa č-čādir	and water has entered the tent.

– Quatrain 1 is repeated –[42]

	qāl	He said:
4	ᶦ*Mḥammad bāʕaq yā bayyē:*	Muhammed screamed: Daddy!
	w ᶦ*lḥaqne yā b*ᶦ*n xayye*	Come with me, nephew!
	w ᶦ*lḥaqne yā b*ᶦ*n xayyē:*	Come with me, nephew,
	š-šawši qabʕēt ič-čādir	the wind has destroyed the tent!

– The first two lines of quatrain 1 are repeated –

– Quatrain 3 is repeated[43] –

– The first two lines of quatrain 1 are repeated –

---

[40] < Turkish *çavuş* (Barthélemy, 1935: 133).
[41] Cf. Turkish *çadır* and Persian *čādor* (Barthélemy, 1935: 133).
[42] The word *gbiri* is pronounced slightly differently in the repetiton, i.e. *gbīrī*.
[43] A word, *wlak* 'hey!', indicating impatience, is added in the beginning of the third line of quatrain 3.

5   *ǧāna ʕibdaḷḷa ʾāġā*   The landlord, Abdullah, came to us.
       w qilnālo bāʕⁱd sāʕa   We said to him: [We can pick] after an hour.
       šūf id-dinya limmāʕa   Look, there are flashes of lightning,
       w il-mayye fātit ʕa č-čādir   and water has entered the tent.

– Quatrain 1 is repeated –

6.4. The Workers

Apart from their own *fanns*, *finnāns* might also perform works by other *finnāns*. For instance, Salim Delioğlu/Salim Riḍwān id-Dāli (1941–), a *finnān* from Yeniçağ/Ṭawaqli village, performed a *fann* that seems to have been composed by the ʕAli ʾAḥmad who is mentioned in the *fann*. This *fann*, like the last, is a reflection on the harsh working conditions these labourers had to endure. The following presents the first three quatrains as well as the final one of this *fann*:

1   *baḷḷa stimʕo yā ḥiḍḍār*   Please listen, O audience!
       ʕa lle ǧēri ʕlayna w ṣār   to what happened to us.
       ʾⁱw lākin šū ṭāliʕ bi l-ʾīd   Yet what we can do?
       hāda min ʾaḷḷa mqaddār   This is God's will.

2   *qaddār ⁱw kētib hīkē*   He has ordained, and has written [our fate] thus:
       w baḥdāli mā hattīkē   What a miserable situation [...]![44]
       ʾⁱskit yā wāḥid ya šrīkē   Shut up, my workmate!
       fʕālitnā killa qiṣṣār   All our workers are weak!

3   *fⁱ ʕālitna killa wlaydāt*   All our workers are children!
       mā lin qidrā yā ḥayfāt   They have no power – the pity of it!
       rūḥo banna rrūḥ[45] ʕa l-bāt   Come on, let us go home.
       w ⁱsmaʕ minni w ṣār iṣ ṣār   Pay heed to me: what has happened has happened.

18   *w in-nāẓim hāza[46] l-ʾabyāt*   And the composer of these verses
       ʕāle ʾaḥmad yā sādāt   is Ali Ahmad, O Sirs.
       sallim timmo w id-dayyāt   Well said and well done!
       rattab hal-ġinnī tiskār[47]   He composed this song as a remembrance.

6.5. The Korean War

Turkey sent soldiers to the war between North and South Korea in 1950-1953. Among these soldiers there were members of the community. The following is a

---

44 It was not possible to give an exact transcription or translation of the second phrase due to unclarity in pronunciation. It is presumably related to the verb *hatt* 'to taunt'.
45 < *baddna nrūḥ*.
46 Very occasionally the *finnāns* use a classicism (a word or pronunciation from Classical/Standard Arabic).
47 < *tizkār*.

selection of the quatrains of a *fann* by an anonymous *finnān* dealing with the aforementioned soldiers:[48]

1	*balla stimʕo yā ʾinsāːn*	Please listen, O people!
	ta nġannē w ⁱnqaddi ḥzāːn	Let's sing and pour out our grief
	lā xābār ille ġānāː	about the news[49] that has reached us
	w il-qālᵘb ʕannow ġiflān	of which the heart had been unaware.
4	*ḥaṭṭūnā ġiwwa l-bābūr̰* [50]	They put us on the steamship
	ⁱw maššūnā ġiwwā li-bḥūr	and made us travel upon the seas.
	qilna yā xēḍⁱr dastūr̰	We said: O Khiḍr, please
	ⁱtraġġiʕna b xēr ⁱw sālam	bring us back safe and sound.
6	*w ⁱlḥiqna ʕāla qōrāː̰*	We arrived in Korea
	w šifna d-dāwal maḥrūrā	and saw the countries fighting.
	yā ʾalla nqaddi šhūrāː	Please God let the months pass [quickly] for us
	yirġāʕ il-ʕaskar tāmān	and the soldiers return safe.

6.6. The Cow

Livestock played a crucial role in the community's life. They relied mainly on cows, oxen, chickens, sheep, and donkeys. These were considered valuable property that, consequently, had to be properly fed and taken care of. The death of some animals was, therefore, regarded as a serious loss to the family. For instance people would offer their condolences to a family that had lost a cow, using the expressions commonly used after a person's death.[51] *Finnān* Hasan Kültekin related that he had composed a *fann* after the death of his cow, and described how his wife would not stop weeping and how their neighbors would visit them to present their condolences. The following are a selection of the quatrains of this *fann*, as performed by him:

1	*ʕⁱla lla ya xūyi ʕla lla*	We put our affairs in God's hands, my brother.
	w ⁱxsirna w biʕawwēḍ alla	We made losses, but God will compensate.
	mātit ʕinna hal-baqra	Our cow has died.
	w ⁱnšalla la nšuf daqra	God willing, we will meet no further trouble.
3	*mātit mā hiyi b-bāle*	She has died. Such is life.
	ʾiš-šakwi lā rabb il-ʕāle	Pleas [should be directed] to the supreme Lord.
	– The previous two lines are repeated. –	

---

[48] As performed by Cemile Bal (1936–) from ʕsēkra village, which is today–together with Nʕayri and Bsētin il-ʕāṣi–officially in the neighborhood of Aknehir.

[49] I.e. the news that they were to be sent to war.

[50] Cf. French *vapeur* and Turkish *vapur*.

[51] E.g. *nšalla tislamu wlādik* lit. 'May God grant your children life.' This expression is also used as a euphemism to express that someone is dead. For instance: *ġibna wlād walad waldān tislamu intēw* lit. 'We brought children, one child, two children, may you live.' in the meaning of *I gave birth to two children and they both died* (Ağbaht & Arnold, 2014: 22, fn. 38).

	ᵃw qādir yirziqna ᵓaḷḷa	God is able to provide for us.
	qādir yirziqna ᵓaḷḷa	God is able to provide for us.
4	mātit ma b qalbe nīrān	She died. But my heart isn't burning.
	w ⁱltammu ʕlayyi ǧ-ǧīran	Our neighbours gathered.
	– The previous two lines are repeated. –	
	ᵃw qālo biʕawwēḏ aḷḷa	They said: God will compensate.
	qālo biʕawwēḏ aḷḷa	They said: God will compensate.

6.7. The Ox

Sometimes *finnāns* would spontaneously compose and perform a *fann* about an event directly after it took place. For instance *finnān* Naif Koç/Nāyif il-Qūči (1927–2018) from Bsētīn il-ʕāṣi[52] went one day to the livestock bazaar with an ox. He wanted to leave the bazaar as soon as he finished his work, but the municipality officer forced him to wait. It was a cold and rainy day and he was growing cold and bored. He tied the ox to a pole, and stood in front of it, then slapped the ox between its horns and started to perform a *fann* that, eventually, drew attention to his plight. The following are the first two quatrains of this *fann*, as performed by him, followed by his narration of what happened next (translated into English).

1	ᵓaḷḷa yʕinak ᵓābu qrūn	For God's sake, Horned One!
	la ṣṣir[53] miṯ⁴l xuk malʕū:n	Don't be like your ill-tempered brother!
	kaⁱⁱt maṭrā min wiččā:k	Because of you I have been caught in[54] such a rain-shower
	ʕimri mā kalta b kānūn	that I have never been caught in in a January.

"They [the municipality officers] turned to me, saying: 'What is this [man] saying to the ox?' The salespeople gathered around."

2	ᵃw xattak[55] minšaʕ[56] li-flāḥa	I bought you for ploughing.
	w il-ᵓārⁱḍ waḷḷa mirtāḥa	And really, the field is a comfortable one.
	ᵃw kinⁱt bī birǧ ir-rāḥā	You have been in a palace of ease.
	w ⁱnšaḷḷa bṣir minnak mamnū:n	I hope you will please me!

"He [the municipality officer] turned to me. He said: Countryman, farewell! Release the ox and goodbye to you! Sir [to the interviewer], I pulled the ox away. I went out from the western gate. Two people [the municipality officers] were waiting. One of them said: Hey, countryman, where are you going? […] The other one said to him: Leave him, leave him free, let him go. […] Then we got it [the ox] in the truck and brought the ox home. […] This happened about forty years ago, more than forty years ago."

---

52 Officially in the neighborhood of Aknehir.
53 < tṣīr.
54 Lit. 'I ate a rain.'
55 < xadtak.
56 < minšan.

6.8. Smoking

Smoking was usually not tolerated in the Alawi community of Hatay province. In some villages the first person who started smoking in the village is still remembered by the old people, just like the first people to buy a radio, television or car in the village. Smokers were not allowed to take care of a holy tomb (*zyāra* pl. *zyārāt*) or to help cook *hrīsi*—a special dish made with wheat and meat for religious festivals.[57] Some *fanns* that vilified smoking became popular. Muhiddin Doğan/Miḥyiddin il-Qāḍi (1930–2011) from Dikmece/Dakimǧa village composed one of these, which criticized smoking in a sarcastic manner. The following are selected quatrains, as performed by him:

6	*sikāra yā maḥlākē*	How beautiful you are, cigarette!
	w hal-ʿālam fiki šrākē	That people are addicted to you.
	ʾāfande[58] yā tiryākē	O, addicted Sir!
	w ḥāyātak killa mrārā	All your life is bitter!
7	*ᵃw had-daxne min timmak bitqūm*	The smoke comes out of your mouth.
	ⁱw bitxirxir ǧiwwa l-ḥalqūm	It flows into your windpipe.
	ᵃbtinzal ʿa l-qālᵗb zaqqum	It goes down to the heart as bitter poison.
	ᵃw killa mārad w ⁱxṣārā	It is all just illness and damage.
8	*w īza ma šribt id-dixxān*	If you don't smoke
	ᵃbyiʿǧibūk in-niswān	women will like you.[59]
	w ⁱtʿammil ḥālak ṣilṭan	You think that you're a Sultan
	ᵃw ʾēxirtak rāʿi krāra	but you will end up a muleteer.

6.9. Fashion

Another remarkable social change experienced by this community involves the 'uncovering' of women's heads. Traditionally, women in the community used to wear a white veil (*šamli* pl. *šamlāt*).[60] Still today, it is worn by most of the old women in the villages. Even uncovered women usually cover themselves when visiting a holy tomb or attending funerals or vigils. In the following *fann*, *finnān* Hamza Turunç/Ḥamza Ṭrinǧ (1934–) from Yeniçağ/Ṭawaqli village not only complains about women who stopped wearing the veil and started wearing 'modern' clothes, but also criticizes men who have long hair. The following are selected quatrains, as performed by him:

---

57 Smoking is still not tolerated, at least in the religious segment of the community in Hatay. For an overview of the topic see Procházka-Eisl & Procházka (2010: 86–87).

58 Today *ʾafandi* does not refer to an official title, as it did in the past (cf. Barthélemy, 1935: 10).

59 Presumably there is a negation particle *ʾa* missing at the beginning of the second line. In that case the translation would be as follows: '[You think that] if you don't smoke, women will not like you.'

60 A thin white muslin cloth.

1	baḷḷa stimŞūli yā nās	Please listen to me, O people!
	ṭār il-ḥāya min ar-rās	People have no more shame.[61]
	libs il-mōḍa[62] zādu ktīr	In wearing fashion they have gone too far.
	ṣar maydūro kašf ir-rās	They have started walking around bareheaded.

2	bi libs il-mōḍa zādow	In wearing fashion they have gone too far.
	libso māt'l mā rādow	They dressed as they wished.
	maḥḥad biwaṣṣi wlādow	No one warns his children.
	w ir-riǧǧal 'a byitnaffās	And the husband does not utter a word.

5	baḷḷa stimŞu ya ḥbāyeb	Please listen, my dears!
	'il-ḥāḍir yiḥki la l-ġāyeb	Those who are present should tell the absent:
	hal-mōḍa mōḍit 'aǧānēb	This fashion is foreigners' fashion
	ma byirḍāha rabb in-nās	which God does not approve of.

6	w 'tŞow yā nas w 'qšāŞow	Come people, and take a look
	Şa l bīkun rēxi zdāġow	at the one who has long hair!
	yā 'aḷḷah mā 'abšāŞow	O God how ugly he is!
	mqašmar ḥālo bēn in-nās	He has disgraced himself among the people.

8	w in-nāẓim hāza l-'abyāt	The one who composed these verses
	ḥamze 'aḥmad bat li-wlād	is Hamza Ahmad from the Wlād family.
	sallim timmo w id-dayyāt	Well said and well done!
	rattab hal-ġinni yā nās	He composed this song, O people.

6.10. The Wife

It is not surprising that some *fanns* are dedicated to the *finnān's* wife. Naif Koç was one of the *finnāns* who composed such a *fann*. The following is the *fann* with some of *finnān's* comments on it (translated into English):

> "Once – I shall sing to you this one as well – I wanted to wake my wife up […] I said: "It's foggy" – I woke up early, and I saw it was foggy [so] I said [the following *fann*]":

1	'ḍbābi yā Şayni ḍbābī:	It's foggy, my dear, it's foggy!
	w qūmi qŞādī ya ḥbābī	Get up, sit up, my darling!
	ǧawzik qāŞid min bakkī:r	Your husband has been up early,
	w iš-šām'l Şa l-Şittābī:	and the sun is on the doorstep.

2	ǧawzik qāŞid min bakkī:r	Your husband has been up early,
	baddo yisraḥ baddu yṭir	He wants to get going, wants to fly.
	baddu yġiblēk 'Şāfī:r	He will bring you some birds
	min wādi bāt il-xābī	from Bāt il-Khābi Valley.

---

61 Lit. 'Modesty flew from the head.'
62 Cf. Italian *moda* and Turkish *moda*.

3 | *baddu yġiblik šaḥrūrāt* | He will bring you quails: |
|---|---|
| | *riddi l-miqli ġalli z-zāt* | Prepare the frying pan, heat the oil! |
| | *qassīsī hā li-wlaydāt* | How lazy the children are,[63] |
| | *ᶦyfaḍḍūli kill ᶦġyābi:* | they [just] come and empty my pockets. |

– Quatrain 1 is repeated –

"[…] It sometimes comes to my mind, so I sing it and make her happy."

6.11. Politics

The period during which the *Demokrat* Party was in power (1950–1960) witnessed a strong political tension between the ruling party and the opposition (*Halk* Party) in Turkey. This tension was reflected in Turkish society, causing several incidents.[64] The next *fann* relates one of these incidents which happened in a village. It was performed by *finnān* Süleyman Yıldız/Slaymān Riḥāni (1923–1982), who was prominent as a performer.[65] Before performing he explained the events that led to the composing of the *fann*.[66] These are reproduced below (translated into English), followed by selected quatrains:

> "Dear listeners, we would like to tell you what happened in our village, Dikmece/ Dakimǧa. Perhaps in every village there are such issues. Some support the *Demokrat* party and some the *Halk* party. If you support the *Demokrat* party and I support the *Halk* party, we do not talk to each other at all. Even if you were married to my sister and I were married to yours, we would stop visiting each other. If I lost a relative, you would not come to the funeral, nor would I go to yours. This is how hostile it was. Dear Sir, I am a supporter of the *Halk* party and the headman of our village and Ḥasan Agha are supporters of the *Demokrat* Party. They removed a 1500 metre pipe that connected my house to the reservoir because I did not vote like them [for the *Demokrat* Party]. They gave the water to the *Zahra* family because they were on their side. They gave the water to all the supporters of the *Demokrat* Party [in the village], and they cut the water from all the *Halk* party supporters. This is why we got angry and composed this song:[67]"

1 | *min qīnī la nṣēb ᶦḥyāt* | Let me dream up some verses[68] |
|---|---|
| | *ʕa l-xālᶦq w ad-dēmoqrāt* | about the *Halk* and *Demokrat* parties. |

---

63 It was not possible to give an exact transcription or translation of the first phrase due to unclarity in pronounciation. The word *qassīsī* (< *qassīsīn*) is probably the plural form of *qassīs* which is used to refer to a person who neglects cutting his hair. The *finnān* here presumably means that the children are lazy.

64 See Mertcan (2013: 238–274) for a description of the political atmosphere in the community during these periods that includes some allusions to the aforementioned incidents.

65 For a reflection on his life, see the documentary film *Sowt* by Evecen & Çay (2015).

66 This *fann* was taken from a cassette presumably recorded at the beginning of the 1960s.

67 Lit. 'We took out for them this song.' *šilnālin hal-ġinnī*.

68 Lit. 'From my imagination let me set up verses.'

The first two introductory lines are repeated by a group of people.[69]

6	*ᵃ̓w ʾawwil sāčim*[70] *yā xwān*	At the first election, O brothers,
	ṣārit fitni mn iš-šīṭān	the devil caused unrest.
	iḍ-dāyᵘʕa nqaṣmat ḥōfān	The village divided into two sides
	ⁱb qāl ⁱw qīl ⁱw kitr ⁱʕyāṭ[71]	with tittle-tattle and lots of shouting.
7	*ᵃ̓b ʾamr il-wālī w il-birṭi:*[72]	By order of the governer, the party,
	w il-mixtar[73] *w il-ʾaʕẓāwi:*[74]	the headman, and the members,
	lā ʕinna ǧallābu mayy	they had water brought to our village
	ⁱw ʕamlūwa tlat ḥanafiyāt	and made it into three fountains.
10	*ᵃ̓w ḥānāfit il-xalqāwi*	And the fountain of the *Halk* party-supporters
	min qilt[75] *il-mayy ⁱmṣaḍḍāyi:*	has rusted through scarcity of water.
	ḥaṭṭ ⁱbtimmā ṭappāyi:[76]	By adding a stopper in its mouth
	w qālu kāfi yā sādāt	they said: That's enough, O Sirs!
21	*silman rīḥāni w miḥyiddin*	*Silmān Rīḥāni* and *Miḥyiddin*[77]
	naṣbūwa w yaḷḷah li-mʕīn	composed this, and God is their helper.
	ʾaḷḷā yilʕān it-tintayn	May God damn them both:
	il-xāᵈq mēʕ ad-dēmoqrā:t	the *Halk* and the *Demokrat* parties!

7. Conclusion

The *fann* is a genre of oral poetry attested among the Alawi community in the Turkish province of Hatay (Antioch), which is composed in the vernacular Arabic of the community by people known as *finnāns*. It consists of a variety of themes, often humorous, but sometimes tragic, and was performed publicly on various occasions and in a variety of places. All composers of *fanns* that thus far have been encountered are men; but on the other hand, the *fanns* may be performed by either men or women. The manner of performance lies somewhere between song and speech, which is reminiscent of *sprechgesang* or *melodized speech*. Traditional instruments, such as flutes, drums and *darbukas*, might accompany the performer. The *finnāns* were the main providers of entertainment in the past

---

[69] Their role in the performance of the *fann* could be considered that of a chorus. The last word is pronounced slightly differently by the chorus, in a more dialectal pronunciation, i.e. *w id-dēmiqrāt*.

[70] < Turkish *seçim*.

[71] The *ṭ* is not audible.

[72] Cf. Turkish *parti*.

[73] Cf. Turkish *muhtar* and Classical/Standard Arabic *muxtār*.

[74] Cf. Turkish *aza* and Classical/Standard Arabic *ʾaʕḍāʾ*.

[75] < *qillit*.

[76] < Turkish *tapa*.

[77] *Finnān* Muhiddin Doğan/Miḥyiddin il-Qāḍi was a close friend of Slaymān Rīḥāni. To what extent his friend contributed to this *fann* is not clear (Nihat Çay, personal communication, 23 November 2017).

and were popular in the community. They reported all kinds of events and also played the role of expressing public opinion.

The *fanns* consist of several quatrains and display particular rhyming patterns. In the main pattern, the first three lines of each quatrain share the same rhyme, while all the fourth lines within a *fann* share one rhyme. Some *fanns* also have introductory lines at the beginning of the *fann*. A few of the *fanns* present the name of the *finnān* in the last quatrain. There is a noticeable amount of repetition in the *fanns*, sometimes of a whole quatrain, sometimes of two lines. The metrical structure of the *fanns* is syllabic, based mainly on seven syllables per line. It seems that the syllables permitted are Cv, Cv̄, CvC and Cv̄C, and some changes in the vowels may occur in order to match one of these.

The *fanns* are very rich sources reflecting many aspects of the cultural, daily and social life of the community from the 1930s until recent decades. They may indeed be the best source available for the community's life during that period. The rich and lively tradition of the *fann* has been declining over several decades and most surviving *finnāns* are old. Some *fanns* have been recorded for posterity, but additional documentation is urgent. While the present study gives an overview of the form and content of the *fanns*, as well as their social and cultural context, further studies are also needed for a wider analysis of the social, formal, and stylistic aspects of the *fanns*.

References

Ağbaht, M. & Arnold, W. (2014). Antakya'nın Dursunlu köyünde konuşulan Arap diyalekti. *Nüsha (Şarkiyat Araştırmaları Dergisi)*, 39, II, 7–26.

Amy de le Bretéque, E. (2016). Self-Sacrifice, Womanhood, and Melodized Speech: Three Case Studies from the Caucasus and Anatolia. *Asian Music*, 47 (1), 29–63.

Arış, Y. (2009). *ElkiHil B@aynek*. İstanbul: Emre Matbaacılık.

— (2012). *Ene @niyni @el Ġeli*. İstanbul: Emre Matbaacılık.

— (2014). *Dürüvb El@aşk Me ReHmit Hede*. İstanbul: Oğul Yayıncılık.

— (2017a). *Ye Tayr*. İstanbul: Oğul Yayıncılık Cafer Hayta.

— (2017b). *Khaltit RüvHi Biy RüvHa*. İstanbul: Oğul Yayıncılık Cafer Hayta.

Arnold, W. (1998). *Die arabischen Dialekte Antiochiens*. Wiesbaden: Harrassowitz Verlag.

— (2000). The Arabic dialects in the Turkish province of Hatay and the Aramaic dialects in the Syrian mountains of Qalamûn: two minority languages compared. In J. Owens (Ed.) *Arabic as a Minority Language*, (347–370). Berlin: Mouton de Gruyter.

— (2002). Code Switching and Code Mixing in the Arabic Dialects of Antioch. In A. Youssi, F. Benjelloun, M. Dahbi, Z. Iraqui-Sinaceur (Eds.), *Aspects of the*

Dialects of Arabic Today: Proceedings of the 4th Conference of the International Arabic Dialectology Association (AIDA) Marrakesh, Apr. 1–4, 2000. In Honour of Professor David Cohen, (163–168). Amapatril, Rabat.

– (2010). Pausalformen in den arabischen Dialekten Antiochens. In S. Talay & H. Fischer (Eds.) *Arabische Welt: Grammatik, Dichtung und Dialekte*, (227–235). Wiesbaden: Reichert Verlag.

Bağı, R. (2007). *Hatay İli Harbiye ve Şenköy Beldeleri Müzik Kültürü*. (Master's thesis). İstanbul Teknik Üniversitesi. https://tez.yok.gov.tr/UlusalTezMerkezi/ (accessed 18 October 2017).

– (2014). *Türkiye'de Yaşayan Arap Alevilerinin Etnik ve Müzikal Kimliği*. (Doctoral dissertation). İstanbul Teknik Üniversitesi. https://tez.yok.gov.tr/UlusalTez Merkezi/ (accessed 18 October 2017).

Barthélemy, A. (1935–1969), *Dictionnarie Arabe-Français (Dialects de Syrie: Alep, Damas, Liban, Jérusalem)*. Paris: Libraire Orientaliste Paul Geuthner.

Çay, N. (2010). *Carte cara*. (Music album). Production: Kom Müzik.

Doğruel, F. (2005). *"İnsaniyetleri Benzer..." Hatay'da Çoketnili Ortak Yaşam Kültürü*. İstanbul: İletişim Yayınları.

Durand Zúñiga, E. P. E. (2015). *An Instrumental Study of Pausal Vowels in il-Ǧillī Arabic (Southern Turkey)*. (Doctoral dissertation), The University of Texas at Austin.

Evecen, G. (2012). *Finnên*. (Documentary). Translated into Turkish, English, and German by Mahmut Ağbaht, Hüsne Akgöl, and Bahar Yeniocak. Turkish subtitle: https://www.youtube.com/watch?v=RUvJW4OHgak, English subtitle: https://www.youtube.com/watch?v=bvSgrccbmkM&t=1s, German subtitle: https://www.youtube.com/watch?v=FMYpy7T5zs8 (accessed 4 May 2018).

Evecen, G. & Çay, N. (2015). *Sowt*. (Documentary). https://www.youtube.com/watch?v=Xsv26b9NrZ4&t=29s. (accessed 4 May 2018)

Jastrow, O. (1983). Beobachtungen zum arabischen Dialekt von Adana (Türkei). Zeitschrift für Arabische Linguistik, 11, 72–79.

Kruk, R. (2006). Sīrat ʿAntar ibn Shaddād. In R. Allen & D. S. Richards (Eds.), *Arabic Literature of the Post-Classical Period*, (292–306). Cambridge: Cambridge University Press.

Mertcan, H. (2013). *Türk Modernleşmesinde Arap Aleviler (Tarih Kimlik Siyaset)*. (1th edition). Adana: Karahan Kitabevi.

Okay, A. (2010). Bir cinayetin 40. yılı Roma köprüsü'nün yıkımı. *Hatay Güney Rüzgarı*, 128, 9–14.

Özbay, E. (2008). Bir halk kahramanı Cemil Hayek. *Hatay (Aylık Kültür ve Keşif Dergisi)*, 18, 12–15.

– (2009). Bir halk kahramanı Cemil Hayek. *Evrensel Kültür (Aylık Kültür, Sanat, Edebiyat Dergisi)*, 207, 18–21.

– (2017). Kültürel bir fenomen ve imge olarak halk kahramanı Cemîl Ḥâyek ve hakkında söylenegelen halk destanı. In H. Mertcan (Ed.). *Asi Gülüşlüm Ah Güzel Antakya*, (97–11). İstanbul: İletişim Yayıncılık.

Procházka-Eisl, G. & Procházka, S. (2010). *The Plain of Saints and Prophets: The Nusayri-Alawi Community of Cilicia (Southern Turkey) and Its Sacred Places*. Wiesbaden: Harrassowitz.

Procházka, S. (1999). From language contact to language death: the example of the Arabic spoken in Cilicia (Southern Turkey). *Orientalia Suecana* 48, 115–125.

– (2002a). Contact phenomena, code-copying, and codeswitching in the Arabic dialects of Adana and Mersin (Southern Turkey). In A. Youssi, F. Benjelloun, M. Dahbi, Z. Iraqui-Sinaceur (Eds.), *Aspects of the Dialects of Arabic Today: Proceedings of the 4th Conference of the International Arabic Dialectology Association (AIDA) Marrakesh, Apr. 1 – 4, 2000. In Honour of Professor David Cohen*, (133–139). Amapatril, Rabat.

– (2002b). *Die arabischen Dialekte der Çukurova (Südtürkei)*. Wiesbaden: Harrassowitz Verlag.

– (2009). Women's wedding songs from Adana: Forty quatrains in Cilician Arabic. *Estudios de Dialectología Norteafricana y Andalusí* 13, 235–255.

– (2016). The story of sālim az-zīr abū laylā al-muhalhil in Cilician Arabic (Southern Turkey). In Z. Gažáková & J. Drobný (Eds.), *Arabic and Islamic Studies Honour of Ján Pauliny*, Bratislava: Comenius University, 149–177.

Reyhani, M. (1997). *Gölgesiz Işıklar - II Tarihte Aleviler*. (2nd edition). İstanbul: Can Yayınları.

– www.albabtainprize.org/encyclopedia/poet/1683.htm (accessed 18 October 2017)

Reynolds, D. W. (2006). Sīrat Banī Hilāl. In R. Allen & D. S. Richards (Eds.), *Arabic Literature of the Post-Classical Period*, (307–318). Cambridge: Cambridge University Press.

Rosenhouse, J. (2000–2001). A comparative study of women's wedding songs in colloquial Arabic. *Estudios de Dialectología Norteafricana y Andalusí* 5, 29–47.

Smith-Kocamahul, J. (2003). *Language Choice, Code-Switching and Language Shift in Antakya, Turkey*. (Doctoral dissertation), University of Canterbury. https://ir.canterbury.ac.nz/handle/10092/2839 (accessed 20 September 2017).

Sönmez, E. (2015). Şeyh Mahmut Reyhani ile. *Ehlen (Kültür, Sanat, Siyaset Dergisi)* 5, 46–48.

Wehr, H. (1979). *A Dictionary of Modern Written Arabic*. J Milton Cowan (Ed.). (Fourth Edition). Wiesbaden: Otto Harrassowitz.

Yakto (2008), issue 12.

Yakto (2009a), issue 13.

Yakto (2009b), issue 14.

"Hüseyn'im Vay!":
Voice and Recitation in Contemporary Turkish Shi'ism

Stefan Williamson Fa

Kars is quite unlike any other city in Turkey. What is most immediately striking is the city's grid-like pattern based around eight principal roads, and its Imperial Russian architecture. At the geographical intersection between Anatolia and the Caucasus, Kars has a long and complex history under different empires, rulers and people. Like many other borderlands, this has led to a complex history of migration, emigration, settlement, coexistence and conflict, all of which have left marks on the city and its soundscape.

Historically, the movement of people and culture between Anatolia and Caucasus has been relatively fluid, a fact which is exemplified in the tradition of *âşık*s, bardic minstrels who once travelled between the urban centres of Kars, Tbilisi, Yerevan and beyond, reciting poetry and epics and playing the long necked lute known as the *saz*. Even during the Soviet period, the sound of *âşık*s travelled across the relatively sealed border with people in Kars reportedly tuning into radio broadcasts from Yerevan and Baku every Sunday to listen to the latest recordings of *âşık*s from the Soviet Caucasus. Cassette recordings of folk and popular singers from Iranian Azerbaijan were also present in stores in the city centre at that time (Erdener, 1995).

The city and wider province has long been home to different religious communities and denominations. Late 19th century Russian censuses show that the city's population consisted predominantly of Armenians and Russians, with smaller numbers of Turks and Caucasian Greeks. Today, the city is composed of an ethno-linguistically diverse, yet almost entirely Muslim population. The population is said to be just under 80,000, made up mostly of three self-differentiating Turkic groups: *"yerli"* (literally: 'natives' but referring to 'unmarked' Sunni Anatolian Turks), Azeri (who are mostly the descendants of immigrants who arrived in the city from present day Armenia during the period 1878 to 1920 and distinguish themselves on the basis of sectarian, *mezhep*, affiliation), and Terekeme (who trace their origins to the Caucasus but are predominantly Sunni) as well as Kurmanji speaking Sunni Kurds.

In this chapter, I introduce the genres of lament that are central to Azeri Shi'i (*Caferi*) ritual life in Kars[1]. I begin by arguing the need for these genres to be un-

---

[1] Research for this chapter is based on over a year of fieldwork between 2014 and 2016, largely focused in the town of Kars, as well as other parts of Turkey, Iran and Azerbaijan. In

derstood along a wider nexus of oral performance traditions in the region. After providing a brief summary of the Shi'i community in Turkey I go on to describe the rituals and oral performance genres central to Muharram ritual mourning. The final part of the chapter deals directly with the changing practices of Shi'i recitation in Turkey and the influence of transnational media and professional reciters, known as *meddah,* from Iranian Azerbaijan and the Republic of Azerbaijan. By presenting this material here, I highlight the significance of vernacular oral performance in devotional life in Eastern Anatolia. Rather than rigid, fixed and unchanging, a deeper ethnographic understanding of these forms of oral performance expose the changing, dynamic and often creative nature of ritual and religiosity.

Oral Performance

The singer poet traditions of *âşık* and *dengbêj* bards, still popular today, with their emphasis on storytelling and the recounting of epics are a testament of the importance of oral performance in Eastern Anatolia and the Caucasus. The popularity of *âşıks* often transcended ethnic and sectarian divisions as a common form of entertainment. These bards came from different backgrounds and participated in the song duelling traditions of *âşık* coffee houses and often could only be distinguished by their accents or the themes of their lyrics. Erderner (2015 pers.comm) recalled an incident in which a Sunni Terekeme *âşık* travelled to a Shi'i Azeri village. Upon realising that the audience was not interested in the tales he was reciting the *âşık* began improvising lyrics on the theme of Imam Husayn to which he received great admiration and left the village with a handsome fee.

Such an incident also reminds us of the fact that oral traditions have rarely been neatly divided into categories of secular and sacred. *Âşıks* would often draw on Islamic and mystical themes in their performance and as ways of legitimising their practice (Erdener, 1995). Within this larger soundscape of multi-ethnic multi-denominational singer poets in Eastern Anatolia the lesser known devotional genres of Shi'i oral performance have received little scholarly attention. The various forms of vocalised melodic lamentation performed to commemorate the martyrdom of Imam Husayn, the grandson of the Prophet and third rightful Imam in Shi'i belief, at Karbala, are arguably part of this larger shared aesthetic and poetic register of oral performance found across the region.

Within Shi'i communities across the world, the central and shared sounds of the recitation of the Qur'an and the adhan (*ezan*), exist amongst vocalised suppli-

addition to regular participant observation at mosques, private *meclis* and other gatherings, much of the material presented here was obtained via interviews with a broad range of individuals and members of the community, including professional *meddah* and amateur reciters.

cations (*dua*), laments (*mersiye, sinezen, noha*) and songs of joy and celebration (*molodi, ilahi*), which are connected to time and place and generally focus on the remembrance of the Ahl al-Bayt[2]. Within Twelver Shi'ism there is a surprising consistency in content and form of these genres worldwide. Yet, a huge diversity in style correlates with the wide geographic distributions of these communities. Many of these genres go beyond the fixed holy scripture of the Qur'an and Hadith and represent vernacular devotional traditions with diverse influence and currents. Lyrics are drawn from diverse sources, including specialised poets. While instruments are generally not used to accompany recitation, the melodisation of texts often involves highly aestheticised techniques and styles of vocal performance.

These forms of devotional recitation share certain characteristics with other singer poet traditions in the region. As oral performance their embodied nature can be contrasted with printed text and literature. They share similar performance context as they are fixed in time and space as unrepeatable events which involve the physical presence of audiences and performers. The nature of performance entails a certain fluidity of text and content which is due to the unpredictability of the interactive feedback cycle between listeners and performers. Like the bardic traditions of *âşık* and *dengbêj*, the forms of recitation discussed here tend to rely on memory—the ability to remember lyrics and narratives are central to the art of successful performance. While the oral component of vernacular recitation is central to its transmission and performance, it is important to note that the "oral" and "written" are never mutually exclusive (Sterne, 2011; Hess, 2015). As shown below, recitation involves the combination of textual and oral transmission and, more recently, diverse new forms of media.

Shi'ism in Eastern Anatolia

Azeris[3] are Turkic-speakers whose language is mutually intelligible with Modern Turkish, living mainly in the Republic of Azerbaijan and in Iran[4]. In Turkey, they are estimated to number between 500,000 and 2 million (Shaffer, 2002: 221), though figures are hard to verify given the fluidity of the concept of ethnicity in the country. Azeris in Turkey are predominantly followers of *Caferi* (Ja'fari jurisprudence) Twelver Shi'ism, while Turkey is a majority (Hanafi) Sunni country.

---

[2] Ahl al-Bayt (Turkish: *Ehli Beyt*) is a phrase meaning, literally, "People of the House" or "Family of the House". The term refers to the family of the Prophet Muhammad.

[3] Azeri and Azerbaijani are often used interchangeably though since the independence of the Republic of Azerbaijan Azerbaijani has come to signify citizens of that Republic. Azeris in Turkey refer to themselves as *Azeri* or *Azeri Türkler* (Azeri Turks).

[4] In the Republic of Azerbaijan, ethnic Azerbaijanis account for close to 91% of the population of 8.1 million. In the neighbouring Republic of Georgia, there are approximately 300,000 Azerbaijanis. The largest number of Azerbaijanis today, up to an estimated 20 million live in the Islamic Republic of Iran. (Shaffer, 2002: 224)

Turkey's Azeri community has historically settled in the area which today borders Armenia, Nakhchivan and Iran; the largest city being Kars. They make up around 30–40% of the total population of Kars city and province, and are the largest group in the neighbouring province of Iğdır (Üzüm, 1993). Those living in Kars are mostly descended from the population expelled from Soviet Armenia following the exchanges of 1918–25 (Andrews, 1989: 74). Since the 1970s, parallel to the rising migration in Turkey from rural to urban areas, there has been a steady flow of migration to the industrialised city centres of Western Turkey.

The spread of Shi'ism in Eastern Anatolia and the Caucasus is inseparable from the Islamisation of the area but became particularly strong during the initial years of the Safavid state and Shah Ismail's patronage of Shi'ism in the region. Shi'i identity today in Turkey is not formally forbidden. Yet, the sheer diversity of Shi'ism and the homogenous ethnic and religious character of the official narrative of national identity, have worked to suppress knowledge or visibility of Turkish Shi'ism[5]. Eastern Anatolian Azeris are fairly unknown within Turkey and few appreciate the sectarian difference between Azerbaijanis and other Turks. Within the literature on ethnic and religious groups there also appears to be some confusion. For example, van Bruinessen (1996) incorrectly includes Azeri Shi'ah within his description of Alevi groups of Turkey. Azeris generally reject labelling of their beliefs and practices under Alevism, and prefer to distinguish themselves as *Caferi*. Obviously, not all Azeris embrace Shi'ism or Islam as part of their identity, and amongst those who do, not all participate in the mourning rituals or show interest in the genres of recitation I refer to in this text.

Lamenting Karbala

The martyrdom of Husayn b. 'Ali b. Abi Talib, the grandson of the Prophet Muhammad and third Imam, is a historical and cosmological turning point for Shi'ah. The massacre in the desert of Karbala, present day Iraq, was born out of the continued dispute over political and spiritual succession to the Prophet Muhammed after his death in 632CE. After Yazid had demanded that Husayn abdicate his right to succession Husayn was encouraged by his supporters to travel to Kufa where they could organise and lead a challenge to the caliph. On the way, Husayn and his seventy-two followers, were surrounded and besieged for three days on the desert sands of Karbala, near the banks of the Euphrates River. Husayn's party were deprived of water during the siege and attacked by thousands of Umayyad soldiers who brutally dismembered and decapitated the Imam

---

[5]   Shi'ah in Turkey have struggled over the status of their mosques as the Religious Affairs Department does not recognise the status of *Caferi* (and other non-Hanafi Sunni) communities, and have attempted to bring their mosques under state control. Since the 1980s several *Caferi* organisations and associations have come into existence. In Kars there are three Shi'i mosques, the first having been founded in 1952.

and his supporters on the tenth day of the month of Muharram, the day now referred to as Ashura (*Aşura Günü*). The massacre was much more than the slaughter of those loyal supporters of the family of the Prophet by an overwhelming military force. Instead the tragedy is seen as an ideological battle between the just over the unjust, the principled over the corrupted, making Husayn into the figure of the ultimate tragic hero. Husayn's innocence, infallibility and holiness, in the minds of the Shi'ah, adds to the cosmological significance of his martyrdom.

The commemoration of Imam Husayn's martyrdom began soon after the tragic event and Shi'i practice and theology has developed in contemplation of the historical details of the narrative. Within Shi'ism an understanding of redemption and mediation has for centuries inspired the development of tradition. Through its many vernacular variations, different rituals have been developed to maintain communication between the mundane and spiritual worlds. The use of aesthetic expressions to elicit lamentation and weeping in Muharram rituals is a well documented phenomenon (Ayoub, 1978).

In Turkey, commemorations of Imam Husayn's martyrdom were held on and off by Iranian traders in the Sunni Ottoman capital Istanbul (And 1979: 238–254) until 1923 when such enactments were forbidden for being 'too violent and unworthy of a civilised country' according to both Persian intellectuals in the city and the young Turkish Republic (Zarconne and Zarinebaf, 1993). However, mourning during Muharram was not restricted to the Shi'i traders in the city. Within Ottoman Turkish literature the genre of *mersiye* is said to have developed from the 15th century onwards. From its Arabic and Persian origins *mersiye* poetry became a broad genre, used to lament the deaths of important individual figures including sultans, as well as close friends and family members (Isen, 1993). *Mersiye* dedicated to Imam Husayn appear in Ottoman divan literature as well as in the more popular literature of the sufi lodges (*tekke*) from the same time (Çağlayan, 1997). A strong tradition existed of the vocalised recitation of *mersiye* within the Sufi lodges of various orders. This was especially common at ceremonies during the period of Muharram. These recitations, unlike some other forms of hymns (*ilahi*), would be recited in a melodised form without the use of any instruments out of respect for the martyrs of Karbala. Sebilici Hüseyin Efendi (1894–1975), of whom recordings still exist, is often referred to as the last Ottoman *mersiyehan*, a specialist in reciting *mersiye*.

The diverse Alevi-Bektashi[6] communities living across Anatolia have also maintained a wide range of traditions and forms of lamenting Karbala. The genre

---

6   The amalgamation of Shi'ism and Alevism is extremely problematic and often rejected by Alevis themselves. Scholars within Turkey and beyond have long emphasized the distinctiveness of Alevism and the history of Shi'i ideas in Turkey (Zarconne, 2004; Cahen, 1970). Shi'ah and Alevis have a number of beliefs in common, but distinguish themselves very clearly in their religious rituals.

of *mersiye* features prominently in Alevi Muharram rituals and in the central communal worship service (*cem*) held throughout the year (Özdemir, 2016). *Mersiye*, here, communicates the same narrative and event, but differs significantly in style and form from both the Twelver Shi'i and the Ottoman forms. The Alevi *mersiye* represents a distinct but connected oral tradition in which the poetic lament is often accompanied by a long necked lute (*bağlama*).

The Meclis-*Voice and Space*

The ritual commemoration of the Battle of Karbala during Muharram is fundamental to Azeri Shi'i religious expression and identity in Kars, yet has long been affected and restricted by the social and political climate at the time. Locals often recount how during the early Republican period and years of military rule, all Muharram rituals were forced underground and carried out in secret at people's homes or out of the town and village centres. However, over the last 20 years, these rituals have gradually moved from the private sphere of houses to mosques and, since 1992, an Ashura procession has been held annually through the streets of the city centre, attracting thousands of participants and onlookers.

Amongst Azeri Shi'ah in Kars, mourning begins on the first night of Muharram with mourning gatherings (*matem meclisi*) which are held for nine nights, ending on the eve of Ashura (*tasua*), at the three mosques across the city and at the private houses of sayyids (*seyid*), direct descendants of the Prophet. Families fill the mosques as the sun begins to set with the *meclis* commencing after the evening prayers (*akşam namazı*). The mosques are physically transformed during the month of Muharram, black banners and flags, usually brought back by pilgrims returning from Iran and Iraq, are draped from the minarets and cover the walls of the interior prayer space. Ad hoc sound systems are also set up in the mosques during this period; speakers, microphones and amplifiers are brought in by different members of the congregation to ensure the volume of the recitation is adequate for the event.

The *meclis* typically consists of three main parts, the recitation of *sinezen*, a sermon and the recitation of *mersiye*: The genre of *sinezen*[7] is one of the most widespread sounded forms of religious expression in the Shi'i world. *Sinezen* is a form of poetic lamentation which aligns rhythmically with the beating of the chests or self-flagellation with chains by a group of participants known as a *deste*. Different movements and methods of beating the chest or hitting the back with the chains are adopted to match the different metres of the text of the vocal recitation.

---

7   *Sinezen* comes from the Persian *Sine-zani* meaning striking the chest. In Turkish the verb *sine vurmak* is used for the action of beating the chest while *sinezen* refers to the genre of rhythmic recitation.

During the *sinezen* portion of the *meclis*, a single reciter stands at the head of the *deste* narrating the rhythmic verses to which those gathered often join in call and response sections or during repeated choruses. The repertoire of *sinezen* varies from night to night, often corresponding to a particular figure among Husayn's companions at Karbala, though the most popular texts and melodies tend to be repeated throughout the ten days.

Reciters in Kars, generally known as *sinezenci* or *destebaşı*, are usually chosen for their vocal skills; some are also popular local wedding musicians who give up secular music for the period between the start of Muharram and Arba'een[8]. *Sinezen* at these gatherings are particularly loud and energetic, being especially popular with the younger male members of the congregation whose vigorous body movements are in sharp contrast to the somber poses of the older men seated around the mosque. The reverb-soaked recitation of the *sinezenci* is punctuated by the percussive rhythms and fleshy thuds of hands beating chests or the rattle and whip of chains hitting the cloth on the men's backs, sounds which are not contained by the thin walls of the mosques but resonate onto the streets. Through voice and embodied rhythm the martyrs of Karbala are commemorated, remembered, amplified and sounded throughout the neighbourhoods of Kars.

Melodised narrations of the Battle of Karbala, known as *mersiye* are the climax of *meclis*. They are the emotional and ritual heart of the evening. Originating from the Arabic word for lament (*marṣiyya*), *mersiye*, as seen above, is the general name used and given by Shi'ah and Alevis in Turkey and Azerbaijan to the intoned recitations recounting the battle of Karbala and the life and suffering of the family of the prophet (*Ehli beyt*). While in Iran and Azerbaijan *mersiye* and *sinezen* are recited by specialised *meddah*[9], in Turkey, *mersiye* are almost exclusively recited by imams or sayyids who have received religious education in Iran or Iraq. The recitation can be either melodised or non-melodic, yet it is deeply emotional and draws on both wider Shi'i Islamic traditions and Azeri sounded and poetic forms. *Mersiye* focuses specifically on the suffering of Imam Husayn and his companions at Karbala; it is more descriptive than the *sinezen* and the narrative form expresses the suffering from thirst and hunger of Husayn and the bravery and daring deeds of the battle. The vocalisation combines the recitation of poetry, often in the first person, of those who were at Karbala, with loud weeping, again heavily amplified, aimed at provoking an emotional response from the listeners sitting in the mosque.

---

8   Arba'een, known as Erbain or İmamın Qırxı locally, occurs forty days after the Day of Ashura and marks the end of the mourning period for Imam Huseyn.

9   The Turkish word *meddah* comes from an Arabic word which means "panegyrist" and was used by Ottoman Turks and Persians to designate the professional story-tellers of the urban milieux. The *meddah* originally recited episodes from the Shahname but later came to be known for relating the acts and deeds of important figures in Islam (Boratav, 2012).

The *meclis* combines different forms of melodised and narrated speech and poetry, moving between different registers of speech in different languages. The opening sermon explaining the topic and meaning of the *mersiye* is given in formal Turkish and in a direct style. This is followed by the melodised and emotionally charged first person narrative of the *mersiye* recitation, which is based on Azeri Turkish poetry and uses the informal local Azeri dialect to create a sense of emotional intimacy. The *meclis* ends with a reading from the Qur'an the religious efficacy of Arabic concluding and asking for the prayers and tears of those gathered to be accepted. Those congregated leave the mosque, shaking hands and departing with the phrase '*Allah kabul etsin*', 'may God accept your prayers'. The *deste* groups are often invited to houses after the *meclis* to recite and beat *sinezen*, with the aim of bringing blessings to the house for the rest of the year.

Genres of Lamentation

Unlike other parts of the Shi'i world where literary and written texts circulate as part of a high culture of mourning, in Eastern Anatolia the poetry for lamentation has generally been transmitted through oral performance. Despite the existence of many examples of Turkish language *maktel*, martyrdom texts, and literary works around the theme of the martyrdom of Imam Huseyn in Karbala, Shi'ah in Kars have had relatively little access to this literature and have instead relied on lyrics from anonymous poets that have been transmitted orally across generations.

Until recently, the genre of *sinezen* in the Shi'i villages and centre of Kars and Iğdır were limited to fairly simple rhymes and rhythmic patterns of chest beating, which were repeated year after year and transmitted orally. This type of call and response *sinezen* (Table 1.) is known as "*şahse vahse*", or "*şak-şe*".[10] To recite these the *deste* would form two lines facing each other. One line would call out a verse or phrase and the other respond; for example one side would say "*Şah Hüseyin*" the other would reply with "*Vah Hüseyin*".

---

[10] The popularity of the slogan "*Şah Hüseyin, Vah Hüseyin*" has also led to these older *sinezen* being referred to as, a corrupted shorter version of the phrase coming from the vocalised form.

Table 1. An example of lyrics (anonymous) from the older call and response style of *sinezen*. Collected in Kars, Turkey, in October 2015.

Sinezenci:	**Sinezenci:**
Yezid minip danasına,	Yezid rides a cow,
Deste grubu:	**Deste group:**
Nehlet onun anasına	May his mother be damned
Sinezenci:	**Sinezenci:**
Ay ışığı süt kimin	In the light of the moon,
Deste grubu:	**Deste group:**
Yezid uluyur it kimin	Yezid howls like a dog
Sinezenci:	**Sinezenci:**
Kanlı kılıç Kerbela'da pas tutar!	The bloodied sword rusts in Karbala!
Deste grubu:	**Deste group:**
Melikeler ağam için yas tutar!	The angels mourn for my master!
Sinezenci:	**Sinezenci:**
Ey bi kefen	*A shroud*
Deste grubu:	**Deste group:**
Hüseyn Vay!	*Oh Husayn!*
Sinezenci:	**Sinezenci:**
Susuz olan	The thirsty!
Deste grubu:	**Deste group:**
Hüseyn Vay!	Oh Husayn!
Sinezenci:	**Sinezenci:**
Mazlum Olan	The wronged!
Deste group:	**Deste group:**
Hüseyn'im Vay!	Oh my Husayn!

These examples and others like it suggest that the prevalent form of *sinezen* in the past was based on simple rhymes and used everyday language, with little melodic and lyrical elaboration or depth. The simplicity of such recitation meant that the role of the *sinezenci* was not specialised. The reciter was only required to have a good voice and memorise the simple lyrics. These were transmitted orally from year to year and little effort was made to elaborate on the texts. As mentioned above, the role of *sinezenci* has often been taken on by musicians, yet, an important distinction is made between the recitation of lament poetry and singing. This is particularly clear in the verbs used distinguishing the reading (*okumak*) of *sinezen* and *mersiye* and singing (*şarkı söylemek*). In practice, however, there is slippage between the secular and the sacred as *sinezenci* may appropriate melodies from 'sad' (*hüzünlü*) songs with little opposition. Examples of this range from the use of folk melodies, such as *Sarı Gelin,* to the more surprising and not so subtle adaption of pop lyrics and melodies, including the song *Usta* by Arabesk singer Müslüm Gürses.

The recitation of *mersiye* elegies today is mostly left to local clergy members as their longer narrative form relies on a more detailed knowledge of the events at Karbala, as transmitted orally or written in Turkish, Persian or Arabic texts. According to local elders, in the past the recitation of *mersiye* would often take place at homes and were performed by specialised *mersiyehan* who would be commissioned to narrate the suffering of the *Ehli Beyt* in poetic form as a spiritual vow or offering. The recitation of *mersiye*, is not based on a single literary text rather, a combination of improvised (*doğaçlama*) lament and lines of memorised text or orally transmitted poetry. The recitation of the narrative of Karbala in the form and function of *mersiye* is much more complex than the recitation of *sinezen*. Affective recitation relies on the complex weaving of poetry, narrative with vocal technique to ensure an emotional response from listeners.

As mentioned above, the *mersiye* begins with a spoken introduction which takes on a familiar sermonising tone, similar to the Friday sermon (*hutbe*), in which lessons and meanings are explicated from the events at Karbala. The narrative or particular incident from the Karbala events for the *mersiye* is introduced slowly in spoken voice in this section, often referencing the *mersiye* recited at the previous *meclis*. On each of the first nine nights of Muharram the reciter adds and builds on the larger narrative which climaxes in the account of Husayn's martyrdom, usually recited on the night of *Tasua*. As the narrative begins to take prominence a clear transition is made from the spoken non-melodic introduction into the melodised recitation, which is announced and marked with the intoned Arabic phrase '*Assalamu alaika ya Aba Abdillah*' (meaning 'Peace be upon you, Oh Imam Husayn!'). Unlike the more elaborate melodisation of specialised *meddah* elsewhere, discussed below, the local recitation tends to follow a very simple melodic style repeating a descending mode[11] within a small pitch range, identical to folk funeral lamentation in the area. In this section the reciter may incorporate verses from written *mersiye* poetry, usually from sheet of handwritten notes copied from printed volumes of poetry prepared for each night. The most popular references for *mersiye* recitation are collections of Azeri Turkish devotional poetry originating in Ardabil, Iran, by specialised poets (*Ehli Beyt Şairi*) such as Rahim Monsevi (1937–1991), Abbas Gholi Yahyevi (1901–1979). Books of poetry by these authors are quite scarce locally as they were brought back by individuals who travelled to Iran for their studies or pilgrimage. Despite the shared language, the Perso-Arabic script used in these publications makes such texts relatively inaccessible to lay people, adding to the significance of the oral recitation during the *meclis*. Like many other forms of poetry the text of *mersiye*

---

[11] Reciters of *mersiye* in Kars have no formal musical education and do not recite according to any fixed mode. Despite the fact that recitation of *mersiye* is not categorised as a form of music the terms *makam* and *avaz* are used locally to refer to the melodisation.

poetry is written to be read aloud to an audience where the performance of listening, communal weeping, vocalised responses, such as the exclamation of remorse for Husayn ('*Vay Husayn*') and condemnation of the perpetrator ('*lanet olsun Yezid'e!*'), are intrinsic to the *meclis* and create a dynamic feedback cycle between reciter and listener. The emotional impact of the recitation derives from both the words/text and the quality of voice, melodisation and weeping.

Blum's (2005) work on singers in *ta'ziyeh* highlights the complexity of these forms of religious lamentation, as they are required to learn and invent melodies that can accommodate verses in specific metres. As in Blum's study, many of the individuals who recite *mersiye* acquire a sense of how to coordinate tunes and poetic meters without any formal education or instruction and do not engage in sustained discussion on the topic. The way that individuals recite *mersiye* has similarities with other singer poet traditions, especially as their long narrative structure is not dissimilar to epics. In Parry (1987) and Lord's (1960) groundbreaking work on the oral composition and performance of epics they observed how oral poets weave texts together by using formulas, themes, meters, rhythms, and repetitive structures, conventions which also operate in the performance and tradition of *mersiye*. Yet, these forms of performance and tradition are not unchanging. In what is left of this chapter I discuss the changes in contemporary lamentation with particular attention given to the influence of new media and transnationalism in these practices.

Meddah, *Music and Media*

The last few decades have seen widespread changes which have led to widespread changes in Shi'i recitation in Turkey. The increase in the number of people going to study in Qom and on pilgrimage to Iran, Iraq and Syria meant that more individuals from Turkey began to come into contact with other Shi'i ritual traditions. During the 1980s and 90s, cassettes of Shi'i lamentation were often brought back from such travels and they were copied and shared. Recordings of Azeri language *meddah*, such as Salim Muezzinzade from Ardabil, Iran, became particularly sought after. Since the late 1980s moreover, local poets began writing poetry which, together with the relaxation on censorship of religious material, the opening of Shi'i publishing houses and the ubiquity of cassette recordings, contributed to the spread of a distinct repertoire of Azeri Turkish poetry across Shi'i communities in Turkey.

One of the most popular poets of this era was a librarian from Iğdır, Hüseyin Yalçın (b. 1953 d. 2014), who took on the title of poet of the Ahl al-Bayt (*Ehli Beyt Şairi*) and dedicated himself to writing and publishing his own works commemorating Imam Husayn and the lives of the Ahl al-Bayt. Yalçın's poetry

marked a move away from the simple rhyming call and response style of traditional *sinezen* and proved extremely popular (Table 2.).

Along with a move away from the use of local dialect and to a more formal
register of language influenced by Modern Turkish, his poetry contained intricate
references to details and figures from the Karbala narrative, no doubt a result of
his own religious studies. These poems were written explicitly for recitation as either *sinezen* or *mersiye*. This is seen in the rhythm and structure of the texts, where
chorus sections (*nakarat*), for *sinezen*, were often marked in publication, but he
was also known to recite himself during Muharram or instruct reciters on how to
melodise the texts. Despite the move towards publication of poetry and texts
since the 1980s the vocalisation, melodisation and recitation of these texts has
remained their central purpose.

Table 2. Lyrics from a popular *sinezen* '*Şahı vefa Ebelfez*' (The king of loyalty 'Abū al-
Fādl) about 'Abū al-Fādl Al-Abbas, Husayn's half-brother, written by Hüseyin Yalçın.
The chorus (*nakarat*) and melody is taken from a Persian language recording of a *sinezen* which circulated in the early 1990s. A recited version of Yalçın's text was recorded
and produced in a studio by a contemporary *meddah* from Kars, Halil Çelik, in 2014
and has circulated widely amongst Azeri Shi'ah in Turkey and the diaspora making it
one of the most regularly recited *sinezen* during Muharram.

Şahı vefa Ebelfezl	**The King of Loyalty 'Abū al-Fādl**
Şahı vefa Ebelfezl [Nakarat]	The King of Loyality 'Abū al-Fādl *[Chorus]*
Ebelfezl Ebelfezl Ebelfezl	'Abū al-Fādl 'Abū al-Fādl'Abū al-Fādl
Kim bu pehlivan?	Who is this heroic man?
Alem olup heyran	The standard bearer
Zehra eşgine	Who gave his life
Huseyn'e veren can	for the tears of Zehra and Husayn
Huseyn'e veren can	for the tears of Zehra and Husayn
Soyu Heyder-i	The son of *Haydar*
Vefanın Zirvesi	The peak of loyalty
İsmi Ebelfezl	His name is 'Abū al-Fādl
Huseyn'in nökeri	Husayn's comrade-in-arms
Huseyn'in nökeri	Husayn's comrade-in-arms
Aşk meydanında	On the battlefield of love,
Safları yanında	side by side in their ranks,
Babası Heyder	as though his father, *Haydar,*
Sanki Kerbela'da	were in Karbala
Sanki Kerbela'da	were in Karbala
Hayrandır herkes	All admire him
Ama beni bilmez	But they don't know me
Divane oldum	As I have gone mad
Eşgine Ebelfezl	For the tears of 'Abū al-Fādl
Eşgine Ebelfezl	For the tears of 'Abū al-Fādl

The independence of the Republic of Azerbaijan in 1991 also led to new contact between communities in Turkey and both the bordering Azerbaijani enclave of Nakhchivan and the Azerbaijan mainland. By the early 2000s, those travelling to Azerbaijan from Turkey were able to collect CDs of *meddah* and books containing Latin alphabet Azerbaijani collections of *sinezen* and *mersiye*, which were much easier to read than Arabic alphabet Azeri texts from Iran.

The most significant development has been the recent spread of videos and recordings online. Today, videos of Muharram ceremonies, mourning assemblies and studio recordings of *meddah* from Iran, Republic of Azerbaijan and other parts of Turkey are widely available on online video platforms, such as Youtube, and are constantly shared on social media. The quality of these audio and video recordings and montages is extremely diverse. They range from high quality studio productions, usually 'a capella' accompanied by the sound of chest beating or snare drums to camera-phone recordings of *meclis* gatherings. In addition to the abundance of amateur recordings, many Shi'i organisations and mosques in Turkey have an active web presence. Over the last decades a number of Shi'i television channels have opened in Turkey and are another source of the spread of recordings of popular *sinezen* and *mersiye*.

The proliferation of recordings has had a profound effect on practices of recitation, listening and devotion at a local level. The more devout may listen to these recordings throughout the year. However, during Muharram the recordings take a more prominent role in the soundscape of Kars, where they can be heard blaring out of car windows and out of the speakers at mosques and homes. These recordings have also become a central tool for *sinezenci*, who listen to them obsessively, copying down the words in notebooks and learning to recite them by ear.

The influence of high quality recordings of recitation from Azerbaijan and Iran has led to the re-specialisation of recitation in Turkey. Since the 1990s young reciters from Kars and Iğdır have began to write and recite their own poetry during Muharram, with some, the most popular being Halil Çelik (b. 1985) and Ali Kaçan (b.1986), even producing full length albums of *sinezen* in studios in Ankara and Istanbul. This process of writing, reciting and recording has reenergised recitation and transformed the *meclis* in Turkey to the extent that some individuals have begun to refer to themselves as *meddah*. This new wave of *meddah* have taken huge influence from Shi'ah reciters and eulogists from across the globe but are also involved in their own creative processes of appropriating, translating, writing and composing. Through this process they have revived and reconfigured the craft of devotional performances in ways that represent meaningful ways of lamenting Karbala in contemporary Turkey.

Concluding Remarks

In this chapter I have described the vernacular performative traditions of Shi'i mourning in Kars, Turkey. I began by tracing the oral traditions of Muharram mourning in Turkey before offering a more ethnographic description of practices of lamentation amongst Azeri Shi'ah in the city of Kars. I then traced the recent changes in these performance traditions, in terms of the development of poetry, form and the use of media. The recent re-specialisation of recitation in the community brought about as a result of these new media forms and technologies raise many further questions for the study of these sonic forms of devotion. Though the circulation of texts, reciters, melodies and ideas are not new in this border region the development of new media has had a profound impact on forms of oral performance. Studying and observing these changes and transformation are central to questions of embodiment in religion and the role of sound and music in devotional life.

Furthermore, by discussing these practices of recitation in the framework of other singer poet traditions in the region, I have drawn attention not only to the need to engage seriously with the oral, acoustic and aesthetic in the lives of Muslims but also to the wider connections and influences between vernacular religious practice and other forms of performance, poetry and expression.

Citations

And, M. (1979). The Muharram Observances in Anatolian Turkey. In P. J. Chelkowski (Ed.). *Ta'ziyeh: Ritual and Drama in Iran*. New York: New York University Press.

— (2002). *Ritüelden drama: Kerbelâ, Muharrem, Ta'ziye*. Istanbul: Yapı Kredi Yayınları.

Ayoub, M. M. (1978). *Redemptive Suffering in Islam: A Study of the Devotional Aspects of Ashura in Twelver Shi'ism*. Berlin: Walter de Gruyter.

Andrews, P. (1989). *Ethnic Groups in the Republic of Turkey (Vol. 1)*. Wiesbaden: Reichert.

Blum, S. (2005). Compelling Reasons to Sing: The Music of Taziyeh. *TDR/The Drama Review*, 49(4), 86–90.

Boratav, P.N. (2012). Maddāḥ. In P. Bearman, Th. Bianquis, C.E. Bosworth, E. van Donzel, W.P. Heinrichs (Eds.). *Encyclopaedia of Islam*, Second Edition. Consulted online on 26 November 2017 <http://dx.doi.org/10.1163/1573-39 12_islam_SIM_4728>

Bruinessen, M. van (1996). Kurds, Turks and the Alevi Revival in Turkey. *Middle East Report* 200, 7–10.

Cahen, C. (1970). Le Problème du Shî'isme dans l'Asie Mineure Turque Préot-tomane. *Le Shi'isme Imâmite: Colloque de Strasbourg (6-9 mai 1968).* Paris: Presses Universitaires de France, 115–129.

Çağlayan, B. (1997). *Kerbelâ Mersiyeleri.* (Unpublished doctoral thesis)

Erdener, Y. (1995). *The Song Contests of Turkish Minstrels: Improvised Poetry Sung to Traditional Music.* New York: Garland.

Hess, L. (2015). *Bodies of Song: Kabir Oral Traditions and Performative Worlds in North India.* Oxford University Press, USA.

Isen, M. (1993). *Acıyı Bal Eylemek. Türk Edebiyatında Mersiye.* Akçağ: Ankara.

Lord, A. B. (1960). *The Singer of Tales.* Harvard University Press.

Özdemir, U. (2016) *Kimlik, Ritüel, Müzik İcrası.* Istanbul: Kolektif Kitap.

Parry, M. (1987). T*he Making of Homeric Verse: The Collected Papers of Milman Parry.* Oxford University Press on Demand.

Shaffer, B. (2002). *Borders and Brethren: Iran and the Challenge of Azerbaijani Identity.* Cambridge, Mass.: MIT Press.

Sterne, J. (2011). The Theology of Sound: A Critique of Orality. *Canadian Journal of Communication,* 36(2), 207.

Üzüm, I. (1993) *İnanç Esasları Açısından Türkiye'de Caferilik.* Unpublished Doctoral Thesis, Marmara University.

Zarcone, T., & Zarinebaf, F. (1993). *Les Iraniens d'Istanbul.* Paris: Peeters Pub & Booksellers.

Zarcone, T. (2004). *La Turquie moderne et l'islam.* Paris: Flammarion.

The *Aşıq Saz* in West and East Azerbaijan Provinces of Iran

Farhad Shidfar

Introduction

*Ozan*s and *aşıq*s were and still are known as the minstrels in the Turkic world and related countries. Iran, with its population of about 35–40 million Azerbaijanis can be regarded as one of the biggest and most important Turkish populated countries after Turkey. Within the culture and literature of the Silk Road among the Turkish people inhabiting Iran, the musical poetic art of the *aşıq*s is one of the oldest. Iran and Azerbaijan are the only two countries where stories, anecdotes and legends of the Silk Road are still recited and sung lively in oral tradition and in a rural and traditional atmosphere, such as in *qəhvəxana*s (coffee houses) and wedding ceremonies by *aşıq*s or *ozan*s who have preserved this oral popular culture and tradition.

Today, a wide gap can be observed between the former passing from one generation to the other to an overthrowing of the older generation and a disregard of a younger generation towards Turkish traditions. The tradition of *aşıq*s is actually struggling to survive in Iran, while at the same time being related to other traditions in Anatolia and elsewhere. The study of this culture hence is urgent and important. As no compilations and written documents exist, there is no hope for this rich culture to survive. Since the Azerbaijani *aşıq saz* and *aşıq* music has to be regarded as one of the main columns of Turk nations and culture, this would mean to loose a part of history which obviously threatens Turkish art, literature and ultimately Turkish culture in general.

The present article tries to focus on *aşıq saz*, *saz* or *kopuz*, which is regarded as one of the oldest musical instruments in the history of Turks.[1] The *saz* and similar instruments including the *dutar* or *dombra* are found throughout Turkic Central Asia. Moreover, the music performed on these instruments has a number of common features. These include the use of drones, chromatic scales and a modal concept involving tetrachords and pentachords along with a hierarchy of pitches. The music played by singer-poet like *aşıq*s on their respective long-necked lutes has always remained a separate entity. Today, *aşıq*s generally are aware of the musical

---

[1] In 2015 the author of the present article completed his Ph.D. thesis on the *aşıq saz* and *aşıq* music in Azerbaijan provinces of Iran at the State Conservatory for Turkish Music of Istanbul Technical University (Shidfar, 2015). The author's personal background (who grew up in Urmia the capital of West Azerbaijan province of Iran), his performing ability to play the instrument *aşıq saz* since childhood enriched his ethnomusicological research journey in an invaluable manner.

modes (*dastgah*s, *makam*s etc.) and can even perform parts of them. Nonetheless, they analyze their own music in separate regionally varying traditional terms.

Elements such as *aşıq* poetic forms and *aşıq* melodic structures constitute the roots and the richness of the culture and consequently where in the focus of the present research of *aşıq* music and literature. Ethnomusicological research furthermore includes theories concerning issues such as dissemination and interpretation of this tradition. For example the word *se* in *setar* means "three" and hermeneutically represents Allah, Mohammad and Ali, who are symbolized by the three stings of the instrument. Likewise, dozens of traditional nomenclatures are used within the *aşıq saz* and its music, related to beliefs, rituals and traditions, weddings and dances, agricultural terms, instruments, songs and lyrics etc. Musicological analysis of *aşıq* music includes the following topics in music and terminology:

> Terminology of traditional tuning systems, including *baş*, *orta*, *osmanlı*, *qarı*, *ruhani*, *segah*, *qemli* etc.
>
> Cadences such as *ayak verme* and *ayak verdi bitirdi* (literary "to give foot") meaning "finishing the melody".
>
> Name of the frets such as *şah perde*, *vezir*, *vekil*, *bayati*, *osmanlı perdesi*, *beçe perdeler*, etc.
>
> Melodic characteristics like the use of *hava* with its all conveying meanings such as drone, reciting tone or *karar*, accidentals, etc.
>
> Rhythmic characteristics including *deve dabanı*, *dik dabanı*, *ayak dövme*, *deve yürüyüşü*, *axsama* or *topallama* etc., i.e. the "walking style of camel", "laming", "crippling" etc.

Azerbaijan Provinces in Iran

In Iran ethnically different Turkic groups exist, each carrying Turkic musical culture:

> West and East Azerbaijan
> Zanjan
> Ghom and Saveh
> Khorasan and Turkman Sahra
> Ghashghayi Turks

However, among the huge Turkic population covering almost half of Iran, the provinces West and East Azerbaijan are of central importance for Azerbaijani language and culture in Iran. In the present article, *aşıq* music environments in two particular regions in West and East Azerbaijan were selected. West and East Azerbaijan provinces are located in the north west of Iran (see figure 1). The province West Azerbaijan, comprises an area of 43,660 square kilometers, including the Lake Urmia. Its capital is Urmia. The province is divided into 14

Figure 1: Map of Iran provinces. Retrieved from *www.worldofmaps.net/en/middle-east/map-iran/ map-regions-iran.htm* (last accessed February 2018).

*shahrestan*s (counties) including Piranshahr, Urmia, Mahabad, Oshnaviyeh, Miandoab, Naghadeh, Takab, Shahindej, Maku, Chaldoran, Salmas, Khoy, Sardasht and Bukan.

The province East Azerbaijan covers an area of approximately 47,830 km²; it has a population of around four million people, about one million more than West Azerbaijan. Culturally, politically, and commercially most important city of this eastern province is the historical city of Tabriz. According to the latest divisions of the country in 1996, the counties of this province are: Ahar, Ajabshir, Bostan Abad, Bonab, Tabriz, Jolfa, Sarab, Shabestar, Kaleybar, Maragha, Marand, Malekan, Miyana, Heris, and Hashtrood. The province has common borders with the republics of Azerbaijan, Armenia and Nakhchivan. A dense network of roads and railways connects East Azerbaijan with other parts of Iran and also to neighboring countries. In particular Russians have tried to exert a lasting influence in the region over the past 300 years, occupying the area on numerous occasions. In the late nineteenth century the constitutionalist movement of Iran began here. The origins of ethnic tensions in Azerbaijan go back to the colonialist policies of the Soviet Union and Imperial Russia.

Following musical categorization, West Azerbaijan has been divided into Urmia and Sulduz / Naghadeh. Among these two environments Urmia has been focused on here. Following, in East Azerbaijan mainly Tabriz and Gharadagh music environments have been analyzed. While other cities in East Azerbaijan province of course show different styles in *aşıq* music, they represent minorities and in generally follow the *aşıq* music culture of Tabriz and Gharadagh. We will finally compare *aşıq saz* and *aşıq* music in West and East Azerbaijan provinces with each other.

One of the most outstanding features of the region is the language *Azari/ Azerice/Azerbaijani* and the folklore connected to it. There are very hard debates of the roots of Azerbaijani language as either being originally a branch of Iranian languages or belonging to the Turkic language family. The language debates over the question of being "Azeri" or "Azerbaijani" is highly politicized and includes the nationalistic issue of whether it is an independent language or a dialect spoken in Iran. The term "Azerbaijani" understood as a member of the family of Turkic language results in mentioning a nation living there, while the term "Azeri" refers to the people as the tribes of Iran rather than an old huge nation. The discussion finally leads to some political nationalistic and social movements of separation of Azerbaijan from Iran or not. Likewise, nationalistic features are observable in the issue of minstrel music in both West and East Azerbaijan provinces in Iran as the heart of these debates. As language, literature and music are interwoven, it should be analyzed by linguists, historians and musicians / musicologists. It is very clear that the mentioned field deserves for an interdisciplinary approach and comprehensive studies.

The Aşıq Saz

The Azerbaijani *saz* is a long-necked, fretted, plucked lute with a neck either attached to or carved from the resonator (see figure 2). As such, it is a member of a large family of plucked long-neck lutes found throughout the Near East and Central Asia. In Turkey, a number of instruments similar to the Azerbaijani *saz* are played, varying in both their size and number of strings. These instruments are similarly called *saz* along with some specific name such as *cura* or *bağlama*.

The origin of the word *saz* is unclear. *Saz* in Persian generally refers to any musical instrument, particularly to stringed instruments. As an adjective, *saz* means "in good condition", "tuned up". *Saz* is furthermore the present tense stem of the verb *sakhtan* ("to build"). In Turkish, on the other hand, *saz* refers either to a number of long-necked lutes, or to music in general. Since there is no Turkish word where *saz* might have come from, it seems likely that the name *saz* have been borrowed from Persian language.

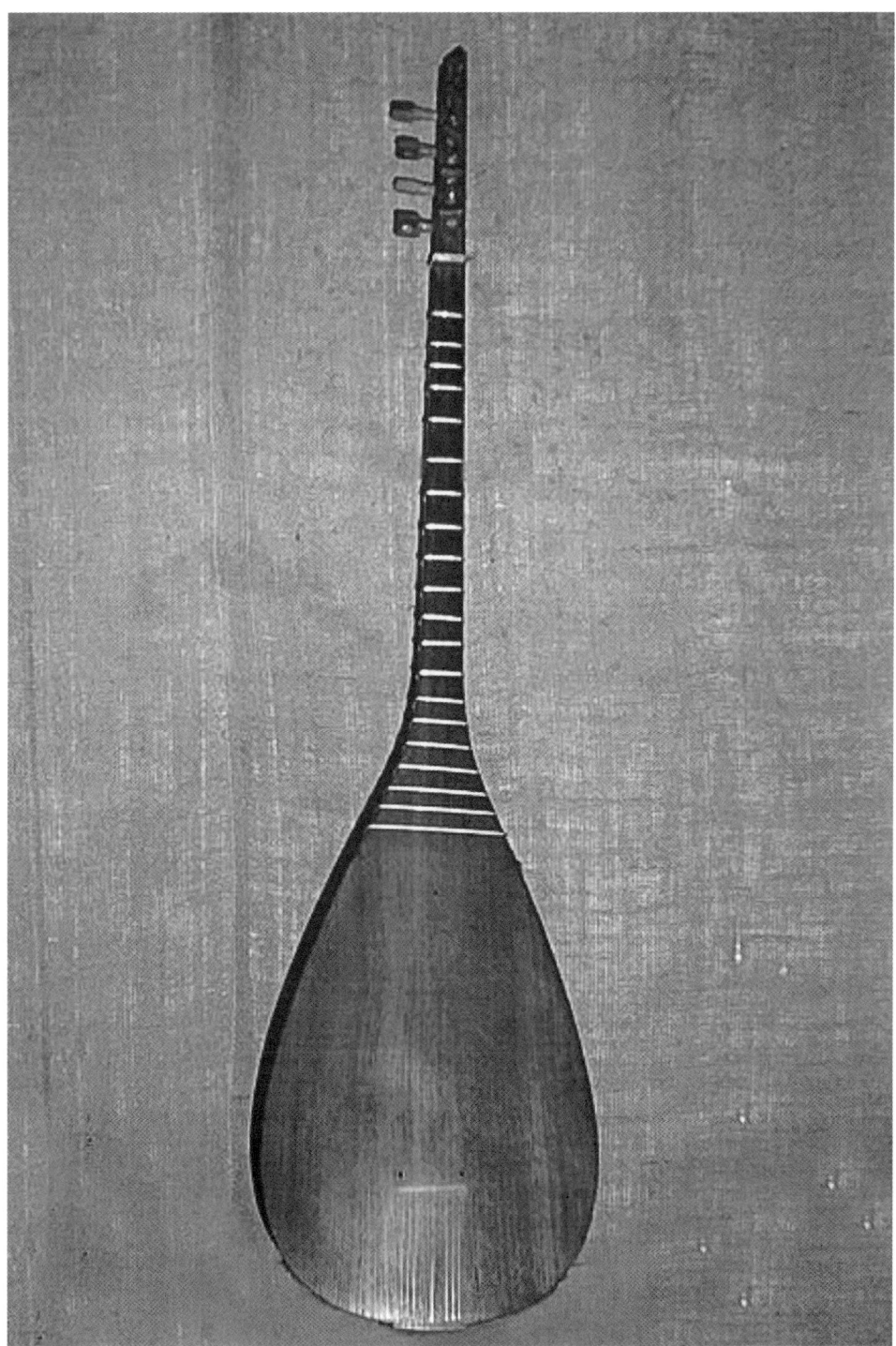

Figure 2: *Aşıq saz*, 2012 (photo by Farhad Shidfar).

Although some of the instruments performed in Azerbaijan have close relatives in neighboring regions, few are exactly the same. The *tar*, for instance, found in Azerbaijan is recognizably a *tar*, but not identical with the Persian *tar*. The Azerbaijani *saz* is similar to, but not identical with the Turkish *saz* or *bağlama*. On the other hand, instruments such as the accordion, clarinet and violin are imported from the western countries, and there is no difference between for example European, Persian and Azerbaijani violins.

Investigating the roots of minstrel music and *aşıqs* in Anatolia reveals not only common roots of *aşıqs* in Azerbaijan or Iran, but also the existence of common cultures including literature, music structure, language, etc. which are visible among the Turkic world in antiquity. Azerbaijani *saz* and *bağlama* are regarded as the grand children of the same ancestors of *kopuz* family. This encompasses all Turkic world countries mostly located along the silk road line over a huge geographical area including middle Asia, Caucasia, Middle East, Caspian Sea regions, even China and the Balkans. In particular Anatolia is seen as the most important region in keeping and preserving this culture before and after Islam. Anatolia, Azerbaijan and Iran have been affected by the appearance of Islam. The similarities of Anatolian *aşıq* music with its Turkic world counterparts are visible in common names of songs, melodic and rhythmic structures, verbal and poetic structures, shapes of instruments and common organological characteristics, social rituals and traditions of Anatolian *aşıqs* especially those of *aşıqs* in Kars and Erzurum: *Aşıqs* in the great Seljuk empire in 1075–1308 AD and afterwards in the Ottoman empire used to play and sing in the time of victories mentioning the heroic characters of the heroes in battles, motivating soldiers who were send to the front; further in wedding ceremonies and funerals, etc. These characters can be found parallel among *aşıqs* of the Turkic world, as for example in the role of *aşıq Qurbani* at the long lasting *Chaldiran* war between the *Safavid* empire in Iran and Anatolia as part of the *Ottoman* empire. Both countries share almost the same minstrel, poetic and cultural characteristics. It may hence be better to launch a parallel research among Turkic world *aşıqs*. However, findings concerning *saz* or *saz* music in one of Turkic world countries like Azerbaijan or Iran may help us to find other yet undiscovered parts of the puzzle of its Anatolian counterpart *bağlama*, and vice versa.

Pickens (1975: 209) described several different sizes of long-necked lutes in Turkey, including, from small to large, *cura*, *bağlama*, *tambura*, *bozuk* (probably a corruption of the Persian word *buzurg* "big"), *divan sazı* ("audience hall *saz*"), and *meydan sazı* ("public square *saz*"). All these lutes, similar to the Azerbaijani *saz*, have three courses, though the number of strings per course varies from one instrument to another. Thus, the lutes may also be classified according to the number of their strings.[2] Turkish lutes use either steel or brass strings. The cours-

---

[2] The big lutes, such as *divan sazı* or *meydan sazı*, can have ten or twelve strings (3 + 4 + 3 or 4 + 4 + 4). These are both called *onikitelli* ("12 strings"), but includes a variant with ten strings. The *bağlama* may have six or seven string (2 + 2 + 2 or 3 + 2 + 2) and is also called

es were traditionally named *zil teli* (high) and *bam teli* (low) while no name was given for the middle course. At present, this nomenclature is not universally used. The middle and low courses of Anatolian lutes are never tuned in unison (Picken, 1975: 211) as they frequently are in Azerbaijan.

In Iranian Azerbaijan the middle course of the the *saz* is only sometimes tuned lower than the high and low courses. However, the Turkish tunings are identical to what is called the *shah perde* tuning. If appropriate transpositions are made, there is, moreover, some indication that this type of tuning is more often used in the Republic of Azerbaijan. Comparing measurements of various Turkish long-necked lutes as given by Laurence Picken (1975, see table 1) with *saz*'s measured in Iranian Azerbaijan (see table 2), we can see that the overall length of the Azerbaijani *saz* falls between that of the *cura saz* and *bağlama*. The *saz* played in Azerbaijan is an instrument of roughly 105 cm length of which 41 cm is the length of the resonator. Length and width of the body, however, are even larger than that of the *bağlama* and in fact rather approximately that of the *divan sazı*. The Azerbaijani *saz* is hence proportionately somewhat shorter and squatter than its Turkish counterpart.

In Urmia the *saz* is the fundamental instrument in *aşıq* traditions. The length of the resonator (*ghazan*) is between 45–50 cm, the neck is 65–70 cm. The length of the instrument is about 110–120 cm. It has about 13 frets (*perde*), the number of strings differs between 7 up and 9, based on the taste of the *aşıq*s. For the

Instrument	Tuning	Overall length	Body length	Body width
cura	(la re sol)	74 (cm)	21 (cm)	13 (cm)
bozuk or *bağlama*	(la re sol)	118 (cm)	36 (cm)	20 (cm)
divan saz	(re sol do)	135 (cm)	45 (cm)	28 (cm)

Table 1: Long-necked lutes in Turkey (Picken, 1975: 210).

	Total Length (cm)	Length of Resonator (cm)	Width of Resonator (cm)	Width of Neck (cm)	Resonator Circumference (cm)	No. of Ribs (cm)
West Azerbai-jan *saz*	107–108	41	23–26	4	57–61	10
East Azerbai-jan *saz*	103	41	26	3	58	9

Table 2: Comparative chart of different parts of Azerbaijani *saz*'s (Farr, 1976: 30).

altıtelli ("six strings") or *yedi telli* ("seven strings"), respectively. The *tambura* and *bozuk* have nine strings (3 + 3 + 3) and might be called *dokuztelli* ("nine strings"). (Picken, 1975: 210).

thickness of the string, the diameter of 20 mm is generally prefered. The Turkish names for the parts of the Azerbaijani *saz* are given by Albright Farr (1976: 30; see figure 3 and table 3).

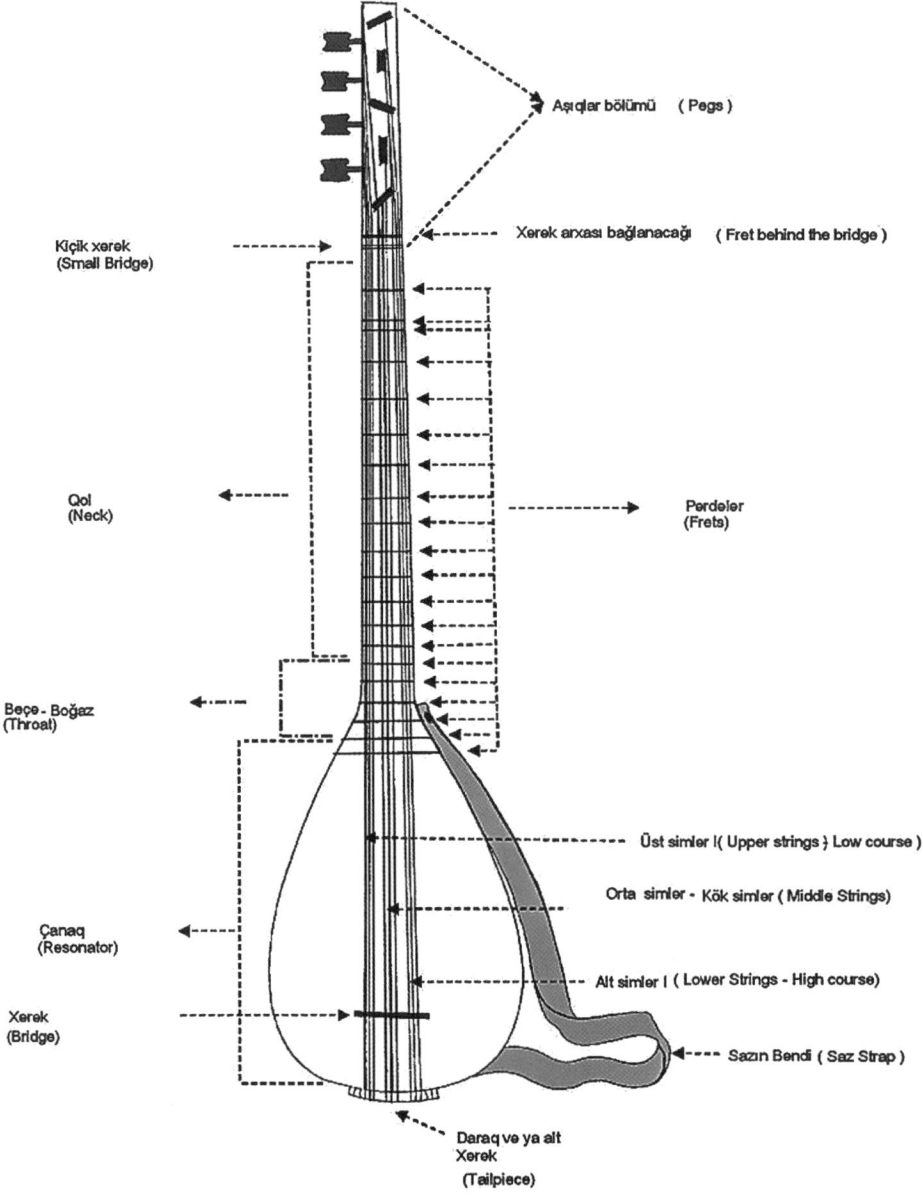

Figure 3: Parts of the *aşıq saz*.

English	Azerbaijani (in Iran)	Translation in English
Bridge	*kharak* (P)	Little donkey
Point at which the strings are attached	*darakh* (T)	Comb
Fret	*parda* (P)	Curtain
Intermediate section of the Saz neck	*boghaz*	Throat
Noise makers	*gushi* (P)	Ear
Neck	*bazu* (P)	Arm
Peg	*gulakh* (T)	Ear
Plectrum	*mezrab* (A)	Plectrum
Resonator	*kasa* (P) *qazan* (T)	Bowl
String	*sim* (P)	Wire

P = Persian word; T = Turkish & Azerbaijani word; A = Arabic word.

Table 3: Parts of the Azerbaijani *saz* (Farr, 1976: 30).

Turkish *saz* makers offer their customers a choice between two types of *saz* resonator. The *oyma saz* features a resonator carved from a single block of wood. These resonators are resistant to high atmospheric humidity. The alternate type (which is the Turkish *saz* lid type used in Azerbaijan) is called *yaprakli* (with leaves), *çemberli* (with hoops) or *dilimli* (with slices). The resonator is constructed by fitting several slats of wood (usually an odd number) together. The carvel-built resonators use less wood, but require more labor. The leaves may open if subjected to high humidity, but the instruments are of lighter weight. The frets on Turkish *saz*s are tied on with tinted nylon string (Picken, 1975: 224f). The knots are similar to those used in Azerbaijan, but they lie on the back of the neck as opposed to the high course side of the neck in Azerbaijan. There are also different types of knots in Azerbaijani *saz*s called *parvane* ("butterfly").

The resonating cavity of the Azerbaijani *saz* is made of nine or ten ribs glued together to form a bowl, which measures about 59 cm around at the widest point. This bowl is then covered with a thin piece of wood. In order to allow the sound to radiate by twenty or so small holes are drilled in the resonator lid and in the ribs making up the resonator. The resonator and its cover are made from mulberry wood. The neck of the *saz* is about 54 cm long. It may be constructed so as to be hollow. This gives the tone of the instrument more resonance. The neck is made of walnut wood because it is harder and more durable than mulberry. Between the neck and body of the *saz* there is an intermediate section curving up from the resonator to the neck. This piece is known as the throat, or *boghaz*, and is about 10 cm long. It is made of walnut wood as well.

Figure 4: Rib curving device (Photo: Farhad Shidfar).

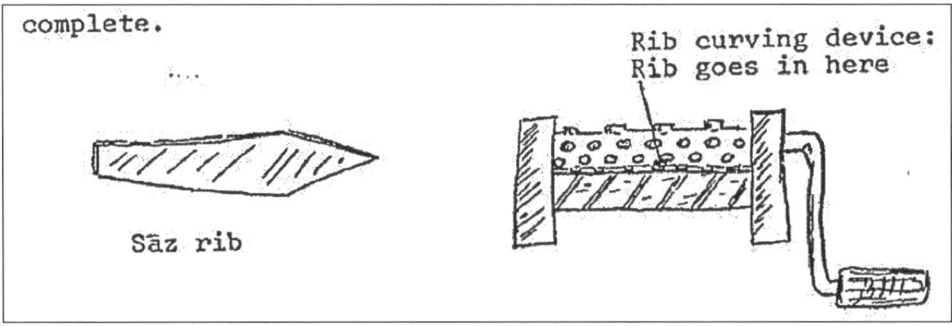

Figure 5: Rib curving device (Farr, 1976: 33).

The most difficult part of making a *saz* is fashioning the ribs that make up the resonator. These are first cut into uniformly shaped pickets. Before the ribs can be glued in place, they must be curved slightly. This is accomplished with a combination of heat and pressure. One side of the picket is heated, and then it is inserted, heated side up, into an ingenious device reminiscent of the wringers on an old-fashioned washing machine.

The top roller is studded metal and the bottom roller is threaded diagonally. When the heated picket has been fed into this device, the studs cause the wood

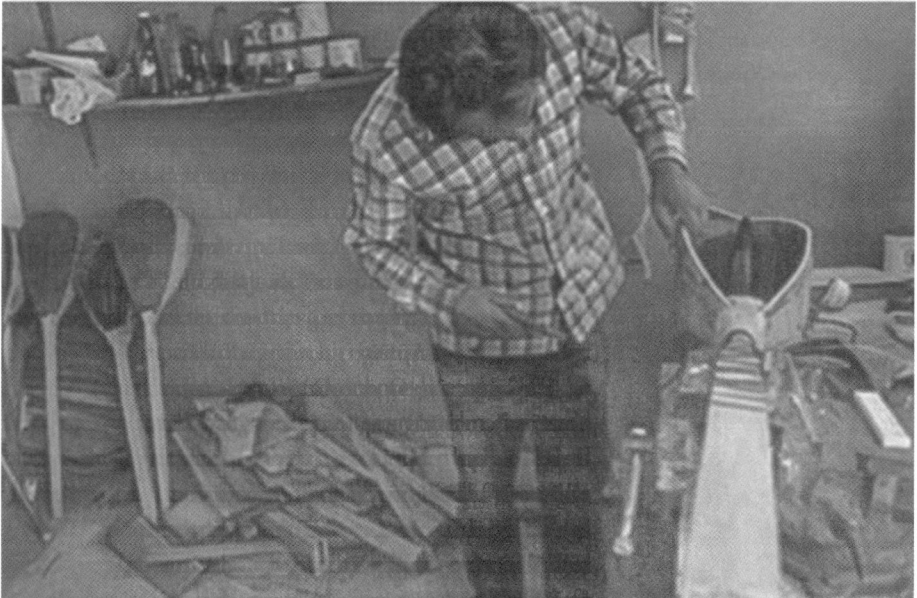

Figure 6: *Saz* making workshop photos (Photo: Farhad Shidfar).

to curve in the direction of the studs. The curved slat must then be further filed or sawed to fit its niche in the resonator body. The slats closest to the resonator cover are glued in place first, and then those adjoining until the entire "dome" of the resonator are complete.

The rest of the *saz* is not too difficult to put together. Holes for pegs must be drilled, the cover attached, etc. If the instrument is decorated with shell work, though, this increases manufacture time considerably and also results in a higher final price (Farr, 1976: 33).

Turkish long-necked lutes are made from a wider variety of woods than the Azerbaijani *saz*. The bow-shaped part of the resonator which Picken calls hemipyriform may be made from alder, cornel, chestnut, elm, hornbeam, juniper, or willow in addition to the favorite Azerbaijani building material, that is mulberry. The lid of the Turkish *saz* has three sections. The biggest part is the *göğüs* (breast), which may be slightly convex and which covers the main part of the resonating cavity. This portion is usually made from some softer wood, such as pine. The other two sections, called shoulders, cover a portion of the resonator on either side of the *göğüs*. These pieces are cut from hornbeam, chestnut, or mulberry (Picken, 1975: 214). The neck is made from some harder wood, walnut or apricot, for instance. (Picken, 1975: 209ff).

The scales produced by the placement of these frets vary. In Turkey, moreover, there is apparently a tendency to use more microtones on lutes played in urban areas. This is due to the influence of the highly microtonal Turkish classical music which is more often heard in cities and towns. Picken (1975: 225) compares a "rural" *cura saz* from Gaziantep with a more "urban" one from Kastamonu. The Azerbaijani *saz* has eleven frets in the first octave (including only one microtone), it hence resembles a "rural" *saz* in Turkey. The *aşıq*s used an oblong, flexible plectrum made from cherry tree bark. Cherry bark plectrums were also employed by Turkish *saz* players (Picken, 1975: 227). Nowadays plectrums are made from plastic for both Turkish and Azerbaijani *saz*s.

For Azerbaijani *saz*s, the resonator, throat, and neck of the instruments are often highly ornamented with gazelle horn, camel bone and mother of pearl. Mother of pearl rattles is also attached to the neck on the side away from the performer. Ornamental work of high quality is the mark of a craftsman, thus, instruments with unusually fine shell work are esteemed by performers (Farr, 1976: 31; see figure 7).

The *saz* has nine steel strings grouped in three courses of three strings each. These courses bear the Persian names for low, middle and high courses: *bam*, *vasat* and *zil* (variant of Persian *zir*). According to Albright Farr, the strings are most often tuned close to the pitches *fa* or *sol* (other tunings will be discussed below). I will consider the high open course of the *saz* as *re* and the low open course as *do*. Notations and transcriptions will be done according to these standarts. The *zil* course is used for the melody, while both the *vasat* and *bam* courses only for the drone. Sometimes the player will use the *bam* course for occasional notes of the melody. To do this, he or she stops the strings with his thumb. Five of the pegs holding these strings are on the front of the neck; the remaining four are on the side of the neck closest to the performer. The strings run from the pegs over a nut at the top of the neck. From there, they go down the neck over a small

Figure 7: Ornaments of *aşıq saz*, Urmia 2010 (Photo: Farhad Shidfar).

bridge, which sits flush with the resonator cover about 1 cm high. The strings are fastened at the base of the resonator onto a piece of gazelle horn (Farr, 1976: 31). In practice, *saz* players in Urmia remove the two strings in the middle course closest to the *zil* course. This allows the player to use the upper *zil* course as a solo course, that is, without the drone strings sounding.

The *saz* has fourteen frets on its neck, while the rest are located on the throat and the resonator. All are originally made of wound sheep gut but nowadays from nylon strings. A fret is known simply as *parda*, *parde*, *perde* or *pardeh*. Farr (1976) considers the low open string as f and the high one as g, and explains the scales used in Urmia and Tabriz (differing slightly from each other) as follows:

	Lo	Ho	1	2	3	4	5	6	7	8	9	10	11	12	13	14
Rezaiyeh	f̲	G̲	a̲	a̲#	a̲#	b̲	c'	c'#	d'	d'#	e'	f'	g'	g'#	a'	bb'
Tabriz	Lo	Ho	1	2	3	4	5	6	7	8	9	10	11	12	13	14
	f̲	G̲	a̲	a̲#	a̲#	b̲	c'	c'#	d'	d'#	e'	f'	g'	a'	bb'	C"

Lo = Low open string; Ho = High open string.

Table 4: Old system of naming strings of *aşıq saz* (Farr, 1976: 32).

Different from Farrs table, however, today the open lower string is generally assumed as c and the open higher string as d. The two basic scales given in table 4 are identical except for the interval between the eleventh and twelfth frets. According to the modern transposed system, in East Azerbaijani *saz* this interval is a whole step between d' and e'. In West Azerbaijan, the interval is a half step between d' and d'#, fret 12 hence one half tone lower than at the East Azerbaijani *saz*. There are only two non-chromatic intervals in the *saz* scale: those between frets 2 and 3, and 3 and 4, which form quarter steps. In practice, though, fret two is not used in melodies except as an ornamental pitch, thus, the scale is essentially chromatic. It is further noteworthy that *aşıq*s in Urmia number the frets on their *saz* from one to fourteen beginning with the highest pitch. East Azerbaijani musicians, on the other hand, number their frets from low pitch to high pitch. Due to the urbanization for the use of *makam shur* in *aşıq* music one fret has been added. If we consider the open string as d, this recently added fret is d# without which *makam shur* cannot be performed.

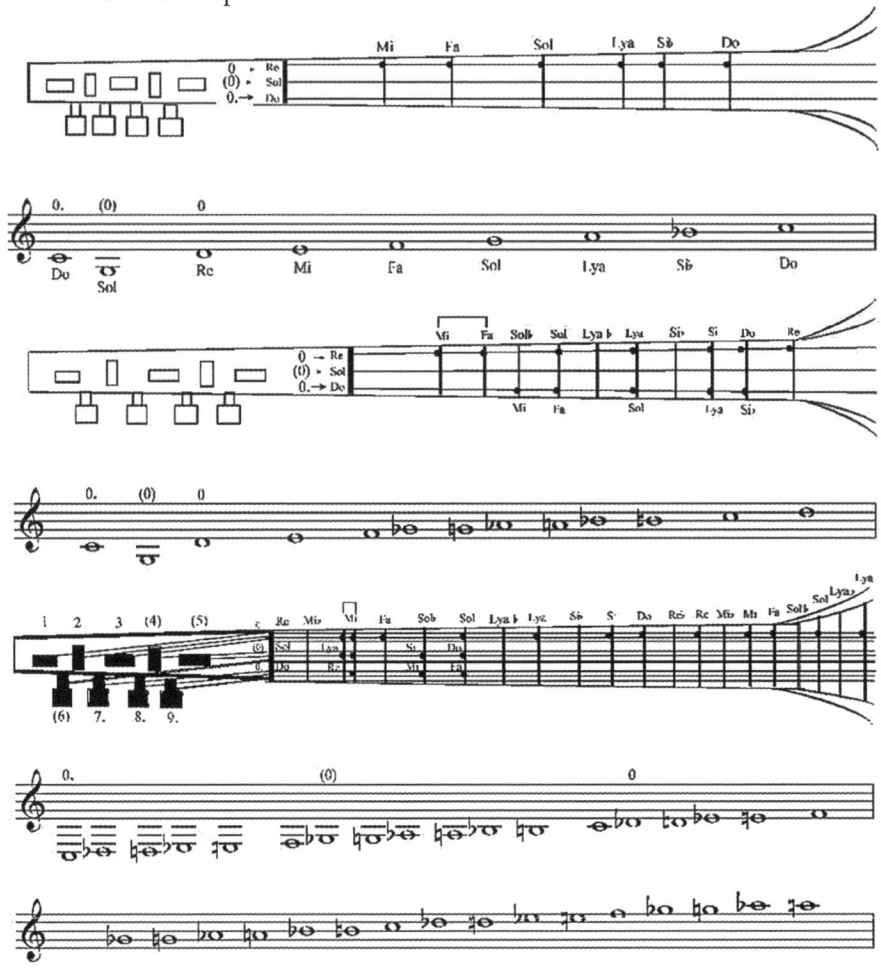

Figure 8: Frets in *aşıq saz*.

Tuning

There are a number of different ways to tune the *saz* depending on both the *hava* (melody) and the taste of the performer. The basic tuning for the *saz* all over West Azerbaijan is where the *bam* (low open strings) and *vasat* (*orta* as middle strings) are tuned to the same pitch while the *zil* (high open strings) are tuned one whole tone higher. This tuning can be used for any of the *hava*s or *aşıq* music melodies.

All other tunings involve the middle course to be tuned either up or down to be in tune with, or an octave lower than, frets 1 (*segah*), fret 3 (*ruhani* or *mahur*), or fret 5 (*shah perde*). This gives the tuning a definite tonal bias and always emphasizes either the pitch that acts as the tonic, reciting or the final note, for the basic melody pattern. The word *kök* comes from Persian *kook* or *kuk* which means "tune".

In East Azerbaijan, since g is the most common reciting tone, the most common alternate tuning for the middle course is g or g' which is *shah perde*. These tunings are used more often in Tabriz than in West Azerbaijan because most Urmia *aşıq*s remove the two strings from the middle course closest to the upper course of their instrument. The *aşıq* with an instrument modified in this way, would gain little tonal boost by retuning his one remaining middle string. Alternate tunings are not totally absent from the Western Azerbaijani scene.

East Azerbaijan *saz* tuning systems falls into four major categories, each named according to changes in the middle strings:

Bash perde or *segah kök* (middle course is tuned to e).

Nim perde / *ruhani kök* / *urfani kök* / *ara kök* (middle course is tuned to f).

Shah perde / *qari kök* / *umumi kök* (middle course is tuned to g).

Osmanli perde / *zarinci kök* / *çoban bayati kök* (middle course is tuned to a or d or both a and d).

Figure 9: East and West Azerbaijan *saz* tuning systems (Mehdizadə, 2012: 32).

Hierarchy of Pitches

Hierarchy of pitches results from the fact that some pitches receive more emphasis than others. Moreover, different pitches have different functions. The *aşıq*s are definitely aware that some pitches in a *hava* are more important than others. The names are fairly descriptive. *Bash perde* means the first, or head fret. *Nim perde* means half fret (between *bash perde* and *shah perde*). *Shah perde* is the most important, or king fret. *Dip perde* is slightly lower than the other important frets when the *aşıq* is playing the *saz*. There are traditionally ways of calling the frets according to the region and history, etc. like; *ayak* (foot), *ruhani* (spiritual), *osmanli perdeh* (ottoman), *beche* (child in Persian) for high note frets, etc.

The use of the lower and middle course of the *aşıq saz* as continued sound is called *dem ses* ("drone"). Since the *saz* is frequently played with a plectrum stroke which sweeps across all the strings, the open strings sounds as a drone. We can divide it into lower course drone as permanent drone as the tuning does not change and middle course drone as flexible drone, as the middle courses change and represent the rank or *makam* of the melody. In West Azerbaijan, drones are usually functionally important, since the open string pitch is a fifth below of the *shah perde* which is c, often a stressed pitch, or an octave below c', which often introduces a *hava* in Urmia. In East Azerbaijan *saz* drone is regarded for middle course beside the upper ones representing the *makam* or rank of the melody as mentioned in the tuning section. Thus, the drone serves to emphasize these important upper course pitches either harmonically or by doubling at the octave.

Rhythms and Meters in Aşıq Music

Saz rhythms in *aşıq* music are actually as complex as those in Turkish music, using several meters including 3/8, 5/8, 6/8, 7/8, 2/4, 3/4, 4/4 12/16, etc. Different from Azerbaijani classical music, however, the meters in *aşıq* music normally are double or triple. Very rarely, other metric patterns occur, such as free meters especially in West Azerbaijan *aşıq* music, reminding to what is generally called *uzun hava* in Turkey. Free meters sometimes occur in the middle of the song where triple and duple meter alternate briefly. Sometimes the whole melody moves on within rhythmic meters while the vocal is performed in free meters. The characteristics of rhythm in *aşıq* music sometimes represent the historical background of the people who were originally nomadic tribesmen. This sort of rhythm hence recalls the sound of horses and hoof-beats, as especially the insertion of 12/16 in the frame work of 4/4 as in *hijran kerem* or *dol hijrani*.

Figure 10: Playing position of the Azerbaijani *saz*. www.youtube.com/watch?v=s_0LogWVc1o (accessed 18 May, 2018).

Playing Techniques, Notation, and Melodic Ornaments

As shown in figure 10, the Azerbaijani *saz* player holds the instrument with the neck in his left hand, in a way that the instrument stands diagonally across his body.

There is usually a leather cord fastened to the *saz* so that the player can suspend the instrument from his shoulder when he plays standing up.

Left hand techniques, as described in general by Farr (1976: 38f) closely remind to those of Turkish *saz* instruments:

> Both the thumb and fingers of the left hand are used to play the saz. The thumb is used only on the *bam* course, whereas the fingers do most of the work playing the melody and ornaments on the zil course. The third finger is also occasionally used to play on the *bam* course. The technique is similar to the one played in *bozuk* tuning system in Turkish *bağlama*. The melody itself is a combination of *zil* and *bam* pitches rapidly interwoven. The first and second fingers play most of the melody notes, while the performer holding *saz*. Third and, less frequently, the fourth fingers play mostly decorative figures. Moreover, if the first finger has played the melody note, the second finger can also add ornamental grace notes one tone higher. (Farr, 1976: 38f).

Most techniques of transcribing and score notation nowadays are common across notation of Turkish *bağlama* and Azerbaijani *aşıq saz*. For the transcription of *aşıq saz* music, some additional notation symbols are explained in *aşıq* music scores:

> The sign "0" stands for the open lower strings (high course), i.e.: d.
> The sign "(0)" stands for the open middle strings, i.e.: g.
> The sign "0." stands for open upper strings (low course), i.e.: c.
> The signs "1 2 3" stand for the positions of fingers on the lower strings.
> The signs "(1) (2) (3)" stand for the positions of fingers on the middle strings.
> The signs "1. 2. 3." stands for the positions of fingers over the upper strings.

In music, ornaments or embellishments are common, which are not necessary part of the overall melodic line, but rather serve for decorating that line. Many melodic ornaments, such as grace notes or trills are performed as "fast notes" around a central note. Trills in *aşıq* music may occur between one and the neighboring half note depending on the intervals defined in the *makam*. Vibrato is produced by sliding a finger back and forth across the neck. The middle course is not used to perform a melody at all. Its function is only that of a drone. The difference between *aşıq saz* and Turkish *bağlama* resides here as *bağlama*'s drone note is generally the upper low open strings.

Also techniques of the right hand closely remind to that of Turkish long-necked lutes:

> The player grasps the plectrum between the thumb and first and second fingers. The strong stroke is down, weak stroke up. Sometimes just the *zil* course is individually struck, but most often all three courses are played so that the melody emerges amid a strong ground pitch. By varying plectrum techniques, meter can be changed from duple to triple. A frequent variation technique is to perform the original melody in triplets. The right hand may also ornament a melody by playing all the original melody pitches tremolo, a technique known as riz. (Farr, 1976: 40)

Three additional symbols are used in transcriptions of plectrum techniques in the *aşıq saz*, indicating the direction of the plectrum downward and vice versa, as well as generating a note without plectrum by hammering or pulling off fingers on the string of *saz*.

(Π) (V) (+)

Figure 11: Downward / upward plectrum strike / hammering or pulling off fingers on or from the strings.

An arpeggio is a musical technique where notes in a chord are played or sung in sequence, one after the other, rather than ringing out simultaneously. An alternative translation of this term is "broken chord". Arpeggios allow monophonic instruments to play chords and harmony and help create rhythmic interest. In other words an arpeggio is a group of notes which are played one after the other, added either going up or going down. Executing an arpeggio requires the player to play the sounds of a chord individually to differentiate the notes. An "arpeggiated chord" means a chord which is spread, i.e., the notes are not played exactly at the same time, but are spread out. In *aşıq saz* it generally sounds based on the tuning system of three set of strings but sounds as many as the individual strings exists in the *saz*, so it means a lot of chords may happen to come up when playing arpeggio in different positions and different tunings of *aşıq saz*.

(⅔)

Figure 12: Arpeggio.

Figure 13: Arpeggio examples played in *aşıq saz* (Mehdizadə, 2012: 189).

Tremolo refers to a rapid repetition of plectrum on the strings of *saz*, one of the most commonly seen uses of the technique are in playing the long notes in the melody. In musical notation, tremolo is indicated by strokes through the stems of the notes that mean it is written with an oblique stroke through the stem.

In the case of whole notes, which lack stems, the bars are drawn above or below the note. Generally there are three slashes or strokes on the stem of the note, because this is the same notation as would be used to indicate that regular repeated thirty-second notes should be played. If there is just one stroke, it means that it needs to be played as many as eighth notes of the note, and if there are two strokes it means that it needs to be played as many as sixteenth notes of the existing note. In Iran it is common to say *riz* or *mezrab e riz* for tremolo. *Riz* means small and tiny which represents small movements of plectrum over the strings of the *saz*.

Conclusion

This chapter deals with the *aşıq saz* in west and east Azerbaijan provinces of Iran. Generally, when we talk about Azerbaijani *aşıqs* or minstrel music of Azerbaijan, one of the major parts of this music and culture, that is the one which has been fallen inside the borderlines of Iran, is neglected. The purpose of this chapter is mainly to reveal the music culture of this area. When we talk about the Azerbaijan provinces of Iran, it includes the majority of the Turk population living in Iran which is more than half of the population of Iran. This chapter focuses on *aşıq saz* rather than *aşıq music* of Azerbaijan provinces of Iran. Further geographical aspects of the region, organological approach to the structure, shape and the origin of Azerbaijani *aşıq saz* in Iran and the comparison with its counterpart Turkish *bağlama*, different parts of the *aşıq saz*, manufacturing of the *aşıq saz*, different tuning systems of *aşıq saz*, rhythms and meters in *aşıq music*, playing techniques, notation, melodic ornamentation and the transcription system of *aşıq saz* has been discussed. On the other hand, I skipped both the historical part of my research and the part on *aşıq music* which has been described in detailed in my PhD dissertation (Shidfar, 2015). The latter includes the verbal, poetic and musical analysis of *aşıq music* repertoire, which was planned to be published as separate articles.

References

Farr, Ch. F. A. (1976). *The Music of Professional Musicians of North West Iran* (Unpublished doctoral dissertation). Washington: University of Washington.

Mehdizadə, Ç. (2012). *Saz Məktəbi*, Baku: Azarbaycan Milli Elmlar Akademiyası Folkolor Institutu.

Picken, L. (1975). *Folk musical Instruments of Turkey*. London: Oxford University Press.

Shidfar, F. (2015). *A Comparative Analysis of Ashik Saz and Ashik Music in West And East Azerbaijan Provinces of Iran* (Unpublished doctoral dissertation). Istanbul Technical University.

Contributors

Mahmut Ağbaht is a PhD student in Semitic Languages at Uppsala University, working on the Arabic dialects spoken in Akkar, northern Lebanon. His fieldwork experience also includes Hatay (Antioch), Turkey. He double-majored in Arabic Language and Literature and Linguistics, and received his M.A. in 2014 at the Department of Arabic Language and Literature, Ankara University. In 2011-2012 he did an internship and study-stay at the Department of Semitic Studies, Heidelberg University through the Erasmus Program. Subsequently he worked as a research assistant at the Department of Arabic Language and Literature, Ankara University, 2013–2017. In 2015 he co-founded in Antakya *Akdeniz Arap Dili ve Kültürü Enstitüsü Derneği* (The Mediterranean Institute of Arabic Language and Culture), the objective of which is to enhance the multilingual and multicultural environment of Hatay. His academic interests include Semitic linguistics, Arabic dialectology, oral literature, and bilingualism.

Stefan Williamson Fa is PhD candidate in the department of Social Anthropology at University College London. His research interests focus on the role of sound in Islamic ritual and religious expression, particularly in Anatolia, Iran and the Caucasus. His PhD research focuses on genres of religious recitation and mourning in the Azeri Shi'ah community in North-eastern Turkey for which he has recently completed a year of fieldwork in the city of Kars.

Martin Greve is a German ethnomusicologist with a focus on music in Turkey. From 2005–2011 he was the coordinator of the Study Program of Turkish Music at the Rotterdam World Music Academy. From 2007–2011 he served as advisor to the Berlin Philharmonic concert hall for the concert sequence *"Alla Turca."* Since May 2011, Martin Greve has been a research associate at the Orient-Institut Istanbul. In 2017, his monograph *"Makamsız. Individualization of Traditional Music on the Eve of Kemalist Turkey"* was published. His latest book *"Yeni Dersim Soundunun Oluşumu: Anlatılamazı İfade Etmek"* (Expressing the Unspeakable: The Emergence of the New Sound of Dersim), coauthored with Özay Şahin, will be published in 2018.

Wendelmoet Hamelink is a Marie Skłodowska Curie Research Fellow at the Centre for Gender Research (STK) of Oslo University. She has an MA and PhD in Cultural Anthropology and Development Sociology from Leiden University. Her book *The Sung Home. Narrative, Morality, and the Kurdish Nation* (Brill, 2016) investigates the lyrics, life stories, and live performances of Kurdish singers that offer fascinating insights into cultural practices, local politics, and everyday life in borderlands. Her methodological and theoretical perspectives consist of narrativity and oral history research, musical anthropology, gender and migration, conflict-studies and nationalism, morality and post-colonial theory. She has long-term fieldwork experience in many countries in the Middle East, Europe and Africa and she speaks Kurdish and Turkish. Her current work includes research on cultural memories and histories of Armenians originating from eastern Turkey, and on cultural resources and resilience of refugees living in Europe. Her research project *Images in Exile* focuses on gender and representation among Kurdish women who recently fled Syria and live now in Norway.

C a n s e r   K a r d a ş   was born in Gercüş, Batman in Turkey. He graduated from Turkish Language and Literature Department at Dicle University in 2002. He received a master's degree at Erciyes University in 2007 and PhD degree at Fırat University in 2013, in both Turkish Language and Literature. Since 2014 he is working as assistant professor at Muş Alparslan University, Faculty of Science and Literature, Turkish Language and Literature Department. He published various works about folklore. He is working on tangible and intangible cultures, mainly *dengbêj* and *âşık* traditions.

U l a ş   Ö z d e m i r   earned his PhD in ethnomusicology from Yıldız Technical University (Istanbul) in 2015. He specializes on musical cultures, organology, historical ethnomusicology and film music in Turkey. He is the author of *Şu Diyar-ı Gurbet Elde: Âşık Mücrimi'nin Yaşamı ve Şiirleri* (2007), *Kimlik, Ritüel, Müzik İcrası: İstanbul Cemevlerinde Zakirlik Hizmeti* (2016), *Senden Gayrı Âşık mı Yoktur: 20. Yüzyıl Âşık Portreleri* (2017) books and several scholarly articles. As a musician, he recorded albums, compilations, soundtracks and he has participated in the various concerts, festivals and lectures all around the world. He is academic staff member of Istanbul University, State Conservatory, Musicology Department.

H a n d e   S a ğ l a m   got her Bachelor degree in composition at Bilkent University Ankara, Magister in music theory from the MDW Vienna and received her doctoral degree in Ethnomusicology from the Department of Folk Music Research and Ethnomusicology (IVE), at the same University with the thesis on "Differences among Alevi and Sunni Âşıks in Sivas". Between 2005 and 2015 she has been working at the MDW on different research projects on music and minorities. Since July 2015 she works as head of the Archive of IVE. Her research interest includes music and minorities, music from Turkey, *âşık* tradition, and bi- and multimusicality.

M a r l e n e   S c h ä f e r s   is a social anthropologist and currently Marie Skłodowska-Curie Fellow at the Department for Conflict and Development Studies at Ghent University, Belgium. She obtained a PhD from the University of Cambridge in 2015 with a dissertation investigating the struggles for voice and audibility on the part of Kurdish women in Turkey. Her research focuses on the impact of state violence on intimate and gendered lives, the politics of memory and history, and the intersections of affect and politics.

Lokman Turgut is an independent researcher on the field of Kurdish Studies, with his research interest on the subject of oral traditions in Kurdistan. He also is a freelance journalist based in Frankfurt. He has a PhD Degree on the Iranian Studies from the Göttingen University with his thesis titled Kurdish Oral Literature in the Regions of Botan and Hekarî. He taught at Göttingen University from 2003 until 2004 Kurdish language classes and classes on the Kurdish oral and written literature, and taught at Erfurt University from 2011 until 2014 subjects related to the Kurdish Question and Kurdish political parties. He published several articles and monographs on Kurdish oral and religious traditions, different oral epic traditions, and different musical traditions on one hand, and on the other he wrote on the history and politics in and around Kurdistan several articles.

Farhad Shidfar was born in Urmia, West Azerbaijan province in Iran. He graduated in English language and literature at Tabriz University in 1998. At the State Conservatory for Turkish Music of Istanbul Technical University (ITU) he received a master's degree in Turkish music (2006) and Ph.D. in Musicology and Music Theory (2015). He is an active musician, playing Azerbaijani *aşıq saz*, *qopuz / kopuz* and Turkish *bağlama*. He gave numerous solo concerts in several countries especially in Iran and Turkey. He published several articles along with translations of books and articles from English to Persian. Besides performing, teaching and academical studies, he has been active in several fields including founding and running a music company and music school in Istanbul-Turkey (www.besiktasmuzik.com), teaching music theory and Azerbaijani *aşıq saz* there, running a shop for ethnic music (www.ethnicmusicshop.com) and a company for music production & record label (www.eastmagic.com) since 2006.

Xi Yang got his PhD on Armenian Studies from UCLA in 2016 with a dissertation on early modern Armenian *ashugh* (bardic) literature, focusing on Sayat Nova, the most accomplished early modern Armenian *ashugh* (bard). He currently works in China's Academy of Social Sciences (CASS), gathering and editing information about studies of literatures in the Persianate World for Chinese readers, and writes on culture studies, including the history of cultural exchange among China, Inner Asia and the Persianate World.

ORIENT-INSTITUT
ISTANBUL

ISTANBULER TEXTE UND STUDIEN

Alle erschienenen Titel sind auch als E-Books erhältlich. Sechs Jahre nach Erscheinen sind sie kostenfrei über www.ergon-verlag.de abrufbar.

1. Barbara Kellner-Heinkele, Sigrid Kleinmichel (Hrsg.), *Mīr ʿAlīšīr Nawāʾī. Akten des Symposiums aus Anlaß des 560. Geburtstages und des 500. Jahres des Todes von Mīr ʿAlīšīr Nawāʾī am 23. April 2001.* Würzburg 2003.

2. Bernard Heyberger, Silvia Naef (Eds.), *La multiplication des images en pays d'Islam. De l'estampe à la télévision (17-21 siècle). Actes du colloque* Images : fonctions et langages. L'incursion de l'image moderne dans l'Orient musulman et sa périphérie. *Istanbul, Université du Bosphore (Boğaziçi Üniversitesi), 25 – 27 mars 1999.* Würzburg 2003.

3. Maurice Cerasi with the collaboration of Emiliano Bugatti and Sabrina D'Agostiono, *The Istanbul Divanyolu. A Case Study in Ottoman Urbanity and Architecture.* Würzburg 2004.

4. Angelika Neuwirth, Michael Hess, Judith Pfeiffer, Börte Sagaster (Eds.), *Ghazal as World Literature II: From a Literary Genre to a Great Tradition. The Ottoman Gazel in Context.* Würzburg 2006.

5. Alihan Töre Şagunî, Kutlukhan-Edikut Şakirov, Oğuz Doğan (Çevirmenler), Kutlukhan-Edikut Şakirov (Editör), *Türkistan Kaygısı.* Würzburg 2006.

6. Olcay Akyıldız, Halim Kara, Börte Sagaster (Eds.), *Autobiographical Themes in Turkish Literature: Theoretical and Comparative Perspectives.* Würzburg 2007.

7. Filiz Kıral, Barbara Pusch, Claus Schönig, Arus Yumul (Eds.), *Cultural Changes in the Turkic World.* Würzburg 2007.

8. Ildikó Bellér-Hann (Ed.), *The Past as Resource in the Turkic Speaking World.* Würzburg 2008.

9. Brigitte Heuer, Barbara Kellner-Heinkele, Claus Schönig (Hrsg.), *„Die Wunder der Schöpfung". Mensch und Natur in der türksprachigen Welt.* Würzburg 2012.

10. Christoph Herzog, Barbara Pusch (Eds.), *Groups, Ideologies and Discourses: Glimpses of the Turkic Speaking World.* Würzburg 2008.

11. D. G. Tor, *Violent Order: Religious Warfare, Chivalry, and the ʿAyyār Phenomenon in the Medieval Islamic World.* Würzburg 2007.

12. Christopher Kubaseck, Günter Seufert (Hrsg.), *Deutsche Wissenschaftler im türkischen Exil: Die Wissenschaftsmigration in die Türkei 1933-1945*. Würzburg 2008.

13. Barbara Pusch, Tomas Wilkoszewski (Hrsg.), *Facetten internationaler Migration in die Türkei: Gesellschaftliche Rahmenbedingungen und persönliche Lebenswelten*. Würzburg 2008.

15. Camilla Adang, Sabine Schmidtke, David Sklare (Eds.), *A Common Rationality: Muʿtazilism in Islam and Judaism*. Würzburg 2007.

16. Edward Badeen, *Sunnitische Theologie in osmanischer Zeit*. Würzburg 2008.

17. Claudia Ulbrich, Richard Wittmann (Eds.): *Fashioning the Self in Transcultural Settings: The Uses and Significance of Dress in Self-Narrative*. Würzburg 2015.

18. Christoph Herzog, Malek Sharif (Eds.), *The First Ottoman Experiment in Democracy*. Würzburg 2010.

19. Dorothée Guillemarre-Acet, *Impérialisme et nationalisme. L'Allemagne, l'Empire ottoman et la Turquie (1908 –1933)*. Würzburg 2009.

20. Marcel Geser, *Zwischen Missionierung und „Stärkung des Deutschtums": Der Deutsche Kindergarten in Konstantinopel von seinen Anfängen bis 1918*. Würzburg 2010.

21. Camilla Adang, Sabine Schmidtke (Eds.), *Contacts and Controversies between Muslims, Jews and Christians in the Ottoman Empire and Pre-Modern Iran*. Würzburg 2010.

22. Barbara Pusch, Uğur Tekin (Hrsg.), *Migration und Türkei. Neue Bewegungen am Rande der Europäischen Union*. Würzburg 2011.

23. Tülay Gürler, *Jude sein in der Türkei. Erinnerungen des Ehrenvorsitzenden der Jüdischen Gemeinde der Türkei Bensiyon Pinto*. Herausgegeben von Richard Wittmann. Würzburg 2010.

24. Stefan Leder (Ed.), *Crossroads between Latin Europe and the Near East: Corollaries of the Frankish Presence in the Eastern Mediterranean (12th – 14th centuries)*. Würzburg 2011.

25. Börte Sagaster, Karin Schweißgut, Barbara Kellner-Heinkele, Claus Schönig (Hrsg.), *Hoşsohbet: Erika Glassen zu Ehren*. Würzburg 2011.

26. Arnd-Michael Nohl, Barbara Pusch (Hrsg.), *Bildung und gesellschaftlicher Wandel in der Türkei. Historische und aktuelle Aspekte*. Würzburg 2011.

28. Kyriakos Kalaitzidis, *Post-Byzantine Music Manuscripts as a Source for Oriental Secular Music (15th to Early 19th Century)*. Würzburg 2012.

29. Hüseyin Ağuiçenoğlu, *Zwischen Bindung und Abnabelung. Das „Mutterland" in der Presse der Dobrudscha und der türkischen Zyprioten in postosmanischer Zeit*. Würzburg 2012.

30. Bekim Agai, Olcay Akyıldız, Caspar Hillebrand (Eds.), *Venturing Beyond Borders – Reflections on Genre, Function and Boundaries in Middle Eastern Travel Writing*. Würzburg 2013.

31. Jens Peter Laut (Hrsg.), *Literatur und Gesellschaft. Kleine Schriften von Erika Glassen zur türkischen Literaturgeschichte und zum Kulturwandel in der modernen Türkei*. Würzburg 2014.

32. Tobias Heinzelmann, *Populäre religiöse Literatur und Buchkultur im Osmanischen Reich. Eine Studie zur Nutzung der Werke der Brüder Yazıcıoğlı*. Würzburg 2015.

33. Martin Greve (Ed.), *Writing the History of "Ottoman Music"*. Würzburg 2015.

34. A.C.S. Peacock, Sara Nur Yıldız (Eds.), *Islamic Literature and Intellectual Life in Fourteenth- and Fifteenth-Century Anatolia*. Würzburg 2016.

35. Burcu Yıldız, *Experiencing Armenian Music in Turkey: An Ethnography of Musicultural Memory*. Würzburg 2016.

36. Zeynep Helvacı, Jacob Olley, Ralf Martin Jäger (Eds.), *Rhythmic Cycles and Structures in the Art Music of the Middle East*. Würzburg 2017.

37. Karin Schweißgut, *Das Armutssujet in der türkischen Literatur des 20. Jahrhunderts*. Würzburg 2016.

38. Stefan Hanß, *Die materielle Kultur der Seeschlacht von Lepanto (1571). Materialität, Medialität und die historische Produktion eines Ereignisses*. Würzburg 2017.

39. Martin Greve, *Makamsız: Individualization of Traditional Music on the Eve of Kemalist Turkey*. Würzburg 2017.

40. Ulaş Özdemir, Wendelmoet Hamelink, Martin Greve (Eds.), *Diversity and Contact among Singer-Poet Traditions in Eastern Anatolia*. Baden-Baden 2018.

41. Oliver Stein, *Nachrichtendienstoffizier im Osmanischen Reich. Ernst Adolf Muellers Kriegseinsatz und Gefangenschaft im Vorderen Orient 1915-1919. Mit einer kritischen Edition seiner Erinnerungen*. Baden-Baden 2018.